Sex Workers, Psychics, and Numbers Runners

THE NEW BLACK STUDIES SERIES

Edited by Darlene Clark Hine and Dwight A. McBride

A list of books in the series appears at the end of this book.

Sex Workers, Psychics, and Numbers Runners

Black Women in New York City's Underground Economy

LASHAWN HARRIS

UNIVERSITY OF ILLINOIS PRESS
Urbana, Chicago, and Springfield

Publication of this book was supported by funding from the Morrill Fund, Department of History, Michigan State University.

Library of Congress Cataloging-in-Publication Data
Names: Harris, LaShawn, 1974– author.
Title: Sex workers, psychics, and numbers runners : black women in
    New York City's underground economy / LaShawn Harris.
Description: Urbana : University of Illinois Press, 2016.
Series: The new Black studies series
Includes bibliographical references and index.
Identifiers: LCCN 2015041914
ISBN 9780252040207 (cloth : alk. paper)
ISBN 9780252081668 (pbk. : alk. paper)
ISBN 9780252098420 (ebook)
Subjects: LCSH: African American women—Employment—New
    York (State)—New York—History—20th century. | Under-the-
    table employment—New York (State)—New York—History—
    20th century. | Informal sector—New York (State)—New York—
    History—20th century.
Classification: LCC HD6057.5.U52 N4843 2016 | DDC
    331.4089/9607307471—dc23 LC record available
    at http://lccn.loc.gov/2015041914

Contents

Acknowledgments

The process of researching, writing, and completing a book is no doubt a long and arduous endeavor. Fortunately, I had the guidance, wisdom, and encouragement of many individuals while finishing this book.

To my family, I extend profound feelings of appreciation and love. To the Cooper-Fleming family (Estella Cooper, Sherema Fleming, Ambrose Fleming, and Leola Cooper), thank you for your constant and unwavering love and encouragement. Thank you for being patient and for not chastising me when I often, and usually without hesitation, chose spending hours at the New York Public Library instead of spending that time with you. Thank you to the Dagbovie and Mullins families. Thank you Frances and Prospero Dagbovie, Chris and Sika Dagbovie-Mullins and Asilah, and Perovi, Kokou, and Be' Dagbovie for your continuous support over the years and for graciously accepting me into your wonderful family. To Pero Dagbovie, one of the hardest working and smartest scholars in the field of African American history, thanks for reading every word of this manuscript, for being my personal copyeditor, for pushing me to embark on unknown territory with this book. While you were working on one of your many monographs, being graduate director, and taking care of three boys, you miraculously always made time to read and comment on my work. You're an inspiration, and I love you.

My love for history was sparked as an undergraduate at Virginia Union University. Thank you Dr. Raymond Hylton for being one of my biggest cheerleaders and for introducing me to the historical profession. Your passion for history was and is infectious and continues to inspire other students. I owe much gratitude to my fellow Virginia Unionites and other close Richmond, Virginia, friends: Nicole and Orlando Douglas, Kim Jefferson, and Yuri and Luretia Stewart, and to Sharon Baptist Church members. Thank you for sustaining me over the years and always sharing your home with me during my research trips to Virginia. Sharon Braithwaite deserves a special thank you for inviting me to be part of TV-One's *Celebrity Crime Files* and allowing me to talk about all things Stephanie St. Clair. Ronald Shelton, thank you for always believing in and encouraging me and for challenging me intellectually. You left this world before the completion of this book; but I know your spirit gently guided me through the final stages of this project—telling me "just get it done."

A host of close academic friends encouraged me and pushed me to complete my book. I am truly grateful for all of the friendships I have fostered over the last two decades. Thank you Sowande Mustakeem, Kennetta Hammond Perry, Talitha LeFlouria, Deidre Cooper Owens, Sasha Turner Owens, Daina Ramey Berry, Siobhan David-Carter, Shannon King, Billie Dee Tate, and Keisha Blain. To my Howard University grad school bestie and sister, Sharita Jacobs Thompson, no words can express my appreciation for your unwavering friendship and support over the past fifteen years. Thank you for being my "ride or die" friend. Thank you Robert Thompson for always being a gracious host during my frequent visits to Washington, D.C.

I am grateful to my Howard University graduate school professors and colleagues: Daryl Scott, Edna Medford, Emory Tolbert, David DeLeon, Elizabeth Clark-Lewis, Louis Woods, Glenn Chambers, Abena Lewis-Mhoon, Christina Jones, Abraham Smith, Jim Harper, Quito Swan, Gordon Gill, David Gosse, Abba Baez, and Brittne Nelson. Since my leaving Howard University in 2007, a host of colleagues and friends at Georgia Southern University, Michigan State University, and within the Greater East Lansing community provided mentorship, friendship, and intellectual engagement. In particular, I would like to thank Jonathan Bryant, Michelle Haberland, Laura Shelton, Linda Collins, Saba Jallow, Renata Newbill Jallow, Alain Lawo-Sukam, Michael Stamm, Mark Kornbluh, Nwando Achebe, Walter Hawthrone, Edward Murphy, Kristina Kelly, Jessica Marie Johnson, Peter Beattie, Jerry Garcia, Maureen Flanagan, Benjamin Smith, Dylan Miner, Estrella Torrez, Brandt Peterson, Casey Williamson, Vanessa Holden, Terah Chambers, David Wheat, Jeanna Whiting, Elyse Hansen, Deborah Greer, Amanda Jenkins, Tama Hamilton-Wray, Jeff Wray, Helen Veit, Christine Root, Ronald Jackson, Jewel Debnam, Bonita Curry, Jenifer Barclay, Rashida Harrison, Richard Mares, Mary Philips, Bayyinah Jeffries, and Terrion Williamson.

This book was tremendously improved by the insightful comments of individuals who read and commented on various parts of the manuscript and by insightful conversations with a host of scholars at conferences. Thank you Francille Rusan Wilson, Ula Taylor, Martha Biondi, Rhonda Williams, Kidada Williams, Jennifer Hamer, Jeffery Anderson, Yvonne Chireau, Jacqueline McLeod, Kali Gross, Sharon Harley, Jeanne Theoharis, Clarence Lang, Gwendolyn Midlo Hall, and Cheryl Hicks for your words of encouragement and spot-on critiques and recommendations about the manuscript and the profession. I am forever thankful to my three external reviewers. They carved out and devoted a significant amount of time to carefully read a raw and unedited manuscript. Their comments, recommendations, and honesty sharpened my analysis on black labor, urban America, and African American women and guided me through the revisions process. Thank you for supporting this project. Both Lisa Stallings and Barbara Bigelow were great copyeditors and a pleasure to work with. They were indispensable to this project.

Much of my research was conducted in my home city of New York and in Washington, D.C. I would like to thank the many archivists, librarians, and staffs at the New York Municipal Archives, New York Public Library, Columbia University, New York State Archives, Schomburg Center for Research in Black Culture, and the Library of Congress for helping me navigate archival collections and photographs. Several New York Municipal Archives staff members, including Kenneth Cobb, Lenora Gidlund, Barbara Hibbert, and Dwight Johnson, deserve special attention. Thank you for assisting me in the research process, and instructing me on how to access some of New York City's richest archival materials. CORBIS staff members Tim Davis, Donna Daley, and Leslie Stauffer were tremendously helpful in researching and locating images for this project. I am beholden to Michigan State University's Office of the Vice President for Research and Graduate Studies for awarding me the Humanities and Arts Research Program (HARP) production grant. HARP funds defrayed the costs of photographs and permissions.

Staff at the University of Illinois Press saw this book go through various incarnations. Thank you Jennifer Clark, Nancy Albright, and Robert Engleman for ushering the book through the production process. Thank you to acquisition editors Larin McLaughlin and Dawn Durante for seeing the potential in this project and for making its publication a reality. Dawn Durante, you have been with this project since the beginning and have shepherded it through the publication process. Thank you for always picking up the phone when I called, for meeting with me at conferences, and for responding to my emails. Thank you New Black Studies Series editor Darlene Clark Hine for bringing this project to the University of Illinois Press, and for always taking the time to offer me professional advice and words of encouragement.

Sex Workers, Psychics, and Numbers Runners

Introduction

Sex Workers, Psychics, and Numbers Runners: Black Women in New York City's Underground Economy interrogates the fascinating lives of New York City black women informal economy laborers during the first three decades of the twentieth century. Gotham's working-class women carved out niches for themselves within the city's noteworthy informal economy as both wage earners and entrepreneurs. These women toiled at a myriad of under-the-table jobs, including street peddling, fencing stolen goods, and drug dealing, and occupied legal service positions as hostesses, coat checkers, cooks, and domestic workers at speakeasies, brothels, and other illegal business establishments; many even became successful entrepreneurs, launching lucrative and modest street vending, hair care and massage, and shoeshine enterprises. Despite black women's multifaceted informal work, this book focuses on the labor patterns and economic activities of those that were part of the city's profitable yet illegal sexual economy, gambling enterprise, and supernatural consulting business. While this book focuses on the nuanced subculture of informal economy laborers, it also delves into reform-minded activists, city politicians, and ordinary New Yorkers' perceptions of off-the-books labor.

In teasing out black women's less familiar modes of labor, this book tackles several important questions. What socioeconomic factors motivated working-class black women's pursuit of informal labor? How did female city dwellers interpret the urban informal economy? How did race and gender shape black women's experiences as off-the-books workers and entrepreneurs? What were the benefits, consequences, and larger implications of unreported labor? How did mounting early-twentieth-century reform organizations, neighborhood associations' anti-vice campaigns, slum clearance programs, and city laws impact—and in some instances obstruct—women's income-producing strategies and efforts toward economic stability and occupation autonomy? More importantly, how did New York black women, those expected to embody turn-of-the-twentieth-century constructions of race and gender and adhere to black reformists' ideas about racial progress and respectability, navigate and survive labor markets that were male-dominated and racially prejudiced, and offered little or no legal recourse or protection?

I argue that New York's burgeoning underground economy served as a catalyst in working-class black women's creation of employment opportunities, occupational identities, and survival strategies that provided financial stability and a sense of labor autonomy and mobility. A number of material and intangible benefits drew women of African descent to New York's informal job market. With its flexible and fluid structure, the informal labor sector offered employment and economic opportunities that complemented black women's desire to secure occupational mobility. Through underground labor, black women imagined and explored the varying possibilities of transforming their immediate socioeconomic circumstances and personal lives. Urban women, according to one scholar, "were reaching beyond their preordained lot in life."[1] City women featured in this book recognized the privilege in achieving labor control and flexibility, which included determining and negotiating the conditions of their work. They envisioned the potential labor benefits that underground work could bring. For many, irregular forms of employment opened the opportunity to juggle the obligations of family and work and to fulfill their traditional roles as caretakers. At the same time, informal labor opened the door for black women to radically disrupt, violate, and push pass the limits of conventional and acceptable public behavior and performances for black women. Notions of public space and uplift politics, constrained economic opportunities, and daily living expenses and necessities attracted black women to illegal and quasi-legal labor that fell outside the scope of domestic work and also to other menial employment reserved for working-poor women of color. Monetary earnings from informal work allowed many to sustain themselves and their families; financially assist relatives living in the South and Caribbean; take care of their unemployed and lethargic husbands and male companions; support black institution building, including financial donations to religious, political, and social organizations; purchase fancy clothes, cars, and other luxury items; and, as New York cultural writer Roi Ottley put it, "to make [their] own way."[2]

But participation in the city's informal labor marketplace was not primarily about personal and community survival or achieving financial stability or success. In other words, prominent African American religious leader Adam Clayton Powell Sr. and others' assertion that poor black New Yorkers were lured to "immoral occupations" as bootleggers and sellers of "hot goods because of [their] low economic status" was not the case for many women.[3] Some New York women did not worry about high apartment and food prices or feeding family members. They had to care only for themselves. Those not necessarily concerned with affording the high cost of city living or economic preservation entered underground work in hopes of escaping dull and monotonous unskilled labor. These women, to borrow from historian Alison Mackinnon, were in "pursuit of purely selfish pleasure or fortune, lured from the self-sacrifice of maternity and the restraints of wedded [and single] life."[4] Inspired by the 1920s and 1930s culture and mood of cheap amusements and sexual experimentation, New York women were unapologetic in their search for joy and pleasure. Many were fascinated by boisterous apartment soirées with live music, food, and alcoholic beverages, all-night restaurants and bars, and they yearned for social and sexual gratification. No doubt, fulfilling individual desires and carving out spheres of pleasure for themselves was a top priority for many women. New York's shadow labor market represented a break from a life of convention and prescribed rules and protocols set by black reformers and moralists and a path toward living in a world in which they chose their own labor and social amusements.

Widening the public gaze and visual images of urban female work in general and black women's labor in particular, the informal work of women of African descent provided unique opportunities for many to assert varying perspectives and outlooks on urban labor, racial uplift ideology, and respectability politics. *Sex Workers, Psychics, and Numbers Runners* makes the claim that black women's nontraditional unlicensed and unlawful work often complicated normative versions of respectability. Female underground laborers intentionally and inadvertently rejected, refashioned, and subscribed to different aspects of propriety politics. Stretching the limits of urban work, women cultivated alternative expressions, visions, and images of outward representations of public decorum, community reform, and female labor.

Workingwomen interpreted respectability politics in varying ways and according to their own sensibilities and economic and social interests. While some black women were far more concerned with economic stability and exciting city amusements than with outward representations of appropriateness, others—certainly cognizant of external models of correctness—used monetary profits earned from illicit labor to support and reinforce traditional aspects of racial uplift.[5] Moreover, for some women, respectability became a fluid concept, practice, and performance that was and could be altered and manipulated at will on a day-to-day basis, depending upon one's socioeconomic circumstances and priorities and situational context. Informal work exposed black women and the African American community's divergent and often conflicting stance on bourgeois respectability, religion

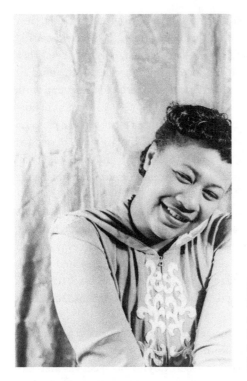

Figure 1: Portrait of Ella Fitzgerald. As a teenager, the future renowned 1930s jazz singer was a Harlem numbers runner for a Manhattan brothel. Courtesy of Library of Congress, Prints & Photographs Division, Carl Van Vechten Collection.

and sexuality, and the appropriate use of public and private spaces. Competing ideologies, as well as tension over propriety politics, were played out in both private and public domains. Urban black neighborhoods, apartment buildings, and street sidewalks became center stages for discussions and debates over neighborhood vice, public displays of proper behavior, and sexual norms. Sometimes lively and spirited conversations and disagreements on individual and community deportment even triggered physical violence.

The personalities, voices, and narratives that emerge from this book do not represent the laboring experiences of all New York under-the-table laborers. Nor does this book employ the voices of urban black women to offer a comprehensive history of New York's underground employment market. Instead, this book calls attention to some women's strategies for dealing with economic disparity and poverty; a restricted urban labor market; thwarted personal dreams of pleasure; and race, gender, and class discrimination. Additionally, this book paints a picture of women's less familiar experiences as service producers operating on the fringes of urban civilization during a time when both the nation and most American cities were experiencing rapid social, economic, political, and cultural shifts. The majority of the black women discussed in the pages that follow were not part of

New York's educated bourgeoisie; nor were they prominent club or community reformers who exemplified and embraced normative definitions of female respectability and labor. Hailing from varying geographical regions including the American South, the Caribbean, and New York City, many of the women profiled in this book were mothers and wives, single ladies, church parishioners, hustlers, and partygoers and were resourceful and naive thinkers and doers simply striving to earn a living wage. Collectively, these seemingly unrespectable, brazen, and incorrigible women—among them Harlem numbers laborers Madame Stephanie St. Clair, supernatural consultant Dorothy "Madame Fu Futtam" Matthews Hamid, and numbers runner turned 1930s jazz musician Ella Fitzgerald (commonly known to the world as the "First Lady of Song" and "Lady Ella")—bypassed legitimate formal wage work altogether or combined industrial and domestic work with that of off-the-books jobs. This diverse cross section of urban female laborer associated with some of New York's roughest hustlers and criminals. They labored in some of the most dangerous public and private labor environments, fought for recognition within their chosen occupations, and constantly faced the potentiality of socioeconomic disappointment, emotional despair, and loss of bodily integrity. Moreover, New York informal laborers and entrepreneurs, united by shared dreams

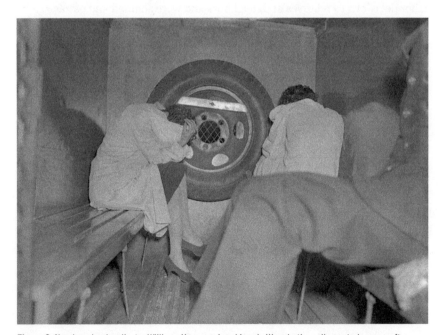

Figure 2: Numbers bank collector Williana Hammond and Lessie Ware in the police patrol wagon after being arrested in a policy raid in 1938. Courtesy of Corbis Images.

of financial permanence and independence, occupation autonomy and dignity, and participating in urban leisure of their choice, courageously charted their own socioeconomic paths. These women stepped far beyond the boundaries of rigid race and gender norms, acceptable forms of employment and amusement, and the behavior expected of early-twentieth-century black female laborers.

This book strives to highlight agency within underrepresented black women's labor. At the same time, this book recognizes the complexities, danger, and unsteadiness of underground work. *Sex Workers, Psychics, and Numbers Runners* underscores both the conspicuous and hidden risks and consequences associated with informal work. Off-the-books employment was far from secure or safe, and indeed, there was much to risk and lose. Engaging in employment that provided little or no legal oversight or protection left black women vulnerable to workplace challenges, inequalities, and dangers. It is also important to note that informal workers were victims and survivors of their own hazardous behavior and questionable decision-making. Because of the nature of their respective occupations, New York women experienced horrendous and heartrending physical, emotional, and psychological traumas. Female underground workers were arrested and jailed, denied payment for their services, and verbally and physically assaulted by police and male and female competitors and customers. They constantly defended their labor decisions to relatives and neighbors and were shamed and ostracized by reformers, community members, and family. Some women, particularly those disappointed in their choice of labor, suffered from emotional strain, severe depression, and low self-esteem. Adding to that, off-the-book laborers, like formal women wage earners, endured structural barriers with New York's informal labor sector. Many, not naive to the limits of under-the-table employment, experienced multiple forms of race, gender, and labor discrimination. The varying contours of race and gender oppression excluded women from well-paying positions, denied many of them well-deserved respect as entrepreneurs, and subjected some to physical and sexual violence. Such labor constraints exposed women's often-veiled vulnerabilities as underground workers and added to the difficulties they already faced living in urban settings.

Navigating challenging labor environments and restrictions and overcoming race and gender bigotry was not easy for black women. For many, surviving and even thriving in unregulated work spaces meant devising workplace strategies and forging partnerships with other informal and formal workers in order to ensure protection for themselves and command respect from competing underground laborers. More importantly, formulating and implementing varying labor resistance strategies permitted some female under-the-table workers to earn money and engage in leisure activities of their choice with little disruption or conflict. Women's vast approaches to tackling labor constraints included, but were not limited to, adopting and performing masculinity, playing on conventional ideas about femininity and protection, employing violence, and creating mutually beneficial relationships and alliances with a host of urbanites. Such initiatives underscore black women's attempts, sometimes successful and failed, at addressing and overcoming work constraints within their respective occupations. In their efforts to carve out space for themselves within New York's underground economy, off-the-books laborers' workplace strategies hardly subverted deeply entrenched race, gender, and class barriers. Nor did their actions obstruct critics' public reform campaigns against their labor or the city's informal labor sector. Their efforts did, however, underscore women's refusal to permit structural constraints and detractors from shaping their labor and personal decisions. Moreover, women's employment strategies illustrate how informal work, to the contrary of city activists, was outlined by both limitation and possibility and power and subordination.

Regardless of the possible economic and social incentives and the collateral consequences associated with under-the-table labor, or how informal workers utilized their earnings, many urban black crusaders, social activists, and ordinary city dwellers alike were troubled by underground work, especially labor connected to the city's flourishing gambling enterprises, sex and drug economies, and any other vice rackets. Prominent leaders and members of New York civil rights organizations such as the National Association for the Advancement of Colored People (NAACP) and National Urban League (NUL) and grassroots neighborhood associations insisted that some extralegal income-generating activities were detriments to community progress and safety and racial advancement. Moreover, working and middle-class subscribers of racial uplift reasoned that involvement in degraded and immoral modes of labor reaffirmed turn-of-the-century racist scientific theories and popular cultural stereotypes that depicted urban blacks as deviant and criminal, hypersexual, and dangerous threats to New York whites and urban civilization. In their minds, certain underground occupations violated traditional ideas about respectable manhood and womanhood. Self-proclaimed "better-class" blacks, those constantly theorizing and utilizing different liberation tactics to eradicate the nation's race problem and white supremacy, naively believed that negative societal interpretations of black life and culture blurred the line between the decent and the immoral and led to incidents of mistaken identities and the victimization and criminalization of urban black bodies, especially those of women. More importantly, urban reformers, moral crusaders, and ordinary folks were deeply concerned about the different ways in which informal labor and vice rackets and their participants—laborers and consumers—impacted family structures and household incomes, neighborhood relations, and community living.

African Americans' opposition to what many considered depraved and unlawful moneymaking schemes was clearly articulated in complaint letters to race activists, private anti-vice agents, newspapers editors, and municipal leaders. Sending grievance letters to New York's premier anti-vice agency the Committee of Fourteen (COF), the Urban League, the *New York Age* (NYA), and city district attorneys, New York residents voiced concerns about suspected informal laborers and their use of private and public space for commercial purposes and about rapacious landlords that permitted vice to flourish in tenement houses. Citizen complaint letters articulated hardworking parents' efforts to protect their children from street violence, nefarious neighbors, and enticing city amusements; described in detail their neighbors' disreputable daily activities; and iterated their heartrending pleas to reside in decent living spaces. Citizen complaint correspondences reflected both individual and collective desires to improve underserved racially and ethnically diverse neighborhoods and to draw city municipal leaders, social activists, and ordinary New Yorkers' attention to the plight of the working class. Moreover, letters affirmed the boundaries of acceptable public and private conduct and delineated the often-veiled intraclass conflicts within urban black spaces. Additionally, grassroots activism of local neighborhood organizations such as the Harlem Citizens Council (HCC) and the reform initiatives of lesser-known New York activists such as South Jamaica, Queens, resident Geraldine Chaney were instrumental in devising anti-vice strategies geared toward neighborhood beautification, slum clearance, and the advancement of community uplift. Already active in the battle against economic and political disenfranchisement, housing discrimination, police brutality, and some city politicians' lukewarm enforcement of antidiscrimination statutes, this vanguard of community leaders signaled urban citizens' unified position and voice on neighborhood and city politics and demonstrated their vested interests in the socioeconomic progress and moral health of their communities.

Filling a void within African American women's labor historiography and presenting a more nuanced perspective on women's work, this book situates black women informal laborers within the larger context of urban female work of the early twentieth century. Scholars of the urban black female experience have produced seminal and insightful studies on the private and laboring lives of black women. Both past and recent studies explore city women's leisure habits, their social and political activism against legal and customary racial segregation and white violence, and their roles as formal wage earners, namely that of domestic, laundry, and industrial laborers. Similarly, historical scholarship on black women entrepreneurs typically chronicles working and middle-class women's failing and successful attempts at creating legitimate formal businesses, including beauty shops, restaurants, insurance companies, boardinghouses, and funeral parlors. Absent from historical interpretations of urban black female labor or female entrepreneurship are the labor experiences and voices of sex workers, unlicensed street and home-based vendors, games-of-chance laborers, magic practitioners, and other extralegal workers. According to historian Jacqueline Jones, "black women employed outside of agriculture, domestic labor, and industry represented a diversity of work experiences, not all of which lend themselves to close historical scrutiny."[6] At the same time, recent studies by Tera Hunter, Kevin Mumford, Irma Watkins-Owens, Sharon Harley, Victoria Wolcott, Kali Gross, Cheryl Hicks, Cynthia Blair, Mireille Miller-Young, Talitha LeFlouria, Sarah Haley, and others challenge scholars to reconceptualize the diverse ways in which twentieth-century black women earned a living wage and how their labor (both free and imprisoned) contributed to New South and northern ideas about labor and modernity and industrialization. Presenting fresh historical narratives and methodological approaches to analyzing female labor, these particular scholars offer new historical accounts and fascinating analyses on urban and rural women, delineating their less familiar experiences as prison laborers, career criminals and confidence artists, pornography workers, sex entrepreneurs, and narcotics dealers.[7]

No doubt, black women's multifaceted employment patterns warrant historical attention and inquiry. This book broadens historical perspectives on urban female labor by shedding light on female labor that fell outside New York's formal wage system. It injects the stories of individuals that have been left out of mainstream historical conversations on urban black women. This book offers a more complicated portrayal of urban women workers in New York, while challenging historians of the black female experience to expand theoretical frameworks on labor and reconsider how city women financially support themselves and their loved ones. By offering another viewpoint on female work, this book underscores the role of black women in the urban labor market as being larger than scholars once thought. An examination of African American women's nontraditional and extralegal labor also contributes to existing urban, social, and cultural histories of New York. It departs from more familiar topics on black New York, such as Harlem's literary and New Negro Movement of the 1920s and 1930s, black women's club reform, and the political activism of African American and Caribbean male intellectuals and activists including A. Philip Randolph, Marcus Garvey, and Hubert Harrison. Scholar Jacob Dorman suggests that New York history, particularly that of Harlem, "has become largely the story of poets, artists, religious eccentrics, political activists, and exclusive clubs and cabarets."[8] Commenting on the scholarly preoccupation with elite black women, historian Cheryl Hicks's work on New York black women during the first half of the twentieth century rightfully states that "scholars and students know far more about the objectives and accomplishments of elite and middle-class black women than about the goals and strategies adopted by the masses."[9] An exploration into working-class black women's overlooked and long-forgotten labor narratives uncovers hidden histories of New York, the black metropolis, and most importantly the dynamics of urban poverty.

Documenting Informal Labor

Delving into the lives, labor aspirations, and world created by New York working-class African American women was an exciting, challenging, and frustrating endeavor. Concerns and even fears about the dearth of primary documentation on women profiled in this book made the thought of archival research daunting at times. As I began recovering and piecing together surviving documents on urban women, I encountered several methodological issues. The paucity and even unavailability of primary material complicated initiatives to excavate women's familial backgrounds, labor patterns, and physical journeys throughout one of the nation's most fascinating metropolises. Textual absences and voids illuminated the many limits of the archive. In her seminal 1987 *Journal of American History* essay, "Mining the Forgotten: Manuscript Sources for Black Women's History," Deborah Gray White rightfully points out that part of the difficulties in resuscitating black women's lives and bringing their stories to the center of historical inquiry is the archival itself. White comments that African American women's "world has been peripheral to those most likely to keep records of any kind," thus making black women's voices and stories scarce within manuscript collections.[10] Considered unworthy of scholarly exploration and excluded from the historical archives, women of color—especially those that lacked privilege and power—have remained on the fringes of history. In their edited volume, *Contesting Archives: Finding Women in the Sources*, scholars Nupur Chaudhuri, Sherry J. Katz, Mary Elizabeth Perry, and others attribute black women's missing, lost, or destroyed primary documentation to "the lack of archival objectivity, neutrality, and disinterested institution[s] that housed historical documents and artifacts."[11] But upon locating rare archival documentation on working-class women's personal and private worlds, which included contradictory, fragmented, and missing biographical sketches and labor accounts, I was reminded of the difficulties of tracing, understanding, and analyzing early-twentieth-century black women's nonlinear footsteps. At the same time and as one scholar notes, exploring such "contradictions and collisions in the documents" presents an opportunity for historians to interrogate black women's multilayered experiences as laborers and urban citizens.[12]

The ensuing omission of economically disadvantaged and nonreformist black women from the historical record lies at the hands of historians of the African

American experience. The narratives and visual imageries of thieving female con artists, numbers-running grandmothers, and single and married sex workers using the urban sex market to satisfy personal sexual fetishes, obviously contravening Progressive-era notions of "what a woman ought to be and do," complicates some historians' efforts to dispel white historical narratives that imagine black women as innately pathological and without sexual restraint. For many, the process of researching, writing, and disseminating African American history to the historical profession and wider public is, as noted by late scholar and cultural critic Manning Marable, "corrective" and represents a "concerted attempt to challenge and to critique the racism and stereotypes that have been ever present in the main discourse of white academic institutions."[13] Some historians' attempts to present positive monolithic images of persons of African descent are certainly understandable. However, as scholar Kali Gross convincingly points out in her seminal work on black female criminality in turn-of-the-twentieth-century Philadelphia, some scholars, in fear of "unwittingly validat[ing] racist stereotypes," often avoid and marginalize "controversial" historical figures and subject matters.[14] Consequently, as explained by labor historian Sharon Harley, "the dearth of traditional manuscript sources and the middle-class biases of many scholars (often regardless of their own familial background) have collectively resulted in few historical studies of the black working-class, [and] rarely do these works address the labor of women in the illegal underground economy."[15]

Working-class black women's erasure from general narratives on African American women's histories downplays class dynamics and privileges the lives, worldviews, and activism of educated middle-class women—those that courageously contested Jim Crow segregation, white violence and brutality, economic and political disenfranchisement, and sexism and rape, and advocated for uniform representations of black womanhood. As a result, black women's histories have become largely about the experiences of a small yet significant group of culturally astute black women, giving the impression that such women's narratives, voices, and experiences were and are representative of all African American women. The failure to situate contentious and perhaps even self-serving and narcissistic individuals within black women's history presents a narrative that is devoid of diversity and complexity and overlooks a rich and intriguing history from below.

Finally, black women informal laborers' absence from the historical record is conceivably attributed to their own efforts. Unlike their middle-class counterparts, informal sector workers did not consciously leave behind diaries and journals, personal papers collections, or any evidence chronicling their inner lives, labor experiences, and leisure activities. They did not believe that their lives or laboring imprints were of any importance to the world, and were far more concerned with their socioeconomic conditions. In other words, documenting their lives was not on their minds. When it came to their labor, many female underground workers purposely concealed their economic activities. They preferred that their personal lives and employment patterns remained hidden from plain view. Applying Darlene Clark Hine's theory of the "culture of dissemblance" is useful in explaining some women's desires to conceal aspects of their public and private worlds. Many underground laborers sought to protect themselves from public scrutiny and the criticism of moral crusaders, race reformers, and ordinary men and women by "creating the appearance of openness and disclosure, but actually shield[ing] the truth of their inner lives and selves."[16] Operating on the periphery of society—out of tenements, on city streets, in the backrooms of nightclubs, dance halls, pool halls, and barber shops—and without official financial records of their business dealings—some black women conceivably chose to live and work in the shadows. For some, invisibility was key to their economic survival. Not drawing public attention to themselves was critical to informal workers' laboring lives. Concealment of irregular labor permitted women to evade detection from law enforcers and meddlesome neighbors and to liberally weave in and out of fluid employment markets. Veiled labor also fulfilled one's prerogative to privately operate independent businesses while still maintaining the outward appearance of respectability. At the same time, labor concealment left informal female laborers vulnerable and masked their labor challenges and restrictions.

This book employs an interdisciplinary approach in reconstructing and analyzing less-privileged black women's labor identities and their power and vulnerabilities as informal workers. In constructing this narrative, I draw upon a wide range of primary materials, including white and black race reform and charitable organizational records; anti-vice investigation reports; Federal Writers' Project (FWP) interviews; immigration and naturalization records; and city and state court and prison records and inmate parole case files. This book also draws on the fiction and nonfiction writings and intellectual and personal critiques and observations of some of New York's most influential writers, journalists, and cultural pundits of the day. Insightful novels, city histories, newspaper editorials, and personal memories of Claude McKay, Roi Ottley, Carl Van Vechten, Wallace Thurman, Marvel Cooke, Thelma Berlack, Vivian Morris, James Weldon Johnson, and others captured the mood, spirit, and pulse of early-twentieth-century New York. Their provocative prose candidly depicted black New Yorkers' socioeconomic and political achievements and circumstances, their individual brushes with urban inequality and encounters with nonwhite city dwellers, and perhaps more interestingly their everyday politics as urban citizens. More importantly, Progressive- and Inter-war–era New York writers offer useful and rare snapshots and commentaries on New York's multiethnic population and their diverse experiences as activists, house- and saloon-hopping partygoers, and hustling underground wage earners and entrepreneurs.

Critical to researching black women's informal labor are national and local white and black newspapers. Urban dailies and weeklies, including the *New York Times (NYT)*, *New York Amsterdam News (NYAN)*, *New York Age (NYA)*, *Chicago Defender*, and others published thought-provoking and sensational news stories that vividly chronicled working-poor men and women's colorful lives. Catchy headlines, racy photographs, and some newspapers' tabloid-style writings exposed the reading public to the gripping accounts of scandalous and courageous prostitutes, wealthy and philanthropic gamblers, deceptive hot-goods vendors, and others' illicit moneymaking activities and schemes. Early-twentieth-century newspapers reported on how working-poor urbanites creatively confronted the vagaries of city living and dangers. More importantly, newspapers of the day provided valuable biographical, labor, and legal arrest information on some women workers, including their name, place of birth and age, marital status, what laws they violated and if they were convicted of a crime, and the physical and emotional traumas they sustained as a result of engaging in unregulated labor.

The classified sections of newspapers, particularly the black press, proved fertile ground for research on informal laborers. Newspapers were integral to black entrepreneurship, enabling the self-employed to advertise and market their businesses, increase their clientele, and appeal to New York's diverse consumer market. Informal businesses not connected to criminal rackets, including nonlicensed childcare providers, hairstylists, and spiritual consultants and self-proclaimed clairvoyants, placed paid advertisements in local city newspapers. Ads highlighted underground entrepreneurs' services, business locations and hours, featured catchy sales slogans and pitches, and sometimes included a flattering and affirmative customer testimonial about the business. For example, supernatural consultants—mediums and healers, crystal-ball gazers, and self-appointed "professors" and "doctors"—employed newspapers to promote their churches and capitalize on the emotional and economic instability of prospective clients. During the 1930s, Madame Reid, the leader of the National Spiritual Church located at 37th West 125th Street, marketed her spiritual counseling services in the *NYAN*. Her ad informed potential customers of her ability to carefully listen to one's problems and alleviate them of emotional and mental grief, illness, and matters of the heart. While Reid's advertisement did not indicate how she intended to resolve clients' issues, it did, along with similar business ads placed by other supernatural consultants, encourage those suffering from mental anguish to try her services. "Don't be depressed. Don't be broken-hearted. Let Madame Reid help you."[17] If curious urbanites were interested in Reid's so-called foolproof spiritual guidance, her *NYAN* ad indicated that her hours of operation were from 1–9 PM on weekdays.

The integration of these primary documents provides a window into the intriguing yet complex and versatile lives and labor practices of New York black women. They allow historians to hear black women's voices. When read together and against each other, diverse primary documentation fills gaps about the women casted in this story and addresses questions that certainly could not be answered by utilizing traditional manuscript collections. Varying primary sources shed light on how some poor black women economically made do and overcame poverty, how different survival strategies paid off or failed, how black women interpreted their own labor, urban space, and respectable politics; how black women took advantage of the socioeconomic and cultural landscape of the urban city to imagine and explore different labor possibilities; and how Progressive- and Inter-war–era reformers and ordinary urbanites responded to informal economy and community vice. More importantly, this rich array of primary evidence reveals the less familiar narratives of a diverse group of understudied urban laborers whose lives were "characterized by victimization [and] agency, dependence [and] independence," and "filled with ambiguities, ironies, and contradictions."[18] On the other hand, primary sources consulted for this book limits endeavors to unearth a broad representation of New York women's underground labor and their familial backgrounds and socioeconomic plans and aspirations for the future. Piecing together extant documentation left me with disjointed or no biographical information and conflicting narratives, and undoubtedly raised a new set of historical and methodological inquiries that could not be addressed in this book.

The chapters that follow chart black women's working experiences, ultimately presenting new perspectives on urban female labor. Chapter 1 offers an overview of black women informal workers both as wage earners and entrepreneurs, positioning their experiences at the center of New York's informal labor market. It highlights working-class black women's socioeconomic conditions and the ways in which economic distress coupled with varying perceptions of urban public space and racial uplift motivated some women's attraction to nontraditional modes of labor. Involvement in the urban informal labor sector illuminated many black women's desires to advance their socioeconomic and private agendas. Understanding the challenges and confines of being relegated to the strenuous menial labor of domestic work, women hoped for employment positions and options that facilitated financial growth and stability for their families, fulfilled social and sexual aspirations, and granted a sense of labor independence and flexibility. New York black women viewed the economic and social opportunities offered by off-the-books labor as a path toward altering the recipe of possibilities for themselves.[19]

But securing extralegal and unlicensed labor that disrupted normative gender roles and racial hierarchies and ideas about public decorum came at a price. Collateral consequences were certainly part of some black women's trajectory as underground workers and entrepreneurs. This chapter also considers the dangers and obstacles associated with self-employment and laboring for employers willing to pay them under the table. Police arrest, sexual exploitation, murder, family and community shame, nonpayment for services, and race, gender, and class inequality were some of the many labor challenges women possibly faced as informal economy workers.

Chapter 2 maps out black women's participation in arguably one of New York's most profitable and contested social and cultural pastimes of the early twentieth century: the illegal numbers racket. This chapter uses the mysterious and unique life of prominent Harlem numbers banker Madame Stephanie St. Clair as a window to illuminate how some black numbers entrepreneurs used the city's gambling enterprise to launch lucrative underground enterprises and as a way to cast a spotlight on black New Yorkers' individual and collective encounters with race, gender, and class prejudice and white supremacy. Throughout the 1920s and 1930s, the fiery "Queen of Numbers," a well-respected and imaginative immigrant from the French Caribbean and perhaps the only black woman to control a Harlem numbers racket, publicly tackled police corruption and white violence against urban blacks and addressed the issue of black immigration and citizenship. Moreover, St. Clair belonged to a community of New York activists and advocates that actively pushed for the reinforcement of turn-of-the-twentieth-century New York State statutes that prohibited racial discrimination. The infamous Numbers Queen was also part of a group of African American and Caribbean policy bankers that waged an infamous public battle against white bootleggers and prostitution racketeers' attempts to take over Harlem's black-controlled numbers businesses. As a community advocate and prominent numbers banker, St. Clair simultaneously embraced and constantly manipulated and shifted bourgeois respectability and racial uplift ideology. On one hand, she boldly and skillfully rejected and refashioned elite versions of propriety. She established a criminal enterprise, affiliated with some of New York's most dangerous vice profiteers, used physical violence against her detractors, and served prison time at several city and state penal institutions. On the other hand, St. Clair's proper outward attire of fashionable dresses, furs, and headdresses and her use of the moniker "Madame" reinforced conventional images of New Negro womanhood and material wealth. St. Clair also embraced aspects of working- and middle-class uplift and respectability that stressed black institution building, race solidarity, and self-help.

Chapter 3 explores the lives of self-professed African American supernatural laborers. Capitalizing on New Yorkers' fascination with the supernatural world and the city's informal-sector economy, African American clairvoyants merged religiosity and spiritual imagery with the lighter fare of underground and commercial amusements. Black women psychics, numerologists, palm readers, and crystal-ball gazers established home-based supernatural businesses, sold magical paraphernalia, published dream books, founded religious temples and churches, and offered curious and impoverished New Yorkers guidance on money, love, and health. This chapter investigates why black women became magic practitioners, surveys the interplay between supernaturalism and New York City's numbers enterprise, and considers the roles of religious leaders, city politicians, and medical professionals in citywide and statewide campaigns against supernaturalism.

Chapter 4 explores black women's multilayered roles within New York's sex commerce, moving beyond widely accepted historical interpretations that position black sex laborers primarily as street solicitors. Identifying black women as madam-prostitutes, casual prostitutes, and sex-house proprietors and entrepreneurs, this chapter addresses the difficulties of documenting sex work within black communities, the broad socioeconomic conditions and personal circumstances outlining black women's entrance into the urban sexual economy, and the occupational benefits of indoor prostitution. Preference for indoor sex work as opposed to street solicitation was informed by a declining brothel system, the 1920s diffusion of sex work into residential spaces and after-hours commercial leisure establishments, as well as possible street dangers and individual sex workers' entrepreneurial endeavors. Labor constraints and potential dangers associated with street solicitation kept many women from plying their trade on city corners. In an attempt to avoid or limit their presence on New York streets, black sex workers—when the opportunity arose—sold and performed sexual services in furnished rooms and hotels, in their own homes, in massage parlors and nightclubs, and in other legitimate and illegitimate commercial businesses. Indoor and residential sexual labor was significant to sex laborers' working and personal lives. Change of labor venue reduced black women's street visibility and chance of arrest, allowed some to establish clandestine and well-known sex businesses, and granted some women the privacy to maintain individual respectability and construct and negotiate diverse sexual landscapes and intimacies.

The presence of numbers runners, sex workers, supernatural consultants, and neighborhood hustlers and con artists hardly went unnoticed by disapproving black New Yorkers. Indeed, morally striving working- and middle-class blacks had much to say about slum conditions, poorly maintained apartment buildings, high rent prices and greedy landlords, municipal leaders' neglect of deteriorating black neighborhoods, and black men and women's extralegal, and what some regarded as demeaning, modes of employment. Relegated to the same underserved communities and dilapidated tenements on account of race discrimination in

New York's housing market, many black seasoned activists, budding politicians, and ordinary men and women were at odds with ghetto and vicelike conditions, particularly the looming presence of illegal economic and social amusements in their apartment buildings and within the broader black community. Although many working-class urbanites had a more complicated and complex relationship with, and connection to, the urban informal economy, many, like their middle-class counterparts, reasoned that particular unlicensed and criminal occupations, including prostitution, bootlegging, and numbers running, were deathblows to race uplift strategies geared at exhibiting community advancement and refuting urban white societal views that black New Yorkers were accepting of immorality and lawlessness in their communities. Chapter 5 draws attention to the multiple ways in which a new vanguard of black political and neighborhoods activists like Jamaica, Queens, resident Geraldine Chaney and members of HCC contested the presence of vice and immoral social amusements and economic activities in their neighborhoods. New Yorkers expressed their concerns and outrage about community conditions and its impact on their families and day-to-day lives through citizens' complaint letters and the formation of grassroots anti-vice neighborhood associations. Grievance letters and community-based organizations, collectively echoing a sense of neighborhood discipline and responsibility, became vehicles for New Yorkers to address the many socioeconomic problems plaguing their communities. Local activism signaled urbanites unified voice on community betterment and their concerns about the socioeconomic progress of black neighborhoods. Local black New Yorkers' activism, part of broader northern civil rights campaigns for citizenship and race, gender, and class equality, underscored visions of wholesome communities and neighborhood safety and their refusal to allow crime racketeers and disorderly neighbors to permeate spaces in which they had to live and work and raise families.

New York City's Informal Labor Market

New York is a fitting location for analyzing the urban informal labor market. Considered the leading commercial and cultural capital of the United States, no urban metropolis surpassed New York's dominance in trade, fashion, finance, manufacturing, and human capital during the early twentieth century. Commenting on New York's growing national dominance during the turn of the twentieth century, historian Angela Blake writes that the city was "the nation's metropolis, the de facto capital of the United States. The city's natural geography and earlier nineteenth-century industrial and infrastructural developments established the foundations for New York's early-twentieth-century dominance."[20] During this time, the popular American metropolis was often described as a city of extremes, recognized for its bustling streets and incomparable nightlife, luxurious mansions and hotels, towering skyscrapers and infamous sweatshops, and its extravagant department stores, restaurants, and apartment buildings. Residents and visitors alike regarded New York as a living picture and symbol of wealth and material consumption, flourishing art, and fascinating urban amusements; many viewed the city as a place where dreams of social and economic prosperity and expanded freedoms and liberties—at least for individuals of certain race, gender, and class backgrounds—could be imagined and realized. At the same time, the famous city, for far too many of its native and foreign-born inhabitants, was representative of lost hope, stifled dreams and unfulfilled destinies, crime and violence, and inequality and unemployment. City dwellers' visions of economic prosperity were circumvented by the harsh realities of urban poverty. Millions of residents lived below the poverty line in dense dilapidated housing structures that were often adjacent to a slew of brothels, nightclubs, and gambling dens. Of the estimated three million urbanites occupying New York in 1900, at least half were impoverished.[21] Even during the 1920s, an era commonly known as a period of mass consumerism, increased employment wages and commercial property values, and national and statewide economic growth, many New Yorkers, particularly working-class urbanites, were impoverished and hardly benefited from post–World War I prosperity.[22] Unsurprisingly, by the 1930s with the emergence of the nation's worst financial crisis, both working- and middle-class city folks hovered at the poverty line.

A growing foreign and racially diverse population, coupled with the migratory crossing of multiethnic values and customs, made New York arguably the nation's "quintessential immigrant city." Throughout the early twentieth century, millions of immigrants poured into New York's Ellis Island with dreams of securing well-paying employment and decent housing, creating new lives for themselves and their families, and taking part in free and cheap city amusements. In 1910, two-fifths of the city's population was foreign-born; the immigration population in 1900 was an estimated 10.4 million and reached 14.3 million by 1930. The vibrant city's fast-growing white foreign-born populace, consisting largely of Germans, Irish, Russians, English, Canadians, Romanians, and Italians, was an estimated two million between 1900 and 1930.[23] Similarly, New York's Asian population, despite turn-of-the-twentieth-century United States immigration policies against Asians, steadily increased during the first four decades of the twentieth century. The Chinese demographics rose from 7,170 to 13,731 between 1900 and 1940.[24] New York's Japanese populace accounted for an estimated 2,312 in 1920.[25] The largest population of African Americans and Caribbean immigrants living in a northern city also called the metropolis home, making it an ideal place to examine the lives of its black female inhabitants. New York's black population, including migrat-

ing southerners, increased from 61,000 to more than 485,000 in the four decades
between 1900 and 1940. Fifty-five percent of foreign-born blacks in the United
States lived in New York City throughout the 1930s, and at least 40,000 Caribbean
immigrants resided in Harlem between 1900 and 1930.[26]

Moreover, New York's cultural and socioeconomic uniqueness was attributed to
its noteworthy informal labor market, which was part of a global phenomenon of
thriving underground employment sectors of the early twentieth century. Scholars
from various academic disciplines have employed and continue to offer a host of
terms, definitions, and theoretical frameworks that characterize informal work.
During the early 1970s, British anthropologist Keith Hart, in his seminal work on
Ghanaian open-air markets and culture, was the first scholar to define the term
informal economy, describing it as an "intricate, fertile web of exchange[s]" or bartering system of services and goods for financial or material compensation that
fall outside formal wage labor.[27] In more recent years, social scientists, including
Manuel Castells, Alejandro Portes, Lauren A. Benton, Saskia Sassen-Koob, Lisa
Maher, Winnifred Brown-Glaude, Sudhir Alladi Venkatesh, and others, have advanced Hart's analysis, offering academic audiences more nuanced perspectives
and interpretations on the informal economy.[28] Discussing the complexity of informal economy sectors in various historical settings and contemporary societies,
scholars have engaged in debates over how to define and identify informal labor
markets and the distinctions, if any, between licit and illicit income-generating
activities. Recognizing the informal economy's heterogeneous nature and its connection to both legitimate and criminal labor markets, academicians collectively
suggest that informal work, also labeled as "off-the-books," "under-the-table," and
"irregular" employment of both wage-earning employees and entrepreneurs, was
and could be quasi-legal, unlicensed, and illegal work that existed outside government oversight and regulations and violated city and state statutes. While there
are some clear distinctions between formal, informal, and criminal employment
sectors and networks, it is important to note that the relationships between these
markets were blurred and often resulted in early-twentieth-century urbanites
varying and conflicting interpretations of unrecorded and illegal work. Borrowing from historian Cynthia Blair's interpretation of the turn-of-the-twentieth-
century informal economies in Chicago, this book contends that the underground
labor market "was a network of economic endeavors and community relations that
supported both the generation of income and the exchange of goods and services
outside officially sanctioned or regulated networks of exchange."[29] Hidden employment sectors—commonly referred to but not limited to—included unlicensed
vending, moonlighting, fencing and selling stolen and counterfeit merchandise,
and laboring for organized criminal syndicates.[30] In pursuit of financial stability

and wealth, employment mobility, and the opportunity to participate in uninhibited social pleasures while simultaneously earning a living wage, New Yorkers consciously evaded city and state laws regarding income reporting, licensing permits, and health and safety and, depending on selected occupations, jeopardized their legal status as free persons and their community and familial reputations.[31]

But New York and other global underground labor markets were not monolithic. Rather, they seemingly possessed characteristics and complexities that were distinct from one another, and over time and space fluctuated according to their geographical locations and respective socioeconomic and political landscapes. Moreover, the functionality of informal labor markets was profoundly shaped by its participants' ethnic backgrounds, gender and class politics, cultural identities and traditions, and overall experiences as urban citizens. Functioning either as laborers or consumers, native-born and multiethnic New Yorkers made their imprints on the city's inimitable informal labor market. Native-born New Yorkers from various cultural groups and newly arrived immigrants and southern black migrants brought to the cosmopolitan metropolis and its clandestine employment market cultural, social, and religious values and frames of reference that derived from their respective ethnic backgrounds, migratory and settlement experiences, and, particularly for blacks, encounters with urban inequalities.

For instance, the emergence of rent parties during the first half of the twentieth century in Detroit, Chicago, New York, and other urban communities were reminiscent of, at least according to Harlem Renaissance writers Wallace Thurman and Zora Neale Hurston, popular southern working-class black after-hours amusements known as "chiddlin switches" and "jook-joint parties."[32] Discussing the cultural migration of black southern amusements and culture to the urban North, Shane Vogel writes that jook-joint parties were "central institution[s] of secular black dance and music [that] developed during and after Reconstruction by rural sharecroppers and migratory workers in the South."[33] Sociologist Ira De A. Reid notes that these social gatherings enabled "certain portions of the Negro group living in Southern cities to supplement the family income."[34] With mass migration to northern city spaces, "black southern migrants brought with them the practices, sounds, sensibilities, atmosphere, movements, and food of the jook" and used the spirit and format of the southern jook to confront personal economic issues in the north.[35] Organized in response to overpriced apartment rentals and race discrimination within urban housing markets, rent parties, also commonly known in New York as "whist parties," were hosted by money-strapped blacks or "whoever might feel the urge during a poverty-stricken interlude to pay exorbitant [weekly or monthly] rent prices."[36] Viewed by urban tenants as avenues toward increasing their household incomes and defraying living expenses, rent parties were not merely "institutions of necessity" or economic survival. Parties evolved into pleasurable and uninhibited after-hours amusements in which hardworking men and women escaped the tenets and judgment of black polite society and the daily drudgery of labor exploitation and white oppression. The historian Robin D. G. Kelley notes that in the darkened rooms of these parties "black working people of both sexes shook and twisted their overworked bodies, drank, talked, engaged in sexual play, and—in spite of occasional fights—reinforced their sense of community."[37] Rent party coordinators charged attendees, which typically included a diverse group of urbanites including maids, truck drivers, laundry workers and shoe-shine boys, seamstresses and porters, a small admission fee for an evening of thrillingly live entertainment. Northern partygoers enjoyed dancing and the musical selections of professional and amateur musicians; engaged in gambling, smoking, and drinking; and dined on home-cooked southern and Caribbean cuisine, such as Hoppin' John rice and tomatoes, gumbo, collard greens, fried chicken and fish, black-eyed peas, and steaming chitterling.

Hosting neighborhood rent parties to stave off the tide of costly apartment living symbolized how diverse income-generating strategies incorporated different aspects of southern black and Caribbean cultures. The varying ways cultural migrations shaped aspects of blacks' moneymaking tactics created subaltern labor markets that were uniquely black and existed within New York's larger informal employment sectors. Subinformal sectors made it possible for laborers to ingeniously address northern racism and restricted employment and meet the cultural and consumer needs of city blacks. Such markets also afforded persons of African descent access to unique services and products, amusements, and cultural practices that were primarily located in black communities. At the same time, black men and women's distinct wage producing and hustling tactics stretched far beyond New York's black enclaves. Black informal economy laborers took advantage of the 1920s mood of unrestrained individual behavior and sexual revolution, and urbanites' search for uninhibited city amusements and the national economic crisis of the 1930s, and sold and marketed services and products to white middle-class slummers and working-class wage earners.[38] Blacks' cultural rituals and their unique economic and survival strategies and leisure activities transcended their original geographical terrains and producers and users. New York white consumers, enthralled by bohemian excursions to black working-class sections of Harlem and Brooklyn and by the prospect of experiencing interracial sociability and cross-racial sex, appropriated and exploited aspects of urban black culture for personal amusements and, in some instances, as a way to fulfill their own economic endeavors. In short, elements of black culture reached new urban geographies and offered the city's ethnically diverse population the opportunity to engage in urban experiences that, at times, reinforced and transcended race, gender, and class hierarchies.

New York's urban informal labor sector transformed, enriched, and endangered the lives of many city women. Urban workingwomen were integral to the city's parallel labor market. Occupying employment spaces traditionally reserved for—and in some instances, dominated by—men, black women's physical presence in particular labor settings, their work patterns and strategies, and their personal economic and social ambitions reconfigured the city's thriving and, at times, treacherous informal labor market. Out of economic necessity, attraction to city amusements, or the search for new occupational opportunities that transcended formal wage labor, women courageously entered labor sectors that reinforced and shifted racial, gender, class, and sexual politics of the day. Whether managing a sex resort, collecting number slips on street corners, or manufacturing and selling alcohol, drugs, and medicine in their homes, urban female entrepreneurs and sellers broadened public images of women and labor, and through their many different labor activities refuted societal views that suggested that unregulated modes of employment furnished economic and social opportunities only for men. Indeed, New York's informal economy sector afforded black women alternative revenue streams, making it possible for many to reimagine and transform their lives and adopt new labor and social identities. African American women made a place for themselves within the complex urban informal sector and, in doing so, created a world that included and allowed them to claim space for themselves as wage laborers, entrepreneurs, and cultural producers.

CHAPTER 1

Black Women, Urban Labor, and New York's Informal Economy

On September 28, 1937, Odile Gonzalez, dubbed by police as the "prima donna of the Harlem hot goods racket," was arrested and accused of being "a notorious receiver of stolen goods." The mid-thirty-something-year-old "Hot Goods Queen," who was previously convicted of prostitution, grand larceny, and felonious assault throughout the 1930s, was one of the purported leaders of a burglary ring that terrorized New York clothing merchants. According to the New York City Police Department (NYPD), Gonzalez and her male associates, including William (Bub) Hewlitt, one of "Harlem's most feared hoodlums" and illegal lottery racketeers' gunman, burglarized several men's department stores, stealing business suits and peddling them to street vendors. While searching Gonzalez's house at 217 West 111th Street, officers discovered sixty-eight men's suits valued at $1,207, all taken from Crawford Clothes, a popular men's store in Harlem. With Gonzalez's arrest, police believed they had captured one of the city's notorious thieves and uncovered the mastermind behind "a citywide chain for distributing stolen property." Upon being apprehended and during her 1937 trial, Gonzalez unsurprisingly lied about her involvement in the "hot stuff" syndicate. To avoid a possible lengthy prison sentence, she informed authorities that her arrest was a case of mistaken identity and that she was not part of a citywide ring of thieves. Gonzalez also, perhaps out of fear of being physically reprimanded, did not implicate her male coconspirators. With the incriminating evidence already in her apartment, Gonzalez did however admit to police that she received the stolen men's suits from a friend and later disposed of the merchandise, selling them to her friends and neighbors for $8 apiece.

Gonzalez's fictitious story about her noninvolvement in the hot goods ring paid off. Rather than being criminally charged with grand larceny or burglary she was tried and convicted of a lesser criminal offense: receiving stolen property. Gonzalez was sentenced to less than one year at New York State's Bedford Reformatory. Upon her release from prison, Gonzalez was not interested in obtaining legitimate formal work and resumed her position as a thief and hot goods vendor. In 1941, Gonzalez again found herself on the wrong side of the law; she violated her parole and was arrested on a burglary charge.[1]

Gonzalez's criminal activities as a thief, con artist, and sex worker were at odds with prevailing black bourgeois perspectives on female labor and perceptibly clashed with conventional images of proper decorum for black women. As a financially struggling working-class woman, Gonzalez was not concerned with black elites' notions of propriety nor did she feel compelled to contest white New Yorkers' prevailing perceptions of urban African American women as dangerous and unlawful "amazons."[2] Her economic circumstances perhaps did not grant her the luxury of worrying about public perceptions concerning her outward behavior or income-producing activities. Like many economically challenged women of the first half of the twentieth century, Gonzalez was more interested in devising wage-generating strategies that addressed her immediate financial circumstance. Gonzalez became one of the many black women who took part in the city's informal and criminal economies, participating in crimes of survival and refusing to wait for and depend upon economic assistance from race leaders, moral crusaders, and local charitable organizations. She relied upon her own survival skills to earn a living wage, illustrating a sense of individuality and commitment to self-preservation. Her participation within both urban criminal and informal labor markets was fueled by a desire to create a future in which her short- and long-standing economic troubles disappeared and conceivably by personal interpretations of urban space, racial uplift, and respectable politics. For her, and other informal economy women, "uplift" and "respectable" were not necessarily construed as a collective concept aimed at empowering the race but rather as a practical strategy that stressed individual empowerment, self-sufficiency, and fiscal stability.

This chapter moves beyond prevailing historical narratives of urban northern black women as formal wage earners during the early twentieth century. It situates the complex and varying labor accounts and economic strategies of black women like Gonzalez at the center of New York's burgeoning informal labor economy. I probe the socioeconomic and personal factors shaping black women's attraction to informal occupations as well as the many challenges and obstacles women faced as off-the-books laborers. Participation in the urban informal economy reflected black women's desire to advance their own socioeconomic and private agendas, including financially providing for one's families, fulfilling sexual and personal needs, and achieving labor independence and flexibility. More importantly, New York black women, taking advantage of the economic and social opportunities furnished by the city's informal labor sector, desired to "alter the recipe of possibilities" for themselves, according to historian Sarah Deutsch.[3] Although different categories of informal labor were considered illegal, quasi-legal, disreputable, and dangerous by urban moral reformers and by disapproving relatives and neighbors, black women readily and grudgingly secured jobs as hostesses, dancers, and waitresses at nightclubs and speakeasies; became unlicensed street peddlers, numbers runners, and narcotics saleswomen and bootleggers; and established home- and street-based gambling, psychic, and sex-related businesses. Wide-ranging categories of under-the-table work benefited many women's lives, enabling some to sidestep menial labor such as household work and others to periodically combine illegal and quasi-legal employment with that of formal wage labor. Nontraditional avenues of labor afforded some black women occupational autonomy, an intangible benefit that made it possible for women to balance their multifaceted roles as workers, wives and mothers, and amusement seekers.

Conversely, laboring in some of the city's grittiest environments and associating with unsavory urbanites came at a price. Depending on the occupation, informal work complicated and at times endangered some women's lives. Informal work in no way guaranteed labor equity or financial stability and success, and it did not always yield social rewards. As informal laborers, black women knowingly and inadvertently sacrificed their neighborhood reputations and risked their personal liberties and safety. Their visions of economic stability and labor autonomy within the city's informal labor market were thwarted by race and gender discrimination, public and family shame, arrest and imprisonment, verbal and sexual exploitation, and death. In spite of such tremendous labor constraints, women struggled to carve out niches for themselves within highly competitive and masculine labor sectors. Consequently, many, for the sake of economic security and to lay claim to urban spaces, developed and relied upon a complex web of survival strategies that allowed them to earn a living and more importantly to navigate the city's informal labor market.

Urban Black Women's Socioeconomic and Labor Conditions

Urban working-class black New Yorkers faced tremendous financial pressure during what Rayford W. Logan referred to as "the nadir" and throughout the Depression era. While a segment of better-class and educated African Americans experienced economic prosperity during the post–World War era and New York's flourishing social, cultural, and literary transformation of the 1920s and participated in urban commercialism, the vast majority of working-class black urbanites residing throughout the city's five boroughs lived under financial distress. The national economic downturn of the 1930s coupled with mounting unemployment, poverty, and race, class, and gender discrimination exacerbated many working-class blacks' existing low socioeconomic status.[4] Discussing the severe impact of the 1930s financial upheaval on African Americans, scholar Cheryl Greenberg writes, "Most African Americans did not have that far to fall when the Great Depression arrived. Even before 1929, the vast majority lived in desperate poverty."[5]

Northern-style racial prejudice and customary forms of race segregation further complicated blacks' financial circumstances and relegated them to crime-infested sections and inadequate housing structures. Black urbanites, according to historian Thomas Sugrue, "faced a regime of racial proscriptions [in the North] that was every bit as deeply entrenched as the southern system of Jim Crow. Economic injustice and pervasive discrimination knew no regional boundaries."[6] Daily encounters with roaches and rats, leaky ceilings and chipped paint, hall toilets, poorly ventilated rooms, and at times nonexistent hot water and heat were representative of many blacks' apartment living experience. Describing black San Juan Hill residents' housing conditions, NAACP activist Mary White Ovington described slum apartments as "human hives, honeycombed with little rooms thick with human beings. Bedrooms open into airshafts that admit no fresh breezes, only foul air carrying too often the germs of disease."[7] Despite such inadequate housing conditions, city blacks paid considerably more money per month for rent than whites residing in the same impoverished communities and apartment buildings.[8] Black New York newspapers of the day routinely reported on the disproportionate amount of rent prices between the races. A 1923 *NYA* article noted that black families living on 145th Street moved into a "five-room apartment paying $80 per month and "former white tenants [paid] $40 per month."[9] In 1925, a judge at a hearing of the Mayor's Committee on Rent Profiteering testified that "colored tenants in [New York, especially in Harlem] pay twice as much as white tenants for apartments" with leaking ceilings, rats, smashed windows, and the daily stench of garbage.[10] Writing about the impact of New York's housing problem on poor wage earners during the late 1920s, *NYAN* journalist and community advocate Thelma E. Berlack rightfully maintained that "New York rents are generally exorbitant; [and] that, all things being considered, a Negro pays rents far out of proportion to that charged a white man in a more exclusive section of the city."[11]

But black New Yorkers were not alone in occupying substandard high-rent apartments. Paying exorbitant rents for dilapidated and rundown housing structures was commonplace for blacks residing in other urban northern and midwestern communities. Black residents in Indianapolis's "Bucktown" paid $25 a month for "flimsy one-story frame row houses that rented to whites for $18"; on average black Chicagoans paid at least $100 more for rent per month than whites between 1909 and 1919; in Detroit, white and black landlords and real estate agents charged black families one-third more for rent.[12] Apartment building proprietors and landlords assumed that blacks, especially those of a low socioeconomic status, could live off fewer amenities and were unworthy of quality housing. Moreover, landlords, particularly those concerned only with monetary gain, cared less about their tenants' poor living conditions or the physical structures of their buildings.

Menial employment wages made it difficult for black New Yorkers to afford exorbitant rents, household necessities, food and transportation costs, and other expenses of city living. According to one resident, "livin' is so high that you've just got to scrub and scrub for the pennies to pay the bills."[13] Racial exclusion in the urban labor market effectively barred black men and women from high-paying skilled positions, including industrial labor. In 1910, only 12 percent of black men worked in mechanical and manufacturing jobs; by 1920 that number increased to 21 percent. At least two-thirds of all gainfully employed black men occupied positions as janitors, elevator operators, waiters, and personal servants.[14] Working-class African American women fared no better than black men. Writing about the burdens of race and gender biases on black female wage earners, educator Elise Johnson McDougald's seminal 1925 essay, "The Double Task: The Struggle of Negro Women for Sex and Race Emancipation," observed that "young Negro girls who might be well suited to salesmanship [or any other well-paying job were] barred from all but the menial positions."[15] Statistic data on black female industrial laborers confirm McDougald's assertions, showing that black women made up 2 percent of professional workers and 23 percent of manufacturing and mechanical industries laborers between 1910 and 1920.

The vast majority of working-class black women engaged in various forms of household work. New York black women labored as cooks, laundresses, domestics, and caregivers for white children. In 1905, National Urban League cofounder and activist George Edmund Haynes reported that 89.3 percent of black women were employed as domestic laborers. Between the first and second decades of the twentieth century, an estimated 70 percent of Manhattan black women labored in white homes at least six days a week, earning between $4 and $6 per week.[16] Even well-educated black women, with "their spirits broken and hopes blasted because they had been obliged to forfeit their training on account of race prejudice" found themselves cooking and cleaning in other peoples' homes.[17] No matter what their academic backgrounds or skilled labor experience was, black women like Florida native and former Mary McLeod Hospital and Training School for Nurses student Blanche Haines had difficulties securing professional labor positions. Arriving in

New York in the 1930s, the thirty-year-old Haines's failure to locate employment that corresponded with her educational training forced her into household work. Haines eventually took a position as a laundress at a Manhattan brothel and later became a prostitute at the same sex resort.[18] Speaking on the "problem of the unemployed negro woman in New York city," white social reformer Frances A. Kellor, in her 1905 *Charities* article on black female urban behavior, labor, and pathology, noted that women like Haines were "unquestionably shut out from many lines of occupation and in many instances [pushed] to rely upon odd jobs and employment in the questionable houses."[19] Indeed, Kellor was right about black women's limited employment options. Haines's jobless status was not unique. Nor was her decision to labor as a domestic worker at a house of assignation easy or uncommon. She was one of many academically trained women that toiled at gambling, drug, and brothel dens, especially as household workers. Actual percentages of women who secured employment as domestics, cooks, and laundresses at underworld establishments are difficult to discern as many intermittently wove in and out of informal labor.

Limited employment opportunities and low wages made it virtually impossible for working-class African American women to navigate the urban terrain. Writing letters to various African American and radical Left newspapers and city politicians throughout the early twentieth century, working-poor single women and mothers publicly expressed their individual and collective frustrations with joblessness, poverty, and low wages, and revealed their day-to-day agony over affording household expenditures. Articulating the sentiments of countless impoverished women during the national economic crisis of the 1930s, one unemployed black mother writing to the Communist Party's *Daily Worker* passionately explained the impact of poverty on millions of households around the country, and poor women's inability to provide their children with the basic necessities of life. "[We are] tired of seeing our children go naked and hungry, crying for bread. We must raise our voices louder against this."[20] Similarly, in a 1938 letter to New York City mayor Fiorello LaGuardia, which was later printed in the NYAN, domestic worker Martina Harris explained the difficulty of stretching her meager $10-a-week salary. "Out of $10 [Harris] was faced with room rent at least $5 per week [and fees for] proper medical care."[21] Lower-class black women's heartfelt testimonials were representative of urban poor women's collective hardships and their tireless efforts to care for themselves and their families. Women's individual writings offer rare glimpses into how poverty and economic hardship framed their daily lives and encroached upon their traditional roles as mothers, wives, and caregivers. Moreover, poor black women's written artifacts, signaling a sense of desperation and hope, illuminated their attempts to bring public attention to less privileged women's economic troubles, as well as their aspirations for decent employment and adequate wages.

Prolonged poverty coupled with the unrelenting stress of possible starvation and unemployment took a serious toll on black women's physical and mental health. Anxiety over poor living conditions and quality of life increased black women's chances of contracting influenza and tuberculosis and experiencing high blood pressure, panic attacks, depression, and other stress-induced health problems. In 1913, a Charitable Organization Society (COS) social worker reported that Agnes Littleton, a single mother of five, was "subject to fits of crying when she allow[ed] herself to think of her troubles" and suffered from "unpleasant sensations in the head." Upon further observation by a medical doctor, Littleton was diagnosed with the "anxiety of keeping the home together, especially anxiety about money." While the doctor noted that Littleton's "present condition [was] nothing abnormal," his medical recommendation for the suffering woman was idealistic and impractical for someone in her economic position. The concerned medical professional proposed that Littleton receive plenty of "rest and [stay] free from worry."[22]

Additionally, ongoing fears of seemingly endless cycles of financial hardship and single parenthood and overall feelings of despair adversely affected some black women's sense of self-worth. At times, the thought of inescapable poverty exhausted and undermined black women's confidence and optimism, clouded their problem-solving abilities, lowered their self-esteem, and resulted in conceptual confusion over how to confront and overcome economic hardship.[23] The tragic story of Nannie Green, a twenty-five-year-old widow and domestic worker in Harlem, underscores the destructive power of lost hope. After the death of her husband, Green, who was overcome by grief and suicidal thoughts, candidly revealed feelings of failure and disappointment to relatives. Green was distressed by the prospect of caring for her eleven-year-old daughter. "Oh, I don't care if [I] live[d] a minute longer. I've had lots of trouble in this world and I see no reason why I should continue to struggle like this.". Single parenthood and the inability to meet pressing economic obligations drove Green to kill herself in 1938; the grief-stricken woman leaped from the East 138th Street Bridge into the Harlem River.[24] Mental stress over family responsibility even provoked some urban African American women to commit violent crimes against friends and even family members. Sixteen-year-old Jamaica, Queens, resident and former domestic worker Lenora Smith was one such individual. Smith's unemployed and single parent status had fatal consequences for her seven-month-old child. In 1939, Smith, by her own admission, walked into the Rockaway Beach police precinct and informed law enforcers that she had murdered her baby. She calmly testified that she "had thrown [her] child into the water because she was destitute and unable to provide for her properly." Smith's act of infanticide demonstrated her and other impoverished parents' frantic attempts to reduce their family sizes and obligations. For some mothers, child murder allowed them to lessen their anxiety, stress, and financial burdens and appeared to be the only way to avoid subjecting their children to further economic distress. In other words, some women perceived the act of murdering their child as an act of maternal love and protection. Women's unimaginable actions against their little ones also revealed the often hidden dramas and emotional pressures plaguing working-class women's lives, particularly that of single parenthood, spousal abandonment, and teenage pregnancy.[25]

Working-Class Black Women, Urban Public Space, and Racial Uplift

Pressing economic circumstances certainly shaped many women's involvement within the urban informal labor sector. On the other hand, the decision to appropriate city streets and apartment building units, stoops, and hallways for labor and leisure pursuits was also profoundly influenced by the multiple ways in which black New Yorkers interpreted and used public and private spaces. Urban blacks, particularly the working class, claimed city spaces for their own purposes, often dismissing and reconfiguring black elite ideas that some urban communities were overcrowded bastions of "loud and vile talking men and women who make no pretense to refinement or decency."[26] Although urban racism confined most black New Yorkers to the poorest sections of the city, many, despite residing in deteriorating apartment structures and crime-stricken communities, made the best out of their congested and impoverished living conditions, especially as they attempted to create meaningful lives for themselves and their families. Blacks understood that the city represented both condemnation and salvation. It was a place where racial and gender biases plagued nearly every aspect of their lives. At the same time, the metropolis provided inventive and hardworking individuals the opportunity to create socioeconomic, political, and cultural landscapes that reflected their experiences with northern discrimination and spoke to their distinct ethnic backgrounds and desire to economically survive and thrive in one of the nation's most fascinating cities. Urban blacks unapologetically and constantly refashioned and used urban public and private settings as they saw fit. This often meant employing geographical terrains to demonstrate a broad range of political and social expressions and imaginative modes of labor.

City streets served multiple functions for early-twentieth-century black New Yorkers. Crowded street corners and pathways were colorful backdrops for leisure and work as well as for political and religious activism. Speaking on Harlem's vibrant street culture, novelist Wallace Thurman observed, "a Hindoo faker here, a loud Socialist there, a medicine doctor ballyhooing, a corn doctor, a blind musician, serious people, gay people, philanderers, and preachers. Seventh Avenue is filled with deep rhythmic laughter. It is a civilized lane with primitive traits."[27] Street strolling on their way to work or church, or even socializing on apartment stoops and fire escapes, black urbanites observed prominent race reform organizations such as the NAACP and Universal Negro Improvement Association (UNIA) leading mass protests against Jim Crow segregation, disenfranchisement, and mob violence down New York streets. On the corners of 135th and Lenox Avenues, Harlemites bore witness to the intellectualism and political activism of radical stepladder orators such as Hubert Harrison, Elizabeth Hendrickson, and Frank Crosswaith. Contributing to Harlem's blossoming cultural and political landscape of the 1920s and 1930s, stepladder preachers used the streets as a testing ground for radical political thought, disseminating to regular and casual onlookers theoretical analysis on the African past, Marxism, and class politics.

New York streets were "public conduits of sociability" and fertile landscapes for impromptu lessons on street protocol and hustling.[28] Using the streets to escape their cramped apartments, ordinary black men and women fraternized on city sidewalks and on their apartment building stoops, in doorways, and on fire escapes—which many perceived as extensions of their overpriced apartments. Laboring under exploitative conditions and constantly under the scrutiny of their white counterparts, urban blacks looked forward to socializing in their neighborhoods. Street landscapes became informal political and educational arenas where blacks candidly discussed politics, racial injustices, and the latest social and neighborhood happenings. Former 1930s Cotton Club performer and communist Howard "Stretch" Johnson recalled, "you'd see thousands of men and women in the streets all day long, playing the numbers or just standing because there was absolutely nothing to do. They just talked about the weather, about women, about poverty."[29] City spaces also became central locations where African Americans perfected the fine art of hustling and learned how to be self-sufficient, quick-witted, and imaginative. Witnessing firsthand the silver-tongued ability of some black New Yorkers, writer Roi Ottley commented that "hustling means starting from the nub and soft-talking yourself into a freebie" and thinking fast on one's feet. In essence, Lenox Avenue and several other New York thoroughfares were fertile training grounds for learning how to make a quick dollar and for acquiring valuable survival skills.

Working black women's outlook on unconventional labor and the appropriation of public and private spaces for either political or social use were anchored in women's refashioning of middle-class interpretations of racial uplift and respectable ideologies. Conflicting notions of such politics operated on various levels within the African American community and most certainly differed and shifted according to one's socioeconomic circumstances and personal politics and aspirations. Racial uplifters—those striving for black liberation, the legislation and implementation of equal rights statutes, and the eradication of Jim Crow segregation—viewed outward displays of cultural refinement and sexual restraint as preconditions toward race and gender equality and against widespread white popular culture images that imagined African Americans as uncivilized hypersexual beings who were unworthy of citizenship. Regardless of their financial status, African American women, for the collective betterment and representation of the race, were expected to adhere to elite definitions of public behavior despite individual viewpoints and quests for self-exploration and discovery.[30] According to scholar Lisa B. Thompson and others, "circulating ideologies such as the Cult of True Womanhood and the Cult of Domesticity, which emphasized piety, purity, and submissiveness, held promise for revising notions about black peoples as immoral."[31]

white woman feminism

Other black women violated, remapped, and subscribed to varying aspects of black bourgeois politics. Their fluid and shifting ideas about public correctness were based on their respective socioeconomic realities and priorities and the desire to live more autonomously and not be confined by societal views of outward behavior or appropriate work and public amusements. For many, racial uplift and public propriety were not necessarily perceived as concepts aimed at advancing African Americans' collective socioeconomic and political conditions, but rather were broadly interpreted as practical strategies that stressed individual economic empowerment and permanence and social independence. Working black women reasoned that personal fiscal soundness and the prerogative to unreservedly select their own occupations and leisure activities trumped projecting public representations of deportment.[32]

Historian Cynthia Blair points out that, as working-class black women articulated alternative and new versions of respectable and uplift politics, they were "neither totally isolated from the values of the families out of which they sprang nor entirely removed from the nearby black community to which many had some familial or social connection."[33] Holding on to childhood lessons of religiosity, chastity, self-help, community building, and other tenets of respectable politics, some black women reluctantly secured extralegal employment that was incongruent with learned and expected family and community values. In fact, many used illicit labor to support respectable behavior, ambitions, and attitudes.[34] One twenty-year-old black single mother sacrificed her reputation in order to care for her tuberculosis-stricken daughter. Deeply ashamed by her line of work yet compelled by family obligation, the woman made the difficult decision to barter sex for money.[35] Similarly, black women like fifty-one-year-old Mary Holmes took portions of their income from illegal work to contribute to black self-help, religious, and educational institutions. A laundress and founder of her 137th Street home-based religious center, St. Mary's Spiritual Church, Holmes used monetary profits from numbers running to finance her church. Holding "good luck" prayer meetings every Sunday and occasionally throughout the week, Holmes collected illegal numbers slips from church attendees, mostly a small group of "women and very young white girls of school age." The interesting fact that Holmes's church was frequented by an ethnically diverse group of young women and girls could indicate that she was operating a sex house—although primary documentation makes no claim of this view. But it does raise the question: Why would young white teenage girls attend Holmes's upper Manhattan place of worship? Nevertheless, in 1927, Holmes, despite attempting to use the unrespectable to support charitable pursuits, was arrested when "332 policy slips were found in [her] Bible." The self-professed spiritual advisor admitted to arresting officers that she collected numbers not to accumulate individual wealth but rather "for the upkeep of the church" and to aid her impoverished community with "welfare work." As a consequence of violating city laws against gambling and possession of numbers slips, the female church minister was sentenced to a three-month jail term in the workhouse on Welfare Island.[36]

Unlike Holmes, urban women like South Carolina migrant Lucille Jones were not concerned with using respectable behavior to uphold or maintain noble endeavors and childhood lessons of respectability. Although reared in morally upright households by parents of unblemished reputations and determined characters, some black women consciously dismissed learned family values or, perhaps in the case of Jones, found it difficult to "combat [bad] influences" once they arrived in urban cities. Although Jones "was a favorite child of her mother and given a great deal," her desire for and fascination with "pretty" luxury items and Harlem's nightlife led her to associate with a "group of men and women of the worst sort." Naive about the perils of city life and enticed by urban consumerism, the newcomer's seemingly unsavory acquaintances introduced her to "drinking parties, casual sexual relations with both women and men, and prostitution."[37]

Black Women and New York's Informal Economy

Early-twentieth-century portrayals of urban underground labor depicted a gendered world of danger and violence, competing masculinities, and sexual exploitation. Often considered masculine territory by prevailing society, the city's informal sector was a socioeconomic and political market in which men of varying class and racial backgrounds labored, socialized, and, more importantly, formulated and articulated their sensibilities about a range of ideas, including the meaning and appropriation of public space and leisure, gender roles and sexuality, and patriarchy. It was, however, inhabited by and produced economic and entrepreneurial opportunities for what some prominent black and white social intellectuals, such as Howard University Professor Kelly Miller, viewed as an increasing "surplus of [Negro] women" in urban cities like New York.[38] This rising community of female laborers took advantage of socioeconomic prospects furnished by rapid urbanization, black migration, European immigration, and mass material consumption of the Progressive era, establishing themselves as buyers, sellers, and consumers of illicit and licit products and services. Urban black women engendered New York's underground sector and were significant to the city's shadow economy. Off-the-books black female laborers widened traditional images of female work, as well as portrayals of women in public and private settings. At times, their labor shifted racial, gender, class, and sexual politics operating within different sectors of New York's informal economy, and allowed many, when necessary, to be aggressive, disorderly, violent, and "act in a manner commonly thought unrefined, even degraded, for their sex."[39] Women's labor decisions reflected their broad beliefs that informal labor markets potentially offered alternative paths toward monetary and social benefits, new labor identities as urban markets sellers, and economic independence.

Informal labor afforded many black women the prospect of bypassing unskilled employment or combining legitimate work with that of off-the-books labor. To make financial ends meet and burdened by the harsh realities of poverty, house eviction, and hungry children, urban women labored simultaneously in multiple occupations. While employed as a janitor at two apartment buildings during the 1920s, thirty-nine-year-old single mother of five Edna Peterson also collected illegal numbers slips, earning 20 percent of collections and averaging $3 to $5 a day.[40] Similarly, the threat of poverty exerted pressure on Pearl Dore to piece together income from several nontraditional sources. Living with her religious sister Vivian Brown, twenty-five-year-old Dore supported herself by selling marijuana cigarettes at a Manhattan "weed joint" and with "day work" she obtained from standing on one of the Bronx's infamous and exploitative "slave markets." Dore's labor selections, particularly her selling of illegal marijuana cigarettes, were motivated by her inability to locate formal wage work during the era of the Great Depression, as well as by her frustrations with being part of what New York political activists Marvel Cooke and Ella Baker identified in their 1935 *Crisis* magazine article as the "paper bag brigade." Dore and other members of the "brigade," unemployed black domestic workers, "patiently [waited] in front of Woolworth's on 170th Street, between Jerome and Walton Aves" for white "housewives to buy their strength and energy for an hour, two hours, or even for a day at the munificent rate of fifteen, twenty, twenty-five, or, if luck [was] with them, thirty cents an hour."[41] Despite Dore's economic and labor hardships, her sister disapproved of her employment hustle. Brown reasoned that her sister's irregular work schedule and fast income from dealing drugs made her idle, discouraged her from securing formal wage work, and placed a strain on their relationship. "She has hardly worked since living with me and many quarrels have taken place because [she lays] in bed until late in the day."[42]

Informal work became a springboard for launching independent businesses, transforming many working-poor and unemployed, yet ambitious, New York black women into survivalist entrepreneurs. Borrowing from scholar Robert L. Boyd's work on early-twentieth-century black entrepreneurship, survivalist entrepreneurs were "persons who [became] self-employed in response to a desperate need to find an independent means of livelihood." This was certainly the case for some Progressive- and Inter-war–era women, who were part of increasing national and local unemployment statistics, and whose dire financial status compelled and even inspired them to create and pursue a variety of economic opportunities for themselves. With little or no economic capital, these survivalist entrepreneurs, refusing to wait for charitable assistance or for someone to employ them, boldly took a chance on themselves. But as the rest of this book shows, urban women saw beyond the economic benefits of underground entrepreneurship and yearned for the intangible rewards and privileges of independent work.[43] Such was the case for street vendor and entrepreneur Lillian "Pig Foot Mary" Harris Dean.

Arriving in New York City virtually penniless in 1896, Dean, a poor migrant from Tougaloo, Mississippi, established her unlicensed-turned-licensed food pushcart enterprise from wages earned and saved from domestic work. Described as a "huge Goliath woman with a deep voice," Dean was celebrated by black Harlemites for her unique business, featuring her savory fried pigs' feet.[44] Dean belonged to an emerging group of black, white, and immigrant pushcart vendors and entrepreneurs who played an integral part in New York's urban commerce during the early twentieth century.[45] Despite urban elites' and city merchants' strong objections to noisy and competitive pushcart businesses, one 1930s writer observed that the "pushcart markets are as characteristic a part of the New York pageant as the skyscrapers."[46] Establishing their businesses with little capital, many pushcart peddlers competitively hawked inexpensive and low-grade products, including shoes, fruits, vegetables, handbags, flowers, and pots and pans, from sunup to sundown at legally designated street markets; others without required city permits and licenses also operated street businesses on city corners.[47] In the fall of 1901, Dean purchased "a dilapidated baby carriage and a large wash boiler. [She] then [talked] the proprietor of Rudolph's, a popular saloon near 61st Street on Amsterdam Avenue, into allowing her to boil the delicacy atop his cook stove. Mounting the steaming boiler of pigs' feet on the baby carriage, she wheeled all her worldly wealth through the swing doors of the saloon and set up business."[48] Laboring on the corner of Lenox Avenue and 135th Street "from early morning until late night" during the second decade of the twentieth century, Dean, wearing "starched gingham dresses," re-created traditional Southern foodways in an urban Northern setting, cooking fried chicken, corn, hogmaws, chitterlings, and her famous boiled pigs' feet. Speaking of Dean's popularity among black and white New Yorkers alike, James Weldon Johnson observed that "everyone who knows . . . 'Mary' and her stand has been tempted by the smell of her pigs' feet, fried chicken and hot corn, even if he has not been a customer."[49]

Lillian Harris Dean was a successful purveyor of southern black culture and cuisine, showcasing her culinary talents and skills on some of New York's most exciting and busiest street corners. Her cooking style symbolized a cultural familiarity and identification with Southern traditions and "facilitated the migration of black Southern foodways to urban Northern and Mid-western centers."[50] For southern migrants, Dean's food was a pleasant reminder of familiar customs and home-cooked meals prepared by relatives. Since the days of slavery, African American women's unique culinary styles were important to their community. Food not only provided the daily nourishment needed to sustain life, it also reinforced family and community connections. Important conversations about family matters, politics and love, respectable politics, and racial injustices were intensely discussed and debated over "soul food." For African American women like Dean, food symbolized a form of cultural work that afforded women economic independence and space to creatively contest race, gender, and class oppression while preserving and forging a distinct culinary custom.[51]

A variety of socioeconomic factors guided Dean's tireless labor on New York streets. The cooking sensation hoped to, and did, create a financially sound future for herself and her family, which included her husband John W. Dean and stepdaughter. Additionally, Dean's street-vending career and business hustle was motivated by her desire "to purchase a place for herself in an old folk's home for respectable colored people."[52] Dean's persistence as an entrepreneur paid off, and she was able to see, experience, and enjoy the fruits of her work. Gaining pecuniary mobility and stability through street labor allowed Dean to travel extensively throughout the United States and abroad and to make monetary contributions to a number of religious, business, and fraternal organizations, including Maggie Lena Walker's Independent Order of St. Luke. Moreover, Dean parlayed her pushcart venture into a substantial real estate business. It was even rumored that the "Pig Feet Queen" paid $42,000 in cash for a five-story building on Seventh Avenue and 137th Street. When Dean died in California in 1929, she was reportedly worth $375,000 and owned real estate throughout Harlem and in Los Angeles.[53]

African American women's informal labor and entrepreneurial experiences were not monolithic. All self-employed women did not attain economic success or financial stability or garner neighborhood respect and popularity like Lillian Harris Dean. Under-the-table labor was erratic and often filled with days of uncertainty and round-the-clock pursuit of customers and business. Even after spending long working hours in their homes or on the streets, many black female informal workers were empty-handed at the end of the day or earned just enough money to pay their bills. Commenting on the daily challenges of self-employment in general, and on street prostitution specifically, New York sex worker Big Bess, in a 1938 interview with writer and Works Progress Administration (WPA) employee Frank Byrd, re-called that the sex trade was "a tough racket. It's got so [bad that] a girl can hardly make a decent living anymore. There was a time when a girl could go out there and pick up a couple hundred a week. But that was a long time ago. You gotta do some tall hustling to even get by nowadays." Even more candidly, Big Bess further expressed her and perhaps other informal laborers' overwhelming frustrations with unsteady employment and earnings. "[I am] getting sick and tired of this life, but what can I do?"[54]

Additionally, many informal wageworkers and entrepreneurs conceivably ex-perienced the common obstacle of nonpaying employers and clients. Consumers that defaulted on payments for rendered services often attempted to renegotiate and haggle for lower prices, concocted stories about affording more pressing liv-ing expenses, and sometimes absconded after informal laborers provided agreed services. Case in point: some self-professed clairvoyants—those in the business of offering clients advice on money, sickness, love, and marriage, lost income and commercial products when clients accumulated an extensive running tab or re-fused to pay because they were unsatisfied with fortune-tellers' services or magical products. Nonpaying clients cost enterprising black women money and time, and placed many in tighter financial positions. Similarly, working-poor unlicensed daycare providers' weekly incomes were compromised by nonpaying parents who found it difficult to afford daily and weekly boarding fees or by destitute mothers who abandoned their children for short and long periods of time, leaving childcare providers with the financial responsibility of caring for someone else's child.

Economic desperation, unproductive working days, and irregular income hardly deterred some New York working-class women from seeking economic opportu-nities within the city's informal labor market. Many black women recognized the monetary limits and dangers of unregulated work but were drawn to the prospect of procuring the intangible benefits, namely labor control and flexibility. Since the end of American slavery, obtaining occupational autonomy, a concept often reserved for whites, was part of black women's perception of and quest for Ameri-can freedom and citizenship. Leslie Schwalm writes that "when freedwomen in-sisted on working 'in their own way and as such times as they think fit,' they were articulating a politics of Reconstruction in which women's experiences of gender, race, and a history of enslavement were inseparable. They made the issue of re-constructing work their own." Black women not only viewed labor autonomy as a way to construct their new identities and family structures and economies but as a weapon against race, gender, and class discrimination and white employers' relentless efforts to undermine their work.[55]

Early-twentieth-century white employers viewed black women's labor as menial, subordinate, and cheap, thus undercutting their claims and rights to fair wages and treatment, decent work environments, and human dignity. White employers expected black female wageworkers to be cheery while working long hours and performing arduous tasks, to be obedient and respectful, and to tolerate maltreatment and exploitative working conditions. Moreover, white men and women demanded that blacks adhere to codes of racial etiquette as prescribed by whites and "display not only civil but often servile behavior" even in the face of physical violence.[56] When twenty-year-old single mother and daytime clerical worker Katherine Herring applied for a part-time domestic servant position (which she was offered) in the home of an elderly Jewish couple, she received a glimpse of her potential workplace conditions as well as her future employers' attitudes toward persons of African descent. After inquiring about proposed weekly wages, the husband, believing that Herring was attempting to negotiate for more money, yelled at her, positing that: "N----rs are all damned thieves and are not good." Even worse, and without regard for Herring as a human being, he spit and struck her in the face and violently threw her out of the house.[57]

Herring's horrific treatment by her white counterparts was not unusual. It was commonplace for whites to verbally and physically abuse black household workers. Belonging to a long-standing tradition of white violence against African Americans, physical and sexual abuse within household labor spaces was used to wield power and authority over supposedly recalcitrant black servants and was integral to the creation and functioning of white supremacy. Spending much of her days cleaning an upper-Westside apartment on 72nd Street, Harlem resident and household worker Jennie Harrison was brutally beaten by her thirty-four-year-old female employer on New Year's Day in 1925. After not being paid for three weeks, Harrison demanded her pay of $45 from her employer, Ziegfeld Follies dancer Evans Burrow Fontaine, who was the former girlfriend of New York millionaire Cornelius Vanderbilt. Harrison's request was met with a coat hanger. She also claimed that Fontaine, "in a rage, thrust a revolver under her nose."[58] In 1939, NYAN journalist Marvel Cooke, writing on the horrors of the Bronx Slave Market, reported that domestic worker Bessie Brown was brutally assaulted by her rich employers "because she had nerve enough to say that she would not leave their home until they had paid her what they owed her."[59] Exercising their presumed right to discipline mendacious and assertive black employees and control their physical movements, white men and women and even their children beat, tortured, sexually assaulted, and in some instances murdered individuals who managed their households and cared for their families on a daily basis. The different ways in which black household workers were treated and devalued, and the "work and terms and conditions under which they did it," according to Jacqueline Jones, "revealed both their place and their possibilities within American society."[60]

Understanding the intersection between white supremacy and the constraints of household labor, African American women actively contested white constructions of black female labor. Despite the threat of being dismissed from their jobs or physical and verbal assault, urban working-class black women constantly strove to maintain their dignity and humanity. Black women wage earners refused to be subordinate and exhibit deference toward their white employers and embodied what scholar Robin D. G. Kelley labeled *infrapolitics*, that is the "daily confrontations, evasive actions, and stifled thoughts" that formed African Americans' resistance patterns. Also a part of their resistance strategies against exploitative labor conditions was recognizing the worth and value of their labor. Publicly and privately, black women defined labor equality and fairness according to their own sensibilities. For many, workplace equity was entangled with broader interpretations of individual and collective liberation, which included demanding inherent rights to dignity and self-respect, economic and income equality, physical well-being, and labor control and mobility.

From a more practical standpoint, occupational autonomy—and, more importantly, flexibility—afforded some black women the chance to manage their hectic lives. On a daily basis, African American women juggled the responsibilities of managing their households, taking care of their families, and maintaining grueling work schedules. Informal labor made it possible for some urban black women to balance their multifaceted lives—something many could not do as household and industrial workers. Depending on the type of labor, some informal workers determined the terms and conditions of their labor and established and negotiated wages and work schedules and locations. For instance, one domestic and casual sex worker explained to an undercover anti-vice agent that she entered and left the informal labor market at will. During times of economic hardship, she took in boarders and prostituted herself on city streets and at a Manhattan nightclub. "[I] used the streets and rented furnished rooms whenever I needed it."[61]

Urban black women who established home-based unlicensed childcare and boarding facilities for low-income black families controlled the pace of their labor and dictated prices for their services. Commonly known throughout the city and the nation during the turn of the twentieth century as "baby farms," illegal childcare centers, which violated New York statutes requiring daycare operators supervising children under the age of twelve to have a state-issued license, offered a much-needed service for working parents with limited childcare options. The scarcity of black nursery programs like the White Rose Missions, Hope Day Nursery, New York Colored Mission, and Katy Ferguson House, and the exclusion of black children from white facilities as revealed by social scientist and Young Women's Christian Association (YWCA) leader Elizabeth Ross Haynes's 1923 study on urban black domestic workers, factored into many working-class women's decisions to utilize the inexpensive services of baby farm operators.[62] Additionally, baby farm facilities appeared to be an alternative option for women who did not want to board their children at the Colored Orphan Asylum and Howard Orphan Asylum, the only two social reform agencies offering institutional care for children of destitute and working black women.[63] Providing a seemingly affordable service for low-income parents, baby farm providers, who were often familiar community members, close friends, and relatives of their clients, charged parents with limited funds a "small fee to care for the [children] during the long hours of the day."[64] For example, during the mid-1920s thirty-year-old Manhattan resident Sadie Howard's rates ranged from "$2 for overnight [to] fifty cents for the day." On a weekly basis, Howard supervised at least seven children in her 144th Street apartment while many mothers maintained long work hours and others took in city amusements.[65] Historian Sherri Broder's work on the urban poor, child protection, and reform in nineteenth-century Philadelphia reveals that: "baby farming was a legitimate occupation that merely formalized the informal childcare arrangements of single mothers and other laboring women. Boarding infants enabled some women to earn a living while remaining at home, while making it possible for others to go out to do the same. [The system] embodied an extensive system of mutual aid among working-class women."[66]

Not all urbanites viewed baby farms as mutually beneficial or as collective child-rearing institutions. Investigating the "baby farms" in Harlem in 1927, *NYAN* staff writer and former UNIA general secretary Edgar M. Grey found some facilities appalling and "destructive to the life" of children and questioned the moral character of baby farm owners. The outspoken writer, pointing out that over one hundred baby farm workers used the classified sections of local newspapers to advertise their businesses, asserted that many "farm keepers" were typically "old, decrepit and sickly women," young married mothers "who desire to boost family income," and women "too lazy to work regularly." Additionally, Grey wrote that childcare facilities that bypassed New York's Department of Health inspections were "used as a 'blind' to cover immoral practices including gambling and selling and manufacturing hootch."[67] Much of Grey's and other working- and middle-class reformers', child advocacy groups', and ordinary urbanites' views held that unfit, nonmaternal, and destitute mothers used the services of mercenary caretakers to get rid of unwanted children—either by selling or murdering them. These views were shaped by sensational newspaper accounts like those written by Grey, by the published reports of the New York Department of Health, and by the public arrest of women accused of starving and abusing children in their care.

Controlling the rhythm of their labor permitted informal economy workers to purposely *exploit* their labor and compromise bodily integrity and their physical well-being. Socioeconomic pursuits, family responsibilities, and the privilege of being self-employed and having labor flexibility compelled some women to maintain long work hours in dangerous sections of the city, to render services to seemingly questionable consumers, and—like Harlem widow and hot-sweet-potato street vendor Madge Wundus—to work in miserable weather conditions. In order to provide professional singing lessons for her young daughter, Wundus toiled in hazardous weather conditions throughout the 1930s. Pushing her heavy food cart through "windblown snow" and strong winds, Wundus, usually "dressed in a man's coat, man's hat, and what appeared to be man's shoes," reasoned working in such severe conditions was a sacrifice she was willing to make for her family. "Easy money," she told herself, "dangerous money too, but money nevertheless. It doubled [my] daily income, [and] enabled [me] to do the things [I] had set to do."[68] In contrast to Wundus, some black women refused to place themselves in precarious and perilous circumstances in spite of the economic incentive. One black sex worker, who jeopardized her well-being every time she offered sexual services to a male client, ironically refused to risk her life and health for what she perceived to be a bizarre sexual encounter with several persons. A white lawyer offered the struggling prostitute "$25 for the night" if she agreed to have rough sex with him and another prostitute. Declining the offer, she cited that "there are many girls who would jump at the chance to make this kind of money, but you know $25 was not enough to risk my health for."[69]

Autonomous and flexible labor spaces bettered the lives of some black women. Occupation control granted women the choice to engage in personal and recreational activities that defined them as black women and fostered family, culture, and community. Informal economy laborers maintained their own homes, cared for their children, spent valuable time with relatives and friends, and attended local church and community events. Moreover, workplace mobility permitted some women the luxury of making labor choices based on family and household circumstances. Taking a nightly waitressing job at a Brooklyn speakeasy, one woman, seeking shelter and employment assistance from the Isaac Hopper Home in Manhattan, informed her case worker that her unreported night job permitted her to spend the morning hours with her sickly mother. Interestingly, while the young woman's flexible work schedule permitted her to fulfill family obligations, her mother, who considered herself to be a "godly" woman, disapproved of her daughter's employment choice.[70]

Moreover, unregulated employment granted some women labor independence and the chance to bypass city and state relief.[71] While an estimated twenty-five-thousand New York black families were receiving some form of public or private relief from various city organizations and agencies, including the Department of Public Welfare or the Emergency Work and Relief Bureau during the late 1920s, other poor blacks refused city relief despite their dire financial circumstance. Pride and having the experience of being disrespected by some relief workers kept some blacks from seeking financial assistance from the city. City relief employees mistreated black relief clients and applicants. Relief recipients and applicants were treated with little or no respect, denied services on account of their race and gender, criticized for their lifestyle choices, and sometimes viewed and regarded as lazy cheats. For public aid recipients, social welfare programs, to borrow from historian Rhonda Williams's work on welfare and low-income housing in Baltimore, Maryland, during the post–World War II era, was a "mixed bag of opportunity and discrimination, possibilities and restriction, freedoms and surveillance."[72] Rather than be part of the city's "army of unemployed," one black female street vendor admitted that she would rather hustle on the streets than receive city money.[73] "It was hard standing on corners swallowing your pride. But it meant independence. Yes, independence. Being independent now meant more than it did when everyone was trying to be independent. So many were satisfied with relief. Well, no relief for [me]. Better to stand out here in the [streets] and be your own boss."[74] Desiring self-sufficiency for herself and her family, another woman chose selling her body on the streets over welfare. According to her longtime male companion, who perhaps was her pimp, prostitution made it possible for them to "never [seek] any help from any charity bureau."[75] Similarly, in 1938, self-employed twenty-eight-year-old street "shoe-shine girl" Louise Wilson informed *NYAN* reporter Dan Burley that she chose the "tough life" of street shoe-shining to "earn daily bread [and to] escape going on relief."[76]

"I Was Hustling for Him, but He Beat Me": The Challenges of Informal Work

The visibility of African American female informal economy workers and consumers engendered New York's underground labor market. Black women strolled redlight districts, smoked cigarettes and drank whiskey at dance halls, socialized and hustled on the streets, and mingled freely with men. As laborers, their presence on the streets, in nightclubs, and in spaces traditionally reserved for men widened prevailing images of urban women and their labor. Functioning in public spaces neither designed nor controlled by women, black women maneuvered as best they could to make a place for themselves. In doing so, they envisioned and created a world that included and allowed them to claim space as laborers and consumers. As wage earners and often the breadwinners of their families, black women felt entitled to explore and take part in urban amusements without approval from relatives, spouses, significant others, or urban reformers. "Why shouldn't I go out some times if I worked?" lamented one nineteen-year-old domestic willing to ignore political activists' rhetoric on the potential dangers of city life.[77] Many believed that earning a living wage granted them authority over their whereabouts, social lives, and how they spent their leisure time. Laying claim to urban space, black women underground laborers, when they could, asserted control over their social, laboring, and sexual lives. Female laborers navigated the city's underground economy sectors, ensured their livelihood and in some cases financial success, and, more importantly, contested male patriarchy.

Early-twentieth-century African Americans newspapers across the nation criticized urban black women's increasing public presence as well as their seemingly inappropriate labor and behavior in after-hours nightspots. In 1908, a writer for the *Colored American Magazine* observed that women's search for nightlife amusements and their bold public personas threatened the "final destruction of our American home, because of its abandonment by its queen, the American woman."[78] In a 1915 article, a *Chicago Defender* contributor reported that, "it is a common occurrence to see girls loitering on the streets late at night or in places where no respectable girl would be seen. The bars of conventionality having been let down is open to the gentler sex. We are not astonished to find them doing the tasks hitherto only assigned to men." The article further suggested that black women's nightlife activities breached gender-specific roles for women, transforming them from decent respectable women into "independent, strong, and sad to say, bold. The modest, retiring effeminate girls that our mothers and fathers knew are almost extinct, [and] their place has been taken by the mannish, tailor-made product."[79]

Commentary on black women's pursuit of social amusements and independence was bound up in the idea that individuality had an adverse impact on black households and circumvented black women's obligation to create wholesome domestic spaces. In other words, the absence of women's physical presence and cultural influence in the home contributed to the social breakdown of their families. According to African American women social and political leaders like Mary Rice Phelps, black women's presence in the home was crucial to maintaining moral households and families. Phelps articulated that, "In the home circle, and around the fireside, her teaching begins with the first dawn of intelligence. She it is who teaches those qualities that are so essential to any race or tribe of beings—morality, the corner stone in the building of any race."[80] Reform-minded African Americans and others, whose rhetoric on family life and household structures was rooted in bourgeois values of race progress, believed that a stable home life was the first step in nation building and that "from pure womanhood must necessarily follow pure homes and from pure homes will spring a people strong in intellect, morals, and religion."[81]

Black elite observations, assumptions, and critiques about urban black women recklessly taking part in extralegal employment hardly coincided with the daily challenges and realities of informal labor. Newfound labor prospects and social pleasures brought a new set of anxieties and obstacles for African American women. Similar to the experience of women in the formal labor market, informal economy women grappled with and encountered overt discriminatory practices and hierarchical systems based on race, gender, ethnicity, and sexuality biases. Because men dominated underground vice, they had access to a broader range of socioeconomic and political opportunities, networks, and occupations. The urban informal economy catered to men's desires and interests, creating a homosocial world that sanctioned and rewarded men's aggressive and competitive behaviors and legitimatized their substantial control over various quasi-legal and illegal labor rackets.[82] In turn, male patriarchy as well as racial exclusion obstructed some women's visions of engaging in labor that fulfilled personal ambitions of financial stability and independence, material consumption, and even sexual gratification. Consequently, female informal laborers faced income disparities, were relegated to less lucrative forms of work, and at times endured demeaning and hostile work environments. For instance, African American women's subordinate position within certain fields of informal labor was evident in New York's illegal lottery racket. On account of race and gender exclusion and male patriarchy, some women were kept at the bottom of the gambling hierarchy. As 1920s and 1930s African American, Caribbean, and white men, such as Casper Holstein, Hyman Kassell, and Alexander Pompez, occupied a wide range of positions within the city's illegal gambling enterprise and amassed wealth and local and national prestige, female laborers, with the exception of some high-ranking women including Rita Munoz and Anita Soas-Howell, rarely secured high-ranking gambling positions as bankers. Like many educated and professional businesswomen of the early twentieth century, female numbers laborers were not perceived by their male counterparts as individuals capable of leading successful business enterprises or delegating responsibilities to men. Nor did men perceive them as formidable entrepreneurs and competitors. Simply put, some men refused, despite the potential monetary benefits, to conduct business with women. In turn, men's traditional outlooks on gender roles and relations kept the vast majority of female numbers games laborers out of positions of power and in low- and midlevel positions as runners, collectors, and clerks.

Coping with male underground workers' violent outbreaks and behavior characterized many women's laboring experience within the urban informal economy.

Some male informal laborers resented women's presence in male-sanctioned public spaces. They were threatened by ambitious women's competitive nature and economic success and by the idea that women were invading their territory and vice rackets. Men credited business-minded women's displays of self-sufficiency as a challenge to their street personas and authority and their failure to control women's physical mobility and choices. Their disapproval of black women's selection of labor and amusements sanctioned the formation of gender and race hierarchies designed to undercut female workers' economic interest and justified the different ways in which men employed violence as a strategy to discipline women for their labor choices. For some men, violence functioned as a weapon against an evolving and gendered informal economy. In other words, men's hostilities with what they perceived as a changing underground sector were mapped out on women's bodies. Asserting their authority over urban women, some men verbally and physically assaulted female laborers and consumers in the privacy of their own homes, on city streets, and in other public venues. In 1929, while attending a speakeasy in a Manhattan apartment, Arthur Williams assaulted fellow partygoer Violet Williams over a quarrel about sex and money. Physically attracted to the thirty-year-old woman, Arthur demanded sex from her after buying her food and drink. An insulted and shocked Violet adamantly resisted Arthur's proposition. Violet's rejection "resulted in an altercation during which [Arthur] suddenly whipped out his gun and fired twice at the woman. One shot went wild and the other found its mark on the left side of Mrs. Williams' chin." An injured Violet was rushed to Harlem Hospital, and her assailant was arrested and charged with felonious assault.[83]

Black women under-the-table laborers were savvy strategists and developed unique tactics to confront racism, male chauvinism, and violence. Blurring the distinction between masculinity and femininity, some informal economy women, both heterosexual and queer, used masculine identities and performances, when needed, as a strategy against male aggression and brutality. Women cross-dressed, took on aggressive masculine personas, and identified as tomboys, and some like mid-twentieth-century Washington, D.C., narcotics dealer and brothel owner Odessa Madre openly expressed same-sex love and passion. Commonly referred to as the "Dope Queen" of Washington, D.C., Madre often appeared at her popular nightclub, Club Madre, with several attractive "sporting women" by her side; it was also rumored that Madre had a sexual relationship with 1950s black comedienne Jackie "Moms" Mabley.[84] Historian Sharon Harley's work on Washington, D.C.'s mid-twentieth-century informal economy posits that Madre and other African American female underground entrepreneurs' exhibition of masculine traits reflected how society viewed their boldness and aggressive personas, their economic success, and their rejection and reshaping of womanhood.[85] Building upon Harley's assessment of the Washingtonian Dope Queen, Madre perhaps purposely, especially as a queer woman and as one functioning in a male-dominated labor space, publicly and privately embraced masculine traits because of their economic and social benefits. For Madre, masculine mannerisms and performances were linked to power and respect and conceivably permitted her to broker business deals with male underworld figures and advance within Washington, D.C.'s illicit drug trade. Interestingly, Madre as a female pimp perhaps employed masculine behavior as an entrepreneurial strategy to manage and physically keep her female labor force in line and avoid competition from male pimps.

Madre and other African American women who openly exhibited masculine identities and performances and violated gender-specific images and sexual politics thrived as informal labor entrepreneurs. Their unconventional personas and behavioral patterns were tolerated and even welcomed by other underground employers, workers, and customers. These women were economically successful and viewed as formidable underground entrepreneurs and competitors. For some, taking on masculine traits made it possible to broker business arrangements with men, assume positions of power, and contravene and refashion traditional imageries of femininity. Adopting different aspects of masculine behavior certainly enabled prominent Harlem numbers banker Stephanie St. Clair to garner respect and make a name for herself within the city's illegal gambling racket. An outwardly fashionable—and what some city spectators considered cultured—woman, St. Clair was known throughout the city as a shrewd and combative businesswoman—someone who readily employed violence against anyone who threatened her business or personally betrayed her. St. Clair was also someone who was on par with her contemporary male numbers bankers. Publicly challenging what many black New Yorkers perceived as white encroachment into Harlem's numbers racket during the 1930s, St. Clair and her staff of male bodyguards verbally threatened and physically accosted white numbers racketeers. In Harlem and among the city's small yet well-known numbers racketeers, she garnered the reputation as someone you did not want to cross. St. Clair socially benefited from manipulating gender-specific behavior for men and women, garnering respect from black New Yorkers and compelling her male adversaries to think twice about contesting her reign as Harlem's Numbers Queen.

Urban African American women's ability to navigate New York's informal labor sector was made possible by the establishment of intraracial and interracial friendships, social networks, and collaborations. Based on their collective experiences with poverty and social interests, black female informal laborers, regardless of their ethnic and religious identities or backgrounds, created both temporary and permanent mutually beneficial relationships, partnerships, and alliances with

African American and white men and women. Such alliances were forged in jail-houses, brothels, nightclubs, rooming houses, and on the streets, and they brought together like-minded individuals interested in creative moneymaking ventures as well as those with a penchant for danger. In times of economic desperation and social isolation, informal economy women lived together, shared clothes and food with one another, and even established street- and home-based economic ventures together. Anti-vice investigative reporter and New York's Committee of Fourteen (COF) agent Raymond Claymes frequented many sex houses that were operated by black madams on a "50–50 basis."[86] Two unemployed eighteen-year-old friends from Baltimore, Helen Day and Clara May Downs, lived in Harlem, enjoyed city amusements, and orchestrated petty crimes together. In 1924, the two women devised a plan to steal money from several women by using the identity and address of Day's former landlady, "Mrs. Emma Woods, an elderly and sickly woman." The scam involved writing notes and requesting money from Woods's friends. Thinking Woods was in financial straits, her unsuspecting friends mailed money to Day and James. The partners in crime, who had a history of stealing and scamming, eventually were arrested for petty larceny and placed on probation.[87]

For the sake of protecting themselves and surviving on the streets, black women underground workers confided in and educated each other on the finer points of street life. They shared personal stories about loved ones, discussed the pains and joys of city life, and traded information on a range of issues, including how best to evade the police and skirt city laws and how to protect themselves from competing fellow underground workers. Investigating Harlem's self-professed clairvoyants and magical healers that violated New York state laws against practicing and prescribing medicine without a medical license, several white police officers observed that some "supernatural" workers developed a "highly organized system of warning each other" about plainclothes police officers' surveillance of their businesses. With the intent of entrapping self-professed practitioners of the magical arts, law enforcers posed as medical patients and visited several "quack" doctors' establishments, requesting health examinations and medical diagnoses and cures for fictitious medical conditions. To protect their businesses and avoid arrest and possibly jail time, some healers developed a strategy of researching the names and addresses of supposed clients in order to determine their true identities. If consumers were found to be fake "clients," medical healers did not inform imposters of their discoveries; they refused to render services to the individual and relayed their findings to fellow clairvoyants in their network.[88]

Documenting black life in New York during the 1930s for the Works Progress Administration (WPA), investigative journalist Vivian Morris found that street prostitutes swapped valuable lessons on men, sex, and health, and how to earn a living and survive on the streets. Morris posed as a streetwalker to understand firsthand the less familiar working lives of streetwalkers. Attempting to gain the trust and advice of one "fellow" sex worker, Morris informed the woman: "I don't know sumbody. I don't know one square from the other. So I come over t' you. Nothing wrong in that is there?" While the streetwalker was suspicious of Morris, perhaps viewing her as possible competition but nevertheless understanding the trials and tribulations of being a new "working girl," she offered to school Morris on street life and protocol and on the urban sex world. "Well, c'mon, sister; let's go ova t' my bung hole an' I'll show yuh th' ropes." But Morris's new "friend" also warned: "don't cha go pickin' up on nis block. We' strict on territory."[89] Patterns of partnering and sharing stories and experiences about street life, unreported labor, and self-protection signaled black women's dependency on their fellow underground laborers. Black women informal economy workers did not live or labor in isolation to one another. Instead, they were part of a fluid and in some cases transient community of laborers that knew all too well the potential benefits and perils of their work. Recognizing the erratic nature of New York's informal economy, women collaborated in order to gain insight on their respective occupations, to understand the politics of informal work, and to protect one another from potentially dangerous situations. For instance, 1930s streetwalkers and drug addicts Lethia Walker and Blanche Simms not only worked Harlem streets together, but both women made sure they knew each others' whereabouts whenever they were with male clients. And, if one "was taking longer than usual" with a customer or failed to return to their designated meeting location, the other searched apartment building hallways and alleys for her friend and coworker.[90]

Shared experiences of personal struggles and common survival interests did not always allow a diverse cross section of black female underground workers to forge bonds, friendships, or partnerships. Much like Timothy Gilfoyle's analysis of rival New York street children, many informal laborers failed to develop a "long-lasting system of reciprocal obligation fundamental to group cohesion and solidarity" or embody "a large conception of mutuality and shared suffering."[91] Because of the competitive and unpredictable nature of informal labor and some underprivileged women's dire economic circumstance, hustling became an individual journey based primarily on self-preservation and personal monetary gain. Vying for consumers' pocketbooks, rival and jealous informal workers gossiped and created vicious rumors about their competition and publicly demonstrated their resentment toward one another's economic success and conspicuous displays of prosperity. Competition and envy over potential customers and money sometimes exploded into violent confrontations. Former schoolteacher turned domestic worker and marijuana seller Bessie Bizzell, commonly known as "Cigarette Bessie," stabbed her fellow drinking partner Gertrude Williams over a money dispute in a Manhattan speakeasy in 1936. The public brawl erupted after Bizzell boasted about receiving relief money. Feeling entitled to a share of her friend's money, Williams demanded that Bizzell hand over $2. When Bizzell refused, Williams knocked her down and drew a knife. Shocked by Williams's behavior, Bizzell, in self-defense, stabbed Williams in the throat with a hat-pin. Bizzell was later arrested and charged with assault.[92]

Off-the-books employment forever altered some black women's lives. Female workers risked their personal safety and reputations and were often without legal protection or recourse.[93] Countless black women faced police harassment and brutality, were verbally and physically assaulted by male handlers and clients, and were publicly and privately shamed by disapproving urban reformers and relatives. Undoubtedly, many black women informal workers were aware of the consequences of their labors. Family members, close neighborhoods, and local reformers warned women about the pitfalls and limitations of informal work. In addition, local newspapers' publication of stories about underground female workers' tragic deaths and assaults and police arrest and jail convictions served as cautious tales for city women. But for some women, individual desire for economic stability, material consumption, and personal pleasures compelled them to dismiss the advice of loved and concerned ones and ignore the countless stories about fallen urban women. For instance, one working mother, who was also a devout Catholic, constantly warned her teenager daughter about the dangers of premarital sex and "immoral associations" with men and women. Her advice, however, fell on deaf ears as her daughter, at least according to her, became rebellious and more interested in fulfilling individual desires. The wayward teen skipped school, stayed out past her curfew, smoked cigarettes, and engaged in premarital sex with older men and teenage girls. Trading childhood lessons of respectability and religious instruction for disreputable social pastimes, the wayward teen occasionally labored as a prostitute as a way to satisfy her desires for expensive clothes and sexual gratification.[94]

At the same time, some informal workers were ignorant and naive about their chosen occupation and tragically experienced consequences far beyond their imagination. Sixteen-year-old Jamaica, Queens, resident Mary Lee Moore's tragic quandary epitomized the impact of underground work on black women's lives. Manipulated into sex work by her twenty-nine-year-old lover, Theodore McKenzie, in 1934, Moore routinely endured her male handler's verbal and physical abuse. A husband and father of two children, McKenzie prostituted Moore out of his mother's Queens apartment, having Moore "submit to all comers who had money." Recounting her horrific ordeal as a "child sex slave" to police officers, Moore recalled that she "hustl[ed] for [McKenzie], [and] he beat and berated me when [I] didn't bring enough money." Objecting to her own sexual exploitation and desperately longing to escape her tormentor's physical, verbal, and emotional abuse, Moore, perhaps feeling a sense of powerlessness and rage, fatally stabbed

McKenzie with a large potato knife. Moore's use of lethal violence delineated her way of protecting her body, her revenge against McKenzie for months of sexual and emotional abuse and captivity, and her attempt to secure long-awaited personal justice—especially when legal protection seemed beyond her reach. For Moore, ending McKenzie's life offered some measure of relief, and more importantly ended her daily despair and victimization. Although Moore was arrested and tried for first-degree murder, an all-white male jury cleared the teenager of the killing.[95]

Harlem resident Cecelia Sargent was hardly concerned with the consequences of her labor. Living a lavish lifestyle, wearing expensive clothes, and separating men from their wallets overshadowed her concern for her well-being and survival on city streets. The "pretty and vivacious" Sargent "prided herself on [her ability to deceive others] and to take care of herself [and] lived by her wits." Arriving in New York City from the British West Indies in 1916, twenty-four-year-old Sargent found "there was no need to work [because] men were easy marks."[96] Sargent became a dealer in stolen merchandise and was a charity girl, embracing the culture of treating. Elizabeth Alice Clement posits that "treating emerged from the tension between girls' desire to participate in commercial amusements and the working community's condemnation of prostitution."[97] Charity girls like Sargent exchanged physical affection and sexual favors for clothing and shoes, public amusements, and financial stability. Reporting on Sargent's intriguing yet complicated life for the *NYAN*, communist activist and journalist Marvel Cooke noted that the materialistic con woman paid a heavy price for "living by shady means."[98] In May 1931, an unknown male assailant strangled Sargent to death; her lifeless and surprisingly pregnant body was discovered on a bed under a pile of expensive clothing in her Harlem lodging house. Newspaper accounts reported that several of Sargent's jilted male lovers and scam victims, who believed that the beautiful scam artist got what she deserved, were suspected of her murder. Cooke wrote that Sargent "had too many affairs. Had she been content with a simple life, she might still have been alive today, or at least, her murder[er] might have been apprehended."[99] Considered one of Harlem's most mysterious killings of 1931, Sargent's murder was never solved, leaving Harlemites to believe that her deceptive and conniving ways caught up with her.

The perils of informal work not only adversely shaped the lives of some of its participants but also the individuals for whom African American women were financially providing for, particularly their children. Like many formal wage-earning mothers with limited childcare options and irregular work schedules, some female underground laborers reluctantly left their children with relatives or neighbors and sometimes, as a last resort, locked their children in their tiny cramped apartments.[100] Lacking appropriate adult supervision, some children were sexually and physically abused by those caring for them, and others were pressured by peers into participating in illicit street amusements and trades, including gambling and pickpocket games. Roi Ottley observed that street kids "deprived of home supervision naturally congregate on street corners, where they witness the most sordid forms of crime. They seek the society of vicious gangs and try to emulate the overdressed underworld figures seen parading the streets."[101] Writing on the interplay between unsupervised children and black parents' relentless efforts to make a living, Willetta Simonton's *NYAN* editorial echoed Ottley's remarks: "The demands for making a living are so great [on black parents], that the boys [and girls] are not properly trained. If the parents are struggling and just making a penurious living, they have neither time nor energy to make their apartment a home or make their children responsible members of society."[102] In a 1931 interview with a social worker, a Brooklyn sex worker affirmed Ottley and Simonton's observations, noting that "lack of supervision" due to her mother's working schedule was to blame for her wayward behavior and entrance into prostitution.[103]

Tragically, some unsupervised children became victims of violent crimes. In December 1929, the *NYAN* reported on the brutal assault of fifteen-year-old Harriet Beecher Stowe student Almer Sutton. Some time after ten P.M., the teenage girl walked her mother Minnie Sutton to her night job at the Lenox Club on 143rd Street, and stopped at a neighborhood drugstore for medicine for a sick relative. After leaving the pharmacist, an unaccompanied Sutton continued home and entered the darkened hallway of her apartment building. "When she reached the stairway floor she was grabbed by the throat from behind. Her attacker "told her [if] she made an outcry, he would choke her to death." Despite the assailant's threats, Sutton "bravely fought the man, but he was too strong for her and she was dragged to the back of the apartment building." The teenage schoolgirl was then severely beaten, raped, and nearly strangled to death. After her attack, a seminude Sutton managed to drag herself into a neighbor's apartment. Despite receiving medical attention, Sutton died several days later from injuries sustained from her assault. Before dying, Sutton managed to furnish police with a description of her attacker: "5 feet 8 inches in height and weight about 165 pounds." The assailant, however, was never apprehended.[104]

Newspaper accounts and urban reformers and moralists scripted informal laborers' tragic tales of sexual exploitation, physical abuse, and death as inevitable consequences for individuals who lived by shady means and, according to historian Victoria Wolcott, "undermined a community identity that placed women in the role of mother, homemaker, reformer, and 'respectable' worker."[105] Simultaneously invoking a spirit of sympathy and judgment, newspapers and respectable advocates rendered victimized sex workers, numbers runners, con artists, and other informal economy women as poverty-stricken, fallen, or naive individuals, whose "low economic status," according to Adam Clayton Powell Sr. and Frances A. Kellor, lured them into "immoral habits [and] occupations" and "vice and laziness."[106] Informal laborers were also publicly identified as individuals that had little regard for law and order and were devoid of respectability, moral guidance, and proper home training. Because print media coverage of women's harrowing work experiences was ingrained with such criticism, the reports also indirectly functioned as cautionary tales, describing the pitfalls and future implications of taking part in unwholesome amusements and labor. In several *NYAN* opinion editorials, Edgar Grey, disdainfully describing Harlem's nightlife and the white slumming craze of the 1920s, posited that underground workers and pleasure seekers were inevitably doomed to a life of misery and despair. "When they have retired from this dishonorable life and this devastating experience, can anyone be so innocent as to expect them to be honest fathers and mothers, husbands, and wives? They cannot be. The natural resistance had been broken; the innate moral restraint dissipated and destroyed, the respect for self and for the race supplanted by the hard and distorted social carelessness which grew from their early experiences."[107] For Grey and other critics of informal labor, once an individual succumbed to unsavory habits and associations there was no turning back, no matter what the economic or social motive was; he/she could not be redeemed. Black newspaper reports of the sordid details of sex crimes, robberies, murders, and other sensational stories were intended to warn urbanites—especially new migrants from the South and individuals contemplating the prospect of earning quick money—about inappropriate public and private behavior and the tragic cost of illegal and disgraceful income-producing labor. But for the sake of community betterment and social control, polite society imagined a world that was different from the actual experiences of underground laborers. While their accounts were laced with some elements of truth, they undermined the possibility that alternative labor choices were potential avenues toward occupational autonomy and new labor identities. Their portrayals illuminated, while revealing urbanites' anxieties about urban society and female work and behavior, a far less complicated depiction of New York black women's varying experiences as informal economy workers.

Conclusion

New York underground black female laborers certainly struggled to negotiate a terrain between their visions of personal autonomy and the realities of informal labor, between self-sufficiency and economic dependence, and between self-perception and societal views that mischaracterized their lives and labor. Indeed, African American women deliberately or inadvertently worked, lived, and socialized outside bourgeois paradigms of normative perceptions of female civility. Part of a community of workers, entrepreneurs, and buyers and sellers, urban black women employed the city's burgeoning underground sector to confront pervasive economic disenfranchisement and discriminatory barriers and to take part in city amusements. More importantly, New York laboring women viewed under-the-table employment as an unconventional route toward fashioning new economic possibilities for themselves and their families. Notwithstanding personal shaming and public criticism from urban reformers, family members, and friends, city women created and secured inventive income-generating labor and entrepreneurial opportunities, reaffirming their resourcefulness and the risks they were willing to undertake in the name of economic permanence, personal ambition, and work autonomy.

Fulfilled aspirations of occupational autonomy hardly described all New York black women's underground work experiences. Indeed, informal labor was a complex blend of opportunities and oppression, possibilities and restrictions, and freedoms and surveillance. Different categories of informal labor brought different sets of challenges, anxieties, and dangers to black women. Working long hours on city throughways or in brothels and gambling dens, New York informal laborers encountered both predictable and unforeseen nonpecuniary impediments, including race and gender exclusion, violence and arrest, male hostility, emotional and psychological trauma, and public and private shame. Undoubtedly, many informal women workers were tragically bested by rival competitors and clients and by their precarious lifestyles, becoming infamous—or nameless—rape and murder victims. Experiencing and witnessing physical and verbal trauma and, in some cases, lethal violence, many informal women laborers embraced masculine identities and forged diverse networks in order to survive and confront the many difficulties brought by informal labor. Nevertheless, unregulated work with all its uncertainties and complexities highlighted both the multiple ways in which race, class, and gender inequalities shaped black women's urban experiences and also how alternative economic opportunities enabled some women to create new economic patterns.

CHAPTER 2

Madame Queen of Policy

Stephanie St. Clair, Harlem's Numbers Racket, and Community Advocacy

On December 9, 1930, Harlem policy banker Madame Stephanie St. Clair was released from the workhouse on New York City's Welfare Island after serving a little over eight months for possession of policy slips.[1] According to the *NYAN*, the forty-something-year-old St. Clair, "a militant enemy of the Harlem police," emerged from prison and "threw a bombshell in the investigation of the policy racket, police, and Magistrates Court when she declared she paid $6,000 to a lieutenant and plainclothes officers." Commonly known throughout Harlem as the "Queen of Policy" and "Queenie," St. Clair's release from jail signaled her desire to resume her position as one of Harlem's preeminent numbers bankers and to launch a public crusade against the NYPD and expose law enforcers' participation in New York's multimillion-dollar numbers racket.[2] St. Clair was one of few black policy bankers and was probably the only female immigrant numbers banker to control Harlem's numbers business during the early twentieth century. Throughout that time, her carefully crafted outward persona, dazzling lifestyle, and reputation as a shrewd, dangerous yet ladylike figure captured the imagination and curiosity of local city dwellers and non–New Yorkers intrigued by Harlem's gambling enterprise. Despite St. Clair's national prominence as an underground entrepreneur, many scholars have ignored how she and other urban women of African descent carved out space for themselves within New York's male-dominated gambling enterprise. St. Clair's fascinating career and public life, however, has been portrayed in mainstream American cinema and television. Dramatizing the mood and pulse of New York's underworld of the 1930s, Francis Ford Coppola's 1984 *Cotton Club* and Bill Duke's

1997 *Hoodlum* illuminate various aspects of St. Clair's life. In 2007, Harlem native and writer Katherine Butler Jones's fictional play, *409 Edgecombe Ave, The House on Sugar Hill*, offered a glimpse into the lives of St. Clair and other African Americans who resided in the affluent Sugar Hill section of Harlem during the Inter-war period. Butler's depiction of St. Clair illuminated a popular community icon with a flair for fashion and the dramatic. And more recently, TV-One's *Celebrity Crime Files*, a weekly hour-long investigative documentary series that delves into sensational crime cases involving African Americans of the twentieth and twenty-first centuries, dedicated an entire episode to the "Lady Gangster."

This chapter places the larger-than-life "Numbers Queen" at the center of one of New York's most popular underground amusements: the numbers game. An examination of St. Clair complicates masculine representations of Harlem's numbers enterprise and disrupts the view that urban black women did not figure prominently in the city's gambling racket. More importantly, St. Clair's status as an affluent and well-respected numbers banker reveals that the city's illegal gambling enterprise offered just as many economic opportunities to women as it did to men. I explore St. Clair's unique public persona as well as her presence in one of New York's most well-known cultural pastimes, using her career trajectory as a window into the diverse ways in which African Americans and West Indian numbers laborers used the city's profitable numbers game for their own socioeconomic and political agendas. As a race-conscious yet self-absorbed historical figure, St. Clair viewed the numbers racket both as an opportunity to amass financial stability and wealth and as an economic venture that was independent from white control. Appropriating different aspects of respectable and uplift politics, including community uplift and black institutional building, the "Digit Queen" used her social status as a well-to-do underground entrepreneur and neighborhood luminary to draw attention to the various socioeconomic and political issues plaguing black New Yorkers. A community advocate within her own right, St. Clair, as expressed through her *NYAN* newspaper editorials, articulated her views on a broad range of urban inequalities, including police misconduct, city corruption, and black immigration and naturalization. The duality of functioning as an underground businesswoman and as a race advocate breached normative constructions of urban race women. Her distinct style of community work, one that constantly refashioned blacks' normative ideas about racial uplift, ushered in alternative expressions of neighborhood advocacy.

No doubt, the Numbers Queen was a complex individual who straddled the line between criminality and respectability. Although St. Clair established a successful gambling enterprise, associated with some of Harlem's well-known crime figures including Ellsworth "Bumpy" Johnson, and attempted to murder her estranged husband Harlem activist Sufi Abdul Hamid, she garnered the support and respect of many black working-class New Yorkers. Black urban dwellers viewed St. Clair as a neighborhood celebrity and were captivated by her ostentatious display of wealth and self-crafted public persona, and perhaps by her questionable ethnic background. Harlem residents, including Thelma Wilson, former manager of the historic 409 Edgecombe Building, and Katherine Butler Jones, were impressed with St. Clair's "courage, intelligence, skill," and her unique ability, as a woman, to control the male-dominated numbers racket.[3] Wilson, Butler Jones, and other black Harlemites admired St. Clair because she employed countless persons of African descent as numbers laborers, bodyguards, and domestic workers and secretaries; purportedly financially supported legitimate black businesses; and publicly advocated racial advancement for African Americans and black immigrants. Moreover, black New Yorkers occupying various socioeconomic positions praised St. Clair because she unapologetically violated race and gender norms and hierarchies in order to undermine the business endeavors of some of New York's most notorious and dangerous white criminals.

Harlem's World of Numbers

Harlem's infamous numbers racket belonged to a global phenomenon of gambling practices that existed at the turn of the twentieth century. Games of chance, including public lotteries, cock and dog fighting, card playing, and dice games, flourished in cities around the world. For instance, Brazil's "animal game," known as *jogo do bicho*, was an illegal lottery that gained great popularity and, as argued by Amy Chazkel, was a precursor to the country's massive informal economies of the twentieth century.[4] In parts of the Caribbean, West Indians from varying class backgrounds played *la bolita*, a three-digit numbers games. Betting on horse races was common in England and France, and fan-tan, "a game played upon a mat-covered table, with a quantity of Chinese coins or small objects which are covered with a cup," became popular in late- and early-twentieth-century China.[5] Games of chance were part of global underground economies and cultural pastimes that permeated the world's socioeconomic and political landscapes. Varying gambling practices illuminated the public's fascination with games of chance and their desire to engage in recreational activities that offered the opportunity to transform one's immediate and future financial circumstances and to satisfy individual pleasures and addictions. Moreover, global consumption of gambling reflected the ability of its participants to assert autonomy over their public and private behaviors and recreational practices and expressed their varying perspectives on the intersections between labor and public amusements.

Harlem's complex racial and ethnic makeup, increasing mass consumerism, and fluctuating city economy gave the numbers racket its distinct flavor, setting it apart from other national and international gambling rackets. Many of the city's racially and ethnically diverse residents took part in the highly profitable game, either as players or as workers. Although 1920s Harlem was often regarded by New Negro intellectuals, writers, and activists as the "Mecca of the New Negro" nearly a decade earlier—before the exodus of Harlem's white residents to other parts of New York—the upper Manhattan neighborhood was inhabited by Italians, Finns, Hungarians, and other nonblack residents who lived between 109th and 146th Streets.[6] Beginning in the early 1900s, a growing African American and Caribbean population replaced white Harlem exodusters. The business savvy of Harlem real estate entrepreneur Phillip Payton Jr. and migrating southern blacks' and West Indian immigrants' vision of obtaining wartime employment and decent living conditions and of escaping white violence in the South brought tens of thousands into the black capital of the world. In 1910, an estimated 22,000 African Americans lived in Harlem, a number that nearly quadrupled to 84,000 by 1920 and reached an estimated 190,000 by 1930. That same year, at least 55,000 foreign-born blacks lived in various other sections of New York City, mostly in Manhattan.[7] Coming of age in Harlem during the 1920s and 1930s, African American playwright Loften Mitchell, recalling the influx of black southerners and Caribbean immigrants to the "Black Mecca," wrote that in "Harlem of my first recognition . . . southern Negroes fled from physical lynchings and West Indians from economic lynchings. They met in the land north of 110th Street and they brought with them their speech patters, folkways, mores, and their dogged determination."[8] Commenting on the impact of black urbanization on Harlem during the 1930s, James Weldon Johnson observed that the "black city [was] located in the heart of white Manhattan, and contain[ed] more Negroes to the square mile than any other spot on earth."[9] Enticed by 1920s consumerism, many native and new black city dwellers, satisfying their personal needs and often living beyond their economic means, found themselves purchasing luxury items and engaging in Harlem's blossoming commercial and underground amusements. Consumerism provided urban blacks with the space to remake themselves as buyers and sellers of commercial goods and offered new avenues of economic possibility.

The entrepreneurial spirit of ethnically diverse policy bankers solidified the broad appeal to and uniqueness of Harlem's numbers rackets. While early-twentieth-century black intellectuals, activists, and contemporary scholars identified different individuals as the pioneers of Harlem's numbers games, the city's various numbers leaders, all hailing from different parts of the world, collectively left their imprint on the gambling enterprise. Wealthy African American, Caribbean, and European numbers bankers including Marcellina Cardena, Casper Holstein, and Stephanie St. Clair created a popular pastime that transcended race, gender, and class lines. Garnering both local and national reputations, their respective rags-to-riches narratives, over-the-top soirees, lavish automobiles and clothes, and palace-like homes were featured in *NYT*, *NYAN*, and *Chicago Defender* editorials and in other newspapers throughout the country. No doubt, Harlem numbers bankers' flashy lifestyles and outward penchant for glamour and excitement brought many city dwellers to the game.[10] For many white, black, and Hispanic gamblers and low-level numbers laborers, New York numbers kings' and queens' unprecedented success and wealth, although achieved illegally, demonstrated the possibility of individual wealth creation and social mobility, the prospect of avoiding backbreaking low-wage labor and, more importantly, the potential to become a major player within one of the nation's most popular pastimes.

The functioning of Harlem's numbers games depended on the labor of many individuals. The banker was the central player in the operation. According to one observer of the game, the "banker was a mystery man. The majority of players and collectors often knew that an individual was their banker, without having a speaking acquaintanceship with him."[11] Policy bankers financed his/her numbers operation, staffing numbers bank headquarters with a group of controllers, clerks, messengers, and numbers runners. Numbers runners or collectors played an essential role in the daily functioning of the gambling enterprise. They were primarily responsible for collecting policy slips from gamblers, getting slips to the numbers headquarters, and sometimes paying winners. Numbers runners were characteristically ordinary men and women whose day-to-day interactions brought them into contact with different people. Making it convenient for customers to participate in the popular game, runners, who could potentially earn anywhere between $20 and $30 a day, collected gambling slips at beauty salons and barbershops, churches, candy stores and newsstands, street corners, patrons' homes, and other places players frequented on a daily basis. Commenting on the manner in which some runners conducted their labor, one local New York newspaper noted that runners "employed by the bankers are on a regular schedule each morning, picking up their collections, and there is nothing clandestine or hidden in their movement. [The collector walks] boldly and openly along, picking up the slips with the money from players on the street, or being handed an envelop with money and slips."[12] At the same time, many numbers runners, certainly aware of the illegality of gambling and its negative reputation among some black New Yorkers, consciously concealed their labor, choosing not to collect on the streets or in other public settings.

Contrary to prevailing historical perspectives, numbers collectors were a diverse group of individuals from varying class backgrounds. Working-class numbers runners typically were either jobless or worked full- or part-time and, as observed by Roi Ottley, were "Negroes, who otherwise would be on the relief rolls."[13] Policy col-

Figure 3: A numbers headquarters at 351 Lenox Avenue in Harlem. Courtesy of New York Daily News Archives.

lectors, like Lloyd Jenkins, a bricklayer and father of novelist and journalist Louise Meriwether, became runners as a result of being unemployed or combined formal wage labor with numbers running.[14] To make ends meet during the 1930s, wayward teenager Ella Fitzgerald supported herself by working as a lookout at a "sporting house" and as a numbers collector.[15] Interestingly, labor and recreational opportunities within Harlem's numbers racket attracted middle-class and educated blacks. Sociologist E. Franklin Frazier pointed out: "Wives of Negro college professors are 'writers' or collectors of 'numbers' for the 'numbers racket.'"[16] Contravening aspects of uplift politics that stressed thrift, morality, and productive labor, middle-class numbers laborers viewed gambling as a pastime that offered them the opportunity to pursue personal pleasures and amusements and still preserve outward images of respectability. Additionally, black elites were perhaps attracted to New York's numbers games and other games of chance because of the "exhilaration of risk and flirting with a world governed more by chance and luck than by rational calculation."[17] Howard University graduate and well-known Manhattan physician Perry W. Cheney secretly operated a small numbers bank at his private medical office on 135th Street. Presumably, Cheney established his numbers business to augment his income and to retain existing and attract new patients. In November 1925, Cheney's clandestine numbers operation was made public when his pregnant girlfriend, Harlem resident Elaine Douglas, threatened to shoot him. Douglas, a twenty-five-year-old widow and graduate of Nannie Helen Burroughs's National Training School for Girls in Washington, D.C., believed that the doctor intended to marry her. Because Douglas was under the impression that marriage to the doctor was in the near future, she loaned him $600 to get his numbers runner out of jail. But after learning from several friends that Cheney was engaged to another woman and wanted her (Douglas) to terminate her pregnancy, she demanded a return of her money. Carrying a loaded .25 caliber handgun, Douglas arrived at Cheney's home with the intentions of confronting him about his two-timing ways and with plans of shooting him or threatening him with the gun. Before Douglas had a chance to carry out either plan, Cheney discovered the gun and "grabbed her wrist and knocked [it] to the floor. A tussle ensued and an officer was called in." Local police arrested Douglas and she was charged with violating the Sullivan Law, a 1911 statute that required a license for purchasing and carrying a handgun, and attempted felonious assault. During her March 1926 trial, Douglas was found not guilty; she later successfully sued her former lover for the amount she loaned him.[18]

Political affiliations were critical to the functioning of Harlem's numbers racket. Since gambling was a misdemeanor in the state of New York, it was in the interest of the banker to form alliances with local politicians, judges, and police. Speaking broadly on law officials' and enforcers' active involvement in New York's underground and criminal economies, one city writer noted, "It is an open secret in Harlem that some policemen receive various forms of gratuities from the underworld. To operate unmolested, pimps, prostitutes, dope-peddlers, brothel keepers, and owners of gambling places paid weekly tribute to corrupt police officers & detectives and high-placed political figures."[19] Vice racketeers' monetary payoffs were supposed to ensure that underworld businesses went unmolested by police and to influence city judges and prosecutors to dismiss their cases. Although many African American bankers paid tribute to city officials and police officers, they, unlike their white counterparts, lacked the political clout to neutralize high-ranking New York City politicians such as Tammany Hall leader James J. Hines.

Gambling participants took part in New York's policy racket despite its illegality. "[N]umbers [was] a people's game, a community pastime in which old and young, literate and illiterate, the neediest folk and well-to-do all participate. All of Harlem played . . . the humble laundrywoman and the disrespectable pool player, as well as the respectable schoolteacher."[20] For many black New Yorkers, numbers gambling, especially during periods of personal economic calamity, was significant to one's financial health. At the same time, African American players viewed numbers playing as a recreational activity and understood that winning large sums of money was not always guaranteed. But the possibility of "hitting the number" meant additional income for the household and potential economic stability, if only for a short time. Winning meant paying bills, purchasing necessary and luxury items, and perhaps even financing a business venture. One policy customer explained: "A hit can change a guy's whole life around. They guy who wins sometimes sets himself up in business, in a grocery store or a bar. . . . Others pay off their bills, their mortgages, and some have sent their kids to college."[21] Writing about a Harlem family during the Depression era, Louise Meriwether's 1970 novel *Daddy Was a Number Runner* illuminates the practical and exciting benefits of selecting the winning number. When main character Francie Coffin's father hit the number, she enthusiastically remarked that money was used to purchase essential household necessities and food and clothes and to indulge on lavish items. "We were eating high off the hog. [Daddy] paid up the back rent and Mother hauled us all downtown to Klein's and bought us some school clothes and two pairs of shoes each."[22]

Not all black New Yorkers were captivated by the fashionable amusement of numbers gambling. A segment of Harlem's African American population frowned upon games of chance, numbers bankers and runners, and the countless players eagerly willing to "take their wearing apparel to pawn shops to play a number."[23] Part of blacks' opposition to gambling was rooted in Progressive-era ideas about appropriate and unacceptable labor and amusements. Reformers and moralists argued that labor and leisure activities and spaces should be orderly, efficient, and decent, and markers of Christian values and middle-class values. Games of chance fell outside the boundaries of urban reformers' definitions of respectable labor and amusement. Furthermore, urban reformers maintained that games of chance undermined tenets of uplift politics that stressed prudence, productive labor, and thrift. Such core beliefs were essential to creating stable black communities and to charting race advancement. Bourgeois blacks argued that games of chance, whether it was numbers playing or betting on horses, encouraged false hope for quick profit, contributed to the demoralization of the African American community, and seduced less-privileged and uneducated blacks into squandering their meager incomes. Furthermore, gambling opponents insisted that the only individuals who profited from numbers gambling were the "evil" unreliable numbers bankers and runners who conveniently disappeared when someone hit big.[24] For instance, Adam Clayton Powell Jr., who later launched a citywide campaign against New York City's numbers racket during the 1960s, became an unlucky victim of a numbers game scam. Sometime in his twenties, Powell Jr. engaging in the game for the first time "hit for ten cents" and was quite surprised when "the banker wouldn't pay off."[25] At the same time, even those middle-class uplifters that publicly condemned numbers gambling were players themselves.

Prominent yet financially struggling New York writers and antilynching campaign activists Alice Dunbar-Nelson and her third husband journalist Robert Nelson were occasional numbers players. The couple hoped to use potential winnings to supplement their household income.[26] Some black elites' and reformers' participation in games of chance and other illicit moneymaking strategies revealed their dire economic circumstances as they fought for black liberation. Moreover, it also illuminated the often complex and contradictory relationship middle-class uplifters had with New York's informal economy and their everyday struggles with adhering to racial uplift ideology and respectable politics.

Opposition to numbers gambling transcended African American class lines, building a cross-class coalition against games of chance. Despite their dire economic circumstances, some members of Harlem's black working class refused to relinquish their hard-earned pennies and dollars to what they considered an immoral racket. Similar to many middle-class reformers' outlooks on gambling, working-poor blacks found numbers gambling morally troublesome. They were not necessarily troubled by the impact of games of chance on black urbanites' collective efforts to secure race equality and citizenship. Instead, many opposed gambling for practical and personal reasons, understanding the firsthand dangers and pitfalls of gambling. Working-class moralists maintained that games of chance corrupted their loved ones and were detrimental to their families' financial and moral well-being. One African American woman insisted that gambling encroached upon her husband's ability to financially care for their family. According to her, the family's household earnings were diminished because he spent "a good portion of his earnings" playing the numbers, and did not "have enough left to support [her] and [their] little children." Identifying gambling as the root of her marital and family discord, she requested that city police break up "two gambling clubs [on] 59th Street."[27]

Black women numbers players were frequently blamed for disrupting family structures. Within the pages of black print media, black women players were accused of failing to fulfill gender-specific roles. They were depicted as imprudent gambling addicts who abandoned their obligation as wives and mothers and as models of social responsibility. Several *NYA* editorials compared female players to drug addicts, citing that their helpless habits were a "menace to women's virtue and womanhood." The *NYA* suggested that, in pursuit of their own self-interests, female addicts of the game sacrificed their families' financial and spiritual well-being. Instead of saving "money needed for rent and food," published accounts suggested that black women, having no mental compass, preferred gambling.[28] The *New York Interstate Tattler*, Harlem's popular gossip tabloid, suggested that neglectful black parents were so high from numbers fever that many made their children place their bets; some parents even allowed their "kiddies [to] spend their nickels and dimes with the wild hope of making a 'hit.'"[29] African American newspapers' and gossip rags' scathing and, at times, overexaggerated commentaries on black numbers players, particularly black women, are both telling and troubling. Such wide-reaching public perspectives advanced gambling opponents' assertions that games of chance were immoral and legitimized their initiatives to monitor and control black behavior. Moreover, newspaper editorials stigmatized and raised questions concerning African Americans' recreational choices, hoping that public disapproval would shame participants away from games of chance.

Notwithstanding public criticism, Harlem's numbers racket had economic and cultural significance for New York's black community. Gambling profits made it possible for many numbers barons to reinvest portions of their earnings back into impoverished black communities. Considered local celebrities by some blacks, race-conscious Harlem numbers kings and queens such as Turf Club owner and West Indian immigrant Casper Holstein made monetary donations to various African American religious, educational, social, and political institutions. Holstein, a *Negro World* columnist, made several financial gifts to the Urban League, Universal Negro Improvement Association (UNIA), and the Katy Ferguson Home, a settlement house for unmarried black mothers and children. Holstein's charity

Figure 4: Casper Holstein outside Washington Heights Court. Courtesy of New York Daily News Archives.

extended beyond Harlem and the United States. The West Indian banker donated money to "underfed children of the colored schools" in Hot Springs, Arkansas, where he vacationed frequently, and financially aided Hampton Institute graduate and social and religious reformer Sarah Williamson's missionary work in West Africa.[30] Langston Hughes applauded Holstein's philanthropic efforts. "He was a great help to poor poets [and] he did good things with his money, such as educating boys and girls at colleges in the South, building decent houses in Harlem, and backing literary contests to encourage colored writers."[31] Interestingly, whenever Holstein's name appeared in some black newspapers, particularly the rather conservative *NYA* and the Urban League's *Opportunity*, his occupation as a numbers banker was rarely mentioned or criticized by black elites. However, Holstein's generous contributions to and affiliation with leading black cultural and community reform groups and his role as financier of black literary production continually made newspaper headlines.[32] In the eyes of many city blacks, philanthropic underground entrepreneurs like Holstein were considered responsible race men, individuals interested in the promotion of black upward mobility and capable of taking care of their families as well as leading black New York toward racial and economic progress. Urban black activists turned a blind eye to Holstein's and other charitable number bankers' extralegal activities because of the possible monetary incentive. Holstein and other New York numbers bankers, including Stephanie St. Clair, financially advanced urban reformers' promotion of race progress, self-help, and black institution building. But Holstein's philanthropic work was not unique. He was among a number of black underground entrepreneurs around the nation that reinvested their earnings into black communities. Speaking on Chicago policy bankers' significance during the 1920s and 1930s, historian Davarian Baldwin writes that numbers barons "underwrote a vibrant culture of theaters, dance halls, and athletic and traditional business enterprises." Also speaking on the midwestern metropolis, Elizabeth Schroeder Schlabach explains: "policy became an institutional means as a way of amassing wealth and resources that constitute the ingredients of social mobility and status, and stimulating economic exchange."[33]

Life of a Queen

Given St. Clair's high-ranking status within Harlem's numbers game, few urban female policy workers established their own policy banks or duplicated her level of success. Working to make ends meet or merely enticed by the possibility of earning higher weekly wages, African American and Hispanic women occupied a broad range of positions within New York's numbers racket. Black women secured low-level positions as numbers collectors as well as more lucrative appointments as comptrollers, clerks, and messengers at gambling headquarters. During the late 1930s, former domestic and industrial workers and southern migrants Lessie Ware and Williana Hammond obtained office positions as clerks and messengers with white and Latino policy kings Alexander Pompez, George Weinburg, and Dutch Schultz. Earning between $16 and $34 per week, Ware and Hammond were responsible for calculating numbers slips and at times managing their respective policy bankers' gambling houses.[34] Similar to Ware and Hammond, the reportedly "fiery" and "beautiful West Indian" Rita Munoz was a leading Harlem comptroller and banker throughout the 1930s. Munoz's rise to distinction within the city's gambling hierarchy resulted from her association with Latino numbers baron Jose "Henry Miro" Enrique. Munoz was allegedly the girlfriend of the married Miro, and in 1931 when he received a two-year prison sentence for tax evasion Munoz assumed control of his bank.[35]

Association with influential male policy barons made it possible for underground female workers like Ware, Hammond, and Munoz to circumvent constraints placed upon them because of their sex and race. Recognizing the burdens and limits of their race and gender and the potential dangers of informal work, some black women drew on traditional ideas about masculinity and femininity to ensure their economic survival and personal safety. Early-twentieth-century constructions on masculinity and femininity imagined men as effective authorities over women's physical and emotional well-being, and reduced women's agency and ability to

Figure 5: Policy bank employee Lessie Ware, who worked for Cuban numbers banker and baseball team owner Alexander Pompez, leaves a Manhattan court after testifying for District Attorney Thomas Dewey at the James J. Hines trial in 1938. Courtesy of Corbis Images.

control their own lives. Some female numbers workers benefited when they placed themselves under male control and protection. Close professional and personal relationships with male informal economy laborers sometimes shielded women from legal arrest and convictions and rival male numbers racketeers and increased their chances of obtaining leadership positions. Some women were appointed to labor positions normally held by men and became trusted confidantes of male numbers bankers, using this affiliation with prominent policy men to thrive in male-dominated arenas.

Figure 6: Policy bank employee Williana Hammond leaves court after testifying for District Attorney Thomas Dewey at the James J. Hines trial in 1938. Courtesy of Corbis Images.

Forty-two-year-old Alberta Greene was another prominent yet lesser-known New York policy entrepreneur. Dubbed by some black New York newspapers as the "Policy Queen of South Jamaica, Queens" throughout the mid-1930s, Greene operated a gambling enterprise in her home, employing five to ten numbers collectors and countless numbers runners. Unlike some New York female numbers laborers, Greene lacked male protection, and her ability to function as a successful gambling entrepreneur seemingly was not connected to a masculine figure. By all accounts, Greene established her home-based business venture by herself. Recognizing her gender as an impediment to protecting her business from potential neighborhood ruffians, Greene's "armed fortress" was "guarded by numerous bolts and locks on each door and by two ferocious police dogs in the rear." Greene's reign as a leading numbers baroness in Jamaica, Queens, however, was cut short when police apprehended her in November 1935. On the word of several local criminal informants, city police learned that Greene "handled thousands of betting slips brought to her home daily by a large group of collectors." The NYPD raided Greene's home and discovered "several tally sheets in her coat and eight books of policy slips in her kitchen closet." Attempting to dispose of any incriminating evidence, Greene unsuccessfully "threw white slips of paper from the window." Greene was eventually convicted and sentenced to twenty days in jail.[36] That year, Greene was one of many Queens residents who were arrested during the borough's vice cleanup, a campaign led by religious and community leaders including William McKinley Dawkins, pastor of Abyssinia A. M. E. Church, and Southside Civic Organization leader and politician Geraldine Chaney.[37]

St. Clair's distinct position within Harlem's numbers business eclipsed the notoriety of most New York white, black, and Latina female policy entrepreneurs. But who was this mysterious woman of African descent whose name and image frequently graced the pages of prominent white and African American newspapers, including the *NYT*, *NYAN*, and *Chicago Defender*, of the early twentieth century? Conflicting primary evidence and secondary historical scholarship on St. Clair's life prior to her immigration to New York City complicates efforts to reconstruct her familial background and raises questions about her ethnicity. Surviving but conflicting documentation suggests that St. Clair was born in British or French West Indies or in France sometime in the 1890s.[38] The 1928 U.S. petition for naturalization of George Gachette, an immigrant from Dominica and New York "elevator operator" or "engineer" and social activist who St. Clair legally married at St. Benedict the Moor Catholic Church in New York in 1915, lists her date of birth as December 25, 1891, and her place of birth as the British West Indies. St. Clair's 1936 United States Declaration of Intent for naturalization record (commonly known as "first papers,") lists her name as Stephanie St. Clair Gachette, indicates her date of birth as December 24, 1897, and place of birth as "Moule Granterre France." Widely read newspapers also contributed to the confusion over St. Clair's ethnicity. Writing about her wealth and well-known public battle with white racketeers including Dutch Schultz, the *NYAN* claimed that St. Clair was a "fiery woman of French birth." Likewise, the *Chicago Defender* on several occasions reported that St. Clair was from Africa and Martinique. Certainly aware of the mystery surrounding her birthplace and ethnic background, St. Clair, after several 1930s interviews with New York journalist Henry Lee Moon, "vehemently" denied being from the Caribbean. She adamantly claimed "European France" as her native country.[39]

The 1911 New York Passenger List and a 1915 marriage certificate and 1942 Social Security card application offer plausible evidence of St. Clair's birth year and place as well as her ethnicity background. Extant documentation indicates Stephanie St. "Claire" was one of four children born to Amedia St. Clair and Ancelin Martraux on December 24 in the mid-1880s or 1890s on the French island of Guadeloupe. Her last place of residence was Le Moule, located on the northeast side of the island of Grand-Terre, one of five islands of Guadeloupe. On July 22, 1911, St. Clair, who may have been either thirteen or twenty-three years old, departed from Guadeloupe on the S. S. *Guiana* and arrived in New York City nine days later; her final destination was Terrebonne, Quebec, a suburb of Montreal. Available evidence does not indicate St. Clair's socioeconomic trajectory or living conditions in Canada. The newly arriving immigrant perhaps was part of the 1910–1911 Caribbean Domestic Scheme, a program that recruited one hundred Guadeloupe black women to labor as domestic workers in white Canadian households. Canadian employers paid hired laborers' $80 passageway from Guadeloupe to Canada, and in return employees were expected to labor for one or two years at a monthly wage of $5. Leaving Canada by 1912, St. Clair joined the tens of thousands of southern blacks and Caribbean immigrants that entered New York City during the era of the Great Migration.[40]

Figure 7: Harlem numbers banker Madame Stephanie St. Clair. Courtesy of Morgan and Marvin Smith Photographic Collection, Schomburg Center for Research in Black Culture, New York Public Library.

Sometime in the early- to mid-1920s, St. Clair, who was probably in her mid-thirties and separated from her husband George Gachette, established her numbers operation in Harlem.[41] According to the *NYAN*, St. Clair, "after having made a half-dozen killings" from luck at the numbers racket became a banker.[42] Ralph Matthews, writing in the *Afro-American* noted that St. Clair "came to America penniless, unable to speak anything but French, but possessing a keen mother-wit which enabled her to amass a fortune in the policy racket." Another *NYAN* editorial may explain how St. Clair obtained money to launch her numbers business. In 1923, St. Clair (Gachette) filed a lawsuit against her apartment building owner Ada Howell and a city marshall, claiming she was illegally dispossessed from her apartment on West 135th Street. In her lawsuit, "Mme Gachette claimed dispossess papers by the City Marshall were never served on her" and that her furniture, silverware, cut glass, and other household effects were placed on the street—and stolen by bystanders. Siding with St. Clair, the Seventh District Court rewarded her a judgment of $1,000. Money received from the lawsuit perhaps was used to finance St. Clair's numbers bank.[43]

By the 1930s, journalist Ted Poston reported that St. Clair had a "personal fortune around $500,000 cash and [owned] several apartment houses."[44] Earning an estimated $200,000 a year, she employed forty to fifty runners, ten comptrollers, and several bodyguards and maids, and resided at the exclusive 409 Edgecombe building on Sugar Hill.[45] Located between 145th and 155th Street between Amsterdam Avenue to the west and Edgecombe Avenue to the east, Sugar Hill, according to historian David Levering Lewis was "a citadel of stately apartment buildings and liveried doormen on a rock, [that] soared above the Polo Grounds and the rest of Harlem like a city of the Incas" and "No. 409 Edgecombe Avenue [was] the best-known building."[46] Living side by side with some of Harlem's most influential black intellectuals, writers, and race activists, including NAACP activist Walter White, painter Aaron Douglas, and Manhattan Assistant District Attorney Eunice Hunton Carter, St. Clair did not conceal her occupation, nor was she ashamed of her chosen line of work. Her neighbors knew who she was and how she earned a living. In fact, her larger-than-life personality and extravagant lifestyle made her difficult to miss and a Harlem celebrity.[47] Former 409 Edgecombe resident Katherine Butler Jones recalls that St. Clair was just as fascinating as some of the building's more "respectable" residents. Jones remembers "Madame Stephanie St. Clair breezing through the lobby with her fur coat dramatically flowing behind her. She had a mystical aura about her, and she wore exotic dresses with a colorful turban wrapped around her head."[48]

St. Clair's economic achievement as a numbers baron must be placed within the context of black female immigrants' settlement experiences, particularly those of Afro-Caribbean descent, during the first half of the twentieth century. More than 48,000 black women immigrants resided in the United States and well over half lived in New York City in 1930.[49] Similar to native-born African American women's laboring experiences, black female immigrants, despite their high literacy rates and experiences as skilled laborers, were relegated to nonprofessional and unskilled employment. In 1925, at least 75 percent of Afro-Caribbean women working in Manhattan were household workers, and more than 10 percent secured jobs as garment laborers.[50] St. Clair's New York settlement experience is somewhat ambiguous. Discerning what kind of labor St. Clair engaged in when she arrived in New York in 1912 is difficult. The 1925 New York census listed St. Clair, whom newspaper accounts suggest was a numbers banker by the early- to mid-1920s, as a "designer dresser." Another official state document revealed that St. Clair worked as a dressmaker and seamstress for several private families, earning $50 per week. Conceivably, St. Clair, like many struggling immigrant women trying to make ends meet, may have combined both formal and informal work, and at some point labored as a seamstress and numbers racket banker. It is also possible that St. Clair claimed a fictitious profession, namely that of "designer dresser," on official state records to conceal her unlawful occupation and business activities.[51] Nevertheless, St. Clair engaged in unskilled low-wage labor even if it was only for a short period. Contrary to many black women immigrants' adjustment to new geographical spaces, in a relatively short span of time St. Clair joined the ranks of a small and elite group of wealthy New York black female entrepreneurs. Her rapid socioeconomic transformation from working-class immigrant to successful informal entrepreneur illuminates the diverse ways in which black immigration and urbanization offered economic opportunities and mobility for some city blacks.

The famed Numbers Queen's flamboyant lifestyle caught the attention of New York City police during the late 1920s. St. Clair and her staff of numbers runners, comptrollers, and domestic workers were constantly under police surveillance. In November 1928, St. Clair's housekeeper, twenty-eight-year-old Sarah Scott, who went by the alias "Sarah Willoughby," was arrested for the "possession of about 5,000 policy slips, 2 adding machines, and 2 policy record books." Scott adamantly denied the charges, maintaining that her arrest was "a frame-up" and that her apprehension was a case of "mistaken identity, the officers believing she was St. Clair, her employer." Scott also informed arresting officers that her inability to read or write made it impossible for her to be a banker. Ever loyal to her employer, Scott refused to provide police with information on St. Clair's whereabouts or on her personal and professional business. Scott's silence on St. Clair can be interpreted in multiple ways. Labor equity and fairness may have cultivated a trusting and amicable working and personal relationship between Scott and St. Clair. Scott may have reaped certain benefits under St. Clair's employment; she perhaps was treated well and granted a flexible work schedule and high wages. More importantly, perhaps Scott believed that St. Clair, someone who had members of the NYPD on her payroll, would negotiate her release from jail. Such incentives would have been worth her sacrificing herself for the Numbers Queen. Unfortunately for Scott, her claims of mistaken identity and refusal to provide vital evidence about St. Clair resulted in a charge of possession of policy slips in January 1929. She was sentenced to the Bedford Reformatory prison.[52]

Being employed by some of the city's notorious underground criminals or assuming a household position at a brothel, speakeasy, or drug and gambling den complicated Scott's and other black women's lives. Black household workers' places of employment and affiliation with unsavory figures made them convenient targets for police harassment and arrest. In January 1936, Clara Lewis, a maid for white brothel proprietor Lou Kane, got caught up in one of New York County Special Prosecutor Thomas E. Dewey's prostitution raids. Lewis was not arrested, but Dewey and his team of assistant district attorneys forced her to testify that her place of employment was a house of prostitution.[53]

Not all black women household workers shared Scott's or Lewis's unfortunate labor experience. Working at prostitution houses and in other precarious spaces benefited some black female wage earners' lives. Compared to formal wage laborers, black female servants laboring at brothels often performed light housework, earned higher wages, and were paid under the table; occasionally, they received expensive gifts including clothes and jewelry from well-off informal economy entrepreneurs and their patrons. As a member of the Abyssinian Baptist Church, one of Harlem's premier religious centers, one domestic worker was indifferent about her employment at a sex house. Recognizing the income disparity between household work within the legal and illegal economies, she noted: "[I] knew the type of person for whom [I] was going to work. . . . But the salary was so much better than any [I] could earn on another housework job."[54] Moreover, black household laborers garnered the trust of and protection from their underworld employers. Throughout the 1930s, white madam Polly Adler relied on her black maid, "a tiny, trim, colored woman of about forty, to assist with the domestic and economic management of her Manhattan brothel." In her 1950 autobiography, *A House Is Not a Home*, Adler recounted that "there was no job too big for her to tackle and no one on earth—be it a six-foot-three cop or a pistol-packing drunken hoodlum—whom she feared to face. She [was] my confidante and comforter, and in my absence, a trustworthy assistant manager. [She] held the fort while I went out, did a little drum-beating, and [took] a night to attend night-club openings."[55]

St. Clair, The NYPD, and White Numbers Racketeers

On December 30, 1929, NYPD officers apprehended St. Clair for possession of policy slips. She was arrested at 117 West 141st Street, where an alleged policy bank operated. On January 1, St. Clair placed an editorial in the *NYAN* announcing her arrest; perhaps someone whom she employed placed the editorial in the paper. Claiming police misconduct, a brazen St. Clair informed readers that she had been arrested: "Yes, arrested and framed by three of the bravest and the noblest cowards who wear civilian clothes."[56] During her trial in March 1930, St. Clair, who represented herself, unapologetically admitted to being a numbers banker, claiming she "was marked for a jail term because of her fight for courtesy and freedom from annoyance [of] the police." Ted Poston reported on St. Clair's nearly three-hour court testimony: "because of her desire to retire after she accumulated her fortune or because of jealousy of other policemen who were not in on the 'gravy,' her apartment was raided, $400 in cash taken, and the offending officer allowed to go without punishment. When she threatened to expose the [story], she was told to keep her mouth closed or she would get hers."[57] Despite her revealing and charismatic testimony, an unconvinced jury and judge convicted and sentenced St. Clair to eight months and twenty days in the workhouse on Welfare Island.[58] It is unclear whether St. Clair's numbers business survived her imprisonment or if she made arrangements for her business to be operated by a close associate. What is apparent is that St. Clair's arrest marked an end, at least for a short time, to her dominance over Harlem's numbers games. The Harlem numbers leader's imprisonment also signaled the beginning of her public crusade against the NYPD.

Nearly a year later, St. Clair emerged from prison determined to disclose the NYPD's close business ties to numbers racketeers. Her aim in exposing the NYPD's vice participation was twofold. While she sought retribution for her 1929 arrest and imprisonment, St. Clair also intended to cast a spotlight on the city corruption, particularly police-protected vice rings. Police and municipal corruption within the NYPD was not new to Gotham residents. Both the Lexow Committee of the mid-1890s and the 1913 Curran Committee investigated and revealed political interference with police procedures, incidents of police brutality, and law officers' criminal activities and protection of organized crime.[59] Like many New Yorkers' concern with police malfeasance and misconduct, St. Clair believed and knew firsthand that city lawmakers and enforcers, those who were on the payrolls of crime leaders and handsomely profited from urban vice, were hypocrites for executing legal policies that attempted to crack down on crime. Publicly contesting police impropriety undermined law enforcers' authority over their jurisdictions and exposed the NYPD to inspection, thus revealing the complex relationship between municipal government and urban criminality.

St. Clair's personal conflicts with law enforcers and her unwavering determination to unmask urban profiteering within the NYPD and City Hall placed her in a precarious position. Drawing attention to city malfeasance meant facing possible police retaliation or reprisal from any of the criminal syndicates connected to law enforcement. Regardless of the potential risk, St. Clair appeared before the Samuel Seabury Commission in December 1930. The commission investigated corruption in the Magistrate's Court of the Bronx and Manhattan and in the NYPD. At private and public hearings, testimonies were heard from judges; lawyers; police officers; numbers workers including Henry Miro, Lessie Ware, and Williana Hammond; criminal informants; and prostitutes.[60] Witness testimony revealed corruption within the NYPD and the court system and uncovered a conspiracy of crooked judges, lawyers, and police who extorted money from defendants.[61] Appearing before the commission, St. Clair, "lavishly dressed in her mink coat, chic hat and ever present jewels mounted the witness stand and hurled a series of charges." She readily testified about her experiences as a numbers banker as well as her business relationships with police. According to St. Clair, she "sent payments of $100 and $500 by [way of] a man known as 'Mustache' Jones to a lieutenant of the Sixth Division and paid plainclothes cops a total of $6,000."[62] Despite paying police, St. Clair alleged that she and her employees were constantly under police surveillance and were often arrested by law enforcement officers. Based on her candid testimony, a lieutenant and thirteen other men were suspended from the NYPD.[63]

White crime bosses' interests in Harlem's numbers racket equally troubled the Queen of Policy. Initially, many white organized-crime figures, especially those amassing wealth from the illegal sale of alcohol, were not interested in Harlem's numbers business. Often referring to the game as "nigger pool," white racketeers viewed policy as an unprofitable game consumed by working-poor blacks. Cultural critic Claude McKay recalled that "numbers was the only game on which a penny could be up as a wager. The white world never imagined that the pennies of Harlem's humble folk were creating fortunes of thousands of dollars and 'kings' and 'queens' in Harlem."[64] Furthermore, some white racketeers perceived black numbers bankers as non-threatening petty violators. Crime syndicate lawyer turned numbers banker Richard "Dixie" Davis explained that black "policy bankers were not gangsters. They were merely gamblers running an illegal business on a very peaceful, non-violent basis."[65] Because some white vice leaders were disinterested in policy, it became an economic enterprise that was primarily dominated by West Indian immigrants and African Americans numbers bankers, runners, and players.

With white racketeers' less than dominant presence in Harlem's numbers racket, African American and Latino numbers entrepreneurs such as Wilfred Brunder

Figure 8: Numbers banker and bootlegger Arthur "Dutch Schultz" Flegenheimer, 1935. Courtesy of Popperfoto.

and Henry Miro became some of New York's wealthiest residents during the early twentieth century. According to the Seabury Commission report, Brunder reportedly earned more than $1 million between 1925 and 1930. Published accounts revealed that Miro deposited over $1.2 million between 1927 and 1930.[66] In the mid-1920s, the *NYA* reported the daily turnover on numbers was $75,000, and the annual turnover was about $20 million.[67] As city newspapers reported on black bankers' wealth and their daily numbers turnover, Harlem's numbers game attracted Prohibition-era white racketeers and bootleggers whose economic profits were circumvented with the repeal of the Volstead Act. No longer able to profit from the unlimited markup on illegal alcohol sales, white criminals searched for alternative business ventures and new avenues of wealth, setting their sights on the policy racket. White crime leaders of the 1920s and 1930s had no desire to take a share of Harlem's numbers racket. Instead, nonblack numbers bankers sought to dominate the policy game.

White gangster Arthur "Dutch Schultz" Flegenheimer posed the greatest threat to African American policy bankers during the 1930s. A Bronx native, Schultz was one of New York's and the nation's most ruthless bootleggers and criminals. In 1935, Federal Bureau of Investigation (FBI) director J. Edgar Hoover referred to Schultz as "Public Enemy Number One," listing him among the most dangerous white criminals of the era, along with John Dillinger, Kate "Ma" Barker, and Al

Capone.[68] Several factors made it possible for Schultz and his gang of gunmen to force some black and Latino numbers bankers out of business. First, Schultz's business and political affiliations with organized-crime bosses like Charles "Lucky" Luciano and Owney Madden, and City Hall officials such as James Hines, ensured a successful takeover. Hines, a powerful Democrat and Tammany Hall politician who was on Schultz's payroll, guaranteed that Schultz and his staff of bankers and runners would be protected from police.

Second, Schultz and other white racketeers deployed violent tactics to force nonwhite bankers out of business. Jamaican writer A. M. Wendell Malliet observed, "had the white gangsters not 'muscled in' on the policy game as it was then being operated by the pioneers it would no doubt have continued as an illegal but not an immoral and racketeering enterprise. But when Dutch Schultz and his henchmen [came in] every conceivable method known to be used by gangsters was brought into the policy game."[69] Schultz intimidated black and Latino barons, offering them several unappealing propositions: Nonwhite bankers could relinquish their successful businesses and work for Schultz or they could continue their operation and pay Schultz a portion of their earnings. If nonwhite bankers rebuffed Schultz's threatening scenarios, they faced the possibility of being severely beaten or murdered. Refusing to submit to Schultz, black and West Indian policy bankers such as Panama Francis retired and became legitimate businessmen; others, however, maintained their numbers enterprises and paid Schultz a share of their bank.

More importantly, the failure of New York African American and West Indian numbers bankers, unlike black policy leaders in Detroit and Chicago who resisted white bankers with the formation of the Associated Numbers Bankers and National Brotherhood of Policy Kings, to collectively protest white incursion may have increased some white numbers bankers' control of Harlem's numbers game. Publicly censuring black policy bankers' seeming failure to challenge white numbers racketeers, one African American player "wonder[ed] why the black people didn't form a mob of gangsters to defy Dutch Schultz and his gang when they entered Harlem to take over the 'numbers' racket from them. We are cowards. We stand by and let the whites take the sweepers' jobs, [and the] 'numbers' racket."[70] While black New Yorkers did not collectively organize against white numbers bankers, many occupying various socioeconomic statuses and positions within the African American community publicly contested white racketeers' efforts to control Harlem's numbers enterprise. Resentment over nonblack policy workers' presence on Harlem streets was in larger part due to white New Yorkers' increasing visibility in black neighborhoods and underground leisure spaces during the 1920s and 1930s. Some African Americans' annoyance stemmed from the belief that Harlem and other black urban spaces were perceived as the "devil's playground, an easy prey for depraved joy-seeking whites."[71] Curious about and in search of so-called authentic and exotic black entertainment, affluent white New Yorkers ventured—or as suggested by Chad Heap, slummed—into Harlem and other racially and ethnically diverse working-class communities to experience cross-racial and class and sexual encounters. New York ethnic communities like Harlem provided urban whites with the "anonymity necessary to indulge in the primitive behaviors and desires they associated with blacks" and to "engage in vices which they would not attempt in their own communities."[72] In one of his popularly read *NYAN* editorials, journalist Edgar Grey suggested that whites, particularly underworld gangsters, were attracted to Harlem because of the prevailing assumption that "Harlem [was] an ideal place to operate [illegal vice] because here the supervision was, to say the least, lax."[73]

Black Harlemites from varying socioeconomic class backgrounds mounted a series of protests against white policy laborers and entrepreneurs. During the mid-1920s, *NYA* editor Fred Moore, who often published editorials condemning games of chance and black policy leaders and players, took issue with white encroachment on Harlem numbers and the disturbing reality that black policy workers' arrest rates were disproportionately higher compared to whites' numbers laborers. On the front pages of the *NYA*, Moore and his staff of journalists identified white bankers and their numbers drop locations, attempting to heighten white bankers' and runners' probability of arrest.[74] The *Afro-American* reported that defiant numbers banker Rita Munoz, who even told the "Dutchman to go straight to h-," led a "revolt of numbers writers and controllers" against white numbers bankers.[75] Moreover, many black numbers players refused to interact with nonblack policy workers. Understandably, black Harlemites distrusted white numbers laborers, believing that some were undercover police officers and "stool pigeons" attempting to entrap and arrest them. Adamantly objecting to nonblack policy collectors in his neighborhood, one black numbers player decided that he "made his last play." He stated that he would rather give up the game than "contribute to the bank accounts of Jews, Cubans, and others who are riding around in their big, powerful cars, living in fine houses and using hundred dollar bills as cigar lighters."

St. Clair joined black New Yorkers' individual and collective resistance against white gangsters and boldly waged a public war against Dutch Schultz and other white racketeers who desired to control Harlem's lucrative numbers racket. In a 1960 article in the *New York Post* (*NYP*), St. Clair claimed she was the only "Negro banker" to fight off Schultz, and she criticized black bankers for being intimidated by white racketeers. "I fought Schultz from 1931 to 1935 [and] it cost me a total of 820 days in jail and three-quarters of a million dollars."[76] Running afoul of white organized crime syndicates, St. Clair courageously declared that she was not "afraid of Dutch Schultz or any other living man. He'll never touch me! I will kill Schultz if he sets foot in Harlem. He is a rat. The policy game is my game. He took it away from me and is swindling the colored people. I'm the only one that's after him."[77] Possessing what 1930s journalist and communist worker Marvel Cooke deemed an "intense spirit of [black] nationalism," St. Clair fought to make "the numbers game for Harlem." Recognizing St. Clair's audacious efforts against Schultz, Cooke wrote that "she alone defied the Dutchman. The policy queen fought back when others cringed."[78]

Showing her enemies that she was fearless, St. Clair staged several strategies of opposition against white incursion. First, she unsuccessfully attempted to organize small black policy bankers who were "ignored by the racketeers and operated outside Schultz's influence." Secondly, St. Clair employed violence to make a statement about white numbers racketeers' presence in Harlem. She confronted legitimate white storeowners whose establishments served as numbers drops for Schultz and other white racketeers. "She entered their stores one after the other and single-handed[ly] smashed plate glass cases, snatched and destroyed policy slips and ordered the 'small timers' to get out of Harlem."[79] Moreover, St. Clair encouraged black numbers players to conduct business with only black numbers laborers. Her crusade against white policy bankers, which could be interpreted as a "play black" campaign, was symbolic of the 1930s "Buy Black or Hire" campaign of Harlem civil rights leaders and business merchants. Promoting economic nationalism, drawing inspiration from nationwide "Don't Buy Where You Can't Work" campaigns, and attempting to bolster their own businesses, Harlem African American merchants' Buy Black campaign emphasized "race loyalty" and encouraged local blacks to "buy from Race Enterprises."[80] Buy Black advocates encouraged black urbanites to avoid white Harlem stores and businesses, particularly those that refused to employ them or subjected them to race prejudice. According to black merchants, African Americans' best hope for labor equity, fair wages, and employment outside of household and unskilled work was with black merchants. Recognizing Harlem blacks' purchasing power, race entrepreneurs maintained that African American consumerism in black stores strengthened race businesses and undermined nonblack merchants' dominance in Harlem.

Similarly, St. Clair's "play black" initiative espoused a sense of race solidarity and economic nationalism that stressed boosting black bankers' businesses and weakening white racketeers' attempts at controlling the game. In her estimation, white infiltration of Harlem's numbers racket was an extension of Jim Crow segregation and the continuation of white domination over black life. St. Clair aspired to "show dese niggers how to hold on to ze game. I'll show them how to fight back. I'll show that Dutch Schultz can't muscle in and take ze numbers away from us like that."[81] At the same time and comparable to E. Franklin Frazier criticisms of African American merchants' Buy Black campaign, St. Clair's vision of a black-controlled gambling racket was her way of "reserv[ing] the field of exploitation" for herself and manipulating notions of racial solidarity.[82] As an informal businesswoman, St. Clair was certainly concerned with the impact of white encroachment on her individual wealth. For St. Clair, nonblack control over Harlem numbers possibly meant the loss of black players to white policy bankers and potentially diminished her economic profits. Moreover, white infringement placed St. Clair's status as Harlem's reigning Numbers Queen in jeopardy. Whether St. Clair's motives were rooted in her own self-interests and/or the promotion of black entrepreneurship, her resistance to white encroachment on Harlem's policy racket undermined white policy bankers' economic aspirations and business prospects.

For interfering with his business operations, Schultz, perhaps viewing the out-spoken black female immigrant as someone that ruptured normative expectations of women and challenged white superiority, placed a contract on St. Clair's life and forced her to go into hiding for a short time in 1935. According to St. Clair, she was running for her life and even "had to hide in a cellar while the super, a friend of mine, covered me with coal."[83] It is unclear if St. Clair employed such seemingly extreme strategies to conceal her whereabouts. What is evident is that verbal and physical threats leveled at St. Clair and other informal economy women, particularly those involved in criminal economies dominated by men, were real and caused many to utilize various survival tactics. On October 23, 1935, St. Clair's public battle with Dutch Schultz ended when he was shot at the Palace Chophouse in Newark, New Jersey. As Schultz lay dying in a New Jersey hospital, he received a telegram from the Queen of Policy, which read, "As ye sow, so shall you reap."[84] Dutch Schultz died three days later on October 26, 1935.

After the death of Schultz, St. Clair remained in the headlines of black news-papers throughout the country. Local New York dailies and weeklies as well as the *Chicago Defender*, *Pittsburgh Courier*, and other newspapers captured the details of her unconventional marriage and her unsurprising return to prison in 1938. In August 1936, a forty-nine-year-old St. Clair "married by contract" Sufi Abdul Hamid, the thirty-year-old founder of the Negro Clerical and Industrial Alliance and one of Harlem's more controversial race activists and stepladder orators of the 1930s. St. Clair and Hamid's contract marriage was a nonlegal union that was supposed to marry the "couple for ninety-nine years [and] contains a clause which allows a trial period of one year during which time the feasibility of the plan could be tested. If at the end of that time, the two decided that a continu-ation of the marriage would not be plausible, the contract could be terminated. If, on the other hand, they had decided that the idea was good, a legal ceremony

Figure 9: Sufi Abdul Hamid. Courtesy of Morgan and Marvin Smith Photographic Collection, Schomburg Center for Research in Black Culture, New York Public Library.

would be performed."[85] Born in Lowell, Massachusetts, in 1903, Hamid, whose real name was Eugene Brown, was an imposing figure who stood 6 feet tall and weighed 225 pounds. The colorful political reformer was routinely seen in Harlem streets, wearing a turban wrapped around his head, a black and crimson lined cape, a green velvet blouse, and black riding boots, advocating black separatism and encouraging black New Yorkers to participate in the 1930s Don't Buy Where You Can't Work and Buy Black campaigns.[86] Although spectators claimed that St. Clair and Hamid made a fascinating couple, their "whirlwind romance" and marriage ended at the barrel of a gun.

On January 19, 1938, in an office building on 125th Street, St. Clair shot Hamid after accusing him of having an affair with a young "conjure woman from Jamaica." This "conjure woman" was none other than Harlem occultist leader and dream book author Dorothy "Fu Futtam" Matthews, whom Hamid eventually married later in April 1938—which suggests that St. Clair's suspicions of a cheating Hamid were correct.[87] In her own defense, St. Clair claimed that the gun belonged to her husband and that it went off during a struggle between the two former lovers. She informed police and reporters that she went to confront Hamid because "he had been treating her cruelly" and because of his alleged affair with Matthews. St. Clair's March 1938 trial revealed the details of what transpired between the two former lovers. On the day of the shooting Hamid had an appointment with his attorney and when he reached the third floor of the office building St. Clair was standing with a gun pointed at him. She "demanded he return to her all the clothing and money she had given him. As he approached her, she fired a shot at him. The first bullet went through his mouth and broke a tooth. He grabbed at her hand and as she stepped back, she fired again and the second bullet went through his jacket. The third bullet went over his head." In several newspaper interviews, Hamid admitted that he was not surprised by his former lover's actions. According to Hamid, several weeks prior to the shooting, St. Clair "had threatened his life" after he informed her that he "wanted no more to do with" her.[88]

During the fascinating trial, St. Clair code-switched from a scorned and enraged wife to a remorseful and betrayed woman, claiming that she "only wanted to scare him with [the gun]. If I had killed him I would have died."[89] Cloaking herself in female respectability and crafting herself as a heartbroken and duped woman, St. Clair expected her outpouring of tears and guilt to garner sympathy from both the jury and court spectators. However, St. Clair's seeming contrition proved unconvincing, as she was convicted of first-degree assault and possession of a concealed weapon. She was sentenced to two to ten years at the New York State Prison for Women at Bedford; however, she ended up at the Westfield State Farm, State Prison for Women. Before St. Clair was remanded to police custody, presiding trial Judge James G. Wallace commented that the newly convicted woman was a dangerous and calculating criminal. "This woman [has] been living by her wits all of her life. She has a bad temper and must learn that she can't go around shooting at other people." With a flair for the theatric, St. Clair "kissed her hand to freedom as she was led out of the courtroom." St. Clair's less than convincing courtroom performance revealed her complexity as a shrewd, clever, and apparently dangerous individual and a layered historical figure that used a variety of survival strategies to maintain her socioeconomic status. The legal drama also illuminated an embarrassed and vulnerable St. Clair (an aspect of her personality that the public was not accustomed to seeing) and her inability to control her private life and relationships. Interestingly, St. Clair's desire to either hurt or kill Hamid came to fruition in August 1938. That year, the colorful race advocate was tragically killed in a plane crash in Long Island.[90]

It is unclear how long Stephanie St. Clair served in prison or when she was released. Moreover, the details of her post-prison life are a mystery. Newspaper accounts and her Westfield State Farm prison record suggest that she was released from prison at least by 1940. A 1943 *NYAN* article reported that St. Clair's postprison whereabouts "are not definitely known. Shortly before the start of the war [World War II], she visited relatives and friends in the West Indies. Since then, she has

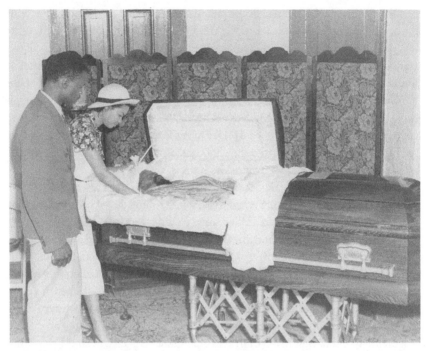

Figure 10: Dorothy "Madame Fu Futtam" Matthews and friend view Sufi Abdul Hamid in casket, 1938. Courtesy of Morgan and Marvin Smith Photographic Collection, Schomburg Center for Research in Black Culture, New York Public Library.

lived in seclusion."[91] In 1960, an aging St. Clair resurfaced in a newspaper interview conducted by *NYP* journalist Ted Poston. Writing about the whereabouts of former 1930s black and Latino policy bankers, Poston informed readers that St. Clair had successfully transitioned from informal economy entrepreneur to "prosperous business woman" and "own[er of] a four-story apartment building in Sugar Hill."[92]

After the Poston interview, St. Clair is rarely mentioned in New York newspapers. The dearth of publicity on her could indicate her lack of relevance and influence during the Civil Rights and Black Power eras, or it might reflect her conscious decision to remain outside the public sphere. In her 2008 autobiography, *Harlem Godfather: The Rap on My Husband, Ellsworth "Bumpy" Johnson* (coauthored by Karen E. Quinones Miller), Mayme Johnson claims that St. Clair left Harlem and relocated to a Long Island mansion "never again getting into the numbers business."[93] While many early-twentieth-century newspapers reported on various aspects of St. Clair's complex public and private life, her purported death in 1969 was not mentioned in the *NYAN, NYA, NYT,* or seemingly in any other newspaper of the era.[94] Similar to the conflicting accounts of St. Clair's ethnic background, her postjail whereabouts and death date and cause of death are unclear, leaving historians of New York wondering what happened to the Queen of Policy.

The obscurity of St. Clair's post–World War II life signals a complex and shifting identity politic. St. Clair was a high-profile urban figure and one who seemingly, according to one journalist, "possess[ed] some indescribable complex and an apparent yen for publicity."[95] However, her extraordinary public lifestyle masked a private persona. A master of manipulation, St. Clair employed a veil of silence when it came to her private life, disclosing to the public only certain aspects of her personal life, her business, and her close relationships. In her numerous newspaper interviews and private testimonies to New York journalists and city officials, St. Clair rarely if ever discussed her family, close relationships, or how she established her underground business. Ambiguity about her private life points to a conscious decision to control, reinvent, and at times present conflicting and multiple public personas.

St. Clair and Community Advocacy

On the surface, St. Clair was not a conventional community advocate or spokesperson, nor did she figure prominently into any of the city's established race- or gender-based reform organizations. Gender exclusion, male patriarchy, and widely accepted ideas concerning black female leadership kept St. Clair and other African American women from obtaining leadership positions within or from becoming public spokespersons for some race reform agencies. Historian Barbara Ransby's analysis on political activist Ella Baker and other African American women during the post–World War II years is useful in exploring how gender inequality impacted black women's reform work of the early twentieth century. "Although women had always been central to community-based campaigns for civil rights, they seldom were accorded recognized leadership roles, and their contributions were often unknown outside the locality and often forgotten after the struggle was over."[96] Moreover, St. Clair's chosen profession, criminal record and time in prison, affiliation with urban criminals, and provocative and ostentatious lifestyle placed her outside of New York's well-established circle of black women community activists and entrepreneurs such as Victoria Earle Matthews and Madame C. J. Walker. St. Clair transgressed black bourgeois definitions of female civility and community activism. Stepping in and out of the confines of standard female behavior was likely a conscious decision that St. Clair made because she was an underground figure. Visions of surviving and financially prospering in the city's male-dominated gambling arena compelled St. Clair and other female off-the-books laborers and entrepreneurs to cast aside, at times, normative images of female decorum and adopt more rapacious and treacherous personas.

The enterprising Numbers Queen's outlook on female propriety was complex and contradictory, and it reflected black women's wide-ranging perspectives on the subject. St. Clair's criminal activity and over-the-top personality indicated multiple and evolving viewpoints on respectable politics. Her perspectives on outward deportment, as expressed through her labor and community efforts, symbolized the appropriation, refashioning, and occasional manipulation of black bourgeois and working-class tenets of respectability. On one hand, St. Clair promoted black middle-class versions of respectability, advocating self-help, black-institution building, and even the projection of proper outward images of black womanhood. For instance, on Harlem streets, the Queen of Policy was often seen wearing expensive attire and jewelry; she presented herself in a manner that commanded respect and admiration. One journalist noted that St. Clair's eye-catching and striking presence "gives [one] the impression that here is a lady who knows her way around."[97] The adoption of the title "Madame" signified her subscription to traditional images of black womanhood. Her use of "Madame" expressed her positive perception of herself and her desire to define herself beyond white racist and sexist parameters. Yet at the same time, St. Clair, once a working-class immigrant, identified with the struggles of less-privileged blacks. Perhaps shaped by her prior financial status, St. Clair, who was undoubtedly concerned with her external appearance and the consumption of lavish items, believed that self-worth and economic permanence were interconnected concepts that took precedence over proper deportment.

St. Clair's race and community consciousness were unquestionably shaped by black New Yorkers' individual and collective experiences with race, gender, and class bigotry and by their continuous campaigns for equality, citizenship, and improved community conditions. Black New Yorkers' distressing personal accounts of poverty and unemployment, inadequate housing, white supremacy and state-sanctioned violence politicized St. Clair, leading her to become one of New York's staunchest yet most unlikely voices against urban inequity.[98] An outspoken community advocate, St. Clair publicly unraveled black city dwellers' socioeconomic and political conditions, particularly their relationship to and treatment by the NYPD. Furthermore, St. Clair's political consciousness and concern for racial betterment was likely impacted by what historians refer to as "personal protests" and battles against race and sex discrimination. In other words, St. Clair's race and political consciousness was informed by her firsthand experience with urban prejudice and police harassment and violence.

Interestingly, the combative numbers banker's expression of community advocacy was similar to that of many African American clubwomen. Her community strategy was rather nonconfrontational and certainly within the boundaries of the law. Given St. Clair's willingness to use violence against white numbers racketeers, her husband, and anyone who threatened her financial well-being, she did not subscribe to armed self-defense as a liberation strategy against racial injustice nor did she encourage black New Yorkers to resort to violence in the face of intense racial oppression and white brutality. Instead, St. Clair used African American newspapers to articulate her positions on race inequity and advancement and on urban white violence. Since the antebellum era, the black press was a "defender of the race, ever ready to counter attacks on African Americans in the mainstream white press, to make the case for black equality and civil rights, [and] to point out the injustices inherent in America's race relations."[99] Undoubtedly, St. Clair and other African Americans viewed the black press as an integral part of the African American experience, believing it was the newspapers' responsibility to speak on behalf of African Americans and to report on black achievement and racial injustices. Writing newspaper editorials during the late 1920s and early 1930s, St. Clair used black print media to express her views on a diverse array of issues, including race advancement, black immigration, city corruption, prospective New York political candidates, and police brutality. Aware of and perhaps influenced by the militancy of Harlem's New Negro activists, St. Clair's opinionated writings rejected African Americans' position as second-class citizens, demanded dignity and respect for black men and women, and insisted that blacks understand their constitutional rights. Not surprisingly, St. Clair used the pages of black newspapers to publicize and sell her own personal story of struggle against the NYPD and to counter false misconceptions about her character. Through her newspaper columns, which consistently featured a photo of a well-dressed St. Clair adorned in fur coats, jewels, and expensive clothes, she hoped to draw attention to urban inequality and city corruption and to remain in the public eye and continue her reign as Harlem's Numbers Queen.

Between September 1929 and February 1930, St. Clair strategically placed paid editorials in the *NYAN*. Her writings included copies of letters she wrote to New York state and local officials, including Governor Franklin D. Roosevelt and New York City mayor James J. Walker, and open letters to black New Yorkers. Addressing state lawmakers about the denial of black civil rights, St. Clair's writings emphasized issues that plagued black New Yorkers' daily lives. In each of her letters, St. Clair seemingly "with tears in [her] eyes" appealed to state and city politicians to address the denial of black civil rights. "Please do something to remedy these terrible conditions of mistreatment to the members of my race."[100] Subscribing to what historian Shannon King identified as "legalism," St. Clair's editorials to lawmakers illuminated her call for African Americans to be treated as first-class citizens and for politicians to enforce blacks' civil rights.[101] By appealing to state and federal

Figure 11: Portrait of Madame Stephanie St. Clair, 1930. Courtesy of Bettmann.

lawmakers, St. Clair, despite her criticism of corrupt law officials, demonstrated some belief and faith, at least publicly, in the legal system and her willingness to employ varying liberation strategies to achieve racial equality.

Police misconduct was a continuous topic within St. Clair's editorials. Her commentary on police malfeasance was part of black and white anti-race activists' broader political conversations on corruption within the NYPD. In several columns, St. Clair accused members of the NYPD of extortion and censured them for their participation in urban vice. She observed: "I don't understand how these police, who are supposed to be the protection of the people, can make raids for so-called policy slips when these same men are participants of the game themselves."[102] In a letter to Mayor Walker in 1929, St. Clair noted that police "sometimes find policy slips in their searches, but if you pay them from $500 to $2,000, you are sure to come back home. If you pay them nothing, you are sure to get a sentence from 60 to 90 days in the workhouse. If they raid a place known as the bank, or where the work is done, and find adding machines and hundreds of the so-called policy slips, they call themselves doing big business."[103]

Both black New York underworld entrepreneurs and race activists affirmed St. Clair's allegations against city police, claiming that law enforcers permitted criminals to operate illegal businesses in Harlem and throughout the city. A 1932 NAACP memorandum claimed that, "it is common knowledge that [gambling, prostitution, speakeasies, and other] rackets would not go on one minute if the police were on their job."[104] Law enforcement officials that sanctioned urban vice throughout working- and middle-class communities were often on the payrolls of criminals and vice racketeers. Former brothel owner turned self-proclaimed prison missionary Hattie Ross, who operated several "high-toned" sex houses employing only white women during the 1890s, testified before the Lexow Committee that she paid NYPD officers at least $100 a month to avoid police raids.[105] Supplementing his modest salary, one police officer received more than $300 each month from various vice businesses. He received $20 from policy bankers, $80 from liquor dealers, and $200 from poolroom owners.[106] Some NYPD officers protected illegal public amusements and vice because they were underworld patrons. Their association with and protection of criminal enterprises enabled them to establish personal relationships with underworld entrepreneurs and receive complimentary services and goods. For instance, one black police officer rarely if ever paid for the many amenities offered at a Harlem brothel owned by a black female. In 1928, an undercover anti-vice agent visited the popular sex resort and was surprised to find the uniformed policeman engaging in unlawful amusements. The female proprietor informed the agent that the officer "like any man that comes around these parts has a good old time," and disregards the illegality of her operation. "He comes here regularly and when off the beat he writes in his notebook that he was at different fictitious places." In exchange for his silence, the officer enjoyed a host of free services and products, including alcoholic beverages, home-cooked meals, live music, and sex with any woman of his choice.[107]

Black New Yorkers' horrific experiences of police brutality and illegal house raids were also topics in St. Clair's *NYAN* columns. During the 1940s, under the stewardship of Adam Clayton Powell Jr., the *People's Voice* argued: "Harlem is damned sick and tired of brutal police who strike first and take prisoners after. We recognize that some police cases require violence, but [we] also insist that too many peaceful persons are vilely maltreated by officers who are unfitted for their jobs and who are stationed in Harlem as the 'Siberia' of the city police department for misconduct elsewhere."[108] From the time of its founding in 1845, the NYPD had a history of misconduct and violence against working-poor Jews, southern and eastern European immigrants, and blacks. The relationship between African Americans and the NYPD was tainted by mistrust, and many blacks perceived law enforcers as perpetrators of violence. In their treatment of New York African Americans, law enforcers employed violence as a standard practice. They had a "tendency to subdue black suspects first and ask questions later became ingrained in police culture."[109]

Black urbanites, whether they were formal wage laborers, criminals, or ordinary housewives, were subjected to police harassment, arrest, physical abuse, and illegal house searches. House crashes were illegal raids in which "detectives, without bothering to obtain evidence, force[d] their way into an apartment" based upon "information and belief that the law [was] being violated there."[110] Adding to the *NYA* and *NYAN*'s coverage of unlawful house raids, St. Clair's November 13, 1929, *NYAN* editorial informed readers of the house "crash," arrest, and physical assault of "Mrs. Davis." Through the column, St. Clair, while attempting to illuminate city black women's often difficult and brutal encounters with police, fails to disclose Davis's full name or her address. Concealing Davis's identity conceivably may have been St. Clair's way of protecting her from further police harassment. It's unclear how St. Clair discovered Davis's story; she could have been St. Clair's personal friend, a loyal numbers patron or neighbor, or a friend of a friend. Whatever the relationship between the two Harlem women, St. Clair used the Davis case to illuminate black women's troublesome relations with the NYPD. Upon visiting Davis at her home, St. Clair found her "face badly bruised, her eyes were black and bloody, and her hand was bandaged." A tearful Davis informed St. Clair that some time in November, five white plainclothes police officers, perhaps on the word of one of their criminal informants, raided Davis's apartment without "saying a word or showing a badge or any papers of any kind. One began to search through my dresser in the bedroom [for policy slips]. One of the men began to beat me and call me vile names." Extant records do not indicate whether Davis filed an official complaint with either the NYPD or city leaders about the police officers' conduct.[111]

Police assaults and other forms of state sanctioned violence was commonplace for many New York black women. On March 7, 1934, Brooklyn resident Pearl Lovell was brutally assaulted by white plainclothes patrolman John A. Johnson. According to Lovell, Johnson entered her "home while she was doing dishes in search of policy slips and without provocation he grabbed her by the arm, twisted it and then forced her to the wall." The officer then "pushed his hand down her bosom to see if there were slips in her bra, and pummeled her when she resisted. Helpless with pain," Lovell told Officer Johnson he "would pay for his conduct." She later instituted a lawsuit for $3,000 damages against the policeman.[112]

Davis's and Lovell's stories of physical and sexual violence were representative of the countless cases where persons of African descent, particularly black women, endured and suffered from police violence. Local New York black newspapers reported on countless incidents where the NYPD verbally, physically, and sexually assaulted black women. Law enforcers pulled their guns on unarmed women and brutally beat them in their apartments, on the streets, and while in police custody.[113]

New York black women's horrific encounters with the NYPD highlighted their vulnerability and lack of protection in urban spaces and the multiple ways in which violence was used to subdue and control black female bodies. More importantly, black women's experience with white violence and brutality illuminated their long-standing tradition of testimony. Despite the possibility of being reprimanded by law enforcement officials, African Americans like Davis and Lovell vehemently contested their abuse as well as violence against other black women. Urban black women courageously informed family members, close friends, and neighbors about their traumatized interactions with law enforcers; reported incidents of police misconduct and brutality to local race reform organizations; confronted their assailants in criminal and civil courts; and employed armed self-defense against what was commonly known as the "Third Degree."[114]

St. Clair joined a coalition of New York race spokespersons and residents that actively fought against police violence. Moreover, St. Clair became one of the many race and community advocates and ordinary black folks that legitimatized black women's claims of physical and sexual abuse at the hands of law enforcers and police informants. While some African American race reformers employed legalism as a strategy against police misconduct, others organized antibrutality campaigns and self-defense organizations, including the Colored Citizens Protective League (CCPL) and the NAACP's New York Vigilance Committee. African American self-defense groups monitored police officers' behavior in black neighborhoods and investigated both police misconduct and incidents where law enforcers violated blacks' civil liberties. For some black political activists, armed self-defense became a legitimate response to police brutality and to the increasing wave of race riots occurring throughout the nation during the Progressive era. Commenting on white violence against African Americans, particularly the Tulsa Race Riot of 1921, black socialist W. A. Domingo argued, "Our aim is to allow those who attack us to choose the weapons. If it be guns, we will reply with guns."[115]

St. Clair probably would have disagreed with Domingo and other New Negro political activists' support of armed self-defense. She refrained, at least publicly, from promoting violence as a method of recourse against white supremacy and violence. Instead, St. Clair advised black city dwellers to organize and stage non-violent mass protests, including rallies and marches, throughout the streets of New York. In St. Clair's estimation, such resistant initiatives, because of their peaceful nature, would compel city officials to equally reinforce city and state statutes concerning civil rights. Moreover, St. Clair argued, perhaps naively, that police brutality could be prevented if African Americans understood their legal rights. Her *NYAN* editorials, similar to public notices issued by the NAACP and published in black newspapers like the *NYA* on the same issue, informed blacks that it was illegal for the police to conduct any type of search without a warrant. In her September 18, 1929, column, she wrote: "TO THE MEMBERS OF MY RACE: If officers meet you on the street and suspect you of anything, do not let them search you on the street, or do not let them take you to any hallway to be searched. If the police should ring your doorbell and you open your door, refuse to let them search your house un- less they show you a search warrant."[116] Having historically experienced various forms of race, class, and gender discrimination and police violence, urban blacks understood their civil and legal rights, often better than those who denied them of such liberties, and did not hesitate to assert their legal rights or publicly call out oppression and inequality when it occurred. St. Clair's public proclamations about blacks' legal rights was hardly new; her public notices brought continued awareness to an already widely discussed issue within black communities and reinforced the important political work of race reforms agencies already in the forefront of contesting illegal apartment searches.

St. Clair's public campaign against city police received mixed responses from black New Yorkers. In September 1929, Harlem resident Samuel T. Floyd wrote an editorial in the *NYAN* applauding her critical assessment of the police, and sug- gested that "everybody in Harlem should agree" with her.[117] However, Richard M. Lee, a Harlem welfare worker and president of the Good People's Club, vehemently disagreed with St. Clair's scathing criticism of the NYPD. A critic of New York's numbers racket and its criminal underworld, Lee, unlike St. Clair, found the "as- sistance of the police [to be] courteous and willing to help me in any way. In fact, I found the police to be Harlem's best citizens."[118] Lee's accommodating remarks were perhaps fueled by an attempt to demonstrate divergent perspectives about the police within the African American community and to appease white New Yorkers and the NYPD. Conscious of escalating racial tension and violence within urban cities, Lee likely hoped that St. Clair's criticism of law enforcement did not result in retaliation against black Harlemites. In her September 1929 column, St. Clair challenged Lee's position as well as his apparent lack of race consciousness, telling him, "You are asleep. Please wake up, for this is the 20th century."[119]

Although St. Clair was not the typical community spokesperson, some aspects of her reform style were symbolic of African American women's tradition of in- stitution building. Some time during the late 1920s, St. Clair and a small group of black Harlem West Indian and African American women established the French Legal Aid Society (FLAS).[120] The organization was part of the many ethnic "home- land" societies and benevolent associations created by New York black immigrants and African Americans during the first half of the twentieth century. Benevolent, church, and fraternal organizations such as the American West Indians Ladies Aid Society "comprised the first line of urban accommodation for Caribbean im- migrants and Southern migrants in Harlem, dealing with individuals' needs from the cradle to the grave." Offering a sense of cultural consciousness and familiarity, ethnic homeland societies offered members a variety of services including sick and death benefits and literary and etiquette classes.[121] Organizations also offered newcomers advice about securing decent and wholesome employment and housing spaces and about the dangers and trappings of urban life.

Little is known about the FLAS objectives, goals, and community activities. Formed in the late 1920s, newspaper accounts reveal that the unincorporated organization promoted the naturalization of black immigrants and proposed to conduct citizenship classes and prepare black immigrants for the naturalization process.[122] However, it is uncertain the number of FLAS instructors and participants or whether participants petitioned for and secured American citizenship. As a FLAS founder, St. Clair believed that American citizenship was crucial to black immigrants' socioeconomic and political lives, and that naturalization was a step toward American political engagement. If naturalized, she reasoned, black immigrants would have the opportunity to take part in electorate politics, using it to throw their support toward political candidates who were willing to enforce New York State laws of the 1880s and 1910s that prohibited racial discrimination in public spaces and addressed urban inequalities and injustices. Or, as suggested by sociologist and author Ira D. A. Reid, St. Clair—perhaps like other black immigrants—viewed American citizenship as a practical strategy for black immigrants to secure employment and economic and social mobility. While St. Clair encouraged naturalization for New York black immigrants, she recognized their hesitation to claim American citizenship. In one of her columns, St. Clair advised black immigrants not to be reluctant about American citizenship, despite intense racial inequality and public accounts of some Immigration and Naturalization Service (INS) officials' mistreatment of black immigrants going through the naturalization. "Dear friends," she wrote, "I want you all to become full citizens of the country. Please do not think about discrimination. It will be for the best if we all became full citizens of the United States."[123] Notwithstanding racial bigotry, many New York black immigrants, in search of socioeconomic and political opportunities in new geographical urban spaces, pursued American citizenship. In the nation, at least 25.6 percent of black immigrants over the age of twenty-one years old became naturalized and an estimated 10.5 percent completed Declaration of Intent applications by 1930.[124]

New York black immigrants, particularly Caribbean political leaders and reformers, articulated diverse opinions on American citizenship. Socialist leader Hubert Harrison and other naturalized blacks shared St. Clair's views on American citizenship. In response to Jamaican journalist A. M. Wendell Malliet's 1927 *Pittsburgh Courier* editorial, "Why I Cannot Become Americanized," Harrison—who was naturalized in 1922—argued that black immigrants, particularly West Indians, had "a fighting chance in [a democratic America] which is denied 'subjects' in the crown countries." Echoing St. Clair's sentiments on black immigrants' role in the eradication of American racism, Harrison admitted in a 1927 *Pittsburgh Courier* editorial that he "became an American because I was eager to be counted in the fight wherever I happened to be, to bear the burden and heat of the day in helping to make conditions better in this great land for the children who will come after me."[125]

Malliet's settlement experience in the United States inspired his denunciation of American citizenship. Coming to the United States in 1917 with "high hopes," Malliet became disenchanted with the prospect of becoming an American citizen after experiencing race prejudice and observing "the Government['s] indifference to lynching, Jim Crowism, and segregation." Malliet's "Why I Cannot Become Americanized" editorials suggested that "strong" racial exclusion and African Americans' "inferiority complex," caused by American race politics, were impediments to citizenship for black immigrants.[126] American race relations and white supremacy, as well as the tangible support that came along with being a British or French subject, also made some black immigrants think twice about American citizenship. Some black immigrants' conscious decision to both employ and claim racial otherness also kept many away from American naturalization. Possessing a variety of accents and fluency in different European languages expanded the racial freedom of some black immigrants and disrupted white Americans' perspective on black foreigners. In some instances, black immigrants, unlike native-born black New Yorkers, gained entrance into racially segregated spaces, obtained better-paying employment, and, according to Ira De Augustus Reid, hardly suffered from American race prejudice."[127]

Naturalization was a personal quest for St. Clair. Her pursuit of American citizenship did not start when she arrived in the United States in the second decade of the twentieth century but rather in the mid-1930s. Archival records reveal that in 1936 St. Clair, using her married surname Gachette, filed a Declaration of Intent, a process that required applicants to renounce allegiance to any foreign governments and demonstrate five years of residence in the United States. It is unclear if she ever filed a petition for naturalization; her ability to file for naturalization was perhaps complicated by her 1938 prison stint at Westfield State Farm. Once released from jail, it is possible that St. Clair continued with the naturalization process. Available immigration records, however, do not show that St. Clair filed a petition for naturalization. Interestingly, the State of New York did issue St. Clair a social security number in 1942—which indicates that she may have become a legal resident of New York.[128]

Conclusion

By the time Madame Stephanie St. Clair entered Harlem's numbers racket during the early 1920s, the lucrative game was in full swing. Harlemites had already witnessed the racket's growth, popularity, condemnation, and intense public battle among racially diverse numbers kings and queens. But residents of the Black Mecca were not unaccustomed to seeing affluent black female numbers bankers or the multiple ways in which women numbers bankers publicly challenged male dominance and manipulated prevailing gender norms to achieve personal economic fulfillment and high-ranking status with the city's illegal gambling racket. In many respects, St. Clair, as a person of color, woman, and immigrant, was an anomaly; her wealth and prominent status within the city's gambling circles was not representative of black female numbers laborers. While she certainly was not the only female numbers banker in New York, her economic success and influence on Harlem's numbers racket was widely known both in New York City and throughout other urban gambling centers across the nation The contentious St. Clair defied the 1920s and 1930s image of the black female policy entrepreneur, rupturing expectations of what it meant to be black and female. Her public battle against Harlem white racketeers and the NYPD thwarted race and gender constructions and hierarchies placed on women and racial minorities. However, the famed numbers baroness was more than just a publicity-seeking informal entrepreneur who, according to one observer, lived "by her wits all of her life."[129] The outwardly aggressive yet sociable Numbers Queen was a complex woman who constantly reinvented herself, shifting at will from criminal to community advocate. As a Harlem luminary and well-to-do businesswoman, St. Clair was one of the many black voices that took part in ongoing conversations on racial advancement and black liberation strategies, urban inequality, and black community–police relations. A neighborhood advocate within her own right, her race and political consciousness were grounded in the changing socioeconomic and political landscape of early-twentieth-century New York; urban blacks' collective struggle with race, gender, and class inequity; and perhaps by her own personal experiences with racial bigotry. Her commitment to racial betterment and to publicly contesting northern-style racism and gender oppression was displayed in her writings and in her promotion of black self-help organizations. Because St. Clair consciously blurred the line between propriety and criminality, her expression of community advocacy was unique and ushered in an alternative image of female reform. Her community work departed from, yet reinforced, aspects of African American women's traditional organizing patterns. St. Clair's distinct style of community work delineates her multifaceted lifestyle and the diverse ways in which urban African American women contested white supremacy and used urban informal markets to make a statement about the marginalization of African Americans.

Black Women Supernatural Consultants, Numbers Gambling, and Public Outcries against Supernaturalism

> There are scores of individuals dealing in herbs, roots, and the power
> of divining, who infest Harlem and reap a fair livelihood from persons
> willing to put some curse on an errant individual, some wife who desires
> to get her husband back to her loving arms, or some husband, tired
> of restaurant victuals, who desires once more to sample the culinary
> wares of an errant mate.
>
> —Ken Jessamy, "Harlem's Fakers," *NYAN*, August 28, 1937

During the late 1990s, self-proclaimed Jamaican "shaman" "Miss Cleo" appeared in nationwide infomercials offering tarot card readings, one-on-one psychic consultations, and spiritual guidance on matters concerning money, family, and love. Miss Cleo and her promoters, the multi-million-dollar syndicate Access Resource Services and The Psychic Readers Network, offered pay-per-call psychic services and attracted consumers via the Internet, direct mail, and infomercials. Known for donning a headdress, Miss Cleo, in a thick Jamaican accent, encouraged television viewers to "Call Me Now" and for $4.99 per minute they could get answers and solutions to burning life questions. Miss Cleo, whose real name was Youree D'Cleomili Harris, was not Jamaican and many people questioned the legitimacy of her self-proclaimed psychic powers. Published accounts suggest that Harris's Miss Cleo persona perhaps originated from a fictitious character from several stage plays based in Seattle. Prior to becoming The Psychic Readers Network's national spokesperson, the Los Angeles and Seattle resident billed herself as a playwright and actress and performed as Miss Cleo, a West Indian woman, in a self-written play entitled *Supper Club Café*. Harris's stage productions were short-lived and unsuccessful and left hired actors and crew-members without pay. Cast members claimed that Harris was unable to pay them because she was suffering from bone cancer: "She said her medical costs would prevent her from paying people immediately, but she wrote each actor and crew member a letter telling him or her how much money she owed. She said [actors and crew] would get a certain amount of money in certain days until we were all paid." Those that crossed paths with Harris believed that her cancer story was a lie and a way to avoid compensating them for their work; many also insisted that the talented actress employed the Miss Cleo character, the image of an all-knowing West Indian shaman, to continue to do what she did best: defraud and con naïve Americans out of their hard-earned dollars.

Monetarily profiting from her large viewership, Miss Cleo and the Access Resource Services and The Psychic Readers Network merged the religious world with that of 1990s American commercial entertainment, and they played on the public's curiosity with, and dependency on, supernaturalism. The Miss Cleo promoters earned millions of dollars from callers desperately seeking spiritual guidance on personal issues. However, in 1999, Access Resource Services and The Psychic Readers Network were accused of fraud and faced lawsuits in several states; in 2002, the Federal Trade Commission (FTC) charged the Florida-based companies with deceptive advertising, billing, and collection practices. In the end, a court order stipulated that Access Resource Services and The Psychic Readers Network pay the FTC $5 million and forgive an estimated $500 million in outstanding consumer charges.[1] Harris's national television gig ended with the FTC lawsuit. Deemed a spiritual fake and con artist, Harris seemingly disappeared from the public eye after the 1990s legal battle and after much public embarrassment. In a 2008 *Jet* article entitled "Where Is Miss Cleo?," the once popular shaman and television personality resurfaced and intended to set the record straight about her spiritual abilities and to refute claims that she was a religious charlatan that swindled millions of people out of their money. In defense of herself, Harris claimed that prior to her associations with the Access Resource Services and The Psychic Readers Network, she earned a living as a spiritual guide and operated a rather successful private practice. Moreover, in her *Jet* interview, Harris insisted that her intention for appearing on national television was not to dupe television viewers. Instead, she hoped to share her spiritual gifts and wisdom with those who yearned to transform their lives.[2]

Youree D'Cleomili Harris belonged to an established tradition of African American women who claimed to possess supernatural abilities. During the antebellum era, some enslaved and free black women were considered conjurers, root workers, and practitioners of magic, often fusing African rituals, traditions, and worldviews with that of Anglo-American religion.[3] According to scholar

Sharla Fett, "as laborers, mothers, and healers, bondwomen grew herbs, made medicines [and] cared for the sick, and prepared the dead for burial," and they "drew their authority from a collective understanding of health and healing integral to African American culture under slavery."[4] In *My Southern Home or the South and Its People* (1882), black abolitionist William Wells Brown observed that "nearly every large plantation had at least one, who laid claim to be a fortune-teller, and who was granted with more than common respect by his fellow slaves."[5] While residing on a Georgia rice plantation during the 1830s, British actress Frances Kemble observed the powerful influence an enslaved "prophetess" named Sinda had over the slave community. Kemble recalled that when Sinda prophesied that the "world was to come to an end at a certain time, the belief in her assertion took such possession of the people on the estate, that they [the slaves] refused to work; and the rice and cotton fields were threatened with an indefinite fallow."[6] For many enslaved African Americans, the supernatural world was integral to the creation of resistance strategies against the system of slavery and allowed many to "construct a psychological defense against total dependence on submission to their masters."[7] Some bonded men and women reasoned that magic practitioners and their homegrown powders, charms, and spells were crucial to helping them cope with enslavement. They viewed the work of plantation magic practitioners as routes toward curing illnesses, preventing physical abuse and being sold, and providing some with the courage and opportunity needed to run away and defy slave owners.

Like their ancestors of the past, some early-twentieth-century blacks viewed supernatural consultants as intermediaries between the spirit world and God and human beings; they believed that hoodoo and conjure practices and other supernatural rituals and paraphernalia were potentially beneficial to their daily lives. Through supernaturalism, believers hoped to ward off evil spirits; secure employment; earn better wages; pick winning lottery numbers; get revenge on an employer, a spouse, or an enemy; and prevent and navigate race, gender, and class discrimination. Commenting on consumers' attraction to supernatural consultants and their products, writer Claude McKay, who was also fascinated by alternative spiritual practices and rituals, observed that "distraught persons resort to them for solace, to get information on finding jobs, love, friendship and conjugal felicity, lucky playing numbers, charm to ward off evil."[8] Moreover, for many individuals, supernaturalism became a conduit for "individual agency and empowerment, and revealed why suffering occurred and indicated who or what was responsible, thus explaining and locating the disease or misfortune within communally based norms and idioms of the spiritual world."[9]

Seeking immediate solutions to their personal struggles as well as aspiring to control some aspects of their public and private lives, many New Yorkers, often out of a sense of hopelessness and curiosity, turned to black supernatural consultants.

Whether legitimate spiritual and religious advisors, those interested in assisting individuals with their spiritual journeys, or confidence artists, those using the guise of religion and spirituality to locate their next mark, urban black numerologists, hypnotists, fortune-tellers, and clairvoyants were in the business of selling optimism and offering guidance on love and marriage, health and sickness, money, and, according to social historian, Shane White "explanations and solutions to what had gone wrong in the lives of ordinary New Yorkers."[10] Marvel Cooke remarked that, "morbidly curious throngs pass through their portals day after day seeking advice on all sorts of problems—primarily during troublous times."[11] Some New Yorkers' dependency on clairvoyants and their occult products was so intense that many were "like drug addicts accustomed to their special stimulant, the devotees must have their occult medicine."[12] Explaining some supernatural believers' unyielding faith in clairvoyants, one observer reasoned, "people seek advice from seers as a way out, [especially those living in] exploited [and] underprivileged communit[ies]. If they are made more hopeful that better days are just around the corner, what real harm is there in it?"[13]

This chapter examines a group of supernatural consultants, who identified as clairvoyants, crystal ball gazers, tarot card readers, hypnotists, numerologists, and magical healers and practitioners.[14] Supernatural consultants created new occupational identities and entrepreneurial opportunities for themselves, selling magical paraphernalia, distributing policy numbers to gamblers, and establishing home- and church-based religious centers and magic and healing businesses. For those in the business of telling clients their futures or curing their illnesses, the supernatural profession was a potentially profitable enterprise, and one of few underground occupations that enabled black women to forge distinct spaces for themselves. Contrary to white monolithic constructions of black womanhood as characteristic of being lazy, licentious, unintelligent, and outside the scope of true womanhood, female supernatural entrepreneurs defied such stereotypes, situating themselves as powerful and all-knowing; as authorities on the past, present, and future; and as individuals who possessed the ability to control others' destinies. Exploring supernatural advisers' working lives, this chapter identifies black women's attraction to supernatural labor, the interplay between supernaturalism and New York's profitable numbers racket, and the varying ways in which black and white urbanites, including race and religious leaders, cultural writers, and city politicians and medical professionals, responded to supernatural advisers' paid labor and religious and spiritual practices. Despite citywide campaigns and state laws against supernatural work, particularly fortune-telling and prescribing medicine without a license, many female magic practitioners merged religiosity and spiritual imagery with that of underground commercial entertainment. They selectively utilized and borrowed secular symbols and aspects of underground culture, especially the numbers enterprise, to launch, market, and expand their supernatural and religious businesses and appeal to New Yorkers' increasing fixation with games of chance.

Divergent Routes to Supernatural Labor

Drawing inspiration from a wide range of spiritual practices, black supernatural consultants subscribed to and fused a variety of organized and orthodox religious philosophies and worldviews with that of magic. For many magic practitioners, supernaturalism was rooted in traditional religions, including Christianity, Hinduism, and Buddhism, and in indigenous African-based spiritual practices. For instance, Harlem medium and community reformer (and former stage performer) Reverend Josephine Becton, founder and pastor of the Allen-Becton Memorial Temple, believed that her gift of mediumship "drew from the rich symbolism of Christianity as well as from a subterranean core of supernatural ideas."[15] I was called at an early age to give the rest of my life to Christian work, and I felt that I could best serve humanity by preaching the gospel." In regards to supernaturalism, Becton proclaimed that "churches teach the resurrection of Christ and life after death, but we [at Allen-Becton Memorial Temple] prove them through the communication of the spirit [with our] psychic messages."[16] Radio evangelist Rosa Artimus Horne, "the incredible and wealthy religious cult leader," also combined elements of Christian ideology with supernaturalism. Born in Sumter, South Carolina, in 1880, the former seamstress better known as the "Pray for Me Priestess" asserted that her ability to "make the blind see" and heal the "sick and lowly" was due to the "miraculous powers of Jesus Christ" and the "mysterious practices of witchcraft."[17] While the relationship between Christianity and magic, as suggested by Yvonne Chireau, were "in conflict with one another," African American women like Becton and Horne frequently navigated between organized religion and various forms of supernaturalism "with little concern for their purported incompatibility."[18]

But not all black supernatural practitioners embraced Christianity. Mme Fu Futtam's religious beliefs and interpretation of magic was rooted in Buddhism and the spiritual rituals of the "Orient." Known in Harlem as the "Negro-Chinese seer," Mme Fu Futtam, whose real name was Dorothy Matthews, was born in Jamaica around 1906 and migrated to the United States some time in the 1920s.[19] In 1938, Futtam and her husband, Harlem activist and religious leader Bishop Amiru Al-Mu-Minin Sufi Abdul Hamid, established the Universal Holy Temple of Tranquillity, Inc. (UHTT), a "Buddhist temple based on the teachings of all the sages and prophets of the ages. The definite purpose is to surmount untested faith and belief with sound knowledge

Figure 12: Dorothy "Madame Fu Futtam" Matthews, Harlem spiritual medium. Courtesy of Morgan and Marvin Smith Photographic Collection, Schomburg Center for Research in Black Culture, New York Public Library.

similar to that practiced by the yogis of India, Tibet, and Japan."[20] Under the leadership of Hamid and Fu Futtam, the UHTT promoted mediumship, spirit possession and reincarnation, and the teachings and philosophies of Gautama Buddha.[21] Assigned by the *NYAN* to write an editorial on the UHTT, and perhaps a bit intrigued by Futtam and Hamid's seemingly unusual religious persuasion and by the fact that the couple had been involved in a scandalous public love triangle with Hamid's former wife Stephanie St. Clair, journalist Marvel Cooke attended several UHTT ceremonies. Arriving Sunday morning to an assembly hall in a four-story building at 103 Morningside Avenue, the curious reporter observed that the dynamic couple opened religious services to nearly 228 attendees. With "a few miraculous manifestations, Chinese incantations, Oriental incense and uncanny sound effects, veering from the Oriental motif," Hamid loudly began his sermon: "Noble sons and daughters let us begin this service in the name of the Absolute, the Compassionate, the astreal and psychic consciousness. It is a privilege to bring the first message of Buddha."[22] Hamid and Futtam's interest in and affiliation with Asian culture and religious customs was not unusual for many black men and women.

Both Hamid and Futtam were part of a group of blacks that subscribed to and combined aspects of Asian religious, cultural, and political ideologies and symbols with that of African American and Caribbean culture. Analyzing black and Asian cultural and political interactions throughout the twentieth century, scholars Vijay Prashad and Heike Raphael-Hernandez maintain that there was a "mutual influence between members of the African and Asian Diasporas in the Americas." This influence was a byproduct of cultural, religious, and political exchanges and interactions between Asians and blacks around the world.[23] Heavily influenced by Asian cultural and religious practices, some black supernatural professionals even claimed that they were born in the "East" and studied under Buddhist and Hindu spiritual workers.

Black magical workers that adopted Asian and other foreign cultures and identities emerged from a small community of black men and women that assumed different racial ethnicities as a creative response to race discrimination and Jim Crow segregation.[24] Taking on new racially foreign personas and performances, urban blacks hoped to expand personal freedoms, manipulate racial barriers, and gain access to segregated public spaces such as hotels, restaurants, social events and clubs, and other places of business that typically excluded African Americans. The 1925 social experiment of Columbia University student Willis Huggins convincingly delineates how sometimes the doors of racial segregation and acceptance widen for ethnically different blacks. Also, intending to prove to his friend, a white "wealthy lad from Pennsylvania that color prejudice," was prevalent in New York, Huggins, his friend, and their two white female companions—all in on the experiment—attempted to gain entrance into a popular nightclub at a white hotel. When the interracial group arrived at the white establishment, Willis was immediately asked by hotel management to leave. A few days later, Willis and his friends returned to the same club and this time were "warmly received" and even "given a round of introductions" by the hotel staff. The Columbia student was even presented to the "manager, his wife and daughter, each of whom insisted that [he] dine with them." Willis's warm reception was attributed to his striking appearance and new identity, a "Hindu dressed in an elaborate costume and armed with a few words . . . which an Oriental classmate" had taught him.[25]

Historian Irma Watkins-Owens writes that black immigrants speaking different European and Asian languages and wearing nonwestern attire disrupted white perceptions of race and blackness. Some whites did not regard black immigrants like they viewed native-born African Americans. They associated black immigration with European culture and lifestyle. Whites were both intrigued and troubled by the racial otherness and exotic sounding speech and unique appearances of the former. Social scientist Ira De A. Reid, who had conducted extensive research on black immigration to the United States during the early twentieth century, posited that Caribbean blacks significantly benefit from their diverse ethnic backgrounds.

Countering arguments that black immigrants suffered from race discrimination, Reid was of the opinion that black foreigners did not "suffer from American prejudice. On the job he speaks French or Spanish and the white boss lets him by." For many black supernatural workers, assuming the personas of the wise, all-knowing, turban-wearing African, Indian, and Caribbean seer was not only about expanded freedoms or manipulating firmly established racial hierarchies. Race, ethnic, and cultural appropriation was also about playing on cultural stereotypes that directly linked nonwhites to nonwestern spiritual practices and gaining creditability and legitimacy as authentic magic practitioners.[26]

While some urban supernatural female consultants were from the Caribbean or nonwestern geographical spaces, or pretended to be, many were working-class native-born New Yorkers and southern migrants, billing themselves as all-knowing and powerful high priestesses of magic. It is important to note that as New York black women entered the realm of supernatural work they neither dominated nor figured less prominently in the profession. Both male and female supernatural laborers marketed and sold magical charms on street corners and in their homes; established home-based occult enterprises, religious centers, and schools; and authored dream books. However, historian Jamie Wilson, in examining "magico-religious workers" who advertised in the *NYAN* during the 1920s, references some distinctions between black male and female supernatural laborers. In promoting their businesses, Wilson notes that men and women branded themselves in different ways, particularly selecting unique honorifics and titles that denoted gender distinctions. Male supernatural workers often referred to themselves as "Professor" and "Masters of Science." Usage of these particular terms set male supernatural consultants apart from their female counterparts. Usually adopted by individuals who possessed or pretended to have advanced educational training, such titles denoted academic superiority, extensive training in a particular subject, and a knowledge base that surpassed that of ordinary men and women. On the other hand, women supernatural workers typically did not use formal educational titles. Women referred to themselves as "Ms.," "high priestess," "Mrs.," and "Madame"—proper female honorifics that were just as significant as men's usage of "Professor." Black female supernatural workers' titles indicated a level of professionalism, authority, and the ability to adopt gender-specific honorifics that were traditionally reserved for white women. Consciously choosing how they branded themselves and advertised their services was an occupational benefit for supernatural entrepreneurs.

Purported divine calling, the gift of prophecy, and the prospect of securing economic wealth and living a lavish lifestyle attracted black women to supernatural work.[27] In her 1931 article "Hoodoo in America," writer and cultural anthropologist Zora Neale Hurston traveled to New Orleans and other southern communities to immerse herself in Hoodoo (and Voudou). She contended: "one becomes a hoodoo doctor [either] by heredity or by the call. The most influential doctors seem to be born to the cult."[28] Native Louisianan Mme Sally Broy, founder of Chicago's and New York City's Righteous Supreme Temple, claimed that she was "born with a veil over her face" and that she "received a power from God to cure any disease on earth."[29] UHTT high priestess Mme Fu Futtam maintained that her "gift for seeing visions and dreaming dreams was handed down from the ancient mystics."[30] Claiming divine calling was a strategy used by supernatural laborers to legitimatize their abilities and labor and profess that their spiritual rituals, prayers, and occult products were sanctioned and blessed by a higher power. Women asserting that they were born with a "veil over their face" created a hierarchy within the supernatural realm, deeming themselves as legitimate seers and distinguishing themselves from practitioners that entered the profession via apprenticeship.

Divine calling was not the only route to supernatural labor. Those interested in the study of supernaturalism attended occult science and esoteric educational programs and schools. Flourishing in the United States during the turn of the twentieth century, occult and esoteric schools were part of the trend to professionalize and legitimatize individual specialized skills. These places of study offered the public secrets and traditions that were once considered hidden, an access to a body of knowledge and spiritual practices and philosophies that were often privately passed down from "a teacher claiming special access to a higher reality to selected followers with the will and the determination to investigate such matters."[31] Supernaturalism was studied at various occult science and esoteric academic centers throughout the nation, and New York was the location of several popular yet unaccredited institutions. City occult schools, including Mattie Norris's Spiritual Church of Christ Teaching on 121st Street, and white occult author Dr. Lauron William De Laurence's National Free School of Spiritualism, offered students, at varying tuition costs, courses of study on crystal gazing, psychic sciences, invocation, and mental healing. Upon completion from some of these programs, students obtained the following degrees: SM (Spiritual Medium), BD (Bachelor of Divinity), DD (Doctor of Divinity), and DSD (Doctor of Spiritual Divinity).[32] With their specialized degrees, students established religious churches and private spiritual businesses and became instructors at occult schools. These schools and other nontraditional educational programs were perceived by some urbanites as fraudulent enterprises and as vehicles for school founders to swindle money from those genuinely interested in supernaturalism as a field of study.[33] Nevertheless, the establishment of occult schools was reflective of some spiritual advisers' views that supernaturalism was a legitimate profession that required academic training.[34]

Moreover, New York black women took on occupations as occult preachers, numerologists, and fortune-tellers not because of a divine calling or because they possessed an interest in studying supernaturalism. Rather, the possibility of alleviating financial hardship and reaping the economic benefits from establishing a supernatural enterprise fueled women's decision to engage in supernatural work. Exploiting and capitalizing on the African Diaspora's diverse religious and cultural practices, these black women were spiritual charlatans, joining the thousands of urban hustlers and confidence tricksters who consciously preyed on and deceived naive and economically stricken New Yorkers. According to scholar Shane White, confidence men and women "were particularly adept at sensing the fault lines in the society and in an individual's makeup. The stories they told relied on, and played with, the culture of their fellow blacks, and the cruel elegance of their schemes laid bare the fears and foibles of their victims. In their own way, the confidence men and women, and their schemes, were often as creative as the much-studied poetry, short stories, and novels of the Harlem Renaissance."[35] Commenting on the scores of black con artists billing themselves as spiritual gurus, writer Winthrop Lane observed, "a towel turban and a smart manner are enough to transform any Harlem colored man [and woman] into a dispenser of magic to his profit."[36]

Langston Hughes's 1950s musical comedy play and later novel *Tambourines to Glory* offer a useful example on how some less-privileged Harlemites used religion and supernaturalism to swindle their neighbors, and as a seemingly viable strategy to avoid poverty and amass extravagant material goods. Protagonists Laura Wright, a "drenched hustler," and Essie Bell Johnson, a single, unemployed mother, billed themselves as the Reed Sisters and established The Reed Sisters Tambourine Temple in Harlem. The two women intended to exploit Harlem's so-called "outcasts." "The ones that drink without getting sick. Gamble away their rent. Cheat the Welfare Department. Lay with each other without getting disgusted—no matter how many unwanted kids they produce. Use the needle, support the dope trade. Them's the ones we'll set out to convert." Recognizing the profitability of their scheme, Laura told a reluctant Essie, we'll make money, and [I can] buy a fur coat and Cadillac." While Laura longed for wealth and luxury items, Essie envisioned financial stability for herself and the chance to relocate her daughter from the South to New York. "Out hustlin in God's name" five nights a week, The Reed Sisters' reputations as fiery preachers paid off as the duo earned $200 a night.[37]

Attraction to supernatural labor and entrepreneurship also transcended class hierarchies and educational backgrounds. Interestingly, some middle-class and formally educated black women created labor identities as fortune-tellers, psy-chics, or numerologists and subscribed to unconventional religious doctrines and spiritual practices that were at odds with black elites' general assumptions about magic and nontraditional religious and spiritual practices. Middle-class blacks criticized supernaturalism, viewing it as a manifestation of black southern culture and African primitivism. They associated alternative expressions of religion with that of con artists, religious cultists, and poor, uneducated, and superstitious Afri-can Americans "whose better judgment has been deadened by worry or sorrow."[38] Despite their peers' critique of unconventional religious and spiritual beliefs, some formally educated women were drawn to supernaturalism and supernatural labor, viewing both as opportunities to personal religious fulfillment and helping others with their spiritual journeys and as ways toward augmenting their incomes. For in-stance, Chicago and New York City club reformer Adena C. E. Minott was among a few middle-class women who publicly acknowledged her ability to read individual characters and personalities. Known as the "Doctor of Metaphysics," Minott was not the typical supernatural consultant. The formally educated social activist did not profess to know the future nor did she read tea leaves or interpret tarot cards. Moreover, Minott, unlike many supernatural consultants, did not participate or encourage any of her clients to take part in New York's numbers racket. On the contrary, Minott was a well-known and respected author, antilynching crusader, and according to the *Chicago Defender,* a "race woman of learning and culture."[39] In 1908, Samuel Watson, writer for the *Colored American Magazine*, praised Minott's educational accomplishments, citing that "every member of the colored race must feel proud of Prof. Minott's achievement, and in appreciation of [such a] brilliant career."[40]

Born in Jamaica some time in the 1870s to working-class parents, Minott emi-grated from Jamaica to New York around the 1890s, joining the first crop of Jamai-can immigrants entering the United States between 1890 and 1920. Minott was educated at the McDonnall College of Phrenology and Psychology in Washington, D.C., where she received a Bachelor of Phrenology and Mistress of Science degree, and at the Fowler and Wells American Institute of Anthropology in New York.[41] Founded by German physician and brain anatomist Franz Gail some time during the nineteenth century, phrenology was the study of the brain and the science of character reading, and involved "assessing [individual] traits and dispositions by measuring the size and location of bumps on the skull."[42] This pseudoscientific field of study, along with Darwinism, reinforced racist ideology that imagined blacks as physically and intellectually inferior and compared them to animals. But the clearly racist theories embedded within phrenology hardly deterred Minott from pursuing the discipline as a field of study. She, perhaps in a similar vein to other nineteenth-century black abolitionists, intellectuals, and medical professionals like James McCune Smith, intended to expose "the scientific fallacy of phrenology . . . and offered scathing criticisms of . . . imputing character and intelligence from physiology."[43] Possessing the "desire to study Phrenology and disseminate it among her people," Minott established the Clio School of Mental Science and Character Analysis in New York City and Chicago in the second decade of the twentieth century.[44] Both schools offered students courses on "character analysis and vocational guidance, phrenology, graphology, and psychology, and private character and analysis or readings."[45] While not a traditional academic institution offering mainstream fields of study, Minott and her Clio School of Mental Science and Character Analysis were part of an extensive and impressive network of northern and southern black female school founders, including club reformers Lucy Laney, Mary McLeod Bethune, and Nannie Helen Burroughs, who established institutions of higher education for African Americans during the Progressive era.[46]

Throughout 1920s New York, Adena Minott became a reputable community activist, holding leadership positions in Victoria Earle Matthew's White Rose and Industrial Association, the National Association of Colored Women (NACW), and the Suppression of Lynching division of the Northeastern Federation of Women's Clubs. Contrary to the negative public reputations of many supernatural consultants, Minott garnered the admiration of prominent race leaders and businessmen, including New York realtor Philip A. Payton, *NYAN* publisher Edward A. Warren, and NACW members Margaret Murray Washington and Elizabeth Lindsay Davis. Middle-class blacks financially supported her Chicago and New York schools and visited on occasion, and according to published accounts Minott was even the spiritual adviser to several influential black New Yorkers. No doubt Minott's popularity within black elite circles was because of her educational background, her ability to align herself with the urban black aristocracy, and, more importantly, her commitment to racial uplift and community advancement. While Minott belonged to New York's small yet important circle of established race men and women, she, like many supernatural practitioners, was not immune from being identified as a con artist or from police arrest.[47]

In 1941, the fifty-eight-year-old phrenologist was arrested for and convicted of first-degree grand larceny. According to the *NYAN,* Minott, one of Harlem's most successful spiritual advisors, was found guilty of "flimflamming" Manhattan white caterer Lucy Terrell out of $1,220. During Minott's two-day trial, Terrell testified that she, having faith in Minott's abilities, willingly gave Minott money she received from an auto accident. Minott insisted that the well-known cook safeguard her money. "Don't let it get away. Put it here in my safe, a vibrational projector-scope safe, and let it make more money for you. All metaphysicians use it. We keep our money in it and the magnetic attraction involved causes the safe's contents to increase several times after nine days. It will make your money double in nine days, providing you don't tell anyone. If you tell, that makes it negative and the safe won't open. You must believe in me and don't tell, if you want the money to grow." The famed spiritual adviser failed to increase Terrell's money after nearly two weeks. While Minott paid Terrell $750 back in five installments, she refused to pay the balance of $450 and was subsequently apprehended by local police. Because of Minott's age, noncriminal background, and community ties to prominent black New Yorkers, she avoided the expected ten-year prison sentence; instead, she received a suspended sentence and was ordered to make full restitution to Terrell.[48]

Crystal Balls, Tea Leaves, and Dream Books

Female supernatural entrepreneurs converted their small tenement apartments and abandoned motion picture houses, lodge halls, and stores into modest temples and chapels, plastering building walls with announcements that were alluring to curious city walkers.[49] Madame Patsy Taylor established her home-based spiritual enterprise in the "basement assembly room of her tenement apartment spiritual haven [where both] white and colored gathered for weekly test meetings, séances [and to] gain knowledge through spirit communication."[50] Clients attested to Madame Taylor's miraculous powers, claiming she "could do almost anything from make you lucky in love, money, healing and restoration to health." Renowned medium Mattie Norris, who "proves without a doubt 'Life Beyond the Graves'," held spiritual and test medium meetings in her home on Sunday, Tuesday, and Thursday, claiming on those "particular days she was able to communicate, lift, and control 'life beyond the grave.'"[51] Writer Claude McKay was intrigued by apartment séances; his *Harlem: Negro Metropolis* (1940) offers a vivid depiction of one of his Harlem séance visits. The Harlem author observed that the rundown apartment walls were "light blue [and] covered with mottos and rubrics—'Trust and Hope,' 'Love and Live,' 'Life is Mystery,'—and embellished with stars, crosses, crescents and hearts cut out of colored paper." A priestess, "a brown woman of commanding height and bulk ... robed in black and white, with voluminous sleeves and a long white train," led the spiritual meeting of supernatural disciples. Communicating with the spirits and performing several healings, the priestess was praised and given $5 by several séance attendees. Implying that the priestess was an opportunist, McKay noted that she, motivated by her devotees' praises, encouraged them to donate more money to the "good spirits. I feel that my inspiration is boundless tonight and those who desire more personal and secret revelation may wait and see me after the meeting. The fee is only one dollar for a private revelation."[52]

Fortune-tellers, palmists, tarot readers, and other supernatural professionals charged clients various prices and accepted monetary donations and freewill offerings for their services and spiritual products. Typically, for private readings, supernatural practitioners charged customers anywhere between $1 and $50. To communicate with the dead, Dorothy "Mme Fu Futtam" Matthews requested patrons pay between $10 and $50. If clients could not afford private consultation or were embarrassed to be seen consulting with a supernatural consultant, they could receive by telegram spiritual messages and affirmations and lucky charms for $10 a month.[53] Supernatural workers, especially those operating scams, informed customers that monetary donations were part of the tradition of thanking and honoring the ancestors and deities for offering valuable life lessons. Customers hoping to receive good fortunes were persuaded to pay supernatural workers additional money for their services.

Monetary sales from occult products sustained women and their businesses. Much of their success in selling magical paraphernalia depended on their ability to be effective salespersons. Magic practitioners' shelves were stocked with homemade concoctions, including incenses, candles, body crystals, dried leaves, figs, flowers, and jars of lotions, powders, oils, and sprays with "colorful and evocative labels offering Strong Love, Domination, Peaceful Home, Money Jackpot, Get Away Evil, Court Case, High John the Conqueror, and Death unto My Enemy."[54] Opening some time in the 1930s, crystal ball gazer Mme Fu Futtam's well-known Harlem candle shop offered lucky charms, candles, lodestones, her widely popular dream and numbers books, and "oriental oils" to regular and new clients.[55] According to their female producers, handmade magical paraphernalia were blessed by a higher power and, if purchased and used properly, ensured prosperity and happiness. For instance, Rev. Mme V. D. S. Armistead, pastor and founder of the 1st Holy Star Psychic Science Church Inc, located in her second-floor apartment on 111th Street, guaranteed her congregation that her prosperity oil, which "sold from ten cents to a dollar a bottle," would improve their socioeconomic circumstances. Armistead's certainty about the power of her product derived from either a lie she concocted to boost product sales or from actually believing that her homemade product was effective in changing consumers' socioeconomic conditions. "I want to tell you 'bout [my] Prosperity Oil. It was because of this oil, that [my] lot in life improved." Use of the oil allegedly resulted in her renting a luxury apartment: "God is no respecter of persons and if He will do this for me, He will do it for you if you only use the oil religiously."[56] Mme Armistead guaranteed parishioners that her prosperity oil was effective if they followed a precise set of instructions. "Anoint the hair three times a day, by applying with the palm of the right hand. And twice a day, that is morning before dressing, anoint the body at night. While doing so, say the Lord's Prayer and the 23rd Psalm and ask in the name of Jesus Christ for what one desires. Use three drops in the bath and seven drops in the water to wash up around where you want prosperity."[57]

Supernatural believers, especially the working poor, trusted that magic para-phernalia would "keep one's wife at home, make women fertile and men sexu-ally appealing," protect them from white oppression and brutality, and ensure newfound happiness and economic well-being.[58] Spiritual products, according to one scholar, were "meaningless when they are removed from the context of belief. The person who has faith may be endowed with self-confidence that can produce successful results."[59] At the same time, magic paraphernalia that failed to produce desired or intended results was "rationalized by saying that it was used improperly, that an enemy was using something stronger, that the user's faith was insufficient, or that the desired outcome was against God's will."[60] In other words, a magical product or supernatural worker's inability to produce guaran-teed outcomes had little to do with the magical paraphernalia or the spiritual adviser. Supernatural workers blamed external forces and circumstances that were beyond their control for preventing communication with the spirit world and for ineffective products—thus diminishing their culpability. Attending a Manhattan apartment séance for a story he was writing for the *NYAN*, journal-ist Ken Jessamy's insufficient faith was blamed for the female host's inability to connect with the spirit world. "After one look at my unbelieving face, the lady conducting the ceremony uttered in a ghostly voice that the spirits will not co-operate. 'There is an unbeliever in the house. Will the gentleman in the back of the room please leave so that the spirits can rise.'"[61] After much protest by the spiritual leader, annoyed séance attendees escorted Jessamy out of the apart-ment—in hopes that the spirits presented themselves. Extant documentation does not reveal if the spirits showed up after Jessamy's departure.

Strongly believing in spiritual products' potency, some supernatural custom-ers squandered their meager incomes purchasing oils, incenses, candles, pow-ders, and amulets. Writing a feature story on Rev. Mme Armistead's Holy Star Spiritual Church in 1939, Marvel Cooke, after attending one of Armistead's ser-vices, observed that her "prosperity oil went like hot cakes. One young woman, sitting just in front of me who looked as though she might do well with a good meal under her belt, purchased a dollar vial."[62] Questioning the authenticity of Mme. Armistead's prosperity oil, Cooke purchased the popular selling oil, a "spiritual balm to awaken slumbering souls."[63] Unsurprising to Cooke, Mme. Armistead's prosperity oil "turned out to be a cheap penetrating perfume augmented by a few drops of oil. The sickening sweet odor was enough to knock you right out of your seat."[64]

While supernatural believers purchased magical products directly from supernatural workers, they also procured such items at neighborhood pharmacies and drugstores and from mail-order distribution companies including the Morton G. Neumann's King Novelty Company of Chicago and the Keystone Laboratories of Memphis, Tennessee. The sale and distribution of occult products by nonmagical believers and corporations were part of the "trend toward the commodification of traditional charms which began around the turn of the twentieth century and accelerated in the 1920s."[65] Often competing with independent clairvoyants, nonmagical merchants sold manufactured supernatural paraphernalia or "curios" such as lodestones, bath oils and crystals, animal bones, perfumes, candles, incenses, and repelling, love, and protective charms. Supernatural professionals maintained varying opinions on nonspiritual occult sellers and the commodification of supernatural products. Many magic practitioners asserted that nonmagical merchants infringed upon their businesses and that factory-produced supernatural merchandises were ineffective, less powerful than homemade concoctions, and not blessed by a divine power. Interestingly, some black supernatural laborers bought directly from the companies, claiming that manufactured products saved them time and labor. To maintain their legitimacy, supernatural workers passed off store-bought items as their own handmade creations.

Recognizing supernatural believers' desire for authentic occult products, nonmagical mail-order companies and white supernatural workers and publishers employed stereotypical images of Native Americans, Indians, Africans, and African Americans, especially black women, to market their products.[66] Nonwhite groups and images were ideal to promote nonmagical merchants' products because they were associated with primitive religions, supernaturalism and superstition, and nonwestern spiritual rituals and practices. Much like the R. T. Davis Milling Company's and the Cream of Wheat Corporation's use of the faithful black servant to advertise hot cereal and fluffy pancakes, white supernatural workers and mail order companies employed images of the all-knowing African American voodoo and root doctors to sell dream and numerology books, healing and harming potions, and incense boxes.[67]

New York City publisher Henry J. Wehman's *Aunt Sally's Policy Players Dream Book* (1889) appropriated the image of an elderly African American woman wearing a headscarf, calico blouse, and apron to sell his dream book.[68] *Aunt Sally* was marketed as a wise agricultural and domestic servant who interpreted dreams and offered lucky numbers to policy players. Throughout the 1930s and 1940s, Morton G. Neumann's King Novelty Company and several other white occult and cosmetic suppliers also employed the Aunt Sally image for their super-natural merchandise and even to promote a line of hair products.[69] The Aunt Sally image, like the "Mammy" trademark was "predicated upon a fascinating interweaving of commerce, memory, and racial nostalgia, while capitalizing on southern black primitive culture and on white appeal and desire of 'brown' hand service."[70] Interestingly, some black supernatural laborers drew on stereotypical black imagery to promote their products, playing on societal assumptions that linked persons of African descent with black magic. The front cover of Dorothy Matthews's 1945 dream book, *Madam Fu Futtam's Lucky Numbers Dream Book*, fea-tured a brown-skinned, overweight, and asexual "Mammy" like image, wear-ing a red handkerchief around her neck and a jeweled headdress. The Jamaican spiritual adviser's physical features were far from the image on her book cover. Harlemites described Matthews as a light-skinned "attractive voluptuous Chi-nese girl" with "hips like a winding road."[71]

Selling Lucky Numbers

The 1920s and 1930s allure and dependency on games of chance, notably New York's contested yet universally played numbers racket, created and bolstered businesses for self-proclaimed spiritual mediums, fortune-tellers, and "professors and doctors" of mystic science. Games of chance afforded supernatural consul-tants new streams of revenue; the opportunity to devise different branding and marketing strategies for their businesses; and in many incidents the chance to take advantage of individuals who were emotionally and economically invested in the city's gambling racket. For many numbers games players, supernatural advisers were critical to helping them select winning numbers, especially when they un-successfully relied upon their own imagination for numbers.[72] Clairvoyants sold and distributed lucky numbers to policy players in different public and private settings: during private consultations in one's place of business, in church, and on street corners. Charging anywhere from ten cents to a quarter for a set of numbers, street "soothsayer[s] take you aside [and] coyly pushes a slip of paper in your hand containing the lucky number and swears you to absolute secrecy."[73] For a private meeting with a supernatural advisor, gamblers paid between $1 and $3 a session, and if the spiritual consultant had a good reputation for predicting winning num-bers, players were perfectly willing to pay top dollar for their services.[74] Princess Claudia's Harlem apartment living room turned occult waiting room was usually filled with those seeking lucky numbers and solutions to life problems. Described as "one of Harlem's most popular card readers," the "small, brown skin woman in her thirties with a nervous energetic air" charged clients $1 for advice and a "card reading."[75] Princess Claudia's clients, mostly working-class, "had so much faith in her that they returned week after week for advice."[76]

Numbers players relied upon supernatural workers' dream books for the selection of winning numbers, believing that "dream books were key to unlocking the city of [winning] numbers."[77] Writer William Forbes observed that many "numbers players wouldn't think of making a play without consulting their treasured dream books."[78] Investigating Harlemites' intrigue with supernaturalism, one New York journalist recalled that, "dream books are as universally read in Harlem as the Bible. At least one-fourth of the population consults them as an aid to hitting the numbers."[79] Dream books were a byproduct of the public's fascination with gambling and the commercialization of supernaturalism. Dating back to the colonial era, American dream books offered solutions to the unknown and served as guides to interpreting dreams and superstitions, and most importantly enabled a dreamer to "turn sleep into capital."[80] Recognizing the economic value of dreams, *NYAN* columnist and well-known Harlem beauty parlor owner Madame Sarah Spencer Washington advised her readers to "keep a pencil and pad at their beside and jot down" their dreams. A committed numbers player like fifty-year-old Mamie Sprinkle "never fail[ed] to dream up a breeze and always sees numbers floating around in the atmosphere."[81] Dream books paired corresponding aspects of life, people's names, natural and man-made symbols, and every imaginable circumstance that might occur in a dream with a particular number or set of numbers. For instance, Mme. Fu Futtam's 1937 dream book *Madam Fu Futtam's Magical-Spiritual Dream Book* suggested that dreaming of a casket "denotes marriage" and the dreamer should play 427. To dream of oranges meant "comfort and relief" and the corresponding number was 213. Dreaming of money meant "that [the dreamer] will be tempted to commit an unbecoming act, and the dreamer's lucky numbers were 565."[82]

Selling dream books became a profitable way for supernatural consultants to earn a living without breaching state gambling laws. Some of New York's most popular clairvoyants and "professors" of mystic science," including Carl Z. "Rajah Rabo" Talbot, Herbert Gladstone "Professor Uriah Konje" Parris, and Mme Fu Futtam, authored dream books.[83] Dorothy "Mme Fu Futtam" Matthews's commonly read dream books including *Madam Fu Futtam's Magical-Spiritual Dream Book* (1937) and *Madam Fu Futtam's Lucky Numbers Dream Book* (1945) sold for thirty-five cents each at local newsstands, at stationery stores, and at her Harlem candle shop.[84] Competing with other popular dream guides, Fu Futtam claimed that her books offered "the newest, most thoroughly practical and authoritative collection of dream and numbers books. Through faith and science we can develop sufficient force to control all that surrounds us, be it poverty, loneliness, business, or love."[85]

Still available in print, *Madam Fu Futtam's Magical-Spiritual Dream Book* is a 112-page publication that not only interprets dreams by subject but also offers readers advice on life issues. The fact that Fu Futtam's work is still in print is telling, revealing the popularity and relevancy of the 1940s book over time and space and its usefulness in helping others tackle and understand personal issues. The section entitled "Things Worth Knowing" includes "valuable" lessons on "How to obtain a lover through dreams," "How to get financial help through the dream process," and "How to be rid of unharmonious conditions and individuals." If one desired to be rid of the latter, Mme Futtam suggests the following ritual: "Put on your shoes, walk a long distance til your feet perspire, then return home in the doorway of your house and throw your shoes out the wide open window and say these words: So my pledge was sealed, so my covenant is broken." To ensure a favorable and effective outcome, Mme Futtam advised customers to precisely repeat the chant while burning her "special candles" and "Egyptian Sweet Air Incense."[86]

Finally, individuals searching for lucky numbers often turned to some of New York's houses of worship, particularly black storefront churches. In the mid-twenties, African American storefront churches "comprised thirty percent of the churches in New York City, and by 1930, seventy-five Harlem churches were considered storefronts."[87] Often housed in apartment living rooms, tenement basements, and abandoned theaters and picture houses, storefront churches—often identified as sanctified and spiritualist churches—were known for their eccentric and unorthodox styles of preaching and religious rituals and ceremonies, including spirit possession, dancing, and speaking in tongues. Sanctified churches had their roots in southern churches and were associated with Holiness and Pentecostal denominations.[88] A byproduct of the black migration to northern urban communities in New York, Detroit, and Chicago, spiritualist churches combined elements of "Catholicism, Voodoo and Hoodoo, and black Protestantism and Islam as well as the messianic and nationalist movements of the 1920s and 1930s."[89]

Alternative places of worship breached black elite ideas of religious respectability and decorum and symbolized what Zora Neale Hurston called a "protest against the high-brow tendency in Negro Protestant congregations."[90] Scholar Lawrence Levine contends that "churches within the black community sought respectability by turning their backs on the past, banning the shout, discouraging enthusiastic religion, and adopting more sedate hymns and refined, concerted versions of the spirituals, [storefront churches, particularly] Holiness churches constituted a revitalization of movement with their emphasis upon healing, gifts of prophecy, speaking in tongues, spirit possession, and religious dance."[91] Traditional Christian ministers and middle-class churchgoers disapproved of storefronts' unorthodox religious expressions of worship, censuring their incorporation of secular music, parishioners' lack of self-restraint during religious ceremonies, and association with the urban numbers racket.

Many storefront preachers condoned and encouraged their congregations to take part in the city's lucrative numbers racket. Compelled by their parishioners' attraction to gambling and the desire to retain and attract church members, some religious leaders abandoned high morals for economic necessity and tolerated churchgoers' numbers playing. Understanding the complexities of urban poverty and even relating to church members' dire economic circumstances, preachers reasoned that gambling offered church members a sense of hope and allowed many to "bring home the bacon" and, more importantly, to pay their church tithes. One preacher noted: "you can't blame the people for trying to better their condition to the best of their knowledge. To give numbers is no sin because the people have to live and to try to win a little money."[92] Preachers took comfort in knowing that they were nurturing both the spiritual and economic well-being of their congregations. One churchgoing black janitress noted that she appreciated receiving both spiritual advice and lucky numbers from her pastor: "I couldn't possibily live on the pay I get as a janitress, and whatever I win on the numbers helps me to get along." Paying her spiritual adviser "50 cents as a fee on each visit," she noted that "the advice I get from the Spiritualist certainly is good and I certainly do believe in them."[93]

Recognizing the numbers racket's profound emotional and economic hold on their parishioners, some religious leaders used their pulpits to operate gambling enterprises and to satisfy their own gambling habits. They did not consider gambling a sin nor did they object to using religious space and spiritual imagery for commercial purposes or economic profit. Commenting on the correlation between the growing numbers of Harlem storefront churches and the policy racket, Claude McKay recalled that city's "occult chapels have multiplied their following by interpreting dreams by numbers and evoking messages from the dead with numbers attached to the messages."[94] Langston Hughes' *Tambourines to Glory* character Laura Wright established her storefront church to promote her "holy numbers racket" and to "inveigle thousands of dollars yearly from the pockets of the unwary in all kinds of ways."[95] Wright's conniving boyfriend insisted that she "give out some holy hymns from the pulpit, or Bible texts with three numbers, and let the folks write the numbers down. From then on, your church will be packed."[96] Pastors unapologetically referenced Bible scriptures and hymns throughout their sermons, tipping off church members to play a particular set of numbers. Rev. Mme Armistead informed Marvel Cooke that her divine numbers were "Psalms nos. 1 and 57." Cooke later wrote in the *NYAN*: "neither 157 nor any combination of that number" ever came out.[97]

Numbers gambling became so integrated in urban black religious spaces that law officials treated them like any other gambling establishments. On the word of paid police informants or concerned neighbors, NYPD officials raided home-based churches and had no problems interrupting church services to apprehend alleged numbers bankers and players. Gustov G. Carlson's 1940 study on Detroit's numbers racket revealed that "it is not uncommon for a congregation to be interrupted in the midst of 'Onward, Christian Soldiers' or 'Nearer My God to Thee' by some burly police sergeant. [The] modern world has witnessed few things more paradoxical than a pastor and his congregation being loaded into a patrol wagon and whisked away to the police station."[98] Similarly, some New York churches became the arresting site of many preachers, evangelists, and congregation members. One Harlem middle-aged married laundress and home-based pastor openly sold policy numbers to her predominately female congregation during the mid-1920s. The numbers-collecting minister's illegal entrepreneurial activity came to local police's attention after a neighbor complained about the heavy foot traffic in and out of her apartment. Possessing over three hundred policy slips, she was arrested by law enforcement officers in front of her unsurprised parishioners.[99]

Conversely, many storefront ministers were troubled by their fellow preachers' tolerant attitudes toward games of chance and the inappropriate use of church space and religious culture for the promotion of illegal gambling and other immoral amusements. Furthermore, many resented the fact that their church congregations were becoming an interesting blend of regular churchgoing folks and individuals who attended church service only in hopes of receiving lucky numbers. Popular Harlem evangelist and husband of Reverend Josephine Becton, George Wilson Becton was an outspoken critic against the city's numbers racket. Known for his ecstatic style of preaching, Becton, also known as the "Billy Sunday of the Race" and the "Dancing Preacher," used his fiery religious revivals to expose the evils of gambling to his followers. Throughout the 1930s, Becton informed his congregation that numbers playing was a lucrative scam that benefited only the ones who financed the game. "You can't win. The whole thing is a racket. It's fixed so that only about one out of every 100 who plays hits. I will give you a number, Say it in your prayers to God. It is 1–2–3. One for God, two for the Son, and three for the Holy Ghost."[100] Opposition to numbers playing revealed Becton's and other church leaders' endorsements of controlled consumerism and uplift rhetoric that encouraged urban blacks to be frugal and mindful consumers. Additionally, controlled consumerism as expressed in some preachers' religious sermons illuminated their anxieties about competing for and losing their parishioners' souls and pocketbooks to city vice.

Opposition to Supernatural Labor
and Alternative Healing Practices

Historically, supernatural work was considered a significant occupation in many nonwestern societies, and spirit mediums and religious guides played an integral role in the everyday lives of ordinary people. Scholar David Lan's examination of Zimbabwe's 1980 independence movement suggests that liberation activists and guerilla soldiers employed supernatural advisors' services in their fight against the British colonial powers. Spirit mediums and religious leaders resided and traveled with Zimbabwean soldiers, counseled political and military leaders, and imposed strict physical and sexual prohibition on combatants. Guerillas trusted that spiritual advisers' words of wisdom and knowledge and stern restrictions would ensure military success and their physical safety.[101] Similarly, in various parts of Cambodia and southern Ghana, spirit guides were considered "superior to humans" and possessed a divine calling to solve everyday problems.[102] Nonwestern societies and individuals from varying socioeconomic and political backgrounds revered supernaturalism. Societal belief in spirit mediums was not primarily motivated by economic calamity or by a desire to understand and control personal destinies. Rather, faith in supernatural counselors emerged from a broad set of cultural and historical philosophies that were firmly rooted in indigenous religions and spiritual practices.

Contrary to the perceptions of spiritual workers in other societies, African American supernatural advisors, whether legitimate seers or con artists, were not considered important vessels to resolving personal problems or societal ills. Nor did many African American clairvoyants garner respect from many black middle- and working-class intellectuals, activists, and religious leaders. Viewed as charlatans and swindlers, black New Yorkers such as social scientist Ira De. A. Reid reasoned that supernatural advisers were "engaged in the business for easy personal gain, and are out and out frauds. Half of the time the messages were wrong, most of the time they were so general they could be applied to anyone, and the rest of the time they were so jumbled nobody could understand them."[103] Marvel Cooke, who had extensively investigated and written on Harlem magic practitioners throughout the 1930s, was also skeptical of supernatural consultants, and publicly questioned their self-professed abilities. "There are an estimated 200 spiritualists in Harlem, most of them hiding behind the guise of religion. Most of these mediums, regardless of the form [of] their readings are clever psychologists. They are adept at reading character from tell-tale marks every person carries with him and they formulate their advice accordingly."[104]

Bourgeois leaders' opposition to supernaturalism and supernatural labor was informed by the belief that alternative and eccentric spiritual and religious practices were a manifestation of slave superstitions and working-poor blacks' lack of educational training, common sense, and respectability. Associating magic with less-privileged blacks, Harlem pastor Adam Clayton Powell Jr. maintained that individuals who wasted money on clairvoyants and subscribed to the religious tenets of storefront leaders like George "Father Divine" Baker "were on the fringes of life, hanging between sanity and insanity and were truly a lost generation."[105] Supernatural laborers' religious and spiritual practices were even negatively portrayed in 1930s radio broadcasts and film newsreels. The Columbia Broadcasting System's (CBS) 1937 "The March of Time: Harlem's Black Magic," a twenty-minute newsreel, highlighted the increasing popularity of the "Black Mecca's" fortune-tellers, psychics, and occult leaders.[106] Movie footage and narration suggests that African and African American alternative and nonwestern spiritual beliefs, namely that of voodoo, was primitive and animalistic, and that some of the city's popular supernatural consultants such as Madame Fu Futtam were confidence men and women that "swept into the Negro communities, set up shop, and began to flourish in a big way."[107] Interestingly, while many black leaders criticized supernaturalism and its appeal to some black New Yorkers, many, including members of the New York chapter of the NAACP, adamantly objected to "The March of Time's" generalization of black spiritual practices and the assertion that all blacks, irrespective of class and educational backgrounds, were wedded to the same religious outlooks. Critics of the 1937 footage posited that "the impression is conveyed that all Harlem is merely a voodoo heaven, that there are no sane, normal, healthy citizens who work hard for a living and despise superstition."[108]

Some storefront church leaders, those not interested in employing or merging religiosity and spiritual imagery with that of underground commercial entertainment for financial gain, voiced concerns about money-oriented supernatural consultants and opportunists pretending to be spiritual advisers. Reverends George and Josephine Becton, as well as others who fused magic and witchcraft with that of organized religion, criticized spiritual leaders that financially profited from their purported gifts from God. They vehemently resented individuals who employed the banner of religion to pose as divine mediums and healers.[109] Throughout the 1930s, the Christ Institutional Incorporation (CII), an interdenominational church based in New York, intended to spread the doctrine of true spiritualism and stop "spiritualism from becoming a racket in the hands of unscrupulous persons." The CII intended to distinguish the "racketeering types of spiritualism from the religious type." CII members asserted that spiritual mediums who "healed for money [were] fakers, while those who heal[ed] by faith, by laying on of hands, and by prayer, without commercializing their gift, are true spiritualists." In October 1935, the CII leaders developed a three-point program, focusing on strategies to prevent "spiritualist racketeers from preying upon the people." The CII's plan "against charlatans and fakers" included educating the public with the true facts concerning racketeer spiritualists, and sending missionaries to every section of the country to spread the doctrine of true spiritualism. CII members "hoped that a constructive work may be accomplished to stop the spiritual racket now sweeping the country by charlatans cloaking under the guise of spiritualism."[110]

While scathing public critiques and cynicism shamed magic practitioners, New York City and state lawmakers criminalized the labor and religious practices of supernatural advisers. Scholar Katrina Hazzard-Donald writes that the establishment of regulatory legislation, including the 1906 Federal Food and Drugs Act and the 1938 Food, Drug, and Cosmetic Act, "modified the public atmosphere in which folk medicine would be regarded and practiced. These two acts addressed issues of truthful labeling and allowed government officials to assert some degree of control and regulation over products and substances that might threaten public safety."[111] State and city ordinances further complicated self-described seers' work. Dating back to the eighteenth and nineteenth centuries, nationwide campaigns against clairvoyants, crystal gazers, fortune-tellers, and other supernatural consultants culminated in the enactment and enforcement of legislation that either restricted or prohibited fortune-telling. For instance, the Pennsylvania General Assembly introduced legislation against fortune-telling in 1861. In 1915, Connecticut lawmakers passed statutes that stipulated that "no person shall by any other means tell fortunes or to reveal the future. No person shall obtain money or property from another in [the] name of palmistry, card reading, astrology, seership, or crafty science or fortune-telling of any kind." By the mid-1920s, at least nineteen American cities required fortune-tellers and clairvoyants to be licensed and pay a special tax. Some municipalities prohibited fortune-telling altogether, while other cities neither forbid nor regulated fortune-telling. Throughout the turn of the twentieth century, New York officials enacted and revised statutes that classified clairvoyants as vagrants and disorderly individuals and made fortune-telling a misdemeanor.[112]

Local newspapers, as part of citywide initiatives to inform the public about money-hungry opportunists and scam artists, routinely reported on supernatural workers' arrests and on undercover police operations that targeted those claiming to possess the gift of prophecy. Facing public embarrassment, jail time, and monetary fines, individuals arrested for fortune-telling were also legally charged with an assortment of other criminal offenses, including petty and grand larceny and possession of policy slips. In 1928, Professor Francis Kingharman, "an ordained minister [and] old master of spiritualism, mentalism, occultism, and psychology," along with "spiritualists" Caswell Hayes and Margaret Coleman, were arrested for fortune-telling by undercover police officer Nettie Sweatman.[113] Kingharman and his co-conspirators charged Sweatman a total of $6 for their services. Hayes charged $2.50 for a reading from a deck of cards and insisted that if she "brings

$25 [next time] I'll fix it so your man won't go out unless you say so." Kingharman requested $2, after informing Sweatman that she was seriously ill: "You look like you might have a tumor or some trouble with your stomach." Female priestess Margaret Coleman warned the officer of her friends, saying that "a tall, brown-skinned woman will meet you on a corner and try to cut you and the man you love will leave you and go to another city with this woman who was your friend [and] smiles at you, but is your bitter enemy." Like Hayes and Kingharman, the prophetess charged Sweatman $2. Hayes and Coleman both were fined $25. Kingharman, who was also charged with possession of policy slips, was held on $500 bail and sentenced to three months in the workhouse.[114]

The 1927 Webb-Loomis Medical Practice Law and other New York state statutes, which prohibit "the use of the title 'Doctor' except by physicians, the sale of a license or diploma, the practice of medicine without a license and advertising under an assumed name," obstructed supernatural work[115] Mediums, herbalists, root doctors, and other supernatural entrepreneurs did not have formal medical training, but this did not stop many from performing standard physical examinations, diagnosing clients with different illnesses, and prescribing healing balms, drinking potions, rubbing lotions and oils, "magic" pills, and other unusual medicines and home remedies to medical patients. One New York writer observed that "there are well-stocked stores in various parts of the community which deal in roots and herbs [and] guarantee to cure any ailment, from consumption to social diseases."[116] The Webb-Loomis Law was somewhat effective in curtailing some supernatural workers' efforts to earn a living. Within a year of its passage, the legislation shut down the so-called pseudomedical practices and businesses of over 1,000 black and white supernatural consultants.[117]

Launching a citywide campaign against medical "quacks," New York's medical community believed that supernatural workers' use of alternative medicine and home remedies undermined medical professionals' expertise and jeopardized the health and lives of urbanites, especially those too poor to afford legitimate healthcare. Dr. R. Dana Hubbard, Head of the Health Department's Bureau of Illegal Practices, insisted that quack doctors contributed to New Yorkers' deteriorating health conditions. "Quack doctors have been bold enough to treat incurable diseases and cases of cancer and tuberculosis, raising false hopes, and subjecting patients to treatment which not only gave rise to delusive hopes but which were injurious, and hastened the end or turned a case which might have been cured by timely treatment into an incurable one."[118]

Harlem Health Center Director and physician and *NYAN* contributor John B. West recalled treating quack doctors' former patients after purported home remedies failed to cure their illnesses. West identified one case where a "woman suffer[ing from] an obscure disease consulted a quack 'Professor' for treatment."

The 'Professor' informed the woman that she had a "belly full of lizards and he would give her religious bananas for them to eat instead of eating her. This went on until the woman's funds were exhausted, and the quack told her that big lizards had hatched out little ones, and they were eating her too fast. It finally developed that she suffered from syphilis, and she is now in an insane asylum." After treating the woman, West insisted that "early treatment by a physician might have avoided this."[119]

Spiritual healer and West-Indian–born Audrey Dayrelle insisted that she could diagnosis and cure all sickness. In August 1930, Lillian Tweed, a working-class factory worker, "lost her life savings [$1,140] to Dayrelle and her team of male swindlers."[120] Dayrelle informed Tweed that she was physically and mentally ill and that evil spirits were threatening her life. To ease some of her suffering, Dayrelle insisted that Tweed offer at least $200 to the spirits. Dayrelle also told Tweed not to divulge their arrangement to anybody. Unable to contain her excitement, Tweed bypassed Dayrelle's warning and confided in a relative. Dayrelle soon learned of Tweed's broken silence, telling her that the "spirits were very angry and needed $200 more to be appeased." Interestingly, Tweed paid the additional money; however, she was conned out of more money by two men. They arrived at her apartment, stating they were sent by the spirits to kill her if she refused to give them money. Out of money and feeling duped by Dayrelle, Tweed informed the police of her misfortune. When the police went to apprehend Dayrelle at her house, she "leaped from the first floor window and landed ten feet below on the pavement. She was slightly injured." Confessing to giving Tweed "medicine to keep her in ill health," Dayrelle was convicted of grand larceny and sentenced to eighteen months to three years in the state penitentiary.[121]

Some unsatisfied magic believers refused to wait for the legal system to reprimand supernatural consultants. Compelled by feelings of financial grief, foolishness, and desperation, individuals like Lawrence Collins and others took matters into their own hands and physically assaulted and killed their supernatural consultants. The stories of supernatural clients' vicious and deathly assaults against their supernatural advisers were chronicled in newspapers around the country. For instance, The *NYA*, the *Pittsburgh Courier*, and the *Chicago Tribune* reported on the highly publicized 1930 murder of Brooklyn resident and Puerto Rican medium Palmira Savala by Lawrence Collins. In 1930, Brooklyn resident Collins, disabled and out of work, employed lethal violence against the twenty-year-old supernatural consultant after she failed to heal his legs. Five years prior Collins was crippled in an elevator accident. He paid Savala $500 in "installments over a period of six months. Twice a week for six months, Collins visited Savala [and] she would place a glass of water between two lighted candles and have some incense burning to create atmosphere." Savala then instructed Collins "to go home and place a glass of water under his bed. He was expected to wash his feet each morning. At one time he was given a bag [of] silk, in which grass and leaves were sewed." Depleted of his life savings and desperate to overcome his disability, Collins even attempted to assign his furniture to an unsympathetic Savala. Refusing the furniture, Savala discontinued treating Collins and "laughed at him when he demanded the return of his money." Plagued by his long physical suffering and mental anguish, Collins, in a fit of rage, shot and killed Savala, and even attempted to murder her husband and child. Collins's desperate longing for physical wellness and revenge against Savala overpowered rational thinking, causing him to enact violence and brutality against the supernatural consultant. For those allegedly duped or swindled by spiritual racketeers, lethal violence seemed like a reasonable way to punish those promising love, money, and physical and emotional healing. Violence also became a vehicle for Collins and other unsatisfied supernatural clients to cope with disappointment, humiliation, and betrayal. The Savala murder is representative of the many labor setbacks supernatural workers experienced as they strove to promote their businesses and earn a living.[122]

Female supernatural consultants hoped that cases of violence against spiritual workers along with negative perceptions of supernatural practitioners would not bring adverse publicity to them as a group.[123] But reported cases of arrests and convictions and violent murders of female supernatural advisers continued to impact some New Yorkers' perceptions of clairvoyants, thus making it difficult for supernatural laborers to defend their spiritual abilities, practices, and labor. At the same time, published accounts against supernaturalism neither collectively hampered women's businesses nor deterred ordinary urbanites from seeking guidance from the scores of individuals dealing in herbs, roots, and the power of divining.[124]

Despite wide newspaper coverage on supernatural workers' legal arrests and convictions and brutal assaults and murders, many New Yorkers praised their ability to cure physical and mental aliments. When fifty-year-old Brooklyn "spiritual healer and life reader" Mme Sally Broy was arrested for practicing medicine without a license in December 1927, her devotees attested and praised her "remarkable powers." During her trial, seventy-five of Broy's black and white clients testified that her homemade concoctions "cured them of tuberculosis and paralysis and other serious diseases and ailments." In a sworn affidavit to the court, twenty-five-year-old Brooklyn resident Eunice Medley claimed that Broy was a "saint sent from God" who cured him of total blindness. "She placed her hand on [my] eyes and said a prayer. She clapped her hands and prayed again and [my] eyes became clear." Despite Medley's and other witnesses' testimonies that affirmed Broy's ability to "cure any disease on earth," the Brooklyn healer was ordered to pay a fine and received a suspended sentence.[125] Supernatural consumers' faith in Broy and other supernatural workers' abilities to cure disease and illness delineated competing societal views on wellness and health and, particularly for those of African descent, illuminated the belief in and use of alternative healing practices—a tradition that dated back to the period of enslavement and reflected larger social, political, and economic issues looming within black communities during the Jim Crow segregation era.

Alternative medicine was practical for those who lacked the financial means to visit doctors or were racially excluded from and Jim Crowed by some urban medical facilities. New Yorkers who had daily interactions, either residing in the same neighborhoods and apartment buildings or attending the same church, with herbalists and root doctors found it geographically convenient to retain supernatural workers' services. Patronizing local supernatural workers enabled African Americans to avoid white physicians, whom they mistrusted, and eased the minds of those who suffered from what scholar Harriet A. Washington called "iatrophobia," a fear of medical professionals and institutions and fear of medicine."[126] Exploring black healers during the period of enslavement, Sharla Fett writes, "twentieth-century eugenics, forced sterilizations of poor women, nonconsensual experimentation, and massive discrimination complete a history of medical abuse built on the legacies of slavery and racism. It is a historical accounting that clearly renders African American distrust of white medical institutions."[127] Black intellectual W. E. B. Du Bois observed that blacks' fear of hospitals, a byproduct of the neglect and the "roughness or brusqueness manner prevalent in many hospitals and the lack of a tender spirit of sympathy with the unfortunate patients," caused many not to seek medical attention when needed. "Many a Negro would almost rather die than trust himself to a hospital."[128] Through supernaturalism and the use of alternative medicine practices, consumers played a significant role within their own healing process. Yvonne Chireau posits that supernatural laborers "emphasized the active role of [the] individual in overcoming the inner, self-inflicted obstacles that could hinder one's progression to good health. The faith that believers placed in Spiritual ministers allowed persons to take charge of their own afflictions, and by extension, to take charge of conflicts that had occurred with their lives as well."[129] This form of spiritual assistance afforded supernatural believers the confidence to transform and take care of their physical and mental well-being and to creatively navigate Jim Crow segregation.

Conclusion

In 2010, thirty-year-old Connecticut resident Jennifer Forness's future appeared bleak. She lost her job as a store clerk, went through a difficult divorce, and suffered from a number of stress-related health problems. Perhaps out of desperation and anxiety over an uncertain future and the need to feel like better days were ahead, Forness purchased hoodoo products online and even consulted a "hoodoo doctor who specialize[ed] in employment matters." Forness hoped that the purchased occult products and supernatural consultants' advice and insight on her personal life would transform her immediate circumstances. Within a year, Forness was convinced that her luck had been radically changed for the better. She secured employment, her health improved, and her seemingly but understandably pessimistic outlook about her life changed. In recent years, especially in the wake of America's economic downturn and slow employment recovery of the mid-2000s, Forness and many other Americans facing unemployment, poverty, housing evictions, and personal turmoil turned to different religious and spiritual products, practices, and supernatural consultants like Youree D'Cleomili "Miss Cleo" Harris.[130] Economically strapped Americans' utilization of occult products is anchored in early-twentieth-century American urbanites' profound faith and trust in supernatural consultants. For those consumers living nearly a century ago, supernaturalism represented a different approach to resolving personal dilemmas, economic issues, and health problems, and the chance to alter undesirable personal circumstances. Supernaturalism and magical products offered optimistic consumers something to hope for and the notion that one could change and overcome personal turmoil.

No doubt, over time and space supernaturalism afforded city dwellers nontraditional strategies toward resolving ordinary everyday problems. Furthermore, supernaturalism presented career opportunities for its female practitioners, empowering many to forge new labor paths and identities. Whether born with supernatural abilities, apprenticing under a seasoned clairvoyant, or adopting supernaturalism as a financial hustle, magic practitioners, particularly those using magic and the spirit realm to earn a living, merged the sacred world and religious imagery with that of underground commercial leisure to establish and bolster their occult businesses and to participate in New York's illegal numbers racket. Providing a wide range of services to seemingly naïve, desperate, curious, and superstitious New Yorkers, supernatural consultants, like many informal laborers and entrepreneurs, unsurprisingly could not predict that their newfound labor prospects and nontraditional spiritual practices would open them up to police arrests, public criticism, and violence.

CHAPTER 4

"I Have My Own Room on 139th Street"

Black Women and the Urban Sex Economy

In 1938, Carol Smith was admitted to the Women's House of Detention, a prison located in Manhattan's Greenwich Village, on a charge of prostitution. Originally from Salisbury, Maryland, the college-educated Smith moved to New York in hopes of finding what black intellectual Alain Locke referred to as "a new vision of opportunity" for herself.[1] A devout Catholic, Smith regarded herself as a religious and respectable girl and never imagined associating with unsavory urban characters or yielding to city vice, premarital sex, and sexual labor. But unable to secure the uninhibited social mobility and the high-paying work she and many other Southern migrants envisioned for themselves, Smith entered the urban sex economy, a decision that reflected both her desperation and bleak economic realities. Sharing her personal story and justification for prostituting herself with a caseworker, Smith admitted that her financial condition and naïveté about city life and dangers and insalubrious urbanites led her to sex work. "[I] had to live, had no money, and therefore resorted to commercial prostitution." Smith was introduced to the urban sex trade by a middle-aged black woman who seemed genuinely concerned for her well-being. As Smith recalled: "I met her as [I] was leaving a moving picture house and [she] invited [me] to her house for dinner and told [me I] was a nice-looking girl and that [I] did not have to worry about money, food, or home, as she would show [me] how to obtain this without any difficulty. [She] showed [me] how to have sexual intercourse with men and gave [me] instruction on how to use contraceptives. [I] was in [her] apartment about one week working as a commercial prostitute and had at least three men each day."[2]

Smith's account of her entrance into New York's sex trade and her day-to-day work as an indoor sex worker reveals, according to one city reporter writing about New York prostitution during the mid–twentieth century, the "story of hundreds of women who have taken to the streets to make their living."[3] Nonexistent employment prospects and naïveté about urban dangers precipitated the entrance of Smith and many other black women into New York's sexual economy. Moreover, as observed in Smith's heartrending testimony to her caseworker, many working-poor and jobless city women found themselves entangled in day-to-day economic situations that caused many to negotiate and at times abandon their individual moral beliefs. Smith's candid account also reveals that the decision to trade money for sex, whether on urban streets or in the privacy of one's home, was not an easy decision. Rather, it was, at least for some, a rational choice that plagued women's consciousness and certainly one that warrants attention by scholars of women's history.

Until recently, scholars have not fully analyzed the complex working lives of Carol Smith and other New York black sex workers of the first half of the twentieth century. Much of what scholars know about urban sex work highlights native-born white American and immigrant women's multifaceted experiences as streetwalkers, sex-house proprietors and inmates, and exotic dancers. Scholarly discourse on the vast dimensions of paid sexual labor situates white women at the center of urban sex economies, offering complicated narratives that tease out the benefits and limitations of their work and how varying forms of sex work impacted city vice and urban and commercial development. Further, literature on white women's sexual labor analyzes how such labor was interwoven into turn-of-the-twentieth-century American public life and culture. While presenting nuance and refreshing interpretations on white sex workers, some historians have excluded and marginalized black female sex workers from studies on prostitution.

When black sex workers' stories are positioned within the larger discourse on sex work, they are often depicted as streetwalkers, paying little attention to their varied occupations and experiences within the urban sex trade.[4] Scant archival material on black sex work may explain black women's marginalization within, and absence from, prostitution studies. Historian Cynthia Blair, whose work places black women at the center of Chicago's sex economy during the early twentieth century, posits that black women's exclusion from prostitution studies offers an incomplete picture of city prostitution. Blair writes that "the omission of black women sex workers has not only led to the analytical neglect of the peculiar experiences of African Americans (who, in many cities, made up a sizable proportion of prostitutes) but also contributed to a lack of attention to the complex role that race played in shaping the turn-of-the-century urban sex economy."[5] Like Blair, recent scholarship by Kevin Mumford, Elizabeth Alice Clement, and Stephen Robertson brings much-needed attention to black sex workers' wide-ranging working experience. Utilizing a variety of primary materials, including red-light district guides, court, police, and reformers' anti-vice records, census data, and newspapers, scholars offer original perspectives on black women's cross-racial and intraracial sexual businesses in northern and midwestern urban centers. More importantly, emerging literature moves beyond the image of black women as streetwalkers and low-level sex workers and instead chronicles black sex workers' less familiar occupations as madam-prostitutes, brothel and call-flat proprietors, and occasional sex entrepreneurs.[6]

Building on historical work that explores how race impacted urban sexual economies and cultures, I use this chapter to bring visibility to the different ways in which black sex workers functioned within Gotham's sex commerce. This chapter specifically highlights the challenges of documenting black prostitution in New York and the broad socioeconomic and personal circumstances outlining black women's entrance into paid sexual labor. Extreme poverty, sexual abuse and trauma, family obligation, and the active pursuit of sexual desire and pleasure brought a diverse yet significant group of black women into sexual labor, a field of work that urban moralists and activists considered damaging to women's bodies and souls and evidence of city women's unbridled and unchecked sexuality. Black women were not limited to one form of sex work. Career and occasional sex laborers occupied varying positions within New York's underground world of commercial sex, functioning as streetwalkers, brothel proprietors and workers, and independent sex entrepreneurs. Engagement in varying sex occupations brought to its participants different sets of labor experiences and narratives and, for some, different measures of occupational control. No doubt, black sex workers recognized and experienced firsthand the constraints of different categories of sexual labor, especially that of street solicitation. Potential street dangers including police arrest, murder, and sexual assault motivated many black women's decision to limit their time on New York streets or to ply their trade in alternative working spaces. Reducing their street visibility, prostitutes rendered services to sex patrons in furnished rental rooms and brothels, commercial businesses including massage parlors, speakeasies, and nightclubs; and within the comforts of their working and middle-class residences. Alternative work environments in private and commercial settings potentially lessened sex workers' chances of arrest and increased their chances of entrepreneurship. Furthermore, paid sexual transactions in residential communities and popular after-hours establishments afforded sex workers the space to explore, negotiate, or depart from normative and unconventional sexual landscapes and intimacies. Women's indoor sexual labor transformed New York's sex geography, shifting prostitution from street corners and alleyways to private residences and semipublic spaces.

Documenting Urban Black Sex Work

Efforts to understand the complex and complicated working lives of New York black sex workers has led many scholars to utilize turn-of-the-twentieth-century reports of vice squads and social reform investigative organizations such as the Committee of Fourteen (COF). Established in 1905 by New York Anti-Saloon League members as a private anti-vice organization, the COF monitored and investigated neighborhood vice conditions, prostitution, and interracial leisure establishments, and lobbied for municipal governments to regulate illegal and unrespectable urban amusements. Moreover, the COF was concerned with urban criminality, sexual immorality, cross-racial sociability, and the spread of prostitution into middle- and working-class communities.[7] Through the employment of white and African American male and a few female undercover agents, who "served as the foot soldiers in the [organization's] campaign against disorderliness and immorality," the COF provided the NYPD with firsthand evidence to allow the identification of suspected lawbreakers and the location of alleged underground businesses. Historian Jennifer Fronc notes that the COF's "pioneering use of undercover investigations yielded new types of knowledge about urban neighborhoods and their residents, which enabled them to intervene and attempt to reconstruct social conditions in New York City and beyond."[8] At the same time, surveillance on undesignated vice districts and their inhabitants prompted police, without questioning the validity of anti-vice agents' investigative methods, to orchestrate raids and entrap assumed underground laborers and to monitor and criminalize New Yorkers' ordinary daily behavior.

The COF's detailed prostitution reports, typically obtained when male investigators posed as potential sex patrons and partygoers, offered both the NYPD and urban reformers a wealth of information on alleged sex workers. COF reports identified the location of sex houses, the various prices women charged for each act of prostitution, the benefits and exploitative conditions of sex work, and the conversation exchanged between agents and prostitutes, pimps, and male johns. "Committee reports," according to one historian, "allow[ed readers] to step into the hotel lobbies, restaurants, taxicabs, massage parlors, and dance halls, as well [as] apartments and other private sites, where the terms for intimacy were negotiated."[9] Moreover, reports provided the aliases sex workers assumed; their age, weight, and ethnic background; and a description of what prostitutes were wearing at the time of solicitation. Black prostitutes were often described as being between the ages of twenty and thirty-five and having "kinky" or "bobbed" hair. COF agents' constant reference to alleged sex workers' bobbed hairstyles, most likely calculated disguises, contributed to societal perceptions that such women were un-Christian, disreputable, and obviously violators of social reformers' ideas about proper female attire and hairstyles. Moreover, pointing out sex workers' hairstyles reaffirmed existing public images of prostitutes and was intended to highlight the physical distinctions between respectable and immoral women.

Throughout the 1920s, bob-wearing women, regardless of their race or ethnic background, were linked to forms of outward conduct that was unbecoming of a proper woman. Short hairstyles were associated with masculinity, late nights carousing at bars, dancing and smoking, scanty attire, premarital sex, unconventional labor, and urban decay. African American Socialist Party activist and writer Chandler Owen maintained that bob-wearing women were unfeminine and posed a challenge to masculinity. Such women, according to Owen, possessed an inner desire to transcend the boundaries of their sex. In a 1926 *Messenger* editorial entitled "Bobbed Hair and Bobbed Brains," Owen posits that bobbed hairstyles were part of a "feminine revolt against masculine tyranny. All in all, the bobbed-hair craze seems to be but a reflection of the general tendency of the woman to become more masculine."[10] For Owen, short, bobbed hairstyles and black women's choice to embrace modern and popular hairstyles was a disruptive phenomenon that undermined conventional gender roles. Owen's critique was also reflective of black New Yorkers' ongoing public and private conversations and debates about outward deportment, proper attire, and the diverse ways in which some black men, while clinging to traditional images and interpretations of gender relations, shunned female individuality. While Progressive-era activists and intellectuals like Owen maintained that bobbed hair breached acceptable hairstyles for women and encouraged women to take on bold attitudes, the controversial haircut symbolized, according to scholar Mary Louise Roberts, a "broader fight for freedom, equality, and the attempt to surmount the high barriers of tradition."[11] Black women with bobbed hair welcomed the ability to freely showcase personalized expressions of femininity and modern-day hairstyles, especially since their individual freedoms were often obstructed by race, gender, and class oppression and criticized by judgmental relatives and moral propagandists. Exhibiting individual representations of beauty was a strategy many black women employed to showcase urban hair culture and to control their bodies. They freely chose what clothes to wear and how to coif their hair, reclaiming their bodies for themselves while refuting stereotypes that cast them as deviant and unrefined. Adorning their bodies the way they deemed fit, urban black women creatively demonstrated meticulous care and pride in their physical appearance.[12]

While COF reports assisted social reformers and law-enforcement officials in their quest to identify sex workers who plied their trade in urban working- and middle-class spaces, many black political reformers questioned the authenticity of their reports and censured COF agents' attempts to shut down so-called disorderly black (and white) businesses that promoted interracial sociability.[13] In several letters to COF General Secretary Frederick H. Whitin, prominent scholar and activist W. E. B. Du Bois adamantly expressed his concerns about the COF's surveillance of African American communities as well as its efforts to defame the reputations of white- and black-owned establishments that catered to a racially mixed clientele. The NAACP cofounder and *Crisis* editor further suggested that the COF's citywide crusade against interracial businesses reinforced racial segregation, violating New York statutes that prohibited discrimination in places of public entertainment.[14]

NAACP New York Vigilance Committee chair Gilchrist Stewart also took issue with the COF, questioning the organization's employment of African American men. In a 1912 letter to Whitin, Stewart argued that the COF was "closing up and bankrupting" black businesses on "the words of colored paid investigators whose testimony would not be worth two cents to an impartial jury." Interrogating the character and motives of African American COF employees, including William F. Pogen and Howard University graduate Raymond Claymes, Gilchrist noted that such men, who were considered race traitors by some African Americans and whom he considered desperate for skilled high-paying employment, retrieved "the kind of evidence they think their employers want." In other words, Gilchrist reasoned that African American COF agents' surveillance work in black neighborhoods had little to do with curbing prostitution and more to do with the "security of their employment."[15] Presumably, black COF agents' labor was motivated by the racial exclusion of urban black men from professional and skilled labor positions and their subsequent relegation to work that was menial and demeaning and denied them of their humanity and dignity.

African American racial uplifters like *NYA* editor Fred Moore disagreed with black leaders' criticisms of the COF, noting the organization's genuine commitment to city reform and the eradication of urban vice. Moore's defense of the COF came as no surprise to COF critics. The prominent newsman was not only a COF supporter but also a COF advisory board member, and he chaired the Committee of Five, the COF's Colored Auxiliary organization, which "assisted in the work of regulating colored saloons and hotels." Furthermore, Moore was instrumental in the employment of several African American COF investigators. Concerned with the moral health and reputation of New York's black communities, Moore, informed by black better-class models of correctness, defended the COF's surveillance of the city's known vice districts, denying allegations that the organization concentrated its efforts on closing black-owned leisure establishments. Responding to black activists' concerns and criticisms, COF executive secretary Walter Hooke in a 1911 *NYA* editorial stated that it was "absurd" for black leaders to suggest "that we are spending most of our time trying to close up colored saloons and hotels and pay but little attention to similar places conducted by whites. We make no exception in closing them whether they be large establishments or small, whether the owners are white or colored." Hooke further explained that their main objective was to make sure "that all saloons, cafes, restaurants, and hotels [be] conducted with a high regard for decency."[16] Historian Jennifer Fronc contends that Moore's partnership with COF officials represented how some urban leaders were somewhat complicit in broadening racial segregation in New York and at times overlooked the COF's undermining of state civil rights laws. At the same time, Moore's collaboration with the COF were political strategies toward eradicating crime in black communities and dismantling white urbanites' perceptions that black enclaves were sites of pleasure for joy-seeking whites.[17]

African American leaders raised reasonable concerns about the credibility of vice reporting and the nature in which the COF and other anti-vice organizations and halfway house and rehabilitative facilities obtained private information about sex workers. There is no doubt that the reports by COF agents and social reformers and caseworkers' descriptive narratives on urban conditions and sex commerce participants were problematic. Their investigative reports were tainted with race and class prejudice, demonstrated their condemnatory views on those about whom they were reporting, and were informed by their own middle-class, racial, and gender biases on less privileged city residents. Complicating anti-vice agents' judgmental attitudes about sex workers and their labor was the authenticity of sex workers' personal narratives. In other words, some COF reports, highlighting some sex workers' biographical accounts and family histories, were conceivably tainted with misinformation. In a conscious effort to protect their private thoughts on their work, family, and sexuality, many sex workers were not always forthcoming or truthful with undercover anti-vice agents or meddlesome caseworkers or prison officials. Instead, women understandably wrapped their lives in a veil of secrecy. Sex workers were uncomfortable with sharing intimate details of their lives with those whom they perceived as strangers and perhaps undercover police officers. When probed about the interior workings of their lives, sex workers concealed or constructed fictitious stories about their real identities, family backgrounds, and sexual histories. One newly released Welfare Island inmate reluctantly discussed her childhood with a prison official. Recorded some time in the 1930s, the administrator observed that the woman "resented being questioned and [that her story] was so hazy as to the details of her early life that it was impossible to obtain a comprehensive background."

By either refusing to answer reformers' questions or determining what questions they would answer, sex workers unexpectedly gained the upper hand on those wishing to dissect various aspects of their lives. In many respects, they controlled the conversation and interview process, intending to convey a narrative they could manipulate.[18] Unable to successfully extract personal information from sex workers, caseworkers, prison officials, and vice agents further stigmatized and vilified supposedly fallen women, documenting them in official city records as physically unattractive, uncommunicative, uncooperative, and disagreeable. Burdening sex workers with such disparaging labels often times impeded their chances of garnering sympathy and of obtaining financial assistance from caseworkers and reformers. Identifying black women's behavioral patterns as unresponsive and bad-tempered reinforced turn-of-the-twentieth-century criminology studies and social scientific theories that suggested that such personality traits were inherent and beyond social workers' and reformers' rehabilitation initiatives.[19]

By withholding or creating fictional narratives about their personal lives, "unresponsive" sex workers fiercely guarded their inner worlds. Unbeknown to hypercritical urban reformers, sex workers intended to maintain a level of anonymity within the context of sexual labor. Furthermore, sex laborers' conscious efforts to safeguard their privacy was based on their indifferent attitudes about societal perceptions of prostitution. Whereas some sex workers used conversations and interviews with city activists and caseworkers to describe the complexities of their lives and socioeconomic circumstances, others reasoned that the various ways in which they conveyed their personal stories did not matter. They believed that overly critical reformers and documentarians of New York vice would distort and misinterpret their narratives and words and script their lives as one-dimensional. Some black sex workers did not view reformers or social workers as individuals they could confide in, but rather as persons who affirmed and advanced political agendas that cast sex workers as women who unrestrained and immoral appetites.

Conversely, other sex workers divulged stories of physical, emotional, and psychological trauma to reformers, undercover vice agents, and sometimes to anyone who would listen to them. Harlem singer Raymond A. Claymes, one of the few African American COF agents hired to obtain information on black nightclubs and speakeasies in Harlem, successfully gained the trust of several black women. Claymes learned sex workers' real names, birthdates, family histories, and reasons for entering New York's sex trade. In May 1928, while investigating the Blue Ribbon Chile Parlor, a Manhattan basement apartment speakeasy frequented by "prostitutes and faggots," Claymes was introduced to twenty-three-year-old sex worker "Miss Clark." Viewing Claymes as trustworthy, "Miss Clark," who was also under the influence of alcohol, revealed her birth name, home address and phone number, and the location at which she plied her trade.[20] Similarly, one brothel workers trusted Claymes enough to disclose private details about her life. The undercover vice agent learned that the gregarious sex worker of British West Indian parentage was "born in Washington, D.C., and traveled extensively between England and the Caribbean." More interestingly, Claymes learned that she was a single mother and was "being kept by her own admission by a prominent married dentist [who gives her free dental work]."[21]

Moreover, some sex workers shared painful and heartrending accounts of physical abuse, rape, and molestation. Speaking to a caseworker at the Isaac T. Hopper Home, a private Manhattan halfway house and charitable organization for destitute women and former female convicts, one woman revealed that several pimps and boyfriends had repeatedly physically assaulted her. She "lived with three men at different times until each of these men became so abusive to her that she found it necessary to leave."[22] Revealing intimate and private details about their lives was therapeutic for many sex workers—it was an opportunity to document emotional, physical, and sexual abuse and to explain their life stories in their own words. At the same time, some sex workers employed personal testimonies in order to garner sympathy and financial assistance from willing listeners and as a way to highlight the complex ways in which unhealthful choices and associations and looming urban inequalities all contributed to their ill-fated predicaments.

Prostitution arrest statistics produced during the early twentieth century by law enforcement, correctional agencies, and social scientists complicates scholarly efforts to construct accurate profiles of black sex workers. Statistic data on prostitution indicate that black sex laborers were over-represented in police arrests and city and state reformatories. According to Bedford Hills Correctional Facility superintendent Katherine Bement Davis, black women, part of New York's 2 percent black population during the second decade of the twentieth century, made up 13 percent of all Bedford inmates serving time for prostitution. Comparably, less privileged American and immigrant women of varying ethnic backgrounds represented the majority of New York sex workers; immigrant women made up 40 percent of the city population and 24 percent of all sex workers at Bedford, and native-born white sex workers represented 67 percent of Bedford inmates.[23] In 1925, the COF and one New York City Magistrate Court reported that black women represented 36 percent of all prostitutes arrested.[24] Political scientist Willoughby Cyrus Waterman's 1930s study on New York vice found that black women made up 46 percent of prostitution arrests. Investigating sex work in Harlem, Waterman maintained that between 1931 and 1935 three-quarters of all black females were arrested for vagrancy and prostitution.[25]

What is troubling about prostitution statistics is that they fail to distinguish actual sex workers from ordinary women who were falsely apprehended and convicted for prostitution. False arrests of black women in New York were fueled in part by white northern anxieties about "blackness" and urban crime and by turn-of-the-twentieth-century stereotypical images that depicted blacks as innately hypersexual, lawless, and free of physical and emotional restraint. Working for the NYPD for more than twenty years, one former cop, recounting his interactions with city blacks, generally believed that African Americans were more "lewd than any other race"; he further suggested that black women "were naturally indolent [and] emotional, [which] tend[s] to make the colored woman a free and easy one in her habits."[26] NYPD Commissioner William McAdoo's characterization of black New Yorkers, particularly those of a certain class background, was negative and indeed problematic. McAdoo referred to some "Tenderloin Negro[es]" as "trouble-some and dangerous characters [that] never work, or earn a living from a life of shame." Additionally, the commissioner depicted black women as "vicious and drunken."[27] All in all, "white police officers," according to one scholar, "believed black women contributed to and exacerbated the problems of a city with a rapidly growing population of southern migrants and foreign immigrants."[28] Disparaging public portrayals leveled at urban African American women left female city dwell-ers like May Enoch, whose false prostitution arrest led to one of New York's most violent race riots of the Progressive era, vulnerable to white brutality and to having their daily behavior and social patterns be deemed criminal. Whether strolling city streets with friends, visiting a relative's apartment, renting rooms to boarders, or operating legitimate businesses, black women faced police harassment and were arrested and convicted for a number of crimes, including possession of numbers slips, loitering and vagrancy, and prostitution.[29]

Black women property owners, landlords, and entrepreneurs were frequent tar-gets of trumped-up police charges. Enterprising female business owners were ar-rested and prosecuted for allegedly using their establishments to promote gambling, bootlegging, and prostitution. In February 1923, city police raided Madame M. E. Hardaway's 128th Street massage and beauty parlor and school after a disgruntled employee claimed Hardaway "permitted her rooms to be used for prostitution." Also caught up in the raid were two of Hardaway's employees: licensed masseuse Pearl Elizabeth Salisbury and beauty culturist Susie Richard; both women were accused of selling sex to white patrons. Vehemently proclaiming her innocence, Hardaway was found guilty of breaching New York City tenement-housing laws of the 1920s and placed on six months' probation. Outraged by her arrest and that of her two employ-ees, Hardaway, a well-respected community advocate, placed a public statement in the *NYAN*, defending her reputation and that of her business. Drawing on her widely known community persona as a reputable and law-abiding entrepreneur, Hardaway declared that those "having worked directly with me in my Beauty School know that I operated a legitimate business and that I take pride in my pupils."[30]

Additionally, destitute and unemployed black women were routinely framed by plainclothes police officers and paid criminal informants. Poor black women like single mother and thirty-one-year-old Ruth Coleman, who were not sex workers but merely accepted drinks, food, or small amounts of money from undercover officers posing as "friendly" male strangers, were repeatedly brought up on prostitution charges. In 1929, Coleman, whose "family was absolutely starving, had gone to a girl's home to beg [for] food." In route to the neighbor's home, "she met a man who offered to buy her whiskey." Thinking only of feeding her family, Coleman refused the drink but agreed to "take the money [to] buy food." Once Coleman accepted the fifty cents, the man revealed himself as an officer and placed her under arrest for prostitution. This was Coleman's first arrest.[31]

Leading race reform organizations and African American newspaper editors publicly criticized black women's false prostitution arrests and police officers' entrapment of impoverished women. The NAACP attributed black women's high arrest rates for prostitution and other crimes to racial bias, avaricious stool pigeons, police corruption, and attempts by city officials to depict African Americans as "more immoral, less decent" than their white counterparts.[32] COF supporter and *NYA* editor Fred Moore condemned the NYPD for falsely arresting scores of black women for sex solicitation. Moore posited that women of African descent were "the favorite prey for frame-up[s] and false charges. If a colorful

Figure 13: Police stool pigeon Chile Acuna.
Courtesy of New York Daily News Archives.

charge of prostitution or keeping a disorderly house can be made to stick against a woman with a few hundred dollars, the legal and official harpies who use the courts for this purpose will usually strip her bare of both money and reputation."[33] Throughout the mid-1920s, Moore used the *NYA* to highlight how urban black women were vulnerable to state-sanctioned violence and to warn urban citizens about some law enforcers' active use of paid criminal informants like black con artist Charles Dancy and Chile Mapocha Acuna.[34] Professional stool pigeon and prostitute procurer Acuna, a thirty-one-year-old immigrant from Santiago, Chile, affirmed black New Yorkers' suspicions that African American women were routinely framed for crimes they did not commit. Testifying before the Seabury Commission some time in 1930, Acuna recalled that police squads throughout the city paid him $150 a week to "shake down innocent women as well as whores," who were then "railroaded and put through the mill." Police informants like Acuna attributed guiltless women's high arrest rates to police officers and detectives' need to fulfill expected quotas of arrests and to rob and extort money from women. Some police officers, after they arrested allegedly soliciting women, "would return to the flats and steal their possessions; some officers [even] had their whole apartments furnished with good[s] stolen from persecuted women."[35]

Urban vice reporting, false arrests, and black women's personal testimonies, which at times were exaggerated and fabricated, present challenges to analyzing the scope of black prostitution in New York. These compelling records and reports reveal more about vice agents, law enforcers, and city social workers and activists' perspectives on sexual labor, morality, and race than they do about sex workers. This does not suggest that such primary sources data are useless in exploring black sex workers' personal lives and working experiences. Indeed, to borrow from Gail Hershatter's work on sex laborers in twentieth-century Shanghai, black sex workers' "daily lives, struggles, and self-perception were surely constructed in part by these other voices and institutions."[36] When judiciously and closely reviewed with an acknowledgment of their shortcomings and coupled with additional archival sources including newspapers and court, prison, and probation records, such extant documentation raises and answers questions about the seemingly ambiguous lives of New York black sex workers. Surviving records shed light on the broad socioeconomic contours outlining black women's entrances into prostitution as well as their multiple labor positions and locations of work. More importantly, such historical artifacts illuminate sex workers' less familiar aspirations, value systems, disappointments, and complex outlooks on sex work and intimacy, and on toiling in one of the most uncertain and dangerous occupations for women.

Entrance into the Urban Sex Trade

Black women's varying testimonials about prostitution reveal that there was no single path into paid sexual labor. Entrance into New York's sex economy during the first half of the twentieth century was precipitated by a myriad of complex and unpredictable circumstances, including the need to procure drugs, alcohol, or luxury items; a history of sexual abuse; the promotion of sexual gratification; manipulation by relatives, friends, and strangers; and the death or abandonment of a spouse or male companion. Despite their disparate routes into sexual labor, many black women reluctantly pursued street and indoor prostitution as a result of economic calamity, family obligations, low wages and unemployment, and male desertion. Urban League social worker and Brooklyn activist Carietta V. Owens's 1914 report on arrested black sex workers appearing before the Women's Night Court in Manhattan observed that the women's "meager salaries and uncongenial surroundings tend to produce a state of dissatisfaction" that led to prostitution.[37] Facing the financial stresses of paying for rent, food, clothes, and city transportation, many urban black women agonized over the prospect of selling their bodies for money. One twenty-eight-year-old unemployed Panamanian dressmaker felt ashamed about prostituting herself and blamed her husband's abrupt decision to leave the family for her unfortunate predicament. "My husband is the cause of all my troubles. He left me and I don't know where he is; he never helped me, I had to work and support him." Her feelings of shame, however, subsided when her funds dwindled. "I owe rent and had to eat, gas and electricity [was] shut down for not paying bills.[38]

Southern black women arriving in New York during the first Great Migration era with visions of high-paying skilled employment, well-kept living spaces, and thrilling urban amusements were perhaps the most susceptible to bartering sex for money, food, and shelter. Fleeing from the rigid confines of Southern oppression, political and economic disenfranchisement, and interracial and intraracial violence, black female migrants' sensibilities about the industrial North as a cosmopolitan place of greater freedom and opportunity were complicated by low-wage work, dilapidated housing facilitates, and customary race discrimination.[39] Black southern transplants, according to historian Thomas Sugrue, "faced a regime of racial proscriptions [in the North] that was every bit [as] deeply entrenched as the southern system of Jim Crow. Economic injustice and pervasive discrimination knew no regional boundaries."[40] Recalling the harsh realities of being a newcomer to the city, one Bedford Hills prisoner, in a 1927 letter to a prison official, expressed that "coming to a big city like New York with no one to help made things much harder. You don't know what girls like me are driven to do. I didn't do them just for fun."[41] Rampant city crime and violence further challenged newcomers' view of northern spaces. Naive residents quickly learned, whether through observation, firsthand experience, or neighborhood talk, that New York was not only a symbol of hope, prosperity, and opportunity. The city, as expressed through New York black and white journalists and cultural critics' newspaper and magazine writings, was plagued by crime, human suffering and exploitation, and hidden dangers lurking on street corners and alleyways and within neighborhoods and apartment buildings.

Alone in unfamiliar urban terrains with limited family and community ties and economic resources, new arrivals like fifteen-year-old South Carolina native Sarah Tyce quickly realized that they "had escaped the horrors of the segregated South only to find themselves adrift and vulnerable in their new home."[42] Five months after arriving in Harlem in 1937, an unemployed Tyce found herself making survival choices that jeopardized her life. The impoverished teen turned to various forms of street work, occasionally bartering sex for money or food and begging. Hustling and laboring on New York streets brought Tyce into contact with Daniel Williams, a twenty-nine-year-old Harlem resident who appeared genuinely concerned with assisting the teen. On the contrary and certainly unbeknown to Tyce, Williams was one of the city's many "cowardly small-time racketeers of [the] race, who preyed upon poor, but respectable looking girls."[43] Sensing the young woman's desperation, Williams played on Tyce's vulnerabilities, offering her a hot meal and a place to rest for a couple of hours in exchange for sexual intercourse. The hungry and tired migrant willingly accepted Williams's proposition. His seemingly nonthreatening gesture, however, turned into a nightmare for Tyce. Once in Williams's 128th Street furnished room, the two engaged in sexual intercourse and Tyce received her promised meal. Upon leaving her new acquaintance's apartment, Tyce was brutally beaten and stabbed by Williams; according to one published account, she "appeared at [a] police precinct bleeding from knife wounds and suffering bruises from a beating." Because of Tyce's young age and brutal physical appearance, city police acted quickly to locate and arrest Williams, apprehending him outside of his apartment.[44] Tyce's tragic story is one of the many stories that outlined how some southern migrant women faired in the urban North, and it speaks to the dangerous day-to-day survival strategies women employed to make their way in the city.

Family and community obligations forced many working-poor black women into the urban sexual economy. As financial contributors to—and often the primary breadwinner for—their families, many sex workers' wages were never their own and were central to helping relatives and close friends maintain economic stability and overcome financial desperation. Contributing economically to their

households was firmly rooted in African American women's tradition of community responsibility and what historian Elsa Barkley Brown dubbed as an "ethos of
mutuality."[45] Entertainer Ethel Waters, who openly discussed her interaction with
sex workers while singing in Philadelphia nightclubs during the 1930s in her 1951
autobiography, *His Eye Is on the Sparrow*, recalled having "great respect for whores."
They "were kind and generous [and] some supported whole families and kept
at their trade for years to send trick babies through college."[46] Waters's observation of family-oriented and nurturing sex workers can be seen in the economic
pursuits of a twenty-one-year-old Harlem brothel inmate. The single mother
of one informed a COF agent that her earnings were not for herself. Unlike some
"women in the life" she did not "foolishly" spend money on fancy clothes or waste
it in after-hours nightspots. Instead, her income "support[ed] her three-year-old
daughter, who was suffering from tuberculosis."[47] The diverse ways she and other
working-poor prostitutes managed their earnings, despite dominant views that
sex workers were materialistic and self-serving, conformed to how working- and
middle-class families reared their children. While sex workers clearly departed
from relatives' dreams of them engaging in legal and nonsexual labor, sex workers adhered to traditional family values that stressed providing for one's family in
times of economic troubles and forgoing personal aspirations for the collective
betterment of the family and community at large.[48]

Kinship and economic responsibilities were hardly a concern for some sex
workers. Their entrance into New York's sex commerce was not precipitated
by family obligation or out of economic hardship. Their attraction to the urban sex trade emerged from a profound desire and passion for sexual pleasure
and fulfillment. Selling sexual fantasies in exchange for money became a viable
option for individuals who were indifferent to prescribed ideas of marital and
sexual norms and who desired to explore what scholar Mireille Miller-Young
calls "illicit eroticism." Similar to Miller-Young's provocative examination of
contemporary African American female porn workers, early-twentieth-century
sex workers consciously "choose to pursue a prohibited terrain of [sexual] labor
and performance and put hypersexuality to use. [They] use[d], manipulate[d],
and deploy[ed] their sexualities in the economy. Commodifying [their] sexuality
[was] part of the strategic and tactical labor black women use[d] in advanced
capitalist economies."[49] Twenty-five-year-old married housewife and occasional
sex worker Martha Briggs interpreted sex work as a path toward economic independence from her unsuspecting breadwinning husband and conceivably as a
path toward sexual fulfillment and experimentation. In her conversation with one
undercover vice agent, Briggs does not offer an explanation about her housewife
status, a position many urban black women did not have the privilege of claiming

since their households were dependent on dual incomes. Briggs's unemployment status may have resulted from a restricted labor market or perhaps was based on a family decision that stressed upholding patriarchal and middle-class ideas about gender-specific roles for married men and women. Nevertheless, Briggs took advantage of her housewife status, using it to "make a little money for herself on the side."[50] Earning money outside their husbands' purviews permitted housewives like Briggs to manage personal finances and spend money according to their own sensibilities and to articulate their opinions on the daily functions of the household. Briggs's clandestine sex business not only exposed her individual quest for financial autonomy. Prostitution and infidelity perhaps exposed marital and sexual dissatisfaction, a desire to transcend monogamous sex, and the absence of emotional fulfillment. Briggs's choice of labor also conceivably revealed a personal commitment to giving and receiving sexual pleasure, a need to overcome her loneliness and boredom as a housewife, and her longing for male companionship. Briggs's need for marital and sexual stimulation from her husband coincided with some black elites' evolving perspectives on and expectations of marriage during the first half of the twentieth century. Historian Anastasia C. Curwood argues that African Americans' views on marriage, profoundly shaped by changing attitudes on sexuality and gender roles, were a "complex blend of older uplifter's mentalities and newer pragmatic standards." Couples shifted from thoughts of marriage as a signifier for conventional gender roles and racial progress to the promotion of emotional satisfaction, sexual pleasure and intimacy, and unions that supported women's personal ambitions.[51]

Finally, the urban sex economy became a potential labor option for individuals hoping to avoid one of the few occupations open to urban black women: domestic work. While many female informal laborers held full- and part-time employment as household servants, others, recognizing the many physical and emotional challenges associated with household labor, refused to work as maids, cooks, or laundresses. In her classic 1956 autobiography *Lady Sings the Blues*, blues legend Billie Holiday revealed her disdain for domestic work. After working in New York as a maid for several months for a "big, fat, and lazy" white woman during the late 1920s, the Baltimore native "figured there had to be something better than [personal service]."[52] Between 1929 and 1930, at the age of fourteen, Holiday was employed by "one of the biggest madams in Harlem" as "a strictly twenty-dollar call girl."[53] While Holiday's contempt for domestic work, like many poor and working-class women of her day, in part motivated her entrance into prostitution, her choice of work was perhaps shaped by other factors. Holiday's brutal sexual assault at the age of eleven, which conceivably led her to become sexually active at a young age, her brief experience as a prostitute at a Baltimore

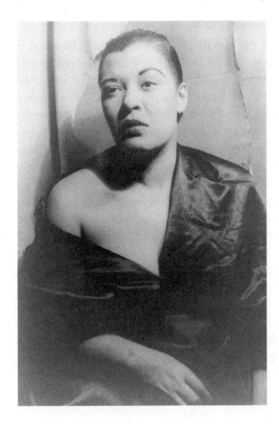

Figure 14: Portrait of Billie Holiday, March 1949. Courtesy of Library of Congress, Prints & Photographs Division, Carl Van Vechten Collection.

sex resort, and seeing or knowing about her mother's (Sadie Fagan) line of work as a sex laborer guided the urban teen into one of New York's oldest professions.[54]

Prostitution was appealing to Holiday and other working-class African American women because they could potentially earn the equivalent of a week's pay of domestic work in an hour or in a single night. Commenting on sex workers' earnings potential, a local newspaper reported that: "some of the ladies of the evening pick up as much as $30 to $50 for a night's work."[55] Bermuda immigrant and Harlem sex worker Bernice Gore informed WPA worker Frank Byrd that she took in boarders, organized rent, and sold sex after her husband ran off and left her with "a sixty-dollar-a-month apartment." Although Gore initially viewed sexual labor as "disgraceful [and] couldn't understand how any self-respecting person could bear" such work, she reasoned that she would be a "fool to go out and break my back scrubbing floors, washing, ironing, and cooking and earn six or seven dollars as a part-time worker when I could earn three days' pay, or more, in fifteen minutes."[56]

While divergent socioeconomic and personal factors influenced women's admission into the urban sex trade, many shared and encountered similar working experiences and certainly endured the burdens of public and community condemnation and personal shame. Interviewing several arrested sex workers at the Women's Night Court, city activist Carietta Owens revealed that many women "showed great concern and shame about [their] situation[s]," exhibiting sorrow and guilt for prostituting themselves.[57] Mortified by their labor choices, some sex workers refused to contact family members when they were arrested for prostitution or hospitalized after an assault. Owens noted that women "admitted to having mothers in New York," but did not want their relatives "to know where they were."[58] Sex workers' refusal to notify loved ones about their legal circumstances or physical conditions stemmed from the understanding that family members disapproved of their lifestyle choices and regarded their work as disgraceful. In many cases, women's families were unaware that they labored as sex workers. Appearing for employment and housing assistance at the Isaac T. Hopper House after completing a sixty-day jail sentence, one streetwalker "refused to give any information about her family," citing that "her people did not [want] to have anything to do with her."[59]

The unbearable realities of sexual labor took an emotional and psychological toll on many African American women, with many suffering from depression, low self-esteem, and alienation—all mental stresses that contributed to alcohol and drug addiction, suicide, and feelings of dissatisfaction with one's life.[60] Internalizing the pain of community shaming and yielding to destructive private thoughts, one sex worker perceived her life as unpromising and wasteful. She lamented: "nothing can be done about it [her life]. Like everyone says, once a prostitute, always a prostitute. [There's] no hope for me."[61] Investigative journalist and undercover streetwalker Vivian Morris's 1939 exposé of prostitution in New York revealed one black sex worker's profound regret for prostituting herself: "I hates it like all hell. I hates myself too fur doin' it. But what the hell are yuh gonna do? What? I ain' got no folks. I'm 22 now, oney 22. Been at it four goddam years. Means I wuz oney 18 when I git started. Why? Cuz I didn't have nobody here an' didn' have no job an' no money. I gotta eat, I gotta live. Hey? I need clothes. Livin' in a stinkin' hole ain' no joke."[62] Exhausted with the nightly grind of street hustling and prostitution, another sex worker commented that she was "getting sick and tired of this life, but what can I do? Christ! I never did anything to deserve a life like this. God! I'd give anything to know what'll become of me!"[63]

Indoor Sex Work

Black women took on varying roles within the urban sex trade, laboring as streetwalkers, brothel proprietors and inmates, and independent sex entrepreneurs—

those without male pimps or handlers. Recognizing the constraints within commercial sexual labor, many black women, when the economic opportunity arose, avoided or limited their work in certain categories of prostitution, namely that of brothel work and street solicitation. Often controlled by madams throughout the Progressive era and later by 1930s New York criminal syndicates, city brothels, which according to scholar Elizabeth Alice Clement experienced a decline by the 1920s with the diffusion of sex work in tenement apartments and nightclubs and an increase in individual sex workers' entrepreneurial spirit, afforded female inmates with relatively safe and semiprivate working and living environments as well as protection from arrest and potentially violent clients. At the same time, brothel work thwarted inmates' visions of occupation control and financial freedom, denying women the ability to select their own clients and placing many in an endless cycle of debt. Visiting a Manhattan "two-dollar [sex] house," a vice agent observed that brothel inmates' wages were hardly their own. Significant portions of women's earnings were paid to brothel madams and proprietors. The vice agent noted that while the "all night price [for a girl was] $20, half of what they earn" pays for food, clothes, and other household provisions.[64] Describing exploitative brothel conditions and organized crime bosses' maltreatment of sex workers, one white prostitute remarked: "All us girls got two meals a day from the madams, but we had to shell out about $18 a week. They worked us six days a week and we received all kinds of men from young punks trying to act like wise guys to old fellas no decent woman would have.[65]

Reinforcing societal patterns of race prejudice and rigid norms concerning interracial sex, some white brothels barred black women, with the exception of those who could racially pass for white, from employment as sex workers at their establishments. But there may be another explanation for black sex workers' absence from white-operated brothels. Recognizing the labor constraints of brothel work, black sex workers perhaps made a conscious decision to avoid this particular work environment. Those considering sex work as a short- or long-term occupation option aspired to engage in labor that afforded them employment flexibility and control and entrepreneurial opportunities. Consequently, labor exclusion from lucrative categories of sex work, as well as financial desperation and the spirit of entrepreneurship pushed many black sex workers into indoor prostitution and onto city streets.

Street-based solicitation afforded independent sex workers, particularly those without pimps or male handlers, employment benefits that were often absent from brothel work. Independent streetwalkers determined their working conditions, retained all their earnings, and interestingly enough catered to some women's propensity for exciting and dangerous lifestyles. Some women, as Christine Ruth Rosen writes, "desired to taste the sporting life," which was a growing part of mid-nineteenth-century urban culture known for gambling, drinking, and brothel and street prostitution.[66] One streetwalker, who enjoyed living on the edge, found "taking any man [she] wanted," and the drama of being pursued by police officers thrilling. "Life on the pavements is rough and raucous, but it has its fascination. The shrill, rasping sound of the police siren or the gruff and commanding voice of the plainclothesmen are elements that give verve to a forbidden career which becomes more glamorous as its futility grows."[67]

The vast majority of streetwalkers, however, were far less enthralled by street-based labor, recognizing the potential dangers of "life on the pavement."[68] Performing what was undoubtedly the most precarious and cheapest form of paid sexual labor, streetwalkers were at the bottom of the sex trade hierarchy and imagined by the public as a "shabby, hunted, exploited group living on the threadbare edge of poverty, victimized by pimps, dope peddlers, and other low elements of the community."[69] Compared to higher-paying sex work, streetwalkers typically earned less income, lacked male protection or often paid underworld figures to protect them, and were expected and known to perform raunchy sexual acts in apartment hallways, taxicabs, darkened alleys, and other semipublic locations. When 1930s sex worker Blanche Simms "didn't have any place" to take male clients she often performed sexual acts in various Harlem apartment building hallways.[70] Observing Harlem street conditions in 1931, one vice officer was taken aback when a twenty-three-year-old streetwalker offered him sex for a dollar in the bathroom of a first-floor apartment building.[71]

A multitude of dangers threatened black sex workers' efforts to earn a living on New York streets. Sex consumers and pimps, police officers, and even competing informal economy workers physically brutalized streetwalkers; these violent and sexual assaults were considered direct consequences of prostitutes' decision-making and often not taken seriously or completely ignored by law enforcers, social workers and reformers, and urban observers. Articulating many urban prostitutes' less familiar reservations and anxieties about street solicitation, one white streetwalker, in an interview with a local journalist, admitted: "you take your life in your hands every time you pick up a guy you don't know. No matter how smart you are, you always run the chance of picking up a bull. And sometimes worse."[72] Black sex workers were certainly aware of the dangers of the street. Many had experienced physical and sexual brutality firsthand or witnessed or heard about other street-walkers' brutal beatings and killings. Speaking to the countless stories of battered streetwalkers, another sex worker maintained that, "terrible things happen to girls in the racket. [They've] been beaten, choked, and one was found dead on a roof. No one ever learned who killed her."[73]

Fear of physical violence and even death prompted many black prostitutes to reconsider and restrict their street presence or when possible avoid street solicitation altogether. But for some economically challenged women, avoiding street labor was virtually impossible, and many found themselves combining street labor with indoor prostitution. One career prostitute, "practicing for about ten years," characterized the majority of her "hustling" as "private." However, when she became "hard pressed for money [she started] solicit[ing] on street corners."[74] Many freelance sex workers preferred indoor prostitution in rented furnished rooms, tenement apartments, and commercial leisure establishments, including nightclubs, speakeasies, and massage parlors. Some women, according to various COF reports, even plied their trade in New York taxicabs. As an alternative geographical space for urban prostitution, indoor sex locations offered black women a variety of socioeconomic opportunities within New York's sex commerce. African American sex workers established and co-managed modest and well-known sex resorts with black and nonblack men and women; they assumed varying positions as madams and madam-prostitutes; labored in less supervised and more causal work environments; and possessed the ability to negotiate working conditions and determine acceptable levels of intimacy with clients. Indoor sex work broadened the urban sex geography, offering sex patrons different sites for sexual pleasure. Moreover, sex work in residential and other semiprivate locations presented black women with the chance to promote and enjoy a wide range of nonmonogamous hetero- and homosexual relationships and sexual activities and performances either openly or privately in their middle- and working-class neighborhoods and households.

The appearance of prostitution in New York's working-class communities and apartments during the early twentieth century was not a surprise to anti-vice reformers. Nor was it uncommon for sex workers and other urbanites to use their living spaces for commercial and labor purposes. "By using their own homes as creative spaces for pay, play, and pleasure," black sex workers were bolstering New York's and African American's blossoming and diverse leisure culture.[75] According to scholar Elizabeth Alice Clement, residential prostitution was a byproduct of several factors that converged in the 1920s, including the selling of illegal alcohol as a consequence of Prohibition and the emergence of rent and buffet-flat parties in tenement apartments. Working in the privacy of their homes or in furnished rooms, some sex workers consciously attempted to conceal their labor from the judgmental gaze of their families, friends, and neighbors. One woman noted that while she sometimes entertained clients in her home, she preferred working out of furnished rooms and hotels. "My reason for that is I don't want the people downstairs who run the place to get on to me, by bringing too many men in. [Sometimes I am] able to sneak the man in without being observed by the people downstairs."[76] Similarly, another sex worker was concerned with her landlady monitoring her behavior and knowing her business. Unable to locate a private place, a sex worker informed her client, an undercover vice officer, that having sex in her apartment was out of the question. Curious about her refusal to have sex with him in her apartment, he asked, "Why can't we do it in your house?" She replied: "the landlady doesn't know much about my business and I can't take you there."[77] Sex workers' refusals to render sexual services in their homes signaled their concerns about their reputations, the spread of neighborhood gossip and community shaming, and perhaps the desire to separate and draw distinctions between their private and professional lives. More importantly, public knowledge about their work and sexual activities could possibly lead to arrest and housing eviction. Under New York state tenement housing laws of the 1920s, building proprietors and landlords, with the blessing of urban moral crusaders and anti-vice crusaders who were concerned about apartment overcrowding, city vice, and the overall quality of urban life, could legally evict tenants who used their living quarters for prostitution, bootlegging, and other immoral purposes.[78]

Black middle-class apartments and neighborhoods were also sites of illegal sexual labor. A 1930s COF investigative report noted that nearly "90% of the tenement speakeasies and the houses of prostitution were located in the well-kept neighborhoods." Sex resorts in fashionable and affluent black communities "offer[ed] "a form of protection under the cloak of assumed respectability."[79] During the late 1930s, twenty-nine-year-old Ida Stokes, who was known as the "colorful and attractive toast of Sugar Hill night life," operated a "disorderly house in one of the Hill's swankiest addresses, 66 St. Nicholas [Avenue]."[80] Similarly, two African American madams jointly operated a "nicely furnished regular eating place and speakeasy" in their apartment on St. Nicolas Avenue. Under the guise of running a "Tea Room," the two sex entrepreneurs, perhaps hoping to double their income, sold "delicious home cooked dinners, [including] sandwiches, salads, steaks, [and] chops." Not only were male clients' sexual desires and fantasies satisfied, so were their stomachs. A plate of chops with a side of salad was as much a part of the clients' party experience as the actual sexual encounter. But the more popular item on the Tea Room menu was sex, which sold for "five dollars plus an additional two dollars for the use of the room."[81]

Clandestine sex work in residential neighborhoods blurred the lines between so-called respectable and fallen women. Residential prostitution made it difficult to distinguish actual paid sexual labor from that of liberated female sexuality. Such indistinct boundaries added to the confusion surrounding women's identities, daily behaviors, labor, and sexual practices.[82] Pleasure-seeking men in search of "reputed joy resorts" failed to distinguish between righteous community women and the "painted concubines" whose company they desired.[83] Additionally, antiprostitution reformers and others in the forefront of vice eradication often mistakenly identified morally upright working- and middle-class black women as prostitutes. In 1927, southern migrant Carrie Adkins's private and sexual conduct came into question when a COF investigator mistook her for a sex worker. Arriving at her Harlem apartment with an armful of groceries, the working-class wife and mother was unexpectedly greeted by a "john" pretending to be interested in purchasing sex. Creating a fictitious story in order to observe Adkins's response, the agent informed her that male patrons at a Harlem cabaret had recommended her place "for a good time." Perplexed by the agent's accusation, Adkins, a self-proclaimed churchgoing woman, adamantly rejected his assumption that she bartered sex for money. In defense of herself, Adkins articulated that she was a model of respectability and domesticity. "I am a Christian woman, 45 years old, the mother of ten children. I am married twice. I have a home in N.Y. and one at Long Branch, N.J."[84]

As residential sex work sometimes resulted in cases of mistaken identities, this form of indoor prostitution provided women like madam-prostitute and brothel owner Lillian Sarati anonymity within their communities. The single thirty-four-year-old Sarati operated a private brothel in her 141st Street apartment. Described by a vice investigator as a "tall and 135 lbs mulatto" with light brown eyes and "bobbed hair," the North Carolina native was born around 1894 and moved to New York some time in the second decade of the twentieth century. Listed as unemployed in the 1920 census, Sarati and her husband Felix Sarati, a mixed-race immigrant from the Philippines who worked as a steward, supplemented their household income by taking in several boarders. Following either the death of or divorce from her husband, Sarati briefly worked in a Manhattan nightclub, continued to take in boarders, and eventually entered the underground labor market. Unlike many widowed or abandoned black women, the absence of Sarati's husband did not put her in financial straits; her "husband left [her] $10,000, but this soon ran through with sporting life, cars, playing races, etc." Pursuit of nightly amusements and luxury material items drastically transformed her financial status from economically comfortable to working poor. To "make a little money" and regain her comfortable lifestyle and material wealth, Sarati operated multiple home-based businesses. The enterprising woman established a brothel with five female inmates, charged white and black sex patrons $2 for a sexual performance, and manufactured and sold illegal alcohol to sex patrons. Few of her neighbors were aware of her line of work or how she, as a single woman, financially supported herself and afforded her extravagant lifestyle.[85]

Discreetly advertising and selling sex in their residential communities, some African American sex workers, regardless of their socioeconomic standing, desired to be perceived in the eyes of their family, friends, and neighbors as decent reputable tenants and even God-fearing churchgoing women. In November 1929, Adam Clayton Powell Sr., pastor of the Abyssinian Baptist Church, was shocked to discover that several seemingly righteous female parishioners were sex workers and buffet-flat organizers.[86] That same month, an *NYA* staff writer informed Powell that members of his ministerial staff and congregation were prostitutes and hosts of immoral social gatherings. In a letter to Powell, the *NYA* journalist charged that prostitution was not only enjoyed by seemingly less-privileged blacks but also by "church members in their homes and buffet flats." The *NYA* writer became privy to the Bible-thumpers' secret sexual activities when he "attended a party [and witnessed] intoxicated women, prominent in society and church, sit opposite men with their feet on the tables smoking cigarettes." He further informed the well-respected Harlem minister that he would provide him with the "addresses of a dozen buffet flats in Harlem, several of them being run by women of your church."[87] Powell interpreted the churchwomen's alleged private social gatherings and sexual activities as a "parody of Christianity" and an embarrassment for the oldest black Baptist church in the state of New York. Confirming some of the writer's allegations, Powell, in his 1938 memoir *Against the Tides*, embarrassingly admitted that one of his dedicated and outwardly devout church members, among "the loudest shouters of the Sunday Morning Praying Band," and her twelve-year-old syphilis-infected daughter were prostitutes. Powell and Abyssinian church members discovered the woman and her child's extralegal labor when the two were arrested and sentenced to four months on Blackwell Island. Tragically, the child sex worker, falling victim to the many consequences of prostitution, died of syphilis at the tender age of fourteen.[88]

Powell's 1938 account does not offer details on the woman and her child or on the nature of their work and economic circumstance. Nor did the prominent Harlem minister offer an insight as to why the woman turned to New York's sex commerce. Given many urban working-class black women's dire economic and unemployment status during the era of the Great Depression, the churchgoing woman perhaps was the sole breadwinner of her household, was unemployed, or needed another source of income to supplement low wages from formal labor. Compared to black and white men and white women, the economic crisis of the 1930s hit black women the hardest, causing many to make often hard and desperate labor decisions. Conceivably, this woman viewed sex work as a last-ditch effort to make fast cash and financially provide for herself and her daughter. Even more telling about this family's economic circumstance was the mother's troubling and more than likely painful choice to prostitute her teenage daughter for money. Side-by-side on New York streets and corners mother and daughter might have selected male clients together and protected one another from police and possibly violent customers. No doubt experiencing feelings of guilt for her and her daughter's predicament, the woman, one of the "loudest shouters" in the church, likely viewed the religious center as a way to cope with feelings of immorality, shame, and disappointment.

Bourgeois, religious, or even educated African Americans who secretly entered New York's sex trade, either as sex entrepreneurs, pleasure seekers, sex party attendees, or organizers, were not uncommon. In 1930, after visiting several Harlem and Brooklyn sex houses, a COF agent reported that his assumptions about urban black sex workers' class and educational backgrounds did not always coincide with his field investigative work. After talking with several women, the agent discovered that some "madam-prostitutes were college trained [and] three were former students of a well-known Negro institution."[89] Factors influencing educated and better-class women's admission into sex work are unrecorded in many surviving documents. Apparently, many failed to conform to prevailing public images of urban sex sellers. Formally educated, middle-class, and churchgoing women did not solicit men on city streets or perform sexual activities in public spaces, and often their violation of normative sexual practices had little to do with finances. Their journey into commercialized sex was fueled by uninspiring and sheltered home lives, sexual curiosity and experimentation, or the belief that sexuality and intimacy, to the chagrin of fellow race advocates, was something that should be explored, especially outside the confines of marriage and heterosexual relationships. By departing from prevailing public images of neighborhood sex entrepreneurs, female parishioners and other educated and financially comfortable women outwardly subscribed to female propriety yet secretly embraced a politics of individuality and pleasure. They used outward performances of morality to conceal behavior inconsistent with organized religious practices and morality. Simultaneously embodying conflicting public and private personas, well-to-do sex workers attended reputable social and religious functions, were held in high regard by their unsuspecting neighbors, and served as leading community advocates.

Some black women were indifferent about maintaining a low profile, caring little about community perceptions of them as prostitutes. These sex workers were unashamed about how they earned a living and publicly advertised their services and their longing for sexual pleasure. Female sex sellers' apathy about their work was often displayed in their behavior in public and semipublic settings. Taking a chance on being apprehended and attempting to increase their clientele, women deliberately flaunted their sexuality. They wore provocative clothes and indiscreetly whistled at and called out to potential male clients from apartment windows, hallways, and entryways. In a 1930s letter to New York Urban League officials, Harlem resident Frances Watkins complained about the "indecent behavior" of a known sex worker living in her building. Watkins observed that the prostitute, who was also the mother of two girls, brazenly "sits on the stoop all day long, [and] attracts the attention of white men as they pass and invites them into her apartment."[90] COF investigations into vice conditions in 1930s Brooklyn reveal that residential prostitutes working either collectively or individually unapologetically solicited in their communities. Scantily clad women dressed in form-fitting dresses and underclothes as outer garments could be seen standing in their apartment doorways waiting for potential customers to pass or running "off the stoops and deliberately bump[ing] into men." The Brooklyn vice agent recalled that his street strolling and observations of the borough's immoralities were interrupted by "three women [who] ran over to me, grabbed me by the arm, and said, 'What do you say, boy, do you want to go upstairs?'"[91]

Commercial leisure businesses, including nightclubs, cabarets, cigar and candy shops, motion picture theaters, and nightclubs and speakeasies, were also integral sites of sex solicitation for women who maintained a bold disregard for public propriety. New York City's 1896 Raines Law inadvertently increased sex workers' presence in urban commercial amusements. Enacted as a temperance statute, the ordinance was intended to curb drinking; it closed saloons on Sundays and prohibited any businesses with the exception of hotels from selling alcohol on the Sabbath. The controversial legislation permitted only those hotels with ten beds or more to serve alcohol to customers. Rather than protecting the Sabbath and controlling alcohol consumption as intended, the Raines Law produced new venues for prostitution. Cleverly evading the city statute, commercial leisure business owners placed ten or more beds in their backrooms, permitting sex workers to rent out beds. Popular leisure establishments served as new sites for sexual transactions and performances and ethnic and racial interactions. In turn, sex workers became major participants in the city's burgeoning nightlife, forging new partnerships with urban business owners and devising new ways of earning a living and asserting control over their professional lives.[92]

Sex workers brokered business arrangements with theater and nightclub proprietors and other business owners who encouraged prostitution at their establishments. During the early twentieth century, "nightclubs, highly dynamic cultural institution[s], were a typical booming service industry" as well as locations for open sexual labor and sexuality.[93] "Nightclubs," according to historian Lewis Erenberg, "helped form the mystique of the big city. They provided a setting for the fantasies money might buy. In the same club could be found socialites, wealthy gamblers, ethnic entertainers, young college folk, and business couples, all enjoying themselves with the social barriers down."[94] Nightclub proprietors, in exchange for an increase in the number of male patrons and boosts in alcohol and food sales, permitted casual sex workers, madams, and brothel inmates to "stroll into their places of establishment" acting as enticing visual advertisements. White madam Polly Adler contended that nightclub solicitation improved her business. "Clubs were a display window" for prostitutes, she stated. "When I'd walk in, surrounded by my loveliest girls, it was always a show-stopper, and as a result of all this publicity business got better and better."[95] Business owners also marketed women's sex resorts, distributing their business cards and providing nightclub patrons and partygoers with the names and locations of nearby sex workers and their houses of pleasure.

New York nightclubs like the Barron Wilkins Exclusive Club—an interracial Harlem cabaret located on 134th Street and Seventh Avenue known for promoting the careers of African American musicians such as Duke Ellington and Ada "Bricktop" Smith and offering its patrons exotic shows and gambling—enlisted and encouraged their female staff of waitresses, entertainers, and hostesses to moonlight as prostitutes and mix work chores. At different city nightspots, it was not uncommon for female nightclub or speakeasy employees to wear multiple laboring hats. Women danced and sang, waited tables, and occasionally offered partygoers sexual pleasure. For instance, in April 1927, a white anti-vice investigator visited the popular club, asking a black waiter about the possibility of "having fun with some sporting girls." Although the waiter initially appeared skeptical of the agent and pretended to "not know anything about that," his suspicions dissipated and he "called a short colored girl entertainer" to the investigator's table." Understanding perfectly the agent's request, the women wrote down her name and address, "239 W. 139th Street," and her price for one hour: "I charge $5" because "I have my own room. This is a furnished room house and all you do is to ring the bell, ask for me and they will call me."[96] In a 1928 COF annual report, vice investigators reported that out of "998 hostesses employed in 380 [Manhattan] resorts, 544 admitted being prostitutes."[97] Twenty-seven-year-old Miss Johnson earned dual incomes at the Blue Ribbon Chile Parlor on 131st Street; she worked as a waitress-hostess and sex worker. Often propositioned for sex by male clients while she waited tables, Johnson increased her nightly wages by promising sex patrons a "little party as soon as [she got] through fixing food" and serving restaurant customers.[98] Performing multiple labor tasks at after-hours establishment was economically beneficial for some women. Many augmented low incomes with customer tips and potentially increased their clientele. However, taking on varying labor positions left women physically exhausted from constantly entertaining club patrons and feeling exploited—by themselves and by their employers.

Selecting Sex Patrons

The freedom to select clients was a benefit of indoor prostitution; it provided a choice often based on race and ethnicity and the ability to discern whether a potential sex patron had money. Although many black sex workers welcomed interracial sexual encounters with white men, others preferred intraracial sex and operated sex businesses that catered to nonwhite men (African American, Asian, and Hispanic). In 1929, after visiting sixty-one Harlem brothels, one vice squad agent recorded that of the fifty-six establishments operated by black madams, at least eight entertained white patrons.[99] [Similar to how many racially and ethnically diverse men were excluded from some white sex houses, some black pleasure resorts catered only to nonwhite men's sexual fantasies and fetishes.] A 1930s COF prostitution report found several black-controlled brothels that managed "colored and white prostitutes almost exclusively for "negro patrons." Preference for nonwhite johns stemmed from the level of comfort black women felt with members of their own race or other men of color. Additionally, some sex workers distrusted and were skeptical of white male leisure seekers in black districts and were reluctant to render services to them, especially in their homes. Certainly aware of the different ways in which law enforcers and anti-vice agents used to curb interracial sociability and urban prostitution, black sex workers believed that white "Good Time Charlies" hoping to "make a little party" with them were plainclothes cops or criminal informants intending to physically assault them or entrap and arrest them for solicitation. Perceptions of urban white men as major actors within the functioning of unbridled state-sanctioned violence against women of African descent caused black sex workers to limit or have no interactions with nonblack men.

Conversely, other black sex workers preferred and welcomed interracial sex and created businesses almost exclusively aimed at white men.[100] Black sex workers' preference for white men stemmed from widespread assumptions that such men were naive and could be easily conned or coaxed into paying more money for sex. A 1938 *NYAN* editorial posited that Harlem sex workers "openly solicit white men into Negro sections and dwellings—all for a few dollars. Negro men are not wanted by [these] Negro women."[101] Black sex workers found it difficult to overcharge and negotiate higher rates for sex with African American men, citing their tendency to haggle for lower sex prices. Assuming that a well-dressed black client (an undercover vice agent) had "plenty of money," prostitute "Bessie Amos," who was the estranged wife of Louis C. Whitfield, "one of the largest Negro real estate dealers in Harlem," informed him that her price was $5. After he complained that the price was too high, Amos, in frustration and hoping to make a quick buck, lowered the price to $1. Feeling cheated by the "male client," Amos "cursed" him "good and strong," telling him she usually "objected to staying with Negros anyway." "[I] could get anything [I] want from a white man, and white men never question [me] anyway."[102] Criticizing some black women's active pursuit of interracial sex with white men, a *Chicago Defender* writer contended that black women "really feel honored to be the garbage can for white men, knowing these men have no intentions for good but only seek their bodies for pleasure of their own selves. Such women should be ostracized from the ranks of our race and left to work out [their own] salvation, as they drag down our race with shame." Some black sex workers' desire for white patrons was closely tied to their economic pursuits.[103]

As white pleasure seekers ventured into African American communities, black sex workers took advantage of white men's desire for "high brown babies" and their curiosities about black female sexuality. Moreover, they strategically played on white clients' perceptions of them as sexual deviants and hypersexual beings in order to command and negotiate higher fees for cross-racial sex.[104] Madam-prostitute Maybelle Curry informed an African American COF agent that: "her price for the act of prostitution varied according to whether the man was white or colored." If he was white, Curry typically charged between $4 and $5; however, if he was African American, "she would commit the act for $3." Black madams Margie Lee and Ida Davis financially benefited from entertaining white men at their Manhattan sex house. One frequent white client of Lee and Davis noted that, "you could come around here with $500 in your pocket and walk out without a penny."[105]

Securing more money from nonblack sex clients was not the primary reason some black women preferred white customers. Sex worker turned renowned blues singer Billie Holiday preferred white sex patrons because she did not want to deal with smooth-talking and narcissistic black men. In her autobiography *Lady Sings the Blues*, Holiday explained that: "with my regular white customers, it was a cinch. They had wives and kids to go home to. When they came to see me, it was wham, bang, they gave me the money and were gone. But Negroes would keep you up all the damn night, handing you that stuff about 'Is it good, baby?' and 'Don't you want to be my old lady?'"[106] "As a general rule," another sex worker avoided "solicit[ing] colored men [and] operated [only with] Chinese, Filipino, and Porto Ricans." She "adopted this policy because someday she might decide to marry a Negro man and no other Negro man [will] be able to say anything about her that her husband might hear. If [I] should marry and pass some of the Chinese or Spanish fellows who know [me] they would talk their language and nothing would be understood."[107] Illicit cross-racial sexual encounters permitted sex workers to protect their names and reputations from neighborhood gossip and to reserve sexual and emotional intimacies for black men. Furthermore, interracial sex did not ruin black women's chances of marrying men of African descent.[108]

By exclusively soliciting white men, African American prostitutes created a hierarchy among black sex businesses that was based on ethnicity and skin complexion. Black sex houses that catered to white men boasted of their selection of beautiful white and light-skinned black women. Recognizing the historical complexities and connotations of skin color and the social and financial advantages of possessing lighter skin, sex houses placed a higher economic value on "mulattoes" and "high yellow complexion" and white prostitutes.[109] Interracial sex offered white men access to African American women's bodies and reaf-firmed their continued domination over black women. Since the era of slavery, white manhood and patriarchy were predicated upon white men's access and ability to debase the black female body. In fact, some white men viewed inter-racial sex with black women, either voluntarily or by force, as a rite of passage into manhood, and as part of a larger patriarchal culture that legitimized and rewarded racial and sexual violence against black women. For instance, white prospective fraternity pledges at The City College of New York were encouraged by organizational members to have intercourse with a black prostitute. Accord-ing to the fraternity brothers, this initiation task would prove their manhood and racial superiority and ensure membership into the organization. "One does not became a man until he has had a black woman and can not be considered for membership in [the] fraternity until [he] becomes a man."[110]

Historian Cynthia Blair suggests that white men's access to and viewing of black female sexual acts, especially those that involved same-sex activities, resembled the racial dynamics of nineteenth- and early-twentieth-century minstrel shows. Performing in blackface, minstrel show performers entertained white audiences by distorting and mimicking African American mannerisms and culture. Highly racist in their depictions of black life, minstrel shows reinforced white supremacy and bolstered whites' belief that persons of African descent were innately inferior and suitable for only menial labor and entertainment purposes. In a similar fashion, black sex workers' public and private sexual performances not only fulfilled white men's sexual fantasies, they affirmed preconceived notions that black women were sexual commodities to be looked at, owned, and demeaned.[111]

But urban white men's closeted desires for black sex workers and fantasies about interracial sex—and in some cases sexual violence—came at a price. Indeed, their sexual encounters with black sex workers left some vulnerable to sex-related crimes, including "creep joint" and "badger games." Badger and creep joint women, either con women who used the pretense of sex to rob men or actually prostitutes that doubled as swindlers, cleverly used their knowledge of urban white men's amusement habits and fantasies and their assumptions about black female sexu-ality for their own economic advantage. According to one high-ranking police official, such women "rob white men with impunity, especially those who look respectable and well-dressed."[112] Playing on outward expressions of femininity and respectability, badger women, some wearing flattering dresses, hats, and jewelry, lured men into their apartments, tenement hallways, and other isolated spaces; their male or female accomplice, usually armed with weapons, hid in the background waiting for the opportunity to deprive hapless men of their money, clothes, and valuables.[113] Creep joint women cunningly distracted men with sexual intercourse while their co-conspirators quietly robbed them. Accomplices went

	No. 13761						Name Loulie Smith

POLICE DEPARTMENT
CITY OF NEW YORK.
Detective Bureau.
No. 53.

Bertillon Measurements.

L. Foot, 23.0
Mid. F. 10.6
Lit. F. 7.8
Fore A. 42.6

Head Length, 18.3+
Head Width, 14.5
Len. 5.6
R. Ear,

Height, 1.60.2
Outer Arms, 1.62.0
Trunk, 84.1

Name Loulie Smith
Alias
Crime Badger
Age 31   Height 5 Ft. 3½ In.
Weight 106 lbs.   Build Slim
Hair Black   Eyes Black
Comp. Dark   Moustache
Born U. S.
Occupation Dressmaker
Date of Arrest October 22, 1907
Officer Joseph Glennon, 23d
Remarks Wears wig and ears pierced

Figure 15a and 15b: Dressmaker and badger Loulie Smith arrested in 1907. Courtesy NYC Municipal Archives.

Figure 16a and 16b: Domestic worker and badger Nellie Vance arrested in 1908. Courtesy NYC Municipal Archives.

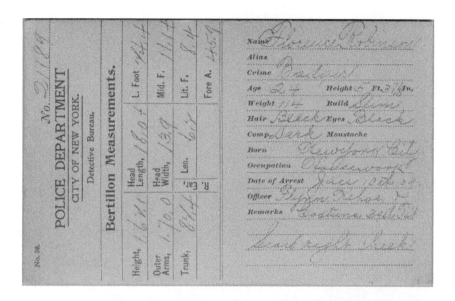

Figure 17a and 17b: Domestic worker and badger Florence Robinson arrested in 1909. Courtesy NYC Municipal Archives.

No. 58   122—09 (B) 65,000

(Sub№.____25380

POLICE DEPARTMENT
CITY OF NEW YORK
Detective Bureau

Bertillon Measurements

		Head			
Height,	1.50.5	Head Length,	17.5	L. Foot,	22.5
Outer Arms,	1.56.0	Head Width,	13.%	Mid. F.	10.6
Trunk,	79.0	R. Ear. Len.	5.6	Lit. F.	8.1
				Fore A.	42.5

Name   Annie Harris

Alias

Crime   Badger

Age 21   Height 4 Ft. 11¼ In.

Weight 105   Build Mod.

Hair Black   Eyes Black

Comp. Dark   Moustache

Born   Virginia

Occupation Housework

Date of Arrest September 1, 1910

Officer Rudly, 32nd pct.

Remarks 2 scars over right brow.

Figure 18a and 18b: Domestic worker and badger Annie Harris arrested in 1910. Courtesy NYC Municipal Archives.

through victims' pockets and wallets and stole valuable effects and money. Creep joint participants then replaced stolen money with "pieces of newspapers cut the size of paper money, and inserted the paper in the wallet in place of the real bills."[114] Both creep joint and badger crimes, often aimed at nonblack men, reflected black women's "broader resentment toward the prolonged denigration of [their] woman-hood and sexuality, and against male patriarchy and racist hypocrisy."[115] Moreover, both creep joint and badger crimes served as an additional way for some economi-cally struggling prostitutes to augment the low wages they earned from sex work.

New York newspapers continually reported on the increasing problem of white men seeking a "good time with colored women and experiencing grief." In 1929, forty-five-year-old Howard King was robbed, beaten, and stabbed when he made the unfortunate decision to have sex with Ethel Jackson, a streetwalker and thief. King's "good time" with Jackson quickly turned violent when her male partners "relieved [him] of thirty-two dollars, one new hat, a pair of eyeglasses, and a pen and pencil."[116] King's unfortunate experience was "only one of many cases reported to the police by men who visit 'creep joints' where harlots rob their victims."[117] White men who reported how "black harlots" victimized them were ostracized for

Figure 19: Harlem sex worker and alleged murderer Blanche Simms. Simms killed white firefighter Frederick Supanic in 1938. Courtesy of Weegee (Arthur Fellig) International Center of Photography/contributor.

breaching racial and sexual mores, engaging in extramarital affairs, and frequenting black districts. One city official maintained that "a [white] man actually takes his life in his hands when he walks through the streets of Harlem." White New Yorkers believed that white men foolish enough to socialize in the city's well-known vice districts searching for urban pleasures got what they deserved.[118]

Sometimes white men's encounters with black sex workers turned deadly. Consider, for instance, the physical altercation between Blanche Simms and white fireman Frederick Supanic. In October 1938, Simms, a twenty-nine-year-old married prostitute and alleged "dope addict," was arrested for killing Supanic.[119] What the reading public understood about the crime derived from Simms's police interrogation and trial testimonies. Confessing to the murder, Simms claimed that she killed Supanic in self-defense during a dispute over money. For $1, Supanic had sexual intercourse with Simms in an apartment building hallway at 205 West 115th Street. Not satisfied with Simms's services, Supanic demanded a refund. The firefighter's request for his money was embedded in the historic notion that white men could assert their authority and superiority over poor and working black women. Additionally, Supanic's request signaled many urban white men's perspective on black women and their formal and informal labor. White men like Supanic imagined black female's labor as cheap and solely for white consumption and as something that was not their own and could be exploited at any time. Vehemently resisting Supanic's demand and asserting her control over her labor, the money-strapped Simms refused to return the fireman's money. Consequently, and according to her police testimony: "he beat me [and] I drew a knife, stabbed him, and ran. He caught me and tried to throw me over a railing, and it was then that [I] sank [the] switchblade into his heart. It was either his life or mine. I did it in self-defense."[120] Claiming self-defense as a legal strategy was problematic for Simms and other African Americans accused of committing crimes against whites. Blacks' assaults on whites violated racial mores intended to subordinate blacks and represented an audacious challenge to white supremacy. Rigid race relations and customs dictated that it was never justified for blacks to use physical force against whites. When Simms physically defended herself from Supanic's alleged attack, she was unconsciously breaking from a tradition of brutality against black women. In November 1938, Simms was charged with and found guilty of manslaughter and sentenced to eight to sixteen years at the Bedford Hills Reformatory.[121]

Black Women's Thoughts on Sexualized Labor

In 1935, Mississippi-born blues singer Lucille Bogan, professionally known as Bessie Jackson, recorded the song "Shave 'Em Dry," a widely popular song that highlighted a sex worker's impenitent description of her sexual prowess and endurance and her overwhelming appetite for physical stimulation and gratification. Purposely pushing and complicating the boundaries of traditional sexual scripts while offering blues listeners diverse imageries of sexualities, Bogan powerfully sang: "Want you to grind me baby, grind me until I cry. Say I fucked all night, and all the night before, baby. And I feel just like I wanna fuck some more. Oh great God daddy, grind me honey and shave me dry. Now if fuckin' was the thing that would take me to heaven, I'd be fuckin' in the studio till the clock strike eleven. My back is made of whalebone, and my cock is made of brass, and my fuckin' is made for workin' men's two dollars, Great God, round to kiss my ass."[122]

Bogan and her provocative lyrics and music were part of a trajectory of 1920s and 1930s African American female blues performers, including Bessie Smith, Ma Rainey, and Bertha "Chippie" Hill, who brazenly affirmed black women as sexual beings and celebrated female eroticism while clearly breaking from standard sexual norms. Scholar Hazel Carby contends that blues women, through their highly provocative songs and stage performances, "play[ed] out and explore[d] the various possibilities of a sexual existence; they are representations of women who attempt to manipulate and control their construction as sexual objects."[123] Exhibiting a more nuanced and perhaps more realistic imagery of black women's wide-ranging sexual experiences and practices, blues women defied turn-of-the-twentieth-century black liberation strategies and performances that directed women of African descent to remain silent about and conceal their sexuality and, as suggested by sociologist Shayne Lee, to "think conservatively about sexuality and scrupulously supervise their representation to avoid participating in the historical legacy of sexual stereotyping and exploitation."[124]

Aside from sexually explicit blues music and performances, evidence of black women's multifaceted ways of articulating and displaying sexual propriety or pleasure and fulfillment appears in a variety of archival materials. Historian Cheryl Hicks's pioneering work on early-twentieth-century black women inmates at several New York State prisons (including Bedford Hills) offers new methodological approaches to extracting working-class black women's veiled perspectives and conversations on sexuality. Examining prison records and private letters from female inmates to family members, close friends, and jail officials, Hicks demonstrates that black female offenders, when discussing their sexual histories, embraced a politics of silence yet openly identified themselves as sexual beings. "Answering the explicit questions that Bedford administrators asked all women during the admissions process," black women "revealed sexual experiences that exemplified a variety of behaviors, including desire, ignorance, and abuse."[125] New York prison women's expressions of diverse sexual scripts exhibited the full spectrum of black female sexuality. Similarly, glimpses of sex workers' varying attitudes about sexual labor, desire, love, intimacy, and sexual violence appears in anti-vice investigative reports, halfway-house admissions and exit records, newspaper accounts, and sex workers' candid interviews with New York journalists and writers. These extant archival records reveal more than black sex workers' silence or openness about their sexual lives. Materials unearth sex workers' aspirations about their labor and economic futures, their subscription to and reworking of traditional middle- and working-class values, and their construction and negotiation of diverse sexual landscapes.

Widely accepted societal views of prostitution portrayed sex workers as women who were promiscuous and depraved, and who had uncontrollable sexual desires. Urban black women that traded sex for financial stability or sexual satisfaction, or in order to obtain narcotics and alcohol, were typically perceived as individuals who defined themselves as purely sexual beings. While some sex laborers embraced the concept of "illicit eroticism," all did not define themselves by their occupation nor did they consider themselves to be impecunious fallen women. In other words, early-twentieth-century sex workers were not what they seemed or appeared to be, and, as scholar Tricia Rose reminds us in her conversation on black women's sexuality, they did not narrowly define their sexuality or sexual experiences. Beyond public perceptions, black sex workers viewed themselves in a variety of ways: as daughters, mothers, and wives; as workers; as pleasure seekers and givers; and as religious and spiritual beings. As multifaceted individuals, they maintained and articulated complex, lucid, and conflicting outlooks on sexual labor and sexuality, intimacy and pleasure, and morality. Speaking to an admissions employee at the Isaac T. Hopper Home during the late 1930s, one sex worker, hoping to receive relief and financial support from the facility, considered herself a spiritual person despite her line of work and her family's and friends' criticism of her labor choices. Raised in what she described as a strict Christian home, her understanding of monogamous sexual relationships fell within the context of marriage. However, the harsh realities of poverty led her at times to temporarily abandon and negotiate personal rigid interpretations of sexual intercourse and moral values, substituting for them ideas that situated sexual relations outside of matrimony. For her and many other women, sexual activities became viable sources of income that could be used in times of economic hardship. Despite succumbing to prostitution, the young woman viewed herself as a spiritual person, "praying daily" that God would remedy her economic circumstances.[126] As prostitutes struggled to maintain individual moral standards, they articulated alternative readings on conventional religious practices. Such nuance perspectives enabled women to justify their participation in New York's sex commerce.

Some black women interpreted sexual labor primarily as a business, making a conscious effort to separate their working life from their private world. Sex workers strove to maintain a level of professionalism with male clients. Professional attitudes on prostitution were fueled by a myriad of circumstances, including but not limited to women's troubling past experiences with johns, same-sex desires, and their decision to reserve intimate sexual relations for individuals whom they loved or cared about. Moreover, some sexual workers' professionalism signaled the belief that prostitution was one aspect of their lives; it was part of their laboring lives and did not represent who they were as individuals. In their interactions with customers, sex workers withheld personal information about themselves, avoided intimate interactions with male patrons, and often performed quick, emotionless, and mechanical sexual acts. Jan MacKell's study on turn-of-the-twentieth-century prostitution in Colorado contends that "when it came to the actual act," some women "removed only the essential clothing to transact their business, then dressed, without even looking" at the client.[127] Physical and psychological detachment from men permitted sex workers control over their work and emotions. For Harlem sex workers like WPA interviewee "Big Bess," also known by Harlem police as "Lenox Avenue Bess," prostitution was merely an economic undertaking and one that rarely yielded any physical or sexual pleasure. Because of her experience with several emotionally and physically abusive men—which led to her being imprisoned in Chicago for five years on a manslaughter charge for killing her former lover—Big Bess felt only disdain for men, regarding them, at least perhaps for moments in her life, as her "pet hate." Although Big Bess made "her living by being nice to" men, her contempt for urban men looking for a few minutes or hours of sexual stimulation fostered her sexual and emotional withdrawal from men. Detachment from the opposite sex did not necessarily mean that Big Bess was sexually attracted to women or desired emotional support from them; it does imply that her detachment from male clients was her way of not conflating her work with her personal life. By all accounts, Big Bess, like many sexual laborers, obtained only what she needed from male patrons: money.[128]

Other prostitutes viewed sex work not only as an economic prospect but also as an opportunity to step outside the confines of mundane and monotonous sex. Sex work offered New York women the space to assert their wide-ranging sexual subjectivities and to explore unfixed and unregulated sexual practices and sites of pleasure. Indeed, as sexual laborers, black women were not only interested in offering erotic amusement to their clients; many were also interested in receiving sexual pleasure. Analyzing urban and rural amusement spaces, scholar Robin D. G. Kelley posits that African Americans' pursuits of social pleasures, including attending dances and parties and participating in nonconventional sexual performances, were part of their attempts "to escape from the world of assembly lines, relief lines, and color lines, and to leave momentarily the individual and collective battles against racism, sexism, and material deprivation."[129] For black women, both formal and underground laborers, escape from the drudgery of household work and family life—if only for a couple of hours or one night—was important to their emotional and psychological well-being. After-hours entertainment spots and other social settings served as supportive spaces that facilitated candid conversations about urban inequalities, labor exploitation, politics, and family issues, and allowed female attendees to check respectable politics at the door. Moreover, such social venues made it acceptable for black women, those expected to confine to the rigid boundaries of female civility and deportment, to actively and unapologetically explore the full range of their sexuality without being criticized.

Black sex workers' desire for labor spaces that offered sexual excitement and variety was evident in their attending and organizing of "pussy parties," "sex circuses," and buffet flats. Popular during the Jazz Age, buffet flats, usually held in tenement apartments, were private parties known for entertaining male and female patrons with gambling, live music, sex shows, and prostitution. According to Stephen Robertson, "buffet flats [by the late 1920s] had become a more important location for prostitution than better-known cabarets and speakeasies."[130] Also part of the 1930s pansy and lesbian craze, buffet flats as well as other private apartment gatherings served as intimate settings for homosexuals to socialize freely and engage in same-sex intercourse without public condemnation.[131] Moreover, buffet-flat party attendees explored and acted out their sexual fantasies and broadened their sense of sexual fulfillment. Early-twentieth-century buffet flats and other private amusements became viable economic venues for women like thirty-five-year-old Harlem madam Virgie "Cotton" Canfield to earn a living. "Buffet flat proprietors [like Canfield] not only claimed new and contested territory for the urban leisure and sex trades but also operated within a competitive context of proliferating commercialized amusements."[132] Canfield operated a brothel house and organized buffet-flat parties, catering to both hetero- and homosexuals. At Canfield's establishment, guests chose from a selection of attractive men and women and engaged in erotic sexual performances and fetishes. Vice investigator Raymond Claymes's 1928 reports vividly described what he considered unusual sexual activities at one of Canfield's "freakish" parties. Claymes, who was also "solicited for an act of perversion by one of [Canfield's male guests]," observed fifteen girls and a "few fairies [men] dancing indecently. The women were dancing with one another and going through the motions of copulation, and the men were dancing with one another. The men were fairies and also dancing indecently. A number of the women had their dresses pulled up to their thighs." One of Canfield's female sex workers, attempting to gauge Claymes's sexual preference and interest, informed him that mostly "everyone in here is supposed to be a bull dagger. A bull dagger was a woman who goes through the motion of copulations with another woman, using her 'boy in the boat' to tickle the other one." Making it clear that he was not interested in sexual encounters with men, Claymes informed the woman that he enjoys sex the "normal way." The twenty-three-year-old sex worker with bobbed hair then solicited Claymes, telling him that she charged $5 to commit an act of prostitution.[133]

Throughout the 1930s, the Daisy Chain was one of New York City's most popular buffet flats. Located at 101 West 140th Street in Harlem, the Daisy Chain, also known as the 101 Ranch, was operated by married Harlem entertainer and chorus dancer Hazel Valentine. A well-known New York actress-singer, Valentine appeared in several local and international musical productions including the 1925 Paris production of *Revue Negre*, starring Josephine Baker, and *Tan Town Topics* (1926) at Harlem's Lafayette Theater.[134] Although Valentine was not a prostitute, her parties served as a space for sex workers to advertise their businesses and pander to partygoers' extraordinary sexual fetishes. Valentine used her professional relationships and connections with fellow chorus girls and jazz musicians, including Thomas "Fats" Wright Waller, Billie Holiday, and William James "Count" Basie to publicize her exclusive parties. Descriptions of Valentine's popular "sex palace" were captured in the testimonials of its patrons and several 1930s Harlem entertainers and journalists. Jazz bassist George "Pops" Foster remembered the Daisy Chain as "a house of prostitution and drinks and everything. Women goin' with women, men goin' with men, nobody paid it any mind, everybody was gay and havin' a ball. [It] was a big railroad flat house, with these rooms over here and rooms over there and a long hall, and you'd see people on the floor getting' their thing. You had to pay $5 apiece, and everybody got buck naked and everybody was ballin. Half coloured, half white. Hell yeah, real integrated."[135] In 1977, *NYAN* columnist Dan Burley recalled that Valentine's "after-hours joint" was known as the "traditional 'Training Camp' in bedroom rodeos for the idle sons of the Park and Fifth Avenue rich."[136]

The Daisy Chain and its fashionable proprietor were even commemorated in song by some of the nation's leading jazz and blues musicians. In 1929, Fats Waller, best known for compositions such as "Ain't Misbehavin,'" composed "Valentine Stomp," and bandleader Count Basie wrote "Swingin' at the Daisy Chain" in 1937.[137] Discussing the Daisy Chain's influence on African American musicians like Waller and Basie, Progressive-era blues composer and musician William Christopher Handy posited that the establishment's endless flow of alcohol, beautiful women, and sex served as a muse for African American singers, composers, and songwriters. "If Fats Waller could be locked up in a room at the 'Daisy Chain' with a piano, a bottle of gin and several beautiful chicks, he would certainly come up with some of the most beautiful music written this side of Heaven." Waller's biographer, Ed Kirkeby, noted that the talented musician spent so much time at Valentine's house of pleasure that he "paid the rent at the Daisy Chain on more than one occasion when things weren't going too well.[138]

During the 1920s and 1930s, Valentine and the "best known buffet flat in Harlem" were entangled in several highly publicized scandals. In July 1926, Valentine was arrested at her 127th Street apartment for shooting her husband, Albert. While the sex- and music-filled Daisy Chain was not established until some time in the 1930s, Hazel Valentine's small apartment soirees were well known among local musicians and entertainers and regular Harlem partygoers. This particular social gathering was in celebration of Hazel's return from performing in Europe. The physical altercation between the Valentines occurred when Albert entered the couple's apartment and discovered that his wife was hosting a small party "attended by [a few female friends] and several men." Objecting to both the party and the presence of strange men in his home, Albert "summoned his wife into an adjoining room and a heated argument ensued" and turned violent. Hazel, perhaps afraid of her husband or frustrated by his attempt to control her social activities, shot him in the upper torso. Albert Valentine was rushed to Manhattan's Mount Sinai Hospital, and his wife was arrested for assault. Initially, Hazel Valentine admitted that she assaulted her husband in self-defense, claiming he struck her several times in the face. During her court appearance, however, Hazel completely denied shooting her husband, declaring she was "excited when she made the admission." Conceivably desiring to privately resolve his marital dispute and prevent his wife's imprisonment, Albert testified that since he was "shot from behind [he] don't know who fired the shot." Consequently, the court Magistrate dismissed the case against the popular entertainer.[139]

In the late 1930s, Valentine's Daisy Ranch was under the watchful eye of city prosecutor Thomas Dewey. Appointed in 1935 to the position of New York County Special Prosecutor by Governor Herbert Lehman, the young attorney, who made a name for himself both as a federal prosecutor and as a Wall Street attorney, waged a legal battle against New York's underworld, particularly numbers and prostitution racketeers, organized Mafia bosses, and corrupt politicians and city police who manipulated city government through bribery, payoffs, and intimidation.[140] In January 1936, Dewey with the assistance of Eunice Hunton Carter and his team of assistant district attorneys, orchestrated a series of raids on eighty city brothels. That spring, Dewey also prosecuted one of New York's most infamous sex racketeers: Charles "Lucky" Luciano. Three years later, Dewey and the NYPD raided Hazel Valentine's trendy nightspot. According to one published account, the apartment raid was part of citywide initiatives to rid working- and middle-class communities of prostitution and other forms of vice. The notorious Daisy Chain was "cracked and its feminine links were sent to prison, while the big-shot procurers who waxed rich off the vice spectacle either went to the penitentiary or skipped town."[141] Limited primary documentation fails to reveal if Hazel Valentine was among the arrested or if she was fortunate enough to evade city officials.

Conclusion

Urban vice squad reports, admission and release records of penal and social work agencies, and newspaper accounts unmask black women's intriguing yet complex experiences within New York's sex trade. While one-sided middle-class investigations into urban prostitution were tainted by race, gender, and class misconceptions and prejudices about sex workers, such reports, when closely scrutinized and combined with archival records, reveal far more than just economically strapped city women searching for a living wage.[142] Primary materials unravel the complicated web of socioeconomic circumstances that shaped black women's decisions to become sellers of sex and erotic fantasies. Spousal abandonment or death, employment discrimination, family obligation, peer pressure, and the longing for uninhibited sexual pleasures and independent work motivated many black women's participation in New York's sex economy. The nature of black prostitution was grounded in part by African American women's vast experiences as streetwalkers, brothel madams and inmates, buffet flat organizers, and residential sex workers. Racial exclusion from white-controlled sex enterprises, precarious street conditions, and entrepreneurship opportunities within the urban sexual economy precipitated black women's pursuit of sex work in tenement apartments, furnished rooms, and commercial leisure businesses. Indoor sex work widened black sex workers' geographical working locations, shifting urban prostitution from urban street corners and apartment-building hallways and alleyways to private and semiprivate spaces. Inconspicuously or openly advertising and selling sexual services in their working- and middle-class residences and in trendy city after-hours clubs and restaurants, black women unreservedly established modest intraracial and cross-racial sex enterprises, selected sex patrons, and articulated and performed acceptable and unconventional sexual practices. For many New York sex workers, however, newfound working opportunities and environments were marked by a variety of obstacles. Individual journeys into sex work were fraught with labor obstacles, including criminalization and legal confinement and gendered violence. Labor hurdles also appeared in the form of community shaming and sex workers' constant struggles to cope with Progressive- and Inter-war–era intellectual discourses and popular culture imageries, which misrepresented who they were as women and as workers. Adding to their public shaming was some women's private struggles with prostitution. Feelings of personal shame and humiliation and the mental and emotional anguish of commodifying their bodies to obtain economic necessities clouded sex workers' work experiences. Black women's internal turmoil was rooted in how their dire financial conditions impacted their decision to negotiate, reconfigure, and abandon moral values. At the same time, sex workers, those embracing a politics of eroticism and placing a price on their bodies and sexualities for money and pleasure, were hardly concerned with urban reformers or their relatives' outlooks on their labor or New York's sexual industry. These sex workers' perceptions of themselves, their work, and appetite for sexual stimulation overshadowed critics' commentaries.

CHAPTER 5

"'Decent and God-Fearing Men and Women' Are Restricted to These Districts"

Community Activism against Urban Vice and Informal Labor

In 1935, forty-two-year-old white Manhattan resident Daisy "Red Light" Sievers was convicted of operating several interracial prostitution houses and sentenced to six months at New York's Bedford Reformatory. The *NYAN* reported that Sievers and her alleged conspirator and husband, a sixty-five-year-old church pastor, were the proprietors of several profitable brothel houses on 112th, 117th, 118th, 119th, and 120th Streets; the duo, according to the Harlem newspaper—perhaps overexaggerating and attempting to convey to the public the severity of the Sievers' business in the community—had two hundred black and white prostitutes working at their establishments. The Sievers' entrepreneurial pursuits and aspects of their private lives became public knowledge after the West 118th Street Improvement Association, an interracial community organization of homeowners, penned several complaint letters to municipal officials. Concerned with the moral integrity of their neighborhood, the advocacy group regarded the Sievers as "menace[s] to the civic pride of the community" and Daisy Sievers "a serious threat to decent womanhood."[1] Headed by Harry Jackson, an African American Manhattan resident, the organization, vehemently protesting the infestation of prostitutes and other undesirables in their apartment buildings and community, notified NYPD Commissioner Lewis J. Valentine about the sex resort owners' legal infractions. Complaint letters detailed the Sievers' daily routines and the impact of their extralegal business on residents: "Such goings on ruin property investments in this neighborhood and leave the community wide open for holdups and other lawlessness. It's a rotten shame that such terrible conditions should exist in a community where Negroes are trying hard to establish decent homes."[2] Moreover, grievance letters stressed group members' frustrations with witnessing half-dressed women and their inebriated sex patrons strolling up and down 118th Street and parading in and out of the apartment building where decent residents lived and attempted to create stable and wholesome homes. Situating their community issues and concerns at the center of New York politics and raising public awareness about the city's troubling vice spots, the West 118th Street Improvement Association's staunch crusade against prostitution and other forms of lawlessness resulted in tangible solutions for organizational members and the community at large. The West 118th Street Improvement Association's antiprostitution stance, coupled with the political activism of other Manhattan community groups and city officials' 1930s citywide campaign against urban vice (including prostitution), culminated in increased police presence and surveillance of the 118th block and ultimately the arrest of the Sievers.

Apprehending urban brothel proprietors like the Sievers demonstrated the collective activism of grassroots neighborhood organizations and their unified stance against city vice, slum districts, disorderly public behavior, and crime racketeers. Moreover, community associations' local initiatives, particularly their complaint letters to municipal leaders and urban anti-vice activists, voiced their concerns about living conditions and public safety and the impact of lawlessness on law-abiding citizens and their families. The West 118th Street Improvement Association and other citywide neighborhood organizations were at the forefront of galvanizing local residents for community transformation and at developing programs aimed at tackling housing and employment discrimination, inadequate tenement structures, and urban vice. Espousing ideals of self-help and community order and discipline, local grassroots associations relentlessly worked to ensure that ordinary New Yorkers' existing socioeconomic conditions, as well as their promotion of quality residential spaces for all city dwellers, were visible to municipal officials.

This chapter draws attention to the multiple ways in which black city dwellers contested the presence of vice, immoral social amusements, and extralegal occupations within their apartment buildings and neighborhoods. Often residing in the same rundown districts, black activists, emerging from various socioeconomic backgrounds, were at the forefront of organizing and implementing anti-vice strategies, policing the social habits and economic pursuits of both men and women, and striving to promote community order and responsibility. Many—despite the possibility of being labeled a police informant or facing threats of violence from underground laborers and vice racketeers for interfering in their business ventures—bravely and unapologetically condemned neighborhood criminality, degrading forms of labor, and horrific housing conditions. More importantly, neighborhood activists criticized some city politicians' neglect of poor and underserved neighborhoods. Black folks' opposition to what many considered depraved and unlawful moneymaking schemes was articulated in neighborhood conversations, expressed in violent confrontations, and highlighted in complaint letters to race activists, private anti-vice agents, newspapers editors, and law officials. Complaint letters expressed residents' anxieties about a wide range of issues plaguing their neighborhoods, including law violators living in their communities, noisy neighbors, greedy landlords, and parents' efforts to shield their children and young adults from street violence, nefarious neighbors, and enticing city amusements. Complaint letters affirmed the boundaries of acceptable public and private behavior and delineated the often-veiled intraclass conflicts and tensions within urban black spaces, especially within the working class. Such written artifacts also confirmed many black New Yorkers' desires to monitor, control, and modify their neighbors' labor and leisure selections, making sure they adhered to middle- and working-class notions of respectability.

Likewise, grassroots neighborhood organizations such as the Harlem Citizens Council (HCC) and the social and political leadership of black New Yorkers like South Jamaica, Queens, activist Geraldine Chaney were crucial to the crusade against deteriorating community conditions and vice profiteering. This chapter uses neighborhood groups like the HCC and the local activism of Chaney as a window into how black New Yorkers employed grassroots activism and black institution building to implement anti-vice strategies geared toward neighborhood preservation and beautification, slum clearance, and the advancement of community uplift. This vanguard of black leadership signaled urban citizens' unified voice on neighborhood and city politics and their vested interests in the socioeconomic progress of their communities. Moreover, their local activism illuminated urban blacks' collective visions of wholesome communities and neighborhood reform and their refusal to allow criminal enterprises, petty criminals, and disorderly neighbors to permeate spaces in which they had to live and raise families.

Black New York activists' initiatives and hope to transform their communities and improve urbanites' socioeconomic and political conditions were part of historic northern civil rights struggles for American citizenship and for race, gender, and class equality. Their political activism had historic roots within a wide range of citywide and national initiatives, drawing inspiration from the formation of black socioeconomic, political, and religious benevolent organizations and self-help groups of the antebellum era and the turn of the twentieth century. Historically, New York black institutions and their leaders, as argued by scholars Leslie M. Alexander, Jane E. Dabel, and others, actively battled against economic and political disenfranchisement, American slavery, housing discrimination, police brutality, city politicians' inadequate enforcement of antidiscrimination statutes, and black criminality.[3] Emphasizing community relief and responsibility and race consciousness, their efforts galvanized and spoke on behalf of their communities and created a legacy for future political activists to follow and advance. Additionally, early-twentieth-century urban black neighborhood reform was influenced by the varying contours of intense racism, gender, and class exclusion and black urbanization and migration. The reform efforts of ordinary black New Yorkers served as a window into a larger landscape of how black urbanites interpreted their place within community politics and some city residents' outlook on urban space, underground labor, and city life.

Black Neighborhoods, Urban Vice, and Stool Pigeons

Urban black children placing gambling bets for their parents, scantily clad prostitutes soliciting prospective male clients from their apartment windows, and smooth-talking con artists searching for their next victim were all part of black urban landscapes and certainly did not go unnoticed by disapproving black urbanites. Being confined to the same communities and living structures made it difficult for blacks not to notice each other's daily behavior and social preferences and habits. Race discrimination in New York's housing and real estate markets relegated blacks of varying socioeconomic stations and backgrounds to the same undesirable living spaces. A diverse cross section of black urbanites, including race activists, Bible-thumping Christians, and charismatic hustlers, settled in the same deprived communities and dilapidated apartment buildings. Viewing the intermingling of various social classes residing in the same living quarters as an impediment to the creation of wholesome and upright black community, the *NYA*, in a short 1908 column, commented that: "it has long been a problem to separate the hoodlum element from the respectable class of colored people, and no one as yet seems to have found an answer." Monitoring prostitution in various sections of Harlem during the 1930s, one anti-vice agent, generally assuming that all black neighborhoods were central housing and working locations for petty lawbreakers and seasoned criminals, observed with surprise the diversity among black residents in Harlem neighborhoods. Contrary to his assumptions, all black Harlemites were not of loose morals; many were individuals "who are of excellent moral standing [and] are forced to live in the districts where the most vice is carried on."[5] Writing about troubling urban conditions in black communities in Chicago and throughout the nation in 1932, historian Drusilla Dunjee Houston commented on the unfortunate reality that law-abiding and self-respecting blacks, those dedicated to community betterment and outward models of correctness, were concentrated in unhealthy housing environments and, on a daily basis, forced to observe the conduct and manners of individuals whom they considered immoral. "It is unfortunate that many decent God-fearing black men and women" are restricted to districts where "prostitution, quarreling and slashing, [and] bootlegging occur."[6] Because of the color line's impact on the housing market, blacks, as suggested by one scholar, "found themselves isolated from the rest of the city, distant from [a] prospective workplace, and virtually forgotten by municipal authorities of urban reformers."[7]

But not all black residents were forced to live in undesirable neighborhoods. Those with some financial resources relocated to what they considered safer residential spaces. For many, migration meant relocating to white and black communities in different boroughs or to better streets or apartment buildings within the same communities they were attempting to leave. This inward or intercommunity and borough migration gave black families the chance to limit loved ones'—especially children's—exposure to neighborhood violence, crime, and illicit amusements. But migration to seemingly more stable and well-mannered homes, particularly to predominately white communities, was a difficult journey for many black families. White property owners and renters, realtors and landlords, and members of racist improvement associations fiercely contested the influx of black bodies to their communities; their objective was to continue the practice of housing discrimination via restrictive covenants and deed restrictions and to confine nonwhites to city ghettos. Concerned with racially changing residential patterns, racial mixing, and depreciating property values, many white New Yorkers reasoned that blacks were undesirable tenants and neighbors, asserting that "Negroes are loud, destructive, unclean."[8] Actively fighting the housing exclusion of black Queens residents, John A. Singleton, "militant dentist-president" of the Jamaica NAACP, maintained that "no decent houses are available for Negroes, and the exclusive policy of whites make it almost impossible for a Negro, regardless of his station, to get a home in a respectable neighborhood."[9] When blacks successfully relocated to more reasonably priced apartments in better neighborhoods, white landlords, tenants, and members of urban domestic terrorist organizations, like the Queens and Brooklyn chapters of the Ku Klux Klan, did not mince words about the prospect of ethnically diverse New Yorkers moving into their lily-white communities. Hardworking black families were often greeted by angry protesting whites carrying large wooden signs reading: "[We] don't want Negroes to inhabit [our] buildings," "Negros—Stay Away, You're Not Wanted," and "No Colored Need Apply." Moving to nonracially diverse residential areas in Elmhurst, Queens, in 1928, two black families received death threats from white residents. One letter stated, "You better move from that house at once, that's no place for you Negroes to live. A few days more and it will be too late for you, do it quick before actions will be taken to throw you out in a way you will regret."[10]

While relocation to improved housing areas was a viable yet complicated process for some black residents, other urban inhabitants, with little or no economic means, remained bound to rundown housing structures and communities and to their neighbors' interesting yet sordid lives. Living in cramped apartments with paper-thin walls and side-by-side front doors, windows, and fire escapes, blacks were privy to each other's private conversations, domestic disputes, and family living and sexual arrangements. Close living quarters denied residents the ability to choose whom they came into contact with and exposed them to individuals who possessed and exhibited a variety of moral practices. Writing about dilapidated Harlem tenements and the area's diverse array of inhabitants in her poignant best-selling 1946 novel, *The Streets*, Ann Petry wrote that "walls were so thin the good people, the bad people, the children, the dogs, and the godawful smells would all be wrapped together in one package."[11]

Urban League activist Lester B. Granger's 1930s *NYAN* column, "As I Remember," affirmed Petry's descriptive portrayal of apartment living. Granger's column humorously described his childhood experience living in a low-income apartment in New Jersey. Growing up in Newark during the second decade of the twentieth century, Granger, whose mother was a teacher and father a doctor, remembers some of his family members being frustrated yet amused by his neighbors' noisy and outlandish behavior and family squabbles. The more respectable Granger clan even seemingly looked forward to their neighbors' regularly scheduled weekend fights. Granger recalls how his family developed creative eavesdropping strategies and protocols in order to listen to their neighbors' conversations. "When Mr. and Mrs. Flaherty stage their Saturday night fight on the fire escape, we rush to the kitchen windows and glue our noses to the panes. When the couple in the next apartment has a Sunday morning row, we promptly shut the radio off. We tiptoe about the flat in scandalized delight, palpitant with fear lest we should lose a syllable of the juicy revelations which our neighbors are making regarding their family relations."[12] Observing and hearing their neighbors' noisy household disputes was a source of entertainment and a guilty pleasure for the New Jersey family. On one hand, the Granger clan was secretly amused by their neighbors' behavior. On the other, they exhibited a sense of moral superiority over them and critically judged them for the same apartment banter they enjoyed so much.

Whether they wanted to or not, on a daily basis black urbanites like the Granger family encountered eccentric unruly neighbors, craps-shooting drug dealers and petty thieves, and more unruly and unsupervised children than they cared to recall. Speaking to a city reporter about the unsavory characters hustling and socializing in her exclusive Sugar Hill neighborhood, one black woman, afraid of being accosted by local hooligans, stated that she dreaded venturing outside her apartment building. "You don't know when you're going to be insulted or have your pocketbook snatched. Something should be done to clean up this community and make it safe for the children who are coming up."[13] Urbanites like this Sugar Hill resident did not shy away from publicly expressing their sentiments about the communities in which they lived or about the impact of lawlessness on law-abiding citizens. Many were unapologetic about conveying their sentiments about intraracial issues, citing that "idleness, drunkenness and gambling are evils that menace the development of the race. We are in many cases, our own worst enemy."[14]

At the same time, other residents who were disturbed by neighborhood vice were often unwilling to report illicit activities, because some believed the legal authorities were dishonest and corrupt, as well as gatekeepers and protectors of the same vice that terrorized their communities. Race activists and intellectuals such as Lester B. Granger attributed some blacks' silence on neighborhood crime to the impact of ghettolike conditions and the absence of visible symbols of appropriate decorum on the black psyche. Granger believed that some individuals living in crime-infested communities were desensitized to vice and accepted criminality as a normal characteristic of underprivileged communities and city living. Granger's recollection of a friend's observation of a violent confrontation between a bus driver and passenger on a crowded Harlem bus in 1946 speaks to some blacks' silence on unlawful acts: "A friend of mine told me the other day of a bus incident in which a colored passenger, enraged because the bus had passed his getting-off corner, walked to the front of the conveyance and deliberately smashed the driver in the face, while the bus was still traveling. Of course the bus was traveling through Harlem; he never would have tried it otherwise. He felt that he had community sanction and protection if the bus driver got rough. This thug's act endangered the lives of all the persons on the bus, and almost all were Negroes. Not a single passenger did more than utter the mildest protest. By the time that some of them had decided to do anything, the offender had left the bus."[15]

The seemingly indifferent attitude toward, or silence about, neighborhood criminality and indecent public behaviors did not indicate black residents' willful acceptance of lawlessness. Those inhabiting less than desirable residential areas were certainly concerned with neighborhood crime and vice and especially troubled by the different ways in which criminality could and did impact their everyday lives. For some black men and women, the fear of reprisal from neighborhood ruffians kept them from reporting unlawful activities to city police. Those who were fearful about publicly challenging or speaking out against neighborhood vice expressed their reservations and anxieties in anonymous complaint letters to city officials, law enforcement, and reform leaders. Identifying themselves as "interested citizens" and "concerned neighbors," complainants requested that city activists and municipal leaders investigate their claims of vice in particular neighborhoods and revealed the names and addresses of suspected and known criminal figures. Moreover, complaint correspondences underscored letter writers' nervousness about possible retaliation and why some refused to identify themselves or go directly to local law enforcement. Many reasoned that physical harassment, death threats, and the "fear of what [street gangs, pimps, and hustlers] might do to [their] children, compelled them to keep still."[16] One single father's grievance letter about his sex worker daughter underscores some city folks' fears about communicating with authorities about neighborhood vice. Writing to New York District Attorney Thomas Dewey, he expressed his anguish about both his daughter's chosen line of work as a madam in a brothel and her association with a dangerous pimp. Concerned for his daughter, he identified her and her male associate by name and described how the couple made a living forcing young women into sex work. The worried parent indicated that his complaint letter, and hopefully the duo's arrest, was the only way to save his daughter from a continued life of crime. The desperate father feared contacting the police in person because his daughter's partner in crime threatened to kill him.[17]

The violent assaults on law-abiding community advocates like Harlem resident Albert Taylor highlight the real consequences some New Yorkers faced when they audaciously notified authorities about illegal activities in their neighborhoods. In July 1928, thirty-six-year-old Taylor, pastor of a home-based Catholic church and an employee of the British American Tobacco Company, was severely beaten when he publicly took "verbal shots at the immorality of Harlem, the openness of speakeasies, numbers playing, and other promiscuous gambling on the streets, the lewd and vulgar language of the younger folk of the town." Trouble began brewing for Taylor when he complained to his building landlord about his neighbor's alleged speakeasy; Taylor threatened to "take his case downtown" to city hall if his landlord failed to address his grievances. Fearful of being investigated by city officials, the landlord evicted the alleged speakeasy proprietor and his apartment boarders. The evicted tenants not only moved to an apartment directly across the street from Taylor, they also allegedly "plotted revenge and began intimidating him." Taylor's public tirade against his neighbors endangered his life, leaving him unprotected from their threats. On July 4, the outspoken preacher, "'accused by gangsters of 'trying to make a church out of the street,' was beaten and slashed with a knife by robbers, pickpockets, holdup men, knifers, and mailbox robbers" in front of his apartment door. Taylor suffered from slash wounds "over the eye, the nose, and left hand." Several men, including twenty-eight-year-old Edward Nichols, were arrested for brutally attacking Taylor.[18]

There is no doubt Taylor paid a heavy price for interfering in his neighbors' social and economic businesses and pursuits. Taylor's brutal attack illustrates the risks some urban blacks faced when they attempted to safeguard their living spaces and articulated their commitment to the socioeconomic well-being of their communities. Unlike well-known New York stool pigeons, Taylor did not partner with city police to frame innocent blacks nor did the trustworthy local preacher receive monetary compensation from law officials. Rather, Taylor's opposition to the presence of prostitution, gambling, and petty thievery was part of 1920s and 1930s urban reformists' visions of community betterment and respectability. At the same time, published reports of Taylor's and other city dwellers' violent assaults as a result of their courageous actions against illicit occupations and amusements fueled some blacks' real and imagined fears about openly contesting neighborhood criminality.

Finally, the fear of falsely being identified as stool pigeons or neighborhood snitches made some urbanites reluctant to speak out against community vice. Black residents detested stool pigeons, regarding them, according to Harlem labor activist Ashley Totten, as "seller[s] of souls" and as "low, degraded human being[s] akin to contemptible skunk[s]."[19] They loathed the ways in which black criminal informants monitored urban blacks' socioeconomic lives and behavioral patterns and provided law enforcers with unsubstantiated information on alleged law violators and on the locations of suspected vice establishments. Police informants, often criminals themselves, provided law enforcement officials with incriminating and fictitious evidence about suspected criminal activity. For their cooperation, informants avoided jail time or faced lesser criminal charges; some, like part-time restaurant worker Chile Acuna, were rewarded financially for complicating the lives and tarnishing the reputations of innocent men and women. Members of the NYPD paid Acuna $7 a day to frame poor women.[20] Throughout the 1920s and 1930s, NYPD officers used the dubious services of several white, black, and Hispanic male stool pigeons, including John "The Human Beast" Smith, George Henderson, Benny Jackson, and the notorious Charles Dancy.[21] Black criminal informants exploited urban whites' anxieties and notions about black criminality and hypersexuality in order to frame innocent black men and women for a number of crimes, including numbers gambling and prostitution, and to assert power and control over black New Yorkers. Their work was integral to the functioning of unbridled state sanctioned violence against New Yorkers. Their work became an invaluable resource for how some New York rookie and vice squad officers and detectives policed working-class communities and justified the criminalization and brutalization of urban black bodies.

Working-Class Sentiments on Informal Labor

While blacks like Harlem preacher Albert Taylor publicly took issue with their neighbors' illicit income-generating economic and leisure activities, others, including informal economy consumers, maintained divergent and, at times, contradictory positions on unreported labor. Patrons possessed a rather multifaceted outlook and complicated relationship with the urban informal economy and its

*integration of
The effect of
the black
psyche*

labor force, articulating varying levels of tolerance and condemnation for different categories of under-the-table employment. Black New Yorkers recognized the
complexities of informal labor sectors, drawing distinctions between noncriminal
and criminal labor. Furthermore, they acknowledged the blurred lines between
legitimate and illicit wage labor and entrepreneurship, and the different ways in
which city dwellers, from all walks of life and various socioeconomic statuses,
regularly and occasionally navigated between formal wage labor and informal and
criminal economies markets. Categorization between noncriminal and criminal
labor produced both broadminded and intolerant attitudes and perspectives on
informal labor. Distinctions were often made between noncriminal and unlicensed
street- and home-based economic ventures, and the income-producing ventures
that were part of the city's criminal economy.[22] For instance, many black New
Yorkers' faithfully took part in games of chance, most notably the city's popular yet
illegal numbers racket, and readily purchased from urban hucksters inexpensive
counterfeit and stolen merchandise on city streets or at pool halls and beauty parlors. Some of these same folks, however, vehemently opposed the selling of illegal
alcohol and sexual labor, viewing such employment as part of the city's flourishing
vice rackets working to undermine family structures and the community at large.
Moreover, they were quick to point out that criminal economy jobs risked individual
safety, compromised one's personal integrity and moral standing within her/his
respective community, contributed to the downfall of black neighborhoods, and
reinforced urban whites' contentions that black life and culture were threats to
urban civilization.[23]

Some informal economy consumers tended to be liberal-minded when it came
to unlicensed household and street businesses and did not necessarily link unreported work with criminality. For some, using their relatives,' neighbors,' or
strangers' informal sewing, clothing, cooking, childcare, and hairstyling services
were economically beneficial to the community, providing affordable products and
services and negotiable bartering systems for low-income families. Noncriminal
economic undertakings were not viewed as immoral pursuits, nor were they considered detrimental to informal laborers' familial and neighborhood reputations
or to their belief in respectable politics. Differentiating between noncriminal and
criminal-sector jobs justified some working-class consumers' active participation within the urban informal economy and allowed many to be sympathetic
toward economically strapped individuals' choice of employment. They refused
to cast judgment on informal economy laborers because they understood, through
firsthand experiences, the financial burdens of urban living and the external race,
gender, and class barriers thwarting urban blacks' efforts to secure financial stability and lead independent and nonconforming lives.

Tolerance of informal occupations, even those of a criminal nature, stemmed in part from working-class blacks' personal connections to underground workers. Urban blacks had relatives and close friends who engaged in criminal labor. Some were longtime brothel inmates or streetwalkers, drug dealers, and numbers racketeers, and others moved fluidly in and out of off-the-books work. In her 1951 autobiography, *His Eye Is on the Sparrow*, Pennsylvania native and blues singer Ethel Waters recalled that her family "had one link with prostitution. This was Blanche, one of Mom's nieces, who was seven or eight years older than I. Though Mom [disapprovingly] shook her head over Blanche's way of life, she was always strongly biased in her favor because she was our relative." Working-class men and women like Waters's mother were perhaps torn between their personal moral convictions and objections to degrading forms of labor and their familial and emotional obligations to wayward relatives. While they disapproved of their loved ones' labor and leisure pursuits, they understood the "economic conditions [and perhaps the emotional and psychological circumstances] forc[ing] people to accept work where they inevitably come in contact with immoral practices."[24] Nevertheless, some black families maintained casual and close friendships with underground economy workers, refusing to disown and shame their relatives or report their extralegal activities to local police. Some even allowed their children to interact with drug-dealing and sex-working relatives and close friends. As a young child growing up in the slums of Chester and Philadelphia, Waters was exposed to prostitution, drunkenness, and other vices and spent a considerable amount of time with her prostitute cousin. Waters fondly recalls: "Blanche often played with me, read me stories, and sang little songs with me. I loved her. There was a great camaraderie between us, and that young prostitute gave me some of the attention and warm affection I was starving for." Additionally, Waters recounts that her time with her cousin provided her with a realistic view of street hustling and prostitution and warned the multitalented future entertainer about the pitfalls of street life. Waters's intriguing personal account fails to reveal the many intimate conversations between herself and her cousin. Waters does, however, acknowledge that her cousin's candid discussions about her seemingly painful and complex life "did more to keep me straight in the tough years to come than any person I ever knew."[25] The two women's close relationship conceivably influenced Waters's sympathetic and less judgmental position on sex work, its female labor force, and the personal circumstances that shaped women's participation in the world's oldest profession.

While many working-poor blacks understood the emotional stresses and financial pressures motivating relatives, friends, and neighbors to engage in unreported criminal and unlicensed labor, others, regardless of their familial and personal connections, vilified and shunned labor that bypassed city licensing ordinances and breached city and state statutes. Viewing themselves as morally upright urbanites, they censured unsavory occupations and amusements, refusing—despite their own low economic circumstances—to engage in underground labor. Even with the grueling demands of exploitative labor such as domestic and factory work, some working blacks adamantly refused to compromise their dignity, self-respect, and neighborhood reputation for economic stability and wealth. Speaking to a friend about the prospect of prostituting herself for money or to better her financial situation, one black woman reasoned that no matter how hard times got she "would rather kill [herself] scrubbing" floors than take to prostitution.[26] Frowning upon questionable income-generating strategies and critically judging individuals who took alternative paths toward economic stability and personal fulfillment, less-privileged and self-righteous blacks maintained that if *they* possessed the moral capacity to endure and overcome poverty and unemployment without compromising or abandoning their moral values, others could do the same. Subscription to different aspects of racial uplift and self-help contributed to some blacks' judgmental attitudes toward informal laborers and their staunch positions on criminal and unlicensed labor. Self-help ideology pushed some men and women to adopt socially conservative perspectives about individual lifestyle choices and to criticize and shame those who departed from or reconfigured conventional ideas about good manners, frugality, and sexual purity. In turn, hypercritical urbanites viewed behavioral modification as a path toward individual respectability and were intolerant of those that made labor decisions based on personal desire, economic circumstances, and labor ambitions.

Working-class blacks' divergent points of view on informal labor revealed intraclass differences on the work, outward propriety, and appropriation of urban space, and illuminated the hidden tensions and power struggles within underprivileged communities. Moreover, black urbanites' varying outlooks on informal and criminal labor and leisure indicated that conversations about morally healthy black living spaces and public and private decorum were not parts of a two-sided discussion or debate between middle- and working-class blacks. Discourse on the politics of respectability was also a complex and shifting dialogue among working-class blacks. Black working-class neighborhoods and apartment buildings, stoops, and hallways became center stages for spirited debates and arguments over neighborhood etiquette, proper social amusements, the black body, and whether or not local hooligans were adversely transforming local communities. Disparate ideologies on urban labor, public conduct, and neighbors' personal use of communal hallways, stairwells, and front entrances even erupted into physical altercations. For instance, the 1923 clash between two black women in an apartment building hallway serves as an example of how competing ideas about outward behavior and the boundaries of private and public spaces resulted in violent disputes. Adamantly opposed to immoral activity in her tenement building, a formal-wage female worker confronted her female neighbor—a working prostitute whom she believed had "no respect for anyone"—about her choice of employment and how she openly solicited men from her window. It is unclear what the neighbor's temperament was like when she approached the sex worker or what was discussed between the two women. Conceivably, the annoyed tenant expressed to the sex worker her disapproval of prostitution and the manner in which she publicly flaunted her labor and sexuality. The sex worker vehemently objected to her neighbor's public shaming and policing and hardly appreciated her unsolicited morality lesson. The sex worker viewing herself as a hardworking and paying tenant felt entitled to use her apartment however she deemed fit, and she was not concerned with her neighbors' thoughts on her, her labor, or her decision to transform private space into commercial labor space. For prying into her business, the prostitute verbally and physically accosted her meddlesome neighbor.[27]

Law-abiding city dwellers like those who confronted their less-respectable neighbors or informed law and police officers about community wrongdoers yearned to physically live "apart from the roughness" and the crime-ridden neighborhood.[28] Confined to urban ghettos yet determined to make the best out of communities in which they had to live and raise children, working-class subscribers to bourgeois respectability made earnest attempts to display—similar to historian Kevin Gaines's discussion of early-twentieth-century black elites and class differentiation—evolutionary race progress and cultural distinctions within their socioeconomic class and working-poor communities. Comparable to middle-class blacks' efforts to distance and distinguish themselves from the black masses, some workingmen and women monitored and contested the unacceptable behavior and lifestyle choices of those within their socioeconomic class and within their household structures.

Working-class racial uplifters concerned with the stability and moral health of their households and their family's neighborhood reputation closely scrutinized their relatives' leisure patterns, particularly those of young black girls. Politicized by both urban reformers' anti-vice campaigns and rhetoric and print media coverage of city crime, and certainly aware of the impact of racial stereotypes on the lives of young black women, parents and relatives worried about their female kin succumbing to urban dangers and amusements and about the threat of interracial and intraracial violence. In turn, New York black parents, as similarly discussed in scholar Marcia Chatelain's work on early- and mid-twentieth-century Chicago black girls, "scrutinized [their children's] behaviors, evaluated their choices, and assessed their possibilities as part of a larger conversation about what urbanization ultimately meant for black citizens."[29] Historian Cheryl Hicks contends that working-class families' anxieties about their young female kin's wayward behavior and "stigma attached to black neighborhoods" led some to turn to Progressive-era New York state wayward-minors laws that intended to regulate and correct juvenile behavior.[30] Wayward-minor laws permitted parents, legal guardians, and law enforcers to commit delinquent girls—those skipping school, participating in premarital sex, socializing with other unruly young adults, and engaging in other transgressive behavior—to private city reformatories and the state penitentiary. Desperate black parents naively hoped that state intervention would ensure household stability and teach incorrigible girls hard but invaluable lessons about appropriate behavior, respecting authority figures, and the perils of urban life.[31]

Working-class blacks' attempts to display evolutionary progress within their own socioeconomic class and opposition to neighborhood criminality and non-respectable social behaviors were intended, in part, to counter black elites' general perceptions of lower-class blacks and demonstrate ideological similarities across class lines. Lower-class blacks' uneducated and low socioeconomic status and questionable choice of social pastimes fueled urban bourgeois assumptions that financially struggling individuals lacked proper decorum, traded morality for economic survival and material consumption and social pleasures, and accepted and ignored the infiltration of vice and indecent behavior in already blighted areas. Moreover, working-class blacks embraced genteel behavior and performances for practical and idealistic reasons. For many, outward representations of propriety were linked to social and economic mobility and to the creation of a hierarchy within their own socioeconomic class. Struggling black residents, perhaps naively, hoped that visual imageries of respectable conduct would lessen the chances of mistaken criminal identities. Based on horrific firsthand experiences within the criminal justice system and encounters with anti-vice agents, working-poor blacks understood that the line between those fighting for community advancement and those more concerned with social pleasures and making a quick dollar was often imprecise and frequently resulted in the criminalization and victimization of urban black bodies, especially those of black women. For instance, in 1910, New York resident and wageworker Edith Williams wrote a compelling complaint letter to Mayor William Gaynor, explaining how she was falsely accused of and arrested for robbery and solicitation and violently assaulted by an NYPD officer. Recalling her painful experience with the law enforcer, Williams wrote: "I was called awful names by the officer and he spit in my face." When Williams vehemently proclaimed her innocence to the officer, her cries were met with pushes and blows to her arms and legs.[32]

A 1914 Committee of Fourteen (COF) report's description of a sexual encounter between a black Harlem woman and several black men illustrates another example of how black female bodies were routinely criminalized and erroneously identified as inherently deviant and promiscuous. While investigating a Manhattan after-hours spot, white COF investigator and former private detective Charles Briggs witnessed a group of black men attempting to have sex (which was likely a gang rape) with a black woman in the establishment's alleyway. Briggs silently watched the rough sexual interaction, which he interpreted as the sexual activities of consenting adults. In his COF report, Briggs referred to "3 buck negroes holding a young wench up against the wall of The College Inn attempting to have intercourse with her. She offered but little objection and [I] believe that all 3 gentlemen had their fun before [the] affair ended." Briggs failed to come to the woman's assistance; his experience as an anti-vice agent and private eye frequently coming into contact with women—particularly of African descent with alleged loose or dubious sexual morals—perhaps framed his perception of that alleyway scene. For Briggs, the black woman in question was not a victim of sexual assault but rather a willing participant. Drawing from negative Euro-American perceptions of black women, Briggs viewed her as unvirtuous and unworthy of protection and as someone who enjoyed being sexually subdued and mishandled by a group of black "gentlemen."[33]

The refusal to view black women as victims of sexual violence is both revealing and troubling and underscores societal perspectives that black women, regardless of their socioeconomic status, were free from sexual restraint. Whites's false interpretation of urban black women undermined women's real experiences of sexual exploitation at the hands of both white and black men; it also highlighted women's day-to-day vulnerabilities and the constant threat of physical assault as well as their lack of protection in urban spaces. Interestingly, Briggs's silence and stillness on what possibly was a sexual crime sheds light on his and other white New York documentarians' own sexual fetishes about women in general and black women in particular. Black women's public brutalization and victimization were part of some white men's erotic fantasies about women of color, and perhaps explains why some voyeuristically watched other men violently defile women's bodies. For some white anti-vice agents, financial compensation for documenting urban immorality conceivably served as a perfect cover for those who were titillated by scenes of sexual domination.

Citizens' Complaint Letters

Working-class black men and women readily voiced their concerns about city vice, as well as their neighbors' illegal and degrading occupations in complaint letters to race reform agencies, anti-vice organizations, newspaper editors, and police and city politicians. Local activists and politicians' organizational and government offices were flooded with both identifiable and anonymous correspondences from ordinary city residents, citing how "the conduct of our people in various parts of the city [and] the very bad habit [of] men congregating on the corners [is] offensive and hurts the race" and makes the casual observer view "Negro communities in New York as the eyesores of our civilization."[34] Citizens' letters called upon urban reformers and municipal leaders, including city prosecutor and organized crime buster Thomas Dewey and Eunice Hunton Carter, the city's first black female assistant district attorney, to investigate their claims of neighborhood vice, and they vividly described the impact of poor neighborhood conditions on their day-to-daily lives. Black residents appealed to city reformers and officials because they viewed them as allies in the struggle against urban vice and supported lawmakers' citywide campaigns to eradicate slum conditions and eliminate organized and petty crime. City dwellers posited that local political leaders had a civic and moral obligation to enact policies that addressed the growing concerns of their constituents. With the massive media coverage of the Samuel Seabury investigations in the 1930s, many New Yorkers praised Dewey and city prosecutors for their legal stance against numbers game and prostitution racketeers, corrupt city politicians, and the metropolis's most dangerous crime bosses.[35] One resident commended Dewey and his team of assistant district attorneys for "the good work [they] are doing to ridden the city of crime." The letter writer also insisted that the prosecutor's office also focus on crime profiteering and lawlessness in various pockets within working-class communities.[36]

Complaint letters articulated a range of daily issues that complicated black New Yorkers' visions of inhabiting crime-free residential districts. Letter writers blamed licentious, depraved, and fraudulent income-producing strategies and public misconduct for manipulating their relatives, for taking away family income, for luring their children into unscrupulous activities, and for bringing public shame to their communities. Moreover, correspondences underscored working-class blacks' thoughts on the appropriation of public space and documented their unwanted daily observations of and encounters with neighborhood lawlessness and disorderly conduct. Complaint letters informed city officials and activists about known and suspected criminals as well as the locations of prostitution houses and gambling and drug dens. In 1910, an anonymous Harlem tenant wrote to Mayor William Gaynor concerning her neighbor's house of ill repute. The tenant requested that Mayor Gaynor and law enforcers "investigate the private house of No. 160 W. 133rd St. [There resides] a large black woman who runs a disorderly house for young colored girls from the age of 14."[37] Similarly in 1936, a distressed black woman notified Eunice Hunton Carter about a brothel that operated in her apartment building on 117th Street. According to the woman, the brothel employed primarily white prostitutes, "catered to black men" only, and frequently had "men in cars drive up Monday and Saturday evenings."[38]

Heartfelt letters and newspaper editorials by black women expressed their frustrations with the presence of prostitutes, religious racketeers, and gangsters living and hustling in and near their apartment buildings. After several unanswered written complaints to law enforcement, Manhattan resident Frances Watkins conveyed to New York Urban League leaders her annoyance with the "indecent behavior of a woman" living in her building. A concerned Watkins informed League activists that the woman in question "wears a red hat and sits on the stoop all day long, [and] attracts the attention of white men as they pass and invites them into her apartment."[39] Similarly, in a 1938 letter to the *NYAN*, a working mother of three daughters living between St. Nicholas and Seventh Avenues explained her exasperation with known prostitutes living and plying their trade in her rundown apartment building. Additionally, her complaint conveyed her objection to her landlord's decision to rent apartments to known sex workers. "I am a tenant in a building in which [the] unscrupulous landlord rents the two ground apartments to women who live by their wits."[40] By renting space to sex workers, the struggling mother believed that her landlord contributed to the demoralization of the neighborhood and the growth of vice in her apartment building.

Watkins's and other women's anxieties about the permeation of vice in residential areas underscored how some apartment building owners and landlords permitted "vice and filth" to thrive in already poorly maintained housing structures.[41] Some white and black landlords were hardly concerned about their tenants' private affairs and occupations or whether they established illegal home-based businesses. Instead, apartment proprietors were more interested in securing timely paying renters, regardless of their occupations, for their high-priced yet dilapidated apartments. Consequently, tenement apartment lessees were often a mixed blend of working- and middle-class folks, including teachers, domestics, chauffeurs, sex workers, and community reformers. In her 1905 Progressive-era study on black New Yorkers, NAACP founder Mary White Ovington observed that apartment building proprietors and landlords, particularly whites, "rarely make any attempt to discriminate" among their applicants, but take in "anyone who will pay his rent."[42] Frustrated with the housing consolidation of better-class and dissolute blacks, Manhattan resident Elsie Peoples's 1936 *NYAN* letter highlighted: "Because the Negro is, as a whole, very poor, and because white landlords do not discriminate between types of Negroes, they pile prostitutes, slovenly people and decent folks together in the same building. The landlord doesn't make any attempts to keep the houses occupied by Negroes in a clean, respectable condition. It is up to Negroes to bring pressure to bear to force owners to clean up the halls and keep loiterers from obstructing the fronts of the buildings."[43]

While black renters' verbal and written complaints vehemently voiced their frustrations with landlords' selection of tenants, their staunch oppositions to the functioning of their living spaces, according to one *NYAN* letter writer, often "fell on deaf ears."[44] Some landlords completely disregarded black renters' opposition to sharing public space with less-than-respectable neighbors. One journalist commented that some landlords were indifferent about the "external [and internal] appearance of his property" and the well-being of their tenants. In some cases, landlords, bypassing tenement apartment laws against the presence of criminal activity in housing structures, were "reluctant in refusing [sex workers and pimps] living quarters" and preferred underground entrepreneurs as tenants. Many, according to *NYAN* reporter Dan Burley, had no problem harboring young hoodlums and other miscreants, or allowing some to "to make a little money on the side by selling moonshine whiskey, and running crap games, renting transit beds to prostitutes."[45] Landlords assumed, despite the many challenges of hustling for oneself in a fluid yet unstable informal labor market, that sex laborers, numbers bankers and runners, and bootleggers had an "endless flow of cash."[46] They viewed such tenants' occupancy as a way to increase their own personal incomes and take part in their tenants' extralegal economic and social affairs. Threatening to evict underground entrepreneurs or inform police of their illegal businesses and activities, some landlords extorted money from tenants, forcing them to pay higher rents in exchange for their silence.[47] Moreover, landlords reasoned that underground economy laborers were suitable tenants because they paid their rent on time and, unlike some formal wageworkers, were less likely to complain about and demand building repairs. In other words, landlords viewed their occupancy as a way to avoid fulfilling their legal obligations to all paying tenants.

Grievance letters also reflected city residents' anxieties about the collateral costs of neighborhood vice on their children and young relatives. Black mothers, especially those with grueling and nonflexible work schedules and limited or no childcare options, worried about the safety of their children walking alone to and from school, running errands around the neighborhood, and leaving their unventilated apartments to play outdoors. Articulating the sensibilities of many parents, one mother explained to COF officials that she "cannot trust [the] safety" of her children on city streets or even near their apartment building. Children's exposure to and adoption of adverse cultural and neighborhood traits, manners and habits, and street protocols were also subjects of concern for letter-writing parents. Complaint letters expressed the widely accepted view that the presence and observation of prostitution houses, gin mills, and other vice dens were potentially detrimental to household structures and disrupted parents' ability to rear upright children. Writing to New York Urban League Executive Secretary James H. Hubert about a "gang of hoodlums [and] women of the streets" in 1937, a group of black women residents living on 126th Street between Seventh and Eighth Avenues collectively articulated the difficulties in "trying to properly raise children under existing [vice] conditions."[49] These working mothers reasoned that black families could not produce "great, good, patriotic and intelligent [children] with the backdrop of low, wicked, filthy, and ungodly homes."[50] Family lessons of morality, frugality, chastity, and righteousness often competed with the lures of street life for the prized possession of young city dwellers' hearts and souls. One single mother's written statement to city prosecutors explained her fear of losing her two sons to street culture. She explained the need to shield her children "from the lure of vicious gangs, fast talking and well-dressed street hustlers, and beautiful women"—perceived by some young blacks as prosperous role models and mentors. Believing that depressing living environments were linked to juvenile delinquency and the breakdown of black households, the stressed parent lamented: "I want to protect them from these men who, to their young eyes, seem to be living the life. And from these women, some of them very beautiful, who lure them into sources of infection."[51]

Parents' concerns for their children's social and moral well-being were not byproducts of their overactive imaginations. Their anxieties about their children's living conditions were based on the realities of urbanization and on their experiences of residing in underserved communities where crime and vice racketeering was rampant and flourished. And sometimes working-class parents' worst fears about their children's exposure to and association with hurtful intimacies and amusements came to fruition.[52] One mother's recollection of her daughter's downward spiral into sex work speaks to how the exposure to unhealthy influences affected impressionable and economically struggling young adults. The once-proud mother recalled that her daughter, despite living in a "district of prostitutes . . . worked hard for a meager salary" as a domestic worker. On a daily basis, the young woman, perhaps resentful and envious, observed how her "unemployed" female peers unrepentantly strolled neighborhood streets wearing expensive clothes and jewelry and hopped into fancy cars. Experiencing the physical challenges and economic limitations of household labor, the young woman, quitting her formal wage job, turned to prostitution. She befriended several neighborhood sex workers, who subsequently schooled her on the urban sex racket and on how to make fast money. To her mother's dismay, the young woman, discarding childhood lessons of morality and chastity and respectable work, traded backbreaking but legal employment for potentially higher wages, high-priced attire, and independent labor.

Finally, working-class blacks' complaint letters revealed how their daily lives and routines were frequently interrupted by noisy music emerging from their neighbors' buffet flats and rent parties, and by the sight of neighborhood hustlers loitering in apartment building hallways and on front stoops. One Harlemite posited that she was constantly irritated by individuals who spend "all day long, and all evening into the early hours of the morning, making noises, molesting passersby who have tried to go about minding their own business." According to the complainant, such a "condition makes it impossible for residents to rest, and creates a public nuisance to those who must go to and through [the] street."[53] Letters complaining about noise shed light on what black city dwellers thought about the varying sounds emanating from their places of residence and on city streets. Examining Inter-war black Harlem, social historian Clare Corbould makes the point that many black urbanites employed different kinds of sounds to distinguish themselves from their white counterparts and "create a counterpublic sphere that was a spatialization of black self-expression." At the same time, black Harlemites also viewed sound, and more importantly silence, as a way to display physical restraint and discipline and to socially and culturally distance themselves from individuals or groups whose behaviors they disapproved of. Critics of loud rambunctious social and economic amusements and activities were annoyed by noise levels that disrupted their daily patterns and reinforced white perceptions that blacks were raucous, primitive, and disorderly.[54]

Local Activism and Neighborhood Vice

Writing about the influences of vice and deteriorating living conditions in black communities, a 1911 *NYA* editorial contended that less-privileged urbanites, those whose daily lives were frequently affected by lawlessness and disorderly public conduct, should be in the forefront of citywide campaigns against housing slums and community indecency. The editorial also posited that efforts to sanitize and improve black districts were primarily the responsibility of individuals residing in the rundown areas. "[City blacks] must look to the good, quiet decent element in our churches and homes, that constitutes the backbone of the real social structure of the community. It is their battle and they must help bear it. Street-walking women and the animals that live upon their dirty money and boldly loaf in the path of good people, must go. Buffet flats, thrones of lewdness and castles of drunkenness must go. And decent people who harbor low characters and sustain their crimes, they must also go."[55] Community betterment and the contestation over urban black public and semipublic spaces were not working-class peoples' issues to bear alone. Neighborhood crime and vice encroached upon the daily routines of all black New Yorkers, from the morally upright household worker struggling to afford the high cost of urban living to the grassroots middle-class reformer. Combating urban vice was the responsibility of all citizens and became a joint initiative in which both middle- and working-class blacks organized local associations and networks aimed at safeguarding their neighborhoods, protecting their children from immoral influences, and stressing the importance of community discipline and orderliness.

Black New Yorkers' individual and collective concerns about neighborhood vice, deteriorating apartment structures, and filthy streets coalesced into the formation of grassroots neighborhood associations. Block-by-block and neighborhood-by-neighborhood local activists, also part of New York and the nation's "New Negro Movement" of the Progressive- and Inter-war eras, diligently worked to improve and protect their living environments. New Negro men and women including political reformers, intellectuals, and visual artists developed and utilized multiple expressions of protest and reform to contest race, gender, and class inequality. As responsible and creative agents of social change, New Negro activists boldly confronted white supremacy, "celebrated their African origins, sought to celebrate race pride in their expressive culture, and asserted the need for black Americans to search for liberation from the prevailing racial order."[56] Black neighborhood activists—those who were already members of the nation's and city's leading race and gender reform agencies, including the NAACP, NUL, YWCA, and UNIA—and those with little or no experience as social and political reformers, spearheaded community-based citizens organizations with clearly defined goals and agendas. Multilayered association platforms sought to better urban black citizens' quality of life; lobbied city government for improved housing, public schools, and city services; and actively contested race prejudice in New York's labor market. Moreover, the formation of neighborhood social and political institutions was intended to raise the moral standards of its communities, monitoring and correcting individual behavioral patterns and altering the physical landscape of urban black spaces. Frustrated with different aspects of the city's underground economy as well as with some municipal leaders' neglect of black communities, neighborhood civic leaders became the vanguard of social and community change, playing a critical role in the shaping of community affairs. Their activism illuminated their views on civic engagement and intracommunity reform, as well as their unwavering commitment to neighborhood sustainability, self-help, and institution building.

Black urbanites' advocation for and right to have safe, clean, and decent residential spaces and neighborhoods culminated in the establishment of the HCC and other community associations. In May 1925, African American and Caribbean residents of Harlem, including physician Charles Butler, Urban League Executive Secretary James H. Hubert, lawyers Myles A. Paige and William L. Patterson, sociologist Ira De Reid, newspaper editor Fred Moore, and political activist Sarah E. Gardner, established the HCC, a community-based organization representing the unification of twenty-two welfare and social workers' groups. A byproduct of the mid-1920s mass migration of black southerners and Caribbean immigrants to the Black Mecca, the HCC was "organized for the purpose of bringing together religious, business, professional, fraternal, and social organizations into one group for the promotion of better community life in Harlem." Understanding firsthand the socioeconomic and political concerns and needs of black Harlemites, the HCC developed a multilayered reform agenda that reflected the complex ways in which race, gender, and class bigotry obstructed black New Yorkers from attaining decent and well-paying employment, quality housing conditions, and sanitary living spaces. Much of the HCC's community initiatives and programs centered on public health, voter registration and civic improvement, child welfare and adequate housing, black immigration and naturalization, and the racial exclusion of blacks from skilled and professional employment.

One of the HCC's successful campaigns was the employment integration of blacks' medical professionals to Harlem Hospital. In 1925, the HCC, led by Dr. Charles Butler and Urban League Chairman James N. Hubert, partnered with the New York Urban League, NAACP, and other local activists to secure employment positions for black physicians and nurses at the predominately white Harlem Hospital and other hospitals within the city's Bellevue and Allied Hospitals system. Despite their impressive academic backgrounds and credentials, black physicians were virtually barred from employment at municipal hospitals until the later years of the second decade of the twentieth century.[57] New York City had an estimated forty-two doctors in 1910, and approximately one hundred and forty-two by the close of 1929. Typically, urban black doctors were self-employed, operating their own private practices and servicing black community members. Black doctors that obtained positions at city hospitals were usually employed at Harlem Hospital and often relegated to low-level positions. NAACP board member Dr. Louis T. Wright became the first black doctor employed at a city hospital and at Harlem Hospital in 1919; Wright was hired as a clinical assistant visiting surgeon in the outpatient department, a low-ranking position that carried little upward mobility and was not reflective of Wright's expertise.[58] By the mid-1920s, Harlem Hospital added at least five black doctors to its staff. The HCC's and other Harlem activists' tireless appeals to city politicians, including Mayor John Hylan, to integrate city hospitals resulted in the promotions of Harlem Hospital's already employed black doctors. Additionally, Harlem Hospital officials proposed to appoint black medical professionals to "several specialists and internees [positions] in the near future" and to offer black doctors the opportunity to "compete on an equal footing with white physicians for all positions."

While Harlem Hospital officials were slow to employ black health professionals, especially in wake of white physicians and nurses' staunch objections to the hospital's new hiring practices, they did hire and promote several prominent black physicians to positions of power. In 1926, Harlem Hospital appointed New York University and Bellevue Medical School graduate May Chinn to a two-year internship; Chinn became the first black female doctor at the hospital. That same year, the hospital promoted Dr. E. R. Alexander, who had already been employed for five years as an assistant physician in the department of dermatology, to physician-in-charge of the department. Increased representation of black physicians at Harlem Hospital represented a small step toward the inclusion of black health care professionals in city hospitals. Other hospitals in the city were slow to follow Harlem Hospital's lead, making minimal commitments to altering their hiring practices or changing their mistreatment of black doctors and patients. Nevertheless, black New Yorkers viewed the HCC's efforts to integrate city hospitals as a "great accomplishment," interpreting the emerging community organization and its members as allies in the battle against urban inequalities.[59]

Community projects centering on the creation of wholesome black households and neighborhoods and the eradication of urban vice was a top priority for the HCC. The local self-help organization's commitment to neighborhood betterment was part of black national reform agencies' intracommunity initiatives to sanitize black public spaces and produce what black intellectuals and activists described as "better homes and purer homes." Reform-minded middle- and working-class political and religious leaders were dedicated to the purification of their black households, believing that the home was crucial to racial advancement. In their public speeches and in their widely read self-help pamphlets, black intellectuals and activists maintained that the household was "the greatest institution on earth for good or evil; you can't make a great, good, patriotic and intelligent race if you live in low, wicked, filthy, and ungodly homes."[60] For many, healthy and morally stable domestic spaces charted individual and familial respectability, produced good citizens, and displayed positive collective images of black urbanites. Moreover, reformers' imagining of reputable households and living districts was a practical matter and, according to one scholar, connected to blacks' long struggle for democratic rights and citizenship.[61]

The HCC's promotion of respectable and sanitized homes and city spaces was articulated at the organization's well-attended weekly forums and mass meetings. Often held on Sunday afternoons at a neighborhood public school or one of Harlem's prominent religious centers, including Abyssinian Baptist Church or Saint Mark's Methodist Episcopal Church, HCC forums focused on a broad range of socioeconomic, political, and educational issues and topics such as "Negroes in Northern Communities" and strategies for achieving "Better Community Life." Attended by seasoned political activists, intellectuals, and working-class blacks, community meetings offered attendees intellectual engagement and thought-provoking dialogue on local politics and racial injustice, and served as political training grounds for those with little or no organizing experience. Additionally, HCC forums provided a space for participants to publicly and without fear express their grievances about deteriorating neighborhood conditions and municipal leaders' neglect of black communities. Public dialogue about pressing neighborhood issues highlighted blacks' shared experiences, anxieties, and dreams about urban life, and allowed citizens to exchange ideas about how to effectively combat vice and work toward neighborhood beautification.[62]

The HCC, striving for a "clean [and] quiet Harlem," routinely launched week-long neighborhood cleanup programs throughout the mid-1920s. Promoting program slogans like "Clean language, Clean homes, Clean streets, Clean parks and Clean amusements," HCC cleanup initiatives did not directly confront or reprimand informal and criminal economy laborers or those individuals that hustled in tenement stairways and stoops and hosted rent and buffet-flat parties in their apartments. Rather, HCC neighborhood cleanup activists focused on the collective rehabilitation of Harlemites' public and private behavior and on improving the physical landscape of black neighborhoods. Bringing awareness to their campaign as well to the organization itself, the HCC distributed thousands of advertising flyers throughout Harlem, placing "a large number of placards, bearing the slogan for the week, in [black] merchants' windows." Looking toward the broader Harlem community for support of its initiatives, HCC members actively recruited local blacks for their cleanup programs. For instance, during the organization's 1925 summer cleanup drive, HCC members Sarah E. Gardner and Dr. E. Elliott Rawlins organized and led "a dynamic group of fifty spirited women," who recruited local people within their respective neighborhoods. Pledging to transform their neighborhoods' physical conditions, the 1925 summer cleanup participants pledged to keep their communities free from "litter, ashes, garbage; baseballs [in the streets], noisy peddlers and honking auto horns after midnight; loud piano and Victrola playing [and] jazz bands or talking from windows after midnight." This particular HCC neighborhood cleanup also stressed that "resident blocks be free from all kind of commercial enterprises." Moreover, the HCC was concerned with urban children's welfare. Playing on gender conventions that posited that mothers were integral to well-manicured communities, HCC activists advised mothers to monitor their children's public behavior on the streets. This meant prohibiting their children from spending long and unsupervised hours on city streets, and not permitting them to destroy and vandalize recreational facilities in black communities, which included "dig[ging] up grass, break[ing] bottles or throw[ing] broken glass on the grass."[63]

The HCC's initiatives to improve Harlem communities did not reduce crime rates or increase legal arrests. Nor did local grassroots activists' active monitoring of individual and community behavioral patterns deter illegal and unrespectable economic and social activities. Neighborhood ruffians, jobless men and women, and leisure-seeking urbanites continued, despite community reformers' public campaigns to transform their neighborhoods, to use their apartments and neighborhoods to generate income and enjoy insalubrious amusements. Ultimately, they used their private spaces and neighborhood hangouts however they saw fit. The HCC's reform work did yield some results. Not discouraged by individuals they considered immoral or by those who were indifferent to community activists' efforts, HCC members continued to organize neighborhood programs aimed at the creation of wholesome neighborhoods. Moreover, the organization's visions of community engagement and betterment galvanized and encouraged ordinary working- and middle-class folks to work toward the elimination of deteriorating neighborhoods and to formulate strategies for local issues that were often ignored by city officials. Interested in reconfiguring Harlem's physical landscape, the formation of the HCC and its multitiered intracommunity activities delineated blacks' relentless initiatives to enrich their living spaces, as well as refute white city folks' views that black enclaves were locations of criminality and devoid of law-abiding people.

Geraldine Chaney and Neighborhood Activism in Queens

Blacks living in New York's largest borough were concerned with the physical landscape and upkeep of their communities. Located across Manhattan's East River, the population of the borough of Queens jumped from over 200,000 in 1910 to approximately 500,000 in 1920.[64] By the late 1930s, the borough's population, consisting of native-born white and black New Yorkers, Germans, Irish, Italian, and other immigrants, reached more than one million. And like Harlem, Queens was considered "one of the fastest growing Negro communities in the World." According to the *NYAN*, Queens's sizeable black population, living mostly in the communities of Flushing, Jamaica, and Corona, was an estimated 5,120 in 1920 and doubled to approximately 13,600 in 1930.[65] Early-twentieth-century blacks poured into the increasing popular borough, viewing the area as an alternative to living in congested and overpriced Manhattan tenement apartments.

The vast majority of black Queens residents settled in South Jamaica. In the second decade of the twentieth century, various sections of Jamaica were developed into "plain but good one- and two-family houses, close together on small plots" for white New Yorkers and immigrant families. By the late years of the second decade of the twentieth century into the early 1920s, such neighborhoods and housing spaces were opened to African Americans.[66] Growing up in Jamaica during the early 1930s, black intellectual Harold Cruse, without romanticizing racial harmony or undermining white violence in Queens, recalled that his former hometown was "not a typical American neighborhood at all. It had [N]ative Americans, Irish, Poles, Jews, Germans, Italians, and blacks, who lived side by side without much visible friction. There was no separate black neighborhoods in Jamaica in the 1920s and the 1930s. Green fields and the pure air and space of Jamaica" attracted southern migrants and native-born black New Yorkers to the borough.[67] In the first two decades of the twentieth century, the housing constructions of real estate developer J. Franklin Patterson's Merrick Gardens and the business strategies of African American realty companies like J. L. Lee's Frederick Douglass Realty Company made it possible for blacks, especially those desiring to relocate from Harlem and other parts of the city that were plagued by congestion and high housing prices, to rent and purchase reasonably priced homes in South Jamaica.[68]

Housing opportunities for blacks made South Jamaica a premier area for black home ownership in New York City. As blacks flooded into South Jamaica, they established social and political organizations—including the Jamaica branch of the NAACP—became involved in community politics, promoted racial uplift, and actively contested racial inequality and white violence. But South Jamaica's steadily growing black populace did not sit well with Queens's white residents. The so-called invasion by blacks purchasing homes in South Jamaica exposed interracial violence and race discrimination and resulted in white flight. Similar to whites' exodus from increasingly black populated areas in Harlem and other urban cities around the nation, Queens's white inhabitants left South Jamaica for other parts of Queens, thus leaving vacant apartments and houses. Real estate agents and landlords, feeling the economic void of white flight, rented abandoned living spaces to blacks and poor whites. For many blacks, the opportunity for homeownership made South Jamaica, according to Urban League activist James H. Hubert and NYAN staff writer Artie Simpson, the "finest Negro colonies of the state" and "the poor colored man's Mecca."[69]

Inter-war–era social activist and budding city politician Geraldine Chaney and her railroad porter husband Robert Chaney were two of the many thousands of blacks who settled in South Jamaica during the second decade of the twentieth century. Born in 1890 in Norfolk, Virginia, Geraldine Chaney passionately promoted civic engagement, community protection and betterment, and racial advancement for Queens residents. An influential political and community reformer, she was the director of Jamaica's Southside House, a settlement house for black children, and a member of several South Jamaica social, political, and religious institutions, including the Brooks Memorial Methodist Episcopal Church, NAACP Jamaica chapter, Committee for Equal Rights, Southside Civic Organization, and the Colored Welfare Organization.[70] Chaney's affiliation with various local reform groups indicated her commitment to organizations that actively engaged in reforming the area's socioeconomic and political landscape and provided economic relief for destitute and working-poor Queens residents. Moreover, Chaney's wide organizational network enabled her to politicize local people about important community issues and mobilize black men and women for neighborhood change. Similar to the HCC and other New York black reform groups, Queens's African American social and political organizations relentlessly placed local community issues at the center of city politics and pressured city powerbrokers to address issues relating to housing conditions, vice cleanup, and the labor exclusion of black doctors and medical professionals from Queensboro General Hospital.[71]

Geraldine Chaney was one of the city's many rising black women who ran for political office during the 1930s. Nearly a decade earlier, the unyielding work of white and black suffragists culminated in the passage of the Nineteenth Amendment, bringing thousands of American women, most notably New York black women like Chaney and others, into electoral politics. According to historian Julie A. Gallagher, black women politicians, belonging to different political parties, developed a "broad vision of politics that included a strategic engagement with various arms of the state, especially the legislative branch of government" and used their various political platforms to confront both Progressive- and Depression-era issues such as "unemployment, poverty, affordable housing, and rising food prices."[72] All in all, New York black female politicians like Chaney entered electoral politics to "reshape one of the most exclusive power institutions in America," to enforce and protect African Americans' inherent rights as citizens, and to expand the boundaries of black freedom.[73] When Chaney entered the 1930s political arena, the Queens resident was in company with a host of New York Inter-war–era black women politicians that called for new legislative directions in New York and American politics. For instance, in 1934, the New York Socialist Party supported Harlem schoolteacher and socialist Layle Lane in her run for the U.S. Congress. That same year, lawyer Eunice Hunton Carter entered state politics, becoming the first African American woman to run for New York State Assembly in the Nineteenth District on the Republican ticket.[74] Socialist activist Alma Crosswaith was a candidate for Board of Alderman Nineteenth Assembly District in 1932, 1934, 1935, and 1938. Communist and Harlem Workers School Director Williana Burroughs ran for city comptroller in 1933 and for lieutenant governor in 1934.[75] Despite strong public support and organizational backing from radical Left organizations and bourgeois civil rights groups, political hopefuls Lane, Carter, Crosswaith, and Burroughs were all unsuccessful in their bids for public office. Nevertheless, New York black women's candidacies for city and state public offices demonstrated their belief that electoral politics was a viable strategy to pursue and fight for racial justice and equality, civil rights, labor equality, and decent schools, and to address the many socioeconomic and political issues plaguing Gotham's multiethnic population.

Part of a lesser-known yet significant coalition of New York black women political candidates of the Depression era, Chaney, although a registered Democrat, ran for City Alderman in the Fifty-eighth District on the Independent Citizens Party ticket in 1935. Chaney ran under the banner of the Independent Citizen Party, a political coalition consisting of independent church, civic, and labor voters, because it allowed her to broaden her constituent base and appeal to city voters who did not affiliate with the nation's traditional two-party system. Chaney's candidacy and her multilayered political platform advocated for city and state tax reductions, the elimination of slum districts, a free college education, decent low-cost housing, recreational playgrounds for Queens residents, and the enforcement of New York state civil rights legislation. Chaney's proposed political policies garnered wide backing from different political coalitions. Noting Chaney's wide-ranging political support, one city newspaper commented that "party lines in Queens County were shattered as Democratic and Republican workers continued to flock to the 'united front' candidacy of Mrs. Geraldine Chaney."[76] Influential black and white New Yorkers such as Harlem real estate developer and Republican politician J. Dalmus Steele and United Colored Democracy leader Walter E. Reifer and other political coalitions, including the Democratic and Republican parties, endorsed Chaney's candidacy. Expressing his enthusiasm for Chaney, Reifer hoped "that Mrs. Chaney is elected. She has my moral support. If I can give any message to the Negro voters, whether they be Democrats, Republicans, Communists, or what not, it is that the political unity of the Negro comes before party regularity." In the spirit of promoting "unity of all laboring people for their common interest, the Communist Party "withdraws its candidate [white organizer August Henkel] in order to support Mrs. Chaney." According to Communist activist Samuel Reed, "the withdrawal of our candidate from the Communist ticket was based on a request from a committee representing Mrs. Chaney for the formation of a united independent ticket. We gladly withdraw in favor of Mrs. Chaney and will put all our efforts behind her."[77]

Chaney's political run for alderman was short-lived. In November 1935, the Board of Elections withdrew the passionate activist's name from the Queens ballot. Chaney and several other prospective Queens officeholders' nominating petitions were deemed fraudulent and invalid by the Board of Elections and the Queens County Supreme Court, including those of Republicans Edward E. Buhler, running for alderman in the 58th district, and Paul Seigel, running for state assembly in the 4th district.[78] Chaney's unsuccessful foray into electoral politics did not deter her from "fighting discrimination on [all] fronts." She continued to publicly agitate for and highlight Queens's much needed political and social transformation, stressing the elimination of "housing horrors, the double rent standards for blacks," and city leaders' neglect of Jamaica's vice district.[79]

South Jamaica, "once identifie[d] as an area of black settlement, attracted poor as well as middle-class blacks, and hard-won respectability existed [next to] areas of extremely distressed housing. There was a steady growth of poorer residents living in poorly constructed, badly overcrowded and dilapidated frame houses."[80] By the late 1920s, local newspapers, reformers, and residents considered South Jamaica to be one of the worst slums in New York, regarding the area as a "human

cesspool badly in need of a cleanup."[81] Chaney's much loved community of mani-
cured lawns and well-kept homes was gradually becoming a site of dilapidated and
abandoned housing structures and a breeding ground for nefarious activities. One
of South Jamaica's most notorious areas, regularly publicized in local black newspapers, was Railroad Avenue.[82] The premier but undesignated red-light district
was known for its widely diverse commercial businesses and thrilling and illicit
amusements. Railroad Avenue's high- and lowbrow bawdy houses, crowded bar-
rooms, numbers gambling headquarters, and rundown coffee shops and beer gardens attracted South Jamaica's regular partygoers as well as inquisitive urbanites.
The popular area was also a working location for "lounging women waiting to steer
a prospect into any one of scores of side street [brothels]" and for neighborhood
con artists eagerly waiting to devise and employ a con game.[83]

Not one to shy away from publicly expressing her views about city politics
and affairs and vice, Chaney was part of a coalition of leading black and white
Queens activists, including members of the Southside House, Committee for Equal
Rights, and the Urban League Jamaica chapter, that proposed "a moral and physical cleanup" of Railroad Avenue, South Jamaica, and the entire borough. The failure of city politicians to provide economic assistance for slum elimination in the
borough inspired Chaney's commitment to building institutions that confronted
the many socioeconomic issues plaguing Jamaica residents. In 1934, black and
white residents, business owners, and religious and community advocates sent
a slum clearance petition to Tenement House Commissioner and Housing Authority Chairman and Slum Clearance Committee (SCC, a citizens organization
that compiled information on city slums) head Langdon W. Post, which serves as
a classic example of how municipal leaders neglected Jamaica and other crime-
stricken areas throughout the city.

New York's 1930s slum-clearance programs were part of New Deal initiatives to
address inadequate housing conditions and eliminate slum conditions in American
cities. In the early 1930s, Public Works Administration (PWA) officials allotted
federal funds to state and city housing agencies to renovate selected sections of
their cities; the New York Housing Authority received an estimated $25 million.
As the head of several important city agencies, Post, with the assistance of the
SCC, decided how federal funds would be distributed throughout the metropolis,
announcing in the mid-1930s that the city would accept proposals from local business and social and political organizations for consideration in its slum clearance
plan.[84] Selected organizations would receive federal funds for the renovation of
slum areas in their districts as well as the construction of low-income apartment
buildings. Black, white, and Hispanic merchant organizations and social and political groups in the city, including Queens's NAACP and Urban League chapters
and Chaney's Committee for Equal Opportunity, all submitted proposals to the

SCC, reasoning that slum elimination was vital to bettering Jamaica residents' socioeconomic landscape and steering "youths and young women of the section from careers of crime and vice."[85]

Although other Queens County communities like those in Flushing had their fair share of rundown apartment buildings, unsanitary street conditions, and slews of unwholesome leisure spots, Queens residents believed that Jamaica, considered by many to be "the worst [slum] in the county," was an ideal candidate for the city's slum clearance plan. To the dismay of many, Post and municipal leaders rejected Jamaica residents' proposal, reserving federal dollars to renovate housing and street conditions in various sections of Brooklyn and Manhattan. While local officials recognized Jamaica's deteriorating physical landscape and residents' aspirations for healthier and affordable housing spaces, they reasoned that government spending would go toward "real slums"—not "pest spots" like those in Queens. Post's and other city officials' views of Jamaica as a district with minimal slum conditions invalidated Chaney's and other inhabitants' frustrations and experiences with living in deplorable conditions.

Queens residents denounced the decision by Post and other urban leaders to exclude Jamaica from the slum-clearance program. In response to Post's decision and comments on Queens, white attorney Joseph Rothman, legal counsel for the 150th Street Merchants and Property Owners Association stated, "Slum conditions in Queens are increasing. These conditions reached their peak in Manhattan and Brooklyn at the turn of the century and are already on the decline. Concentration of slum clearance in other boroughs will accelerate the pace of deterioration of Queens until the borough, already the stepchild of the city, will become a veritable city of slums." Chaney resented city officials' assertion that Jamaica, a district with similar yet unique socioeconomic and political issues compared to other parts of the city, was not a "real slum." To prove that Jamaica was indeed an area in need of state and federal intervention, a facetious Chaney offered to personally escort Post on a "tour" of the area—a vicinity that she considered "worse than that found in Harlem, and [possesses] housing horrors that would require the pen of a Charles Dickens to describe adequately." Disappointed that Queens was denied the political and financial backing it needed to transform its geographical terrain, Chaney encouraged residents "not [to] accept this as a setback. It means merely that we will have to fight all the harder for slum elimination and for playgrounds."[86]

Lack of financial assistance from federal and municipal leaders hardly dissuaded Chaney or Jamaica, Queens, residents and community leaders from developing strategies aimed at eliminating vice. Chaney continued to be in the forefront of community reform, appealing to a diverse cross section of New York black and white business, religious, and political leaders to partner against crime and slum conditions and to conduct surveys on troublesome neighborhoods in Jamaica and throughout the city. Urban activists planned on using survey findings to pressure New York Housing Authority officials including Post and his successor Alfred Rheinstein to initiate cleanup programs in neglected districts. Chaney appealed to varying reformist organizations for several reasons. Drawing from political campaign strategies from her mid-1930s bid for City Alderman, Chaney hoped to garner broad citywide support for Jamaica, Queens, demonstrating that the forgotten community's existing and future socioeconomic circumstances were not only important to Queens residents but to all New Yorkers. More importantly, the unification of different social and political organizations acting in concert against city slums, poor living environments, and other pressing socioeconomic affairs gripping the city symbolized the significance of interborough activism and illuminated how the city's vastly diverse communities were often plagued by similar issues.[87]

Chaney placed before New York community leaders several recommendations to eliminate South Jamaica, Queens's "picturesque but unhealthy streets of women" and men. Chaney proposed that municipal leaders invest financial resources in the construction of new, or the improvement of existing, neighborhood playgrounds and other recreational facilities for Queens children. In Chaney's and other urban race activists' estimation, the creation of appropriate amusements and leisure spaces for children and young adults instilled a sense of morality and respectability and provided urban youth with alternative forms of entertainment, thus lessening their participation in potentially harmful and unlawful social activities. The Queens reformer's main proposal, especially in the wake of Jamaica's exclusion from federal and city slum clearance programs, was the eradication of vice districts and urban ghettos. Drawing from 1920s and 1930s activists' citywide initiatives for housing reform and understanding firsthand Jamaica citizens' desires for restructured neighborhoods and homes, Chaney called for the demolition of substandard housing facilities and the establishment of a police department crime prevention bureau in South Jamaica. Chaney reasoned that these particular recommendations offered citizens a better quality of life, community protection, and the opportunity to partner with local law enforcement against crime and deplorable borough conditions. By forging alliances with the NYPD, despite its reputation for harassing and brutalizing racially and ethnically diverse New Yorkers, Chaney, clearly embracing legalism, articulated that partnerships with law enforcers enabled local folks to actively voice their concerns about neighborhood affairs, provided opportunities for black residents and police to reconfigure community relations, and "demonstrated blacks' adherence to law and order, as well as how some blacks tried to distinguish themselves from blacks engaged in criminal activity."[88] Additionally, such partnerships stifled perceptions that poor urban communities were ideal locations for wrongdoers to pursue their own economic agendas.

Similar to Harlem Citizens Council members' neighborhood reform work, Queens residents' grassroots activism and leadership and long struggle for community rehabilitation did not resolve South Jamaica's socioeconomic issues and failed to hinder individuals' participation in New York's informal economy. But collective activism and written appeals to city officials, especially about slum clearances, did produce some significant changes for Queens residents. Under the leadership of New York City Housing Authority Commissioner Alfred Rheinstein, various sections of South Jamaica received more than $2 million in federal funding for clearing slum districts in 1939. Tackling some of Chaney's recommendations, federal assistance paid for the demolition of dilapidated tenements, erected several recreational facilities, and began the construction of new low-income housing structures. Chaney and other community leaders viewed the city's decision to transform the area's physical conditions as an economic investment in the neighborhood and its inhabitants. In their minds, improved urban communities and better quality housing would attract legitimate businesses, improve the lives of Queens residents, and potentially curb criminality and unrespectable leisure and income-producing activities.[89]

Conclusion

Race bigotry in the urban housing market, whites' anxieties about black migration into nonblack communities, and individual poverty relegated a diverse group of New York blacks to overcrowded and poorly maintained apartments and vice-infested communities. Congested living spaces left city dwellers with relatively little privacy and exposed to neighborhood criminality and to each other's varying social lives, moral practices, and stances on informal labor. Urban blacks, especially the working poor, did not speak with a unified voice when it came to city vice, troublesome neighbors, or the operation of illicit and unlicensed street- and apartment-based businesses. Opinions on extralegal income-generating activities were multifaceted and conflicting, and they garnered different responses from informal economy consumers, participants, and opponents. Less-privileged blacks who took part in the city's underground economy either as laborers or consumers distinguished employment opportunities that were associated with vice rackets from those of lawful but unlicensed labor. Many reasoned that particular forms of illicit labor, namely bootlegging and drug dealing, prostitution, and numbers banking, were detrimental to racial progress and household stability and respectability, and obstructed New York social reformers' initiatives to create wholesome living spaces. Individual expressions of resistance and involvement in collective neighborhood activism outlined their condemnation for undesirable neighbors and lewd and vile behavior.

New York residents' opposition to immoral and unlawful forms of labor and unwholesome neighborhoods and apartment structures was reflected in the scores of citizen complaint letters addressed to race reformers and city officials and their grassroots neighborhood organizations. Ordinary working- and middle-class blacks were central to city reform and neighborhood politics and affairs, especially when elected officials ignored their concerns for community improvement. The desires for slum and vice eradication and the construction of affordable housing structures culminated in the development and implementation of community protest strategies that were intended to transform crime-ridden communities into physically healthy and morally respectable environments and to raise city dwellers' awareness about the socioeconomic and political issues plaguing their communities and the city as a whole. Striving for racial uplift and neighborhood empowerment, individual and collective expressions of neighborhood activism proved beneficial for many urban black communities. They pressured police, municipal leaders, and race reformers to investigate and legally apprehend known and suspected wrongdoers and tenement house law violators; encouraged residents to publicly voice their concerns about lawlessness; and organized public forums and programs focused on vice elimination, neighborhood cleanup, and community policing. Moreover, neighborhood reform fostered interracial and interborough cooperation between varying political, religious, and social organizations. Complaints by neighborhood associations and individuals allowed residents to place local community affairs at the center of city politics.

At the same time, community engagement had varying outcomes and levels of success. Neighborhood activism improved community conditions and raised urban citizens' consciousness about local matters; however, it also resulted in futile attempts at community rehabilitation and sometimes failed to produce substantial outcomes. Grassroots activism did not always impact hindered vice profiteers from hustling and advertising their businesses in apartment hallways, stairwells and alleys, and on front stoops. City reformers' public campaigns against vice rackets failed to thwart some individuals' involvement in illegal or unrespectable labor and certainly did not curtail informal laborers' misappropriation of urban public and private spaces. Instead, local activists' policing of personal and private behavior and bold attempts at addressing lawlessness seemingly complicated and exposed vice racketeers' working patterns, which in many instances drove illegal labor and businesses deeper into black urban spaces. For some underground economy workers, this meant reducing their visibility on the streets—adjusting work locations, routines, and marketing tactics—and developing strategies that not only evaded apprehension by the police but also the watchful eyes of their neighbors.

New York residents were invested in the safety and advancement of their neighborhoods and its inhabitants. Neighborhood advocacy delineated their refusal to wait for public resources and assistance from local politicians, law enforcement, and the city's various anti-vice and black civil rights organizations. Local social reformers and leaders became transformative figures within their residential districts, persistently toiling for the revitalization of urban neighborhoods and for community preservation and discipline. Inspired by the historical traditions and legacies of self-help politics and community sustainability and their experiences inhabiting underserved communities, local grassroots activism underscored broad visions of city life, social mobility, community protection, and public propriety.

Conclusion

In 1992, Aminata Dia emigrated from Senegal to the United States to study business management at New York City's prestigious Columbia University. After nearly one month of study at Columbia, Dia withdrew from the Ivy League school. In an insightful 2001 *New York Times* editorial on New York African braiding hairstylists and the popularity of unique hair-braiding styles, Dia explained that financial difficulties made it impossible for her to continue her education and live in New York. To financially survive in one of the nation's most expensive cities, Dia turned to a highly specialized and in-demand skill that she acquired as a child in her homeland. She became a professional hair-braider. Dia joined thousands of black female New Yorkers who, since the early 1980s and 1990s, specialized in the creation of intricate hair-braiding styles for urban women. Though considered low-skilled laborers by many, the Senegalese native belongs to a highly skilled community of women (and some men) that draws upon distinct cultural and ethnic traditions, making it possible for them to create niches for themselves within the nation's billion-dollar beauty and hair industry. African scholar Cheikh Anta Babou, who researches Senegalese female hair-braiders in the southern and northeastern region of the United States, argues that hair-braiding as a "profession, traditionally reserved for women belonging to endogamic craft corporations ('castes' in Senegal), has become in the diaspora a highly sought-after and valued career, attracting Senegalese of all genders, ethnic groups, and social statures."[1] For West African women like Dia, hair-braiding has become a viable and, in some cases, lucrative short- and long-term employment opportunity. Hair-braiding is especially appealing to those who are restricted by contemporary U.S. immigration policies and labor laws and those who are not proficient in English.[2] At the same time, hair-braiding is "not merely a job of last resort that women were compelled to choose because of their immigration situation or because they lacked the professional skills to find employment elsewhere." On the contrary, "the popularity of Senegalese braiding opened a large window of opportunity for female immigrants."[3]

New York hair-braiders, particularly those without cosmetology licenses, typically offer hair-care services in their homes; some rent chairs in both licensed and unlicensed beauty salons. Furthermore, the city's most visible informal hair-braiders showcase their artistic work on New York streets. Dressed in traditional African clothing, female hair-braiders can routinely be seen sitting by themselves or in small groups of two or three on colorful crates throughout the city, most notably in various sections of Harlem and Brooklyn, asking female passersby if they want their hair braided for a reasonable price. Other braiding specialists sometimes stroll down 125th Street between Morningside Drive and Lexington Avenue and other parts of New York, particularly near city subway stations, distributing business flyers and cards to women entering or emerging from the train stations. While many potential female consumers are receptive to hair-braiders' persistent hustle and marketing tactics, others believe that hair-braiders' advertising strategies are aggressive and a nuisance. Fierce competition among New York's scores of talented braiders and the prospect of earning high weekly and monthly wages often results in round-the-clock consumer solicitation and sometimes the pestering of potential clients.

As cultural producers and businesswomen, hair-braiders are reaping noticeable economic benefits from an exclusive yet expanding labor market. For a hairstyle, African hair-braiders charge clients anywhere between $25 and $500. Hair prices typically depend on the selected hairstyle and the labor and time required to braid the client's hair. In 2009, some New York hair-braiders, working at least six days a week, earned an estimated $1,600 per month.[4] These artistic innovators have certainly fashioned unique positions for themselves within a confined and competitive labor sector. At the same time, urban hair-braiders, like many formal and informal wage earners, face their own fair share of workplace challenges and limitations. Long working hours, lack of short- and long-term benefits, as well as little or no legal and physical protection from employers or unsatisfied consumers pose potential obstacles for hair-braiders. Also, the physicality of hair-braiding adds to some women's laboring experiences. Hair-braiding can be taxing on women's bodies, often leaving many fatigued and suffering from physical pain caused by standing or sitting for long periods of time and from repetitive hand, wrist, and finger movements.

Contemporary New York newspaper editorials and opinion pieces on urban hair-braiders cast a spotlight on modern-day New York women's labor as informal economy workers. Today, New York female underground laborers, consisting of native-born and naturalized New Yorkers, undocumented immigrants, and migrants from across the nation, engage in a wide range of underground vocations for a variety of socioeconomic and personal reasons.[5] These dynamic yet understudied group of city laborers occupy full- and part-time employment positions as sex workers, household cleaners and cooks, childcare providers, hairstylists and nail technicians, cab drivers, street and subway vendors and entertainment performers, and drug dealers. Newspaper articles, with their captivating and eye-catching headlines and striking photographs, offer rare glimpses into the lives of urban workers. They candidly underscore black women's attraction to different categories of informal work and their varying levels of successes and failures as underground laborers. For example, fifty-two-year-old single mother of four and veteran Bronx street sex worker Barbara Terry, whose personal story was featured in a 2011 *NYT* article, entered the trade at the tender age of twenty-one when her husband abandoned the family some time in the 1970s or 1980s. Working as a sex worker on Hunts Point, off the Bruckner Expressway in the Bronx, nearly her entire adult life, Terry describes the pros and cons of prostitution and why she, even in her fifties, continues to walk the streets. Legally arrested over 100 times and spending countless nights at New York's Rikers Island prison, Terry seemingly "loves the excitement of [prostitution and] coming out here [in the streets] and seeing all these beautiful people [clients and fellow sex workers] I know. Even my dates are a comfort. This place has made me strong. It keeps you young."[6] Moreover, recent newspaper editorials and opinion pieces show that some urban black women's entrance into informal work was precipitated by periods of national financial downturns and employment crises. Reminiscent of the 1930s Great Depression's severe impact on poverty-stricken black women, American's great recession of the mid-to-late 2000s adversely affected workingwomen's lives and circumvented their efforts to earn a living in formal labor markets. One *Washington Post* writer rightfully observed that "across the country, black women are bearing a heavier responsibility for family and friends than their white counterparts, even as they struggle to emerge from an economic downturn that has hit them harder."[7]

Recent labor statistics highlight African American women's depressing financial conditions within the nation's free-market economy during one of the nation's worst economic disasters. In 2009, nearly two years after the Great Recession began and the same year that the nation witnessed the inauguration of its first African American president, the national black unemployment rate stood at a striking 16.0 percent; white unemployment was significantly lower than that of blacks and accounted for 9.3 percent. The jobless rates for black men and women were 17.5 percent and 12.7 percent, respectively.[8] Toward the end of 2012, African Americans' national unemployment rate increased slightly, while whites' unemployment rate decreased by a whole percent. That year, total unemployment statistics were 16.2 percent for blacks and 8.1 percent for whites. Nationally, black women's unemployment rate was 10.8 percent.[9] In 2009, New York City's jobless rate was 9.0 percent; in 2012, it was slightly more than 10 percent. Unemployment for black New Yorkers stood at 6.6 percent between 2007 and 2008 and 14 percent between 2011 and 2012; the white unemployment rate was 3.1 percent between 2007 and 2008 and 6.8 percent between 2011 and 2012.[10]

Contemporary unemployment figures underscore that African American women have disproportionately suffered compared to their white counterparts. While black women fare somewhat better than black men, they gradually experienced employment loss during periods of national recovery while black men slightly regained employment. Scholar F. Michael Higginbotham observed that "over the course of the recovery period, black women lost more jobs than any other group in the American workforce. The disproportionately high unemployment rate for black women is particularly alarming, not only because of the dual racial and gender bias implications but also because more than half of all black families with dependent children are headed by black women."[11] Like their working-class predecessors from the first half of the twentieth century, modern-day working-poor and unemployed urban black women often rely upon a variety of economic resources to address poverty and short- and long-term unemployment and to build sound economic futures. Despite federal and state changes and restrictions to the nation's welfare system during the 1990s and 2000s, jobless yet hopeful New York black women received monetary funds and benefits from federally funded assistance programs. Some women continued to search for employment within the city's dismal and variable labor market. Other New York black women, like sex worker Barbara Terry, joined the hundreds of thousands of Americans who earned a living outside the margins of regulated and legal work.

The socioeconomic circumstances and labor choices and experiences of contemporary black female laborers are strikingly similar to those of women featured in this book. Although separated by distinctly different time periods and historical contexts, modern-day representations of New York black women underground workers can be analyzed side-by-side with those of Progressive- and Inter-war–era workingwomen. Present-day black women's laboring narratives reveal much about their foremothers' economic status, their struggle to provide for themselves and their families, their social desires and religious and spiritual belief systems, and their willingness—despite legal consequences and public criticism—to engage in risky and dangerous work. Modern-day black women's overlooked employment accounts offer scholars of the urban black female experience historic snapshots of women's ingenuity initiatives and strategies to live, thrive, and make their way in a city that yielded and restricted socioeconomic and labor opportunities for women of a certain racial and class background.

Black women's expanding and multilayered role within the urban labor market is perhaps best illustrated in New York's informal labor sector of the early twentieth century. A diverse array of socioeconomic circumstances, labor issues, and personal ideologies and aspirations attracted city black women to underground work. Meager wages; limited formal wage opportunities; fluctuating sensibilities on urban public space, racial uplift, and respectable politics; and a culture of white bigotry influenced less privileged black women's decisions to participate in New York's underground economy. Furthermore, working-class black women's role as primary breadwinners of their families and the desire to obtain occupational mobility, earn material wealth, and enjoy urban amusements and pleasures prompted many to transcend prevailing early-twentieth-century ideas that bound them to low-paying formal wage work. For some of the women discussed in this study, hidden and unregulated labor markets represented an opportunity, however limited, to depart from legal labor spaces that denied them occupational mobility and, most importantly, dignity and respect. The possibility of securing employment autonomy and all the rights and privilege that came with it, as well as refashioning new and alternative labor identities, were central to workingwomen's visions of labor inequity.

While personal visualizations of occupational control were within some black women's reach, others' dreams of employment flexibility were obstructed by day-to-day dangers. The collateral costs that accompanied informal work significantly transformed black women's lives. For many, their laboring attempts led to legal arrest and confinement, rape and murder, family and community shame and estrangement, and sometimes violent confrontations with unsatisfied clients and other underground competitors. Moreover, race and gender exclusion from high-paying and lucrative employment hindered black women's best efforts at navigating New York's complex labor market. No doubt, many women stepping out of the confines of conventional work and breaching early-twentieth-century gender relations and politics understood the physical, psychological, and emotional risks associated with unregulated labor. For the sake of financial preservation, work flexibility, social mobility, and personal fulfillment, however, many women were willing to undertake such risks, ignoring the consequences of off-the-books work. To protect and sustain themselves, women, individually or collectively, devised and adopted protective labor strategies that challenged their detractors and safeguarded their lives and social and economic interests. To borrow from scholar Winnifred

Brown-Glaude's work on twentieth-century Jamaican informal economy women, New York's black working women "demonstrated an amazing capacity to understand and negotiate their marginal position and showed a knack for intervening in the micro- and macrostructure of power that shaped their lifeworlds."[12]

Reform-minded political activists, community advocates, and municipal leaders' organized grassroots campaigns, public outcries, and legal statutes posed serious threats to black women's informal labor. In their attempts to tackle urban vice and transform crime-ridden New York communities into respectable neighborhoods, informal economy opponents believed that illegal and degraded labor and social amusements threatened urban stability and traditional working- and middle-class values. For African American race leaders and reformers, certain forms of informal labor debased normative images of female labor and womanhood, religion, and sexuality and countered black elite versions of racial uplift. Furthermore, underground labor disrupted the everyday lives of respectable urban citizens. Ordinary city folks resented having daily encounters with neighborhood sex workers, numbers collectors, and street hustlers who lived and hustled in and around their apartments and communities. Many were also concerned about their children's well-being and exposure to their neighbors' depraved occupations and lifestyles; they prayed that their younger kin would not be seduced or lured down a path of criminality and immorality. Urban parents hoped that family lessons and conversations about morality, respectability, and racial advancement would outweigh visual imageries of material consumption, lively apartment parties, and well-dressed neighborhood ruffians. Viewing proper public decorum as a precondition for racial equality and black civil rights, black activists maintained that African Americans' participation in New York's informal economy reinforced whites' distorted perceptions of blackness. What essentially troubled these activists was urban whites' failure to recognize class distinctions within black communities and to distinguish those individuals committed to collective race advancement from those devoted to satisfying their own personal economic needs and pleasures.

Black women informal workers were certainly aware of the public criticism and citywide campaigns waged against their social lifestyles and labor choices. Female workers responded in a variety of ways to those who indicted them. Some were indifferent about how their neighbors perceived them. Underground workers like 1930s Harlem hot goods vendor Odile Gonzalez and other personalities discussed in this book were unashamed of their choice of labor. They cared little about how their economic activities complicated working- and middle-class efforts toward conveying acceptable public representations of female work and public propriety and urban whites' perceptions of black life. As I have argued, women like Gonzalez were more concerned with devising wage-generating strategies that stressed individual empowerment, self-sufficiency, and fiscal stability. The collective racial and economic progress of urban blacks was far from their minds. Instead, they formulated financial and upwardly mobile agendas for themselves and constantly reconfigured propriety performances and politics on a daily basis and according to their own sensibilities. Conversely, other women diligently worked to keep their personal and laboring lives private. Their labor concealment does not necessarily suggest that they were ashamed of how they earned a living. Many were simply interested in maintaining outward appearances of respectability, and very much concerned with the consequences of their labor. Exterior displays of public propriety permitted many informal laborers the ability to earn a living without public shame and still be regarded as respectable community members. More importantly, masking one's income-producing activities was a survival strategy used to avoid legal arrest and confinement.

New York black women's informal labor was a microcosm of early-twentieth-century urban women's work across the nation. In Chicago, Detroit, Atlanta, Philadelphia, Nashville, and other American cities in this period, working-class African American women broadened the images of female work by creating a variety of employment positions and opportunities for themselves within the urban informal labor market. Gotham women featured in this study and around the nation transcended normative representations of womanhood, respectability, and domesticity. In essence, many surpassed their gender-specific roles and behaviors as formal wage earners; as mothers, wives, and daughters; and as urban citizens, becoming their own agents of socioeconomic change and important cultural sellers and producers within underserved black neighborhoods and other urban communities. An examination of the complex realities of informal female workers underscores the distinct labor experiences and socioeconomic successes and struggles of many urban working-class women. As a diverse group of black women entered the informal labor sector, they brought with them their hopes and visions for a brighter economic future, the desire to alter the recipe of economic opportunity for themselves, and the idea that unrecorded employment was a possible avenue toward pursuing freer economic and social lives.

Notes

Introduction

1. Sudhir Venkatesh, *Floating City: A Rogue Sociologist Lost and Found in New York's Underground Economy* (New York: Penguin, 2013), 24.

2. Roi Ottley, *New World A-Coming* (Boston: Houghton Mifflin, 1943), 238.

3. "Blame Low Pay for Immorality," *NYAN*, February 12, 1930, 3.

4. Alison Mackinnon, *Love and Freedom: Professional Women and the Reshaping of Personal Life* (Cambridge: Cambridge University Press, 1997), 34.

5. Luise White, *The Comforts of Home: Prostitution in Colonial Nairobi* (Chicago: University of Chicago Press, 1990), i.

6. Jacqueline Jones, *Labor of Love, Labor of Sorrow: Black Women, Work, and the Family from Slavery to the Present*, 2nd ed. (New York: Vintage Books, 1995), 179.

7. Sharon Harley, ed., *Women's Labor in the Global Economy: Speaking in Multiple Voices* (New Brunswick: Rutgers University Press, 2007); Sharon Harley, "Working for Nothing but for a Living: Black Women in the Underground Economy," in *Sister Circle: Black Women and Work*, ed. Sharon Harley and the Black Women and Work Collective (New Brunswick: Rutgers University Press, 2002); Victoria W. Wolcott, *Remaking Respectability: African American Women in Interwar Detroit* (Chapel Hill: University of North Carolina Press, 2001); Shane White et al., *Playing the Numbers: Gambling in Harlem between the Wars* (Cambridge: Harvard University Press, 2010); Kali N. Gross, *Colored Amazons: Crime, Violence, and Black Women in the City of Brotherly Love, 1880–1910* (Durham: Duke University Press, 2006); Cheryl D. Hicks, *Talk with You like a Woman: African American Women, Justice, and Reform in New York, 1890–1935* (Chapel Hill: University of North Carolina Press, 2010); Talitha L. LeFlouria, *Chained in Silence: Black Women and Convict Labor in the New South* (Chapel Hill: University of

North Carolina Press, 2015); Cynthia M. Blair, *I've Got to Make My Livin': Black Women's Sex Work in Turn-of-the-Century Chicago* (Chicago: University of Chicago Press, 2010); Mireille Miller-Young, *A Taste for Brown Sugar: Black Women in Pornography* (Durham: Duke University Press, 2014).

8. Jacob S. Dorman, "Back to Harlem: Abstract and Everyday Labor during the Harlem Renaissance," in *The Harlem Renaissance Revisited: Politics, Arts, and Letters*, ed. Jeffrey O. G. Ogbar (Baltimore: The Johns Hopkins University Press, 2010), 75.

9. Hicks, *Talk with You like a Woman*, 3.

10. Deborah Gray White, "Mining the Forgotten: Manuscript Sources for Black Women's History," *Journal of American History* 74 (June 1987): 237.

11. Nupur Chaudhuri, Sherry J. Katz, and Mary Elizabeth Perry, eds. *Contesting Archives: Finding Women in the Sources* (Urbana: University of Illinois Press, 2010), xiv.

12. Kali Gross, "Exploring Crime and Violence in Early-Twentieth-Century Black Women's History," in *Contesting Archives: Finding Women in the Sources*, ed. Nupur Chaudhuri et al. (Urbana: University of Illinois Press, 2010), 57.

13. Manning Marable, *Living Black History: How Reimagining the African-American Past Can Remake America's Racial Future* (New York: Basic Books, 2011), 58.

14. Gross, *Colored Amazons*, 2.

15. Harley, "Working for Nothing but for a Living," 50–51.

16. Darlene Clark Hine, *Hine Sight: Black Women and the Re-Construction of American History* (Brooklyn: Carlson Publishing, 1994), 37.

17. Classified Ad 2, *NYAN*, March 1, 1933, 7.

18. Marilynn Wood Hill, *Their Sisters' Keepers: Prostitution in New York City, 1830–1870* (Berkeley: University of California Press, 1993), 1.

19. Sarah Deutsch, *Women and the City: Gender, Space, and Power in Boston, 1870–1940* (New York: Oxford University Press, 2000), 4.

20. Angela Blake, *How New York Became American, 1890–1924* (Baltimore: Johns Hopkins University, 2009), 5.

21. David Ward and Olivier Zunz, *The Landscape of Modernity: New York City, 1900–1940* (Baltimore: Johns Hopkins University Press, 1997); Lewis A. Erenberg, *Steppin' Out: New York Nightlife and the Transformation of America Culture, 1890–1930* (Chicago: University of Chicago Press, 1984); George J. Lankevich, *New York: A Short History* (New York: New York University Press, 2002); Robert P. Marzec, *The Mid-Atlantic Region* (Westport, Conn.: Greenwood Publishing Group, 2004), 3; Blake, *How New York Became American*.

22. Ward and Zunz, *Landscape of Modernity*; Erenberg, *Steppin' Out*; George J. Lankevich, *New York: A Short History* (New York: New York University Press, 2002); Marzec, *Mid-Atlantic Region*, 3; Blake, *How New York Became American*.

23. Nancy Foner, ed., *New Immigrants in New York*, rev. ed. (New York: Columbia University, 2001), 7, 52; Ira Rosenwaike, *Population History of New York City* (Syracuse: Syracuse University Press, 1972), 93.

24. Foner, *New Immigrants in New York*, 145.

25. Xiaolan Bao, "Revisiting New York's Chinatown, 1900–1930," in *Remapping Asian American History*, Sucheng Chan, ed. (Walnut Creek, Calif.: Altamira Press, A Division of

Random House and Littlefield Publishers, Inc., 2003), 46; Roger Daniels, *Asian American since 1850* (Seattle: University of Washington Press, 1988), 152.

26. Cheryl Lynn Greenberg, *Or Does It Explode?: Black Harlem in the Great Depression* (New York: Oxford University Press, 1997), 13; Gerald Benjamin and Charles Brecher, eds., *The Two New Yorks: State-City Relations in the Changing Federal System* (New York: Russell Sage Foundation, 1988), 85.

27. Keith Hart, "Informal Income Opportunities and Urban Unemployment in Ghana," *Journal of Modern African Studies* 11 (March 1973): 61–89.

28. Regina Austin, "An Honest Living": Street Vendors, Municipal Regulation and the Black Public Sphere," *Yale Law Journal* 10 (June 1994): 2119–2131; Alejandro Porters and Saskia Sassen-Koob, "Making It Underground: Comparative Material in the Informal Sector in Western Market Economics," *American Journal of Sociology* 93 (July 1987): 30–61.

"New York City's Informal Economy," in Alejandro Portes et al., eds., *The Informal Economy: Studies in Advanced and Less Developed Countries* (Baltimore: Johns Hopkins University Press, 1987), 60–77; Jim Thomas, "What Is the Informal Economy, Anyway?" SAIS Review 21 (Winter-Spring 2001):1–11; Donald W. Light, "Migrant Enclaves to Mainstream: Reconceptualizing Informal Economic Behavior," *Theory and Society* 33 (2004):705–737; Sudhir Alladi Venkatesh, *Off the Books: The Underground Economy of the Urban Poor* (Cambridge: Harvard University Press, 2006); Winnifred Brown-Glaude, *Higglers in Kingston: Women's Informal Work in Jamaica* (Nashville: Vanderbilt University Press, 2011); Lisa Maher, *Sex Work: Gender, Race, and Resistance in a Brooklyn Drug Market* (New York: Oxford University Press, 2000).

29. Blair, *I've Got to Make My Livin','* 23.

30. Venkatesh, *Off the Books*, 92–93.

31. Light, "Migrant Enclaves to Mainstream," 710–711.

32. Wallace Thurman, *The Collected Writings of Wallace Thurman*, ed. Amritjit Singh and Daniel M. Scott III (New Brunswick: Rutgers University Press, 2003), 73–74; Valerie Boyd, *Wrapped in Rainbows: The Life of Zora Neale Hurston* (New York: Simon and Schuster, 2003), 95; Kevin Grace, "Juke Joints," in *Alcohol and Temperance in Modern History: An International Encyclopedia*, ed. Jack S. Blocker, David M. Fahey, and Iran R. Tyrrell (Santa Barbara, Calif.: ABC-CLIO, Inc., 2003), 343.

33. Shane Vogel, *The Scene of Harlem Cabaret: Race, Sexuality, Performance* (Chicago: University of Chicago Press, 2009), 51.

34. Ira De A. Reid, "Mrs. Bailey Pays the Rent," in *Ebony and Topaz; A Collectanea*, ed. Cahles S. Johnson (New York: National Urban League, 1927), 144.

35. Vogel, *The Scene of Harlem Cabaret*, 51.

36. Thurman, *Collected Writings*, 73.

37. Robin D. G. Kelley, *Race Rebels: Culture, Politics, and the Black Working-Class* (New York: Simon and Schuster, 1996), 46.

38. Erin D. Chapman, *Prove It on Me: New Negroes, Sex, and Popular Cultures in the 1920s* (New York: Oxford University Press, 2012), 8; Chad Heap, *Slumming: Sexual and Racial Encounters in American Nightlife, 1885–1940* (Chicago: University of Chicago Press, 2000).

Chapter 1. Black Women, Urban Labor, and New York's Informal Economy

1. "'Hot Goods' Cal Faces New Trial," *NYAN*, November 20, 1937, 24; "Cops Nab 'Hot Goods Queen,'" *NYAN*, October 2, 1937, 1; "Bub Hewlitt in 'Hot Stuff' Net," *NYAN*, May 21, 1941, 1; *The People v. Odile Gonzalez, filed 1937*, District Attorney's Closed Case Files (DACCF), Municipal Archives of the City of New York (NYMA).

2. The term *colored amazons* is taken from Kali Gross's book, *Colored Amazons*.

3. Deutsch, *Women and the City*, 4.

4. Greenberg, *Or Does It Explode?* 66.

5. Cheryl Lynn Greenberg, *To Ask for an Equal Chance: African Americans in the Great Depression* (New York: Rowman and Littlefield Publishers, 2009), 2.

6. Thomas J. Sugrue, *Sweet Land of Liberty: The Forgotten Struggle for Civil Rights in the North* (New York: Random House Publishing Group, 2008), 4, 12.

7. Mary White Ovington, *Half a Man: The Status of the Negro in New York* (New York: Longmans, Green, and Company, 1911), 40.

8. Greenberg, *Or Does It Explode?* 13; Benjamin and Brecher, *Two New Yorks*, 85; Dorman, "Back to Harlem," 76; Mark Schneider, *Boston Confronts Jim Crow, 1890–1920* (Lebanon, N.H.: Northeastern University Press, 1997), 4.

9. "High Rents and Overcrowding Responsible for Many of the Ills Suffered by Harlemites," *NYA*, August 11, 1923, 1; "New Building on W. 139th St. to Set High Mark for Rental Prices in Harlem," *NYA*, February 29, 1924, 1.

10. Winthrop D. Lane, "Ambushed in the City: The Grim Side of Harlem," in *Survey Graphic: Harlem: Mecca of the New Negro*, ed. Alain Locke (Black Classic Press; repr., Baltimore: Black Classic Books, 1980), 693; "Forces Negroes to Live in Foul Hovels," *The Hunger Fighter*, September 25, 1933, 2.

11. Thelma E. Berlack, "Housing Problem for Small Wage Earners Demand Immediate Attention," *NYAN*, March 6, 1929, 3.

12. Richard Walter Thomas, *Life for Us Is What We Make It: Building Black Community in Detroit, 1915–1945* (Bloomington: Indiana University Press, 1992), 93; Christopher Robert Reed, *The Chicago NAACP and the Rise of Black Professional Leadership, 1910–1966* (Bloomington: Indiana University Press, 1997), 120.

13. Clyde Kiser, *Sea Island to City: A Study of St. Helen Islanders in Harlem and Other Urban Centers* (New York: Atheneum, 1969), 200.

14. Greenberg, *Or Does It Explode?* 19–20.

15. Elise Johnson McDougald, "The Double Task: The Struggle of Negro Women for Sex and Race Emancipation," in Lane, *Survey Graphic*, 690.

16. Greenberg, *Or Does It Explode?* 20, 23–24.

17. Joint Committee to Study the Employment of Colored Women in New York City and Brooklyn, *A New Day for the Colored Woman Worker: A Study of Colored Women in Industry in New York City* (New York: C. P. Young Printers, 1919), 11.

18. Client BH, Box 82, Women's Prison Association Records (WPA), Manuscript and Archives Division, The New York Public Library.

19. Frances A. Kellor, "Southern Colored Girls in the North," *Charities* 13 (March 18, 1905): 584.

20. "Must Raise Voice Louder Says Sharecropper Girl," *Daily Worker*, June 16, 1934, 4.

21. Martina Harris, "Domestic Workers," *NYAN*, August 6, 1938, 6.

22. Community Service Society, Box 271, Folder R776 (Case #102726), Community Service Society Records, 1842–1955, Columbia University, Rare Book and Manuscript Library.

23. Judith Worrell and Carol D. Goodheart, eds., *Handbook of Girls' and Women's Psychological Health* (New York: Oxford University Press, 2006), 21–22.

24. "Woman Jumps to Death in Harlem River," *NYAN*, June 18, 1938, 1.

25. "Mother Held in Baby Death," *NYAN*, December 30, 1939, 2A; Frances Elizabeth Dolan, *Dangerous Familiars: Representations of Domestic Crime in England, 1550–1700* (New York: Cornell University Press, 1994).

26. "Detroit Now in Danger of Jim Crowism," *Chicago Defender*, July 29, 1922, 1.

27. Wallace Thurman, *Negro Life in New York's Harlem: A Lively Picture of a Popular and Interesting Section* (Girard, Kans.: Haldeman-Julius Publications, 1934), 9–10.

28. Kathy Peiss, *Cheap Amusements: Working Women and Leisure in Turn-of-the-Century New York* (Philadelphia: Temple University Press, 1987), 57.

29. Jeff Kisseloff, *You Must Remember This: An Oral History of Manhattan from the 1890s to World War II* (New York: Harcourt Brace Jovanovich, 1989), 326.

30. Evelyn Brooks Higginbotham, *Righteous Discontent: The Women's Movement in the Black Baptist Church, 1880–1920* (Cambridge: Harvard University Press, 1993), 187; Stephanie J. Shaw, *What a Woman Ought to Be and to Do: Black Professional Women Workers during the Jim Crow Era* (Chicago: University of Chicago Press, 1996); Kevin K. Gaines, *Uplifting the Race: Black Leadership, Politics, and Culture in the Twentieth Century* (Chapel Hill: University of North Carolina Press, 1996).

31. Lisa B. Thompson, *Beyond the Black Lady: Sexuality and the New African American Middle Class* (Urbana: University of Illinois Press, 2009), 3.

32. Wolcott, *Remaking Respectability*, 94.

33. Blair, *I've Got to Make My Livin','* 11.

34. White, *Comforts of Home*, 1.

35. "Tenement—Speakeasy," November 7, 1928, Box 36, Folder: 135th–207th, Committee of Fourteen Papers (COF), Manuscripts and Archives Division, The New York Public Library.

36. "Spiritual Worker Caught in Policy Net," *NYAN*, November 9, 1927, 4; Probation Department Case Files #8599 (1927), Municipal Archives of the City of New York; "St. Mary's Spiritual Church," *NYAN*, January 25, 1928, 17.

37. Client LJ, Box 86, WPA.

38. Kelly Miller, "Surplus Negro Women," *Southern Workman* 34 (October 1905): 522–528.

39. Victoria E. Bynum, *Unruly Women: The Politics of Social and Sexual Control in the Old South* (Chapel Hill: University of North Carolina Press, 1992), 131.

40. Probation File Case #7747 (1925) Municipal Archives of the City of New York.

41. Ella Baker and Marvel Cooke, "The Bronx Slave Market," *Crisis*, November 1935, 330.

42. Probation File Case #13344 (1938) Municipal Archives of the City of New York; Baker and Cooke, "Bronx Slave Market," 330–331, 340.

43. Robert L. Boyd, "Race, Labor Market Disadvantage, and Survivalist Entrepreneurship: Black Women in the Urban North during the Great Depression," *Sociological Forum* 15 (December 2000): 648.

44. Roi Ottley and William J. Weatherby, eds., *The Negro in New York: An Informal Social History, 1626–1940* (New York: New York Public Library, 1967), 187.

45. Daniel Bluestone, "The Pushcart Evil," in Ward and Zunz, *Landscape of Modernity*, 291; Suzanne Wasserman, "Hawkers and Gawkers: Peddling and Markets in New York City," in *Gastropolis: Food and New York City*, ed. Annie Hauck-Lawson and Jonathan Deutsch (New York: Columbia University Press, 2009), 153–173.

46. Ward and Zunz, *Landscape of Modernity*, 293.

47. Ibid.

48. Ottley and Weatherby, *Negro in New York*, 187–188; "Mrs. John Dean, Colorful Character, Buried Here Following Death in West," *NYAN*, July 24, 1929.

49. James Weldon Johnson, "The Making of Harlem," in Lane, *Survey Graphic*, 637.

50. Frederick Douglass Opie, *Hog and Hominy: Soul Food from Africa to America* (New York: Columbia University Press, 2013).

51. Psyche A. Williams-Forson, *Building Houses out of Chicken Legs: Black Women, Food, and Power* (Chapel Hill: University of North Carolina Press, 2006), 33.

52. Ottley, *New World A-Coming* (1943; repr., New York: Arno Press, 1968), 60; "Mrs. L. H. Dean Leaves on Six Months Tour to Far-Off Pacific Coast," *NYA*, August 18, 1923, 8.

53. Ottley and Weatherby, *Negro in New York*, 187–188; "Pigfoot Mary Leaves $75,000 Estate," *NYAN*, August 7, 1929, 3; "Mrs. John Dean," *NYAN*, July 24, 1929, 3; Ottley, "New World A-Coming: Here's What Gave Harlem Its Flavor," *NYAN*, April 15, 1944, A7; Judith Weisenfeld, *African American Women and Christian Activism: New York's Black YWCA, 1905–1945* (Cambridge: Harvard University Press, 1998), 152.

54. Frank Byrd. "The Private Life of Big Bess," in *A Renaissance in Harlem: Lost Voices of an American Community*, ed. Lionel Bascom (New York: Bard, 2007), 186.

55. Leslie Ann Schwalm, *A Hard Fight for We: Women's Transition from Slavery to Freedom in South Carolina* (Urbana: University of Illinois Press, 1997), 188.

56. Jennifer Ritterhouse, *Growing Up Jim Crow: How Black and White Southern Children Learned Race* (Chapel Hill: University of North Carolina Press, 2006), 25.

57. "Spits in Face of Girl Who Asked for a Job," *NYAN*, March 19, 1938, 24.

58. "Beat Maid with Hanger," *NYAN*, January 14, 1925, A1; "Says Dancer Threatened Her with Gun," *Pittsburgh Courier*, January 17, 1925, 1.

59. Marvel Cooke, "Help Wanted for the Help," *NYAN*, October 7, 1939, 11; "Beat Maid with Hanger," *NYAN*, January 14, 1926, A1.

60. Jacqueline Jones, *American Work: Four Centuries of Black and White Labor* (New York: W. W. Norton and Company, 1999), 13.

61. General Secretary of Inspection Thomas J. Kelly to Executive Secretary of the Committee of Fourteen (COF), August 15, 1919, Box 30, COF Papers.

62. Elizabeth Ross Haynes, "Negroes in Domestic Service in the United States: Introduction," *Journal of Negro History* 8 (October 1923): 391–392; Elbridge T. Gerry, *Manual of the New York Society for the Prevention of Cruelty to Children* (New York: New York Society for the Prevention of Cruelty to Children, 1913), 58.

63. Gunja SenGupta, *From Slavery to Poverty: The Racial Origins of Welfare in New York, 1840–1918* (New York: New York University Press, 2009), 211.

64. Ibid.

65. "Seven Children in Flat," *NYAN*, May 20, 1925, 1.

66. Sherri Broder, *Tramps, Unfit Mothers, and Neglected Children: Negotiating the Family in Nineteenth-Century Philadelphia* (Philadelphia: University of Pennsylvania Press, 2011), 159–160, 177.

67. "Harlem's 'Baby Farms,'" *NYAN*, September 7, 1927, 15.

68. "Lives a Double Life to Raise Her Pretty Daughter," *Pittsburgh Courier*, March 11, 1939, 9; "Sweet Potato Lady," *Pittsburgh Courier*, March 18, 1939, 9.

69. Tenement—Speakeasy," November 7, 1928, Box 36, Folder: G-R, COF Papers.

70. Client VB, Box 66, WPA, 1936.

71. Tera Hunter, *To 'Joy My Freedom: Southern Black Women's Lives and Labors after the Civil War* (Boston: Harvard University Press, 1997): 57–58.

72. Rhonda Williams, *The Politics of Public Housing: Black Women's Struggles against Urban Inequality* (New York: Oxford University, 2004), 4; "Magistrate Scores Relief Clients and Declares They Act Worse than Dogs," *NYAN*, January 18, 1936, 1.

73. Greenberg, *Or Does It Explode?* 47–48; A. M. Wendell Malliet, "'Flowers! Flowers!' Harlem Hears Street Hawker Shout," *NYAN*, July 3, 1937, 6.

74. "Madge Wundus," *Pittsburgh Courier*, 9.

75. Client FO, Box 90, WPA.

76. Dan Burley, "Girl Takes to Shoe Shining to Escape Going on Relief," *NYAN*, October 1, 1938, 6.

77. Cheryl D. Hicks, "'Bright and Good Looking Colored Girl': Black Women's Sexuality and 'Harmful Intimacy' in Early-Twentieth-Century New York," *Journal of The History of Sexuality* 18 (September 2009): 432.

78. "How to Keep Women at Home," *Colored American Magazine*, January 1908, 7–8.

79. "Delinquent Girls," *Chicago Defender*, October 2, 1915, 8.

80. Henry F. Kletzing and William Henry Crogman, *Progress of a Race or, the Remarkable Advancement of the Afro-American Negro from the Bondage of Slavery, Ignorance and Poverty, to the Freedom of Citizenship, Intelligence Affluence, Honor, and Trust* (Atlanta: J. L. Nichols and Co., 1903), 198, 478, 609.

81. *National Association Notes*, January 1899, 1.

82. Peiss, *Cheap Amusement*, 20–21.

83. "Woman Receives Bullet in Chin," *NYAN*, May 15, 1929, 1.

84. Harley, "Working for Nothing but for a Living," 60–61; Jesse H. Walker, "Odessa Madre, Once DC Queen, Dies Penniless," *NYAN*, March 4, 1990, 1; Courtland Milloy, "The Odessa Files: The Life and Times of the Queen of Washington's Underworld," *Washington Post*, May 7, 2010.

85. Harley, "Working for Nothing but for a Living," 60–61.

86. "Tenement—Speakeasy," May 29, 1928, Box 36, Folder: G-R, COF Papers.

87. Probation Department Case File #5739 (1924), Municipal Archives of the City of New York; Probation Department Case File # 5740 (1924), Municipal Archives of the City of New York.

88. "Inquiry on Quacks Is Set for Tuesday," *NYT*, March 27, 1926, 19.

89. Vivian Morris, "Commercial Enterprise," in *A Renaissance in Harlem: Lost Voices of an American Community*, ed. Lionel Bascom (New York: Bard, 2007), 199.

90. *People v. Blanche Simms*, filed January 31, 1938, District Attorney's Closed Case Files (DACCF), Municipal Archives of the City of New York.

91. Timothy J. Gilfoyle, "Street-Rats and Gutter-Snipes: Child Pickpockets and Street Culture in New York, 1850–1900," *Journal of Social History* 37 (Summer 2004): 870.

92. "Hatpin Stabbing Jails Teacher," *NYAN*, September 5, 1936, 1.

93. Frank Byrd, "Prostitute," in *Harlem Document: Photographs, 1932–1940*, ed. Aaron Siskind (Providence, R.I.: Matrix, 1981), 68.

94. Client LG, Box 80, WPA, 1937.

95. "Man Is Slain; Seize Beauty," *NYAN*, April 14, 1934, 1; "Tearful Girl Acquitted in Man's Death," *NYAN*, May 12, 1934, 1; Theodore McKenzie Death Certificate # 2512, Department of Health of the City of New York, Bureau of Records.

96. Marvel Cooke, "Woman of Affair," *NYAN*, January 20, 1940, 15.

97. Elizabeth Alice Clement, *Love for Sale: Courting, Treating, and Prostitution in New York City, 1900–1945* (Chapel Hill: University of North Carolina Press, 2006), 45.

98. Venkatesh, *Off the Books*, 18.

99. Cooke, "Woman of Affair," *NYAN*, January 20, 1940, 15; T. R. Poston, "Murder Will Out? Who Was the Strangler of Vivacious Cecelia Sargeant? Young Lady of Many Affairs," *NYAN*, January 17, 1934, 9; Fifteen Census of the United States, 1930, Washington, D.C.: National Archives and Records Administration, 1930; Cecelia Sargent Death Certificate #15942, Department of Health of the City of New York, Bureau of Records.

100. Gilfoyle, "Street-Rats and Gutter-Snipes," 853–862; Peter C. Baldwin, "'Nocturnal Habits and Dark Wisdom': The American Response to Children in the Streets at Night, 1880–1930," *Journal of Social History* 35 (Spring 2002): 593–611.

101. Ottley, *New World A-Coming*, 159; Gilfoyle, "Street-Rats and Gutter-Snipes," 853–862.

102. Willetta Simonton, "This Week's Guest Editor Says: Clean-up," *NYAN*, March 18, 1939, 10.

103. Client FG, Box, 80, WPA.

104. "Harlem Schoolgirl Dies Following Attack by Man in Darkened Hallway," *NYAN*, December 18, 1929, 23; "Girl Dies after Attack by Rapist in Harlem Hallway," *NYA*, December 21, 1929; "15-Year old Girl Dies after Being Attacked by Brute," *NYA*, December 14, 1929, 1; Almer Sutton Death Certificate #29374, Department of Health of the City of New York, Bureau of Records.

105. Wolcott, *Remaking Respectability*, 94.

106. "Blame Low Pay for Immorality," *NYAN*, February 12, 1930, 3; Kellor, "Southern Colored Girls in the North," *Charities* 13 (March, 18, 1905): 585.

107. Edgar M. Grey, "The Devil's Playground," *NYAN*, July 6, 1927, 12.

Chapter 2. Madame Queen of Policy

1. Welfare Island was located in the East River of Manhattan and was formerly known as Blackwell Island during the nineteenth and twentieth centuries. The island was renamed Welfare Island in 1921 and later became Roosevelt Island in 1973. Throughout this chapter and the rest of the book, I use the terms *policy racket/game* and *numbers racket/game* interchangeably. Both terms refer to New York City's illegal lottery system. Rufus Schatzberg and Robert J. Kelley, *African-American Organized Crime* (New York: Garland Publishing, 1996), 62; "Mme St. Clair Bares 'Policy' Protection," *NYAN*, December 10, 1930, 1; Edwin G. Burrows and Mike Wallace, *Gotham: A History of New York City to 1898* (New York: Oxford University Press, 1999), 507–508; Judith Berdy, *Roosevelt Island* (Charleston, S.C.: Arcadia Publishing, 2003), 60, 71.

2. Rufus Schatzberg, *Black Organized Crime in Harlem: 1920–1930* (New York: Garland Publishing, Inc, 1993), 39–40; "Madame Stephanie St. Clair Convicted," *NYAN*, March 19, 1930, 1; "Mme St. Clair Bares 'Policy' Protection," *NYAN*, December 10, 1930, 1.

3. Katherine Butler Jones, "409 Edgecombe, Baseball and Madame St. Clair," in *The Harlem Reader: A Celebration of New York's Most Famous Neighborhood, from the Renaissance Years to the Twenty-first Century* (New York: Three Rivers Press, 2003), 136; Ron Chepesiuk, *Gangsters of Harlem: The Gritty Underworld of New York City's Most Famous Neighborhood* (Fort Lee, N.J.: Barricade Books, 2007), 74.

4. Amy Chazkel, *Games of Chance: Brazil's Clandestine Lottery and the Making of Urban Public Life* (Durham: Duke University Press, 2011), 2.

5. Iris Ofelia Lopez, *Matters of Choice: Puerto Rican Women's Struggle for Reproductive Freedom* (New Brunswick: Rutgers University Press, 2008), 85; Robert Ruck, *Sandlot Seasons: Sport in Black Pittsburgh* (Urbana: University of Illinois Press, 1987), 141; Manuel Lopez-Rey, "Gambling in Latin American Countries," *Annals of the American Academy of Political and Social Science*, May 1950, 134–143; Joao de Pina-Cabral, *Between China and Europe: Person, Culture, and Emotion in Macao* (New York: Continuum, 2002), 88, 89.

6. Alain Locke, ed. *The New Negro* (New York: Atheneum, 1992).

7. Dorman, "Back to Harlem, 76; Greenberg, *Or Does It Explode?* 13.

8. Loften Mitchell, "Harlem Reconsidered," *Freedomways* 4 (Fall 1964): 468–469.

9. James Weldon Johnson, *Black Manhattan* (New York: Arno Press, 1968), 4.

10. Claude McKay, *Harlem: Negro Metropolis* (New York: E. P. Dutton and Company, Inc., 1940, 108.

11. Claude McKay, *Harlem Glory: A Fragment of Aframerican Life* (Chicago: Charles H. Kerr Publishing Company, 1990), 13.

12. "Why Do the Federal Officials Ignore 'Hooch' Violations in Harlem? Why Do Police Let 'Numbers' Men Do Business," *NYA*, July 10, 1926, 2.

13. Ottley, *New World A-Coming*, 155.

14. Louise Meriwether, *Daddy Was a Number Runner* (New York: The Feminist Press at The City University of New York, 1970), 232.

15. Stuart Nicholson, *Ella Fitzgerald: A Biography of the First Lady of Jazz* (Cambridge: Da Capo Press, 1994), 15; Eileen A. Gavin, Aphrodite J. Clamar, and Mary Anne Siderits, *Women of Vision: Their Psychology, Circumstances, and Success* (New York: Springer, 1997), 238.

16. E. Franklin Frazier, *Black Bourgeoisie* (New York: Free Press, 1962), 164.

17. Ann Fabian, *Card Sharps and Bucket Shops: Gambling in Nineteenth-Century America* (New York: Psychology Press, 1999), viii.

18. "Says She Paid for Doctor's Office: Dr. Cheney's Complaint Scored by Attorney for Mrs. Douglas Say," *NYAN*, December 9, 1925, 1; "Evolution of the 'Numbers' Game in N.Y.," January 31, 1925; "1½ to 3 Year Sentence for Dr. Perry Cheney," *NYAN*, October 26, 1927, 1; Probation File Case #7747 (1925) Municipal Archives of the City of New York; "Mrs. Elaine Douglas Freed of Assault," *NYAN*, March 10, 1926, 2; "Court of Appeals Upholds Verdict against Dr. Cheney," *NYA*, June 19, 1926, 1; "Dr. Perry W. Cheney's Life Threatened by Comely Widow Who Charges Him with Loving, Leaving, Withholding Her Money," *NYA*, November 28, 1925, 1; "Verdict for $600 Awarded Mrs. Douglas for Loan Made to Dr. P. W. Cheney," *NYA*, February 6, 1926, 1; Fifteen Census of the United States, 1930.

19. Ottley, *New World A-Coming*, 165.

20. McKay, *Harlem: Negro Metropolis*, 101.

21. Fred J. Cook, "The Black Mafia Moves into the Numbers Racket," *NYT Magazine*, April 4, 1971, 112.

22. Meriwether, *Daddy Was a Number Runner*, 71.

23. "Corruption of Gambling," *NYA*, August 17, 1929, 5.

24. "Numbers Net Catches Only Little Fish," *NYAN*, October 3, 1928, 1; "Numbers Bankers Live in Luxury while Players Are Often without Necessities," *NYA*, June 28, 1924, 1.

25. Adam Powell, *Adam by Adam: The Autobiography of Adam Clayton Powell, Jr.* (New York: Kensington Publishing Corp., 1971), 31.

26. Gloria Hull, *Give Us Each Day: The Diary of Alice Dunbar-Nelson* (New York: W. W. Norton, 1984), 270–271.

27. William Gaynor Papers, Box 35, Folder 4; Box 15, Folder 1; Box 35, Folder 3. Municipal Archives, Department of Records and Information Services, City of New York Mayor's Papers.

28. "'Numbers' Collectors Persuade Women Players to Continue Insidious Habit," *NYA*, March 21, 1925, 2; "Employers Discover 'Numbers' as Source of Unreliability and Neglect of Duty on Part of Their Employers," *NYA*, April 11, 1925, 2; "Spiritualism Cited by 'Numbers' Player as Aid to Keeping ahead of the Game," *NYA*, March 7, 1925, 2.

29. *New York Interstate Tattler*, August 3, 1928, 1; "Comments by the Age Editors on Sayings of Other Editors," *NYA*, August 25, 1928, 4.

30. "Principal of Industrial Mission 60 Miles from Monrovia, Liberia, Writes Donor of Work Accomplished," *NYA*, December 7, 1929, 1; "Casper Holstein Aids School Children of Hot Springs, Ark," *NYA*, April 28, 1928, 1.

31. Langston Hughes, *The Big Sea: An Autobiography* (New York: Hill and Wang, 1993), 215; "Casper Holstein Due Big Share of Credit for Success of 28th Grand Lodge, I. B. P. O. E. of W.," *NYA*, August 20, 1927, 1; "Casper Holstein Gives $100 in Katy Ferguson Fund Drive for $16,000," *NYA*, December 12, 1925, 2; "Principal of Industrial Mission 60 Miles from Monrovia, Liberia Writes Donor of Work Accomplished," *NYA*, December 7, 1929, 1.

32. "Marcus Garvey's Liberty Hall Is Sold at Auction, with Casper Holstein, of the Virgin Islands, the Buyer," *NYA*, January 8, 1927, 1; "The Third *Opportunity* Contest," *Opportunity*, October 1926, 304, 318–319; Casper Holstein to Mrs. Hubert H. Harrison, December 1927, Box 2, Folders 41 and 42, Hubert H. Harrison Papers, Columbia University; Robert Hill, *The Marcus Garvey and Universal Improvement Association Papers*, Volume 6: September 1924–December 1927 (Los Angeles: University of California Press, 1989), 548–549.

33. Davarian L. Baldwin, *Chicago's New Negroes: Modernity, The Great Migration, and Black Urban Life* (Chapel Hill: University of North Carolina Press, 2009), 50; Elizabeth Schroeder Schlabach, *Along the Streets of Bronzeville: Black Chicago's Literary Landscape* (Urbana: University of Illinois Press, 2013), 57.

34. "Extortion Threat and Gifts to Democratic Campaign Fund Are Bared by Ison," *NYT*, August 20, 1938, 8; "Harlem Woes Echoed at Trial; 'Black Wednesdays' Described," *NYT*, August 20, 1928, 7; "Arrest of 2 Stir Hines' Counsel," *NYT*, August 28, 1938, 5; "New Witnesses Due to Testify Today," *NYT*, August 29, 1938, 1; United States Bureau of the Census, Fifteenth Census of the United States, 1930. Washington, D.C.: U.S. Government Printing Office, 1933.

35. "Numbers Kings Basked in Wealth and Beauty," *Washington Afro-American*, August 27, 1938, 31; "Dewey Silent in Calling Rita," *Afro-American and Richmond Planet*, August 27, 1938, 3, 6; Adrian Burgos Jr., *Cuban Star: How One Negro-League Owner Changed the Face of Baseball* (New York: Macmillan, 2011), 97; "Police Trap Numbers Banker in Apartment of So. Harlem Woman," *NYAN*, July 25, 1936, 3.

36. "Queens 'Numbers Queen' Nabbed in Police Drive," *NYAN*, November 16, 1935, 5; "Prison Terms Given in Policy Offenses," *NYAN*, March 23, 1935, 13; "Judge Sets Bail at $500 for Collector," *NYAN*, November 3, 1934, 13.

37. "Policy Drive in Queens Continues Unabated," *NYAN*, November 23, 1935, 5; "Jamaica Vice Drive Opened," *NYAN*, August 11, 1934, 12; "Jamaica Civic Group Opens New Program," *NYAN*, August 9, 1933, 11.

38. White, *Playing the Numbers*, 117–118; Rufus Schatzberg and Robert J. Kelley, *African-American Organized Crime* (New York: Garland Publishing, 1996), 93; Irma Watkins-Owens, *Blood Relations: Caribbean Immigrants and the Harlem Community, 1900–1930* (Bloomington: Indiana University Press, 1996), 141; Helen Lawrenson, *Stranger at the Party: A Memoir* (New York: Random House, 1975), 175; Butler Jones, "409 Edgecombe, Baseball and Madame St. Clair," 137.

39. Passenger Lists of Vessels Arriving at New York, New York, 1820–1897. Year: 1911. Microfilm T715. Roll 1715. Line 20. 28. Washington, D.C.: National Archives and Records Administration; New York, New York, Marriage Index 1866–1937; George Gachette, Petitions for Naturalization, April 3, 1938, *Petitions for Naturalization from the U.S. District Court for the Southern District of New York, 1897–1944*, ser. M1972; roll 0575, National Archives, Washington, D.C.; United States Social Security Index, 1935–2010; New York State Census, 1925, New York County—Enumeration of Inhabitants, Assembly District 21, Election District 15; Fifteenth Census of the United States, 1930. Washington, D.C.: U.S. Government Printing Office, 1930; Alphabetical Index to Petitions for Naturalization of the U.S. District Court for the Western District of New York, 1906–1966. Washington,

D.C: National Archives and Records Administration; New York, New York, Marriage Indexes 1866–1937; "Mme St. Clair Bares 'Policy' Protection," *NYAN*, December 30, 1930, 1; "Mme Stephanie St. Claire Gains Spotlight," *Chicago Defender*, January 28, 1933, 1; "Mme St. Clair 'Guilty,'" *Chicago Defender*, March 19, 1938, 1; Henry Lee Moon, "Files of the *New York Amsterdam News*: Policy Queen," Writers' Project Program New York, N.Y. Collection, 1936–1941, Reel #1, Schomburg Center for Research in Black Culture, the New York Public Library; "Dominicans Give Splendid Ball," *NYA*, April 7, 1910, 7.

40. Agnes Calliste, "Race, Gender and Canadian Immigration Policy: Blacks from the Caribbean, 1900–1932," *Journal of Canadian Studies* 28 (Winter 1993/1994): 131–148; Passenger Lists of Vessels Arriving at New York, New York, 1820–1897. Year: 1911. Microfilm T715. Roll 1715. Line 20. 28. Washington, D.C.: National Archives and Records Administration; Records of the Immigration and Naturalization Service; National Archives at Washington, D.C.; Supplemental Manifests of Alien Passengers and Crew Members Who Arrived on Vessels at New York, New York, Who Were Inspected for Admission, and Related Index, compiled 1887–1952; New York State Census, 1925, New York County—Enumeration of Inhabitants, Assembly District 21, Election District 15; United States Bureau of the Census, Fifteenth Census of the United States, 1930. Washington, D.C.: U.S. Government Printing Office, 1933; *Index to Declarations of Intention, 1817–1950 from the U.S. District Court for the Southern District of New York*, National Archives, Washington, D.C.

41. George Gachette's 1928 petition for American naturalization indicates he and St. Clair were married but estranged. At that time, Gachette was unclear as to St. Clair's whereabouts. George Gachette, Petitions for Naturalization, April 3, 1938, *Petitions for Naturalization from the U.S. District Court for the Southern District of New York, 1897–1944*, ser. M1972; roll 0575, National Archives, Washington, D.C.

42. "Graft on Gambling Laid to the Police by 'Policy Queen,'" *NYT*, December 9, 1930, 1; "Madame St. Clair Believed Ready to Blow Lid Off," *NYAN*, November 17, 1937, 1.

43. Ralph Matthews, "Was It Curse of Father Divine or Did Madame St. Clair Kill Sufi?" *Afro-American*, August 6, 1938, 3; "Mme Gachette Gets Judgment for $1,000," *NYAN*, February 14, 1923, 3.

44. T. R. Poston, "Harlem Shadows: Harlem Moon," *Pittsburgh Courier*, December 27, 1930, 2.

45. Lawrenson, *Stranger at the Party*, 175; Butler Jones, "409 Edgecombe, Baseball and Madame St. Clair," 137; Schatzberg and Kelly, *African American Organized Crime*, 89; "Graft on Gambling Laid to the Police by 'Policy Queen,'" 1; *Final Report of Samuel Seabury, Referee: Supreme Court, Appellate Division—First Judicial Department* (New York: Arno Press, 1974), 137; "Harlem 'Numbers' Woman Is Witness in Investigation of Police and 'Stool Pigeon' Activities in Greater N.Y.," *NYA*, December 13, 1930.

46. David L. Lewis, *When Harlem Was in Vogue* (New York: Penguin Books, 1997), 217; McKay, *Harlem: Negro Metropolis*, 26.

47. Harlem 'Numbers' Woman Is Witness in Investigation of Police and 'Stool Pigeon' Activities in Greater N.Y.," *NYA*, December 13, 1930; Butler Jones, "409 Edgecombe, Baseball and Madame St. Clair," 132; Christopher Gray, "Streetscapes/409 Edgecombe Avenue;

an Address That Drew the City's Black Elite," *NYT*, July 24, 1994; "Mrs. Carter Seen as Only Negro Appointee," *NYAN*, August 10, 1935, 1.

48. Butler Jones, "409 Edgecombe, Baseball and Madame St. Clair," 136.

49. Irma Watkins-Owens, "Early Twentieth-Century Caribbean Women: Migration and Social Networks in New York City," in *Islands in the City: West Indian Migration to New York*, ed. Nancy Foner (Berkeley: University of California Press, 2001), 28–29.

50. Watkins-Owens, "Early Twentieth-Century Caribbean Women," 35.

51. New York State Census, 1925, New York County—Enumeration of Inhabitants, Assembly District 21, Election District 15; D-1970: Stephanie Hamid, Westfield Receiving Blotters/Department of Correction, New York State Archives.

52. Probation Department Case File #9239 (1929) Municipal Archives of the City of New York; "Grandmother, Age 65, Goes Free on 'Policy' Charge 5,000 Slips," *NYAN*, January 16, 1929, 1.

53. Manhattan District Attorney Papers: Charles "Lucky" Luciano Closed Case Files Papers, Box 2, Folder: 110 W. 96 and 203 W. 98th Street; Box 7, Folder: 22, Duplicates Witness Statements. Municipal Archives City of New York.

54. Client CW, Box 81, WPA.

55. Polly Adler, *A House Is Not a Home* (New York: Rinehart and Company, Inc., 1950), 64–65.

56. "Display Ad 4—No Title: Mme Stephanie St. Clair, *NYAN*, January 1, 1930, 2.

57. Poston, "Harlem Shadows," 2.

58. "Confessed Banker of Numbers Given Sentence to Island," *NYAN*, March 19, 1930, 1.

59. Marilynn S. Johnson, *Street Justice: A History of Police Violence in New York City* (New York: Beacon Press, 2003), 50–56.

60. Private hearings were held from October 9, 1930, to October 26, 1931, and 1,059 witnesses testified before the Seabury Commission. Public hearings were held from September 29, 1930, to May 14, 1931, and 299 witnesses testified before the Seabury Commission. *Final Report of Samuel Seabury, Referee: Supreme Court, Appellate Division-First Judicial Department*, 2.

61. John Dewey, *New York and the Seabury Investigation: A Digest and Interpretation of the Reports by Samuel Seabury concerning the Government of New York City* (New York: City Affairs Committee, 1933), 30, 34.

62. "Mme St. Clair Bares 'Policy' Protection," *NYAN*, December 10, 1930, 1.

63. "Harlem 'Numbers' Woman Is Witness in Investigation of Police and 'Stool Pigeon' Activities in Greater N.Y.," *NYA*, December 13, 1930, 1.

64. McKay, *Harlem: Negro Metropolis*, 101–102.

65. *Collier's*, July 29, 1939, 37.

66. Schatzberg and Kelley, *African-American Organized Crime*, 89; "Graft on Gambling Laid to the Police by 'Policy Queen,'" *NYT*, December 9, 1930, 1; *Final Report of Samuel Seabury, Referee: Supreme Court, Appellate Division—First Judicial Department*, 137; "Harlem 'Numbers' Woman Is Witness"; "Miro Policy King Seized after Raids," *NYT*, February 10, 1932, 17.

67. "Numbers Game White Bankers Want Monopoly," *NYA*, June 12, 1926, 1–2.

68. Ray Wannall, *The Real J. Edgar Hoover: For the Record* (Paducah, Ky.: Turner Publishing Company, 2000), 173; Timothy W. Bjorkman, *Verne Sankey: America's First Public Enemy* (Norman: University of Oklahoma Press, 2007), 71.

69. A. M. Malliet, "Predicts Deadlock of Jury on Hines," *NYAN*, August 27, 1938, 1.

70. "We're Losing," *NYAN*, September 3, 1938, 6.

71. Edgar M. Grey, "The Devil's Playground," *NYAN*, July 6, 1927, 12.

72. Heap, *Slumming*, 1; Edgar M. Grey, "Harlem after Dark," *NYAN*, April 6, 1927, 16.

73. Grey, "Harlem after Dark," 16.

74. White, *Playing the Numbers*, 188–191.

75. "Dewey Silent on Calling Rita," 19.

76. Ted Poston, "Inside the Policy Racket: The Cops Had a Share in the Old Days, Too," *NYP*, March 4, 1960, 4.

77. "Harlem Policy Queen Declares War on Rival," *Pittsburgh Courier*, January 5, 1935, 6.

78. Marvel Cooke, "Mme St. Clair Alone Defied Dutchman," *NYAN*, August 27, 1938, 1; Moon, "Files of the *New York Amsterdam News*.

79. Cooke, "Mme St. Clair Alone Defied Dutchman," *NYAN*, August 27, 1938, 1.

80. Greenberg, *Or Does It Explode?* 117–118.

81. Cooke, "Mme St. Clair Alone Defied Dutchman," *NYAN*, August 27, 1938, 1; Moon, Files of the *New York Amsterdam News*.

82. E. Franklin Frazier, "Some Effects of the Depression on the Negro in Northern Cities," *Science and Society* 2 (Fall 1938): 497.

83. Poston, "Inside the Policy Racket," 4.

84. Watkins-Owens, *Blood Relations*, 142.

85. Lou Layne, "Madame Raps 'Black Hitler,'" *NYAN*, November 20, 1937; "Sufi Wooed St. Clair in Darkened Room," *NYAN*, January 29, 1938; "Mme St. Clair Just Wanted Conciliation," *NYAN*, January 22, 1938, 1.

86. Winston McDowell, "Race and Ethnicity during the Harlem Jobs Campaign, 1925–1932," *Journal of Negro History* 69 (Summer-Autumn 1984): 138; Wilbur Young, "Activities of Bishop Amiru, Al-Mumin Sufi A. Hamid," Writers' Project Program New York, N.Y Collection, 1936–1941, Reel #1, Schomburg Center for Research in Black Culture, the New York Public Library.

87. Mme St. Clair 'Guilty,'" *Chicago Defender*, March 19, 1938, 1; "Mme St. Clair Just Wanted Conciliation," *NYAN*, January 22, 1938, 3; Butler Jones, "409 Edgecombe, Baseball and Madame St. Clair," 139; McKay, *Harlem: Negro Metropolis*, 79; "Cult Leader and Pilot Die in Air Crash," *Syracuse Herald*, August 6, 1938, 2.

88. *People v. Stephanie St. Clair*, filed January 31, 1939, District Attorney's Closed Case Files (DACCF), Municipal Archives of the City of New York; "$6,000 Bail for Mme St. Clair," *NYAN*, January 22, 1938, 1.

89. Mme St. Clair 'Guilty,'" 1; "Mme St. Clair Just Wanted Conciliation," *NYAN*, January 22, 1938, 3.

90. Mme St. Clair Gets Ten Years," *NYAN*, March 26, 1938, 1; "Plane Crash Fatal to 'Black Hitler,'" *NYT*, August 1, 1938, 1.

91. D-1970: Stephanie Hamid, Westfield Receiving Blotters/Department of Correction, New York State Archives; Carolyn Dixon, "What's Happened to the Numbers Game? Check-Up Discloses Interesting Facts," *NYAN*, December 18, 1943, 24; "MME. St. Clair Not Released," *NYAN*, April 13, 1940, 1.

92. Poston, "Inside the Policy Racket," 4, 20.

93. Mayme Hatcher Johnson and Karen E. Quinones Miller, *Harlem Godfather: The Rap on My Husband, Ellsworth "Bumpy" Johnson* (Philadelphia: Oshun Publishing Company, 2008), 115.

94. United States Social Security Administration Death Index, 1935–2014, Family Search; https://familysearch.org (accessed June 6, 2012) (Alexandria, Va.: National Technical Information Service).

95. "Policy Queen Fears She Is on the Spot," *NYA*, September 24, 1932, 1.

96. Barbara Ransby, *Ella Baker and the Black Freedom Movement: A Radical Democratic Vision* (Chapel Hill: University of North Carolina Press, 2003), 297.

97. Poston, "Harlem Shadows," 2.

98. Harley, "Race Women: Cultural Productions and Radical Labor Politics," in *Women's Labor in the Global Economy*, 11.

99. William G. Jordan, *Black Newspapers and America's War Democracy, 1914–1920* (Chapel Hill: University of North Carolina Press, 2001), 1.

100. Display Ad 70—No Title, *NYAN*, September 4, 1929, 12.

101. Shannon King, "'Ready to Shoot and Do Shoot': Black Working-Class Self-Defense and Community Politics in Harlem, New York during the 1920s," *Journal of Urban History* 37, no. 5 (September 2011): 759.

102. "Mme Stephanie St. Clair," *NYAN*, February 19, 1930, 7.

103. "Mme Stephanie St. Clair," *NYAN*, September 4, 1929,12.

104. Ferdinand Morton, "Memorandum re: Conditions in Harlem," April 25, 1932, 2–3; Assistant Commissioner of Correction Fishman to Walter White, Memorandum, May 9, 1932, 1–5 NAACP papers, series C, Box 305.

105. New York State Senate, *Investigations of the Police Department of New York* (New York: J. B. Lyon, 1895), 5217–5220; "Woman Aids in Big Expose," *NYA*, February 17, 1910, 1, 5; William McAdoo, *Guarding A Great City* (New York: Harper and Bros., 1906), 100.

106. Marcy S. Sacks, *Before Harlem: The Black Experience in New York City Before World War I* (Philadelphia: University of Pennsylvania Press, 2006), 89–90.

107. "Tenement—S. E. (Colored), July 22, 1928, COF Papers.

108. Ottley, *New World A-Coming*, 164.

109. Sacks, *Before Harlem*, 89–90.

110. "Innocent Girls Arrested: Former Police Aide Says Many Were Convicted on Perjured Evidence," *NYT*, November 27, 1930, 1.

111. Display Ad 70, 12.

112. "Woman Asks $3,000 for Attack by Cop," *NYAN*, April 7, 1934, 11.

113. Ibid.; "Girl Shows Black Eye and Bruised Body at Police Brutality Hearing," *NYAN*, November 7, 1928, 3; "Officer Brutal, Charge Alleges: U.N.I.A. Files Complaint for Woman Who Was Fined by Court," *NYAN*, June 11, 22, 1932, 19.

114. Danielle L. McGuire, "'It Was like All of Us Had Been Raped'": Sexual Violence, Community Mobilization, and the African American Freedom Struggle," *Journal of American History* 91, no. 3 (December 2004): 907, 910; "The Third Degree," *NYAN*, August 18, 1926, 20.

115. King, "Ready to Shoot and Do Shoot," 766–767.

116. "Mme Stephanie St. Clair," *NYAN*, September 18, 1929, 6.

117. "Samuel T. Floyd Agrees with Stand of Mme St. Clair," *NYAN*, September 11, 1929, 20.

118. "Richard M. Lee Says He Has Always Found Them Courteous," *NYAN*, September 11, 1929, 20; "Club Chats," *NYAN*, February 5, 1930, 5; "Honor Richard Lee," *NYAN*, June 4, 1930, 4.

119. "Mme Stephanie St. Clair," *NYAN*, September 25, 1929, 6.

120. Confessed 'Banker' of 'Numbers' Given Sentence to Island," *NYAN*, March 19, 1930; Watkins-Owens, *Blood Relations*, 142.

121. Watkins-Owens, *Blood Relations*, 73.

122. "Mme St. Clair Held on $5,000 Bail for Special Sessions," *NYAN*, January 22, 1930, 1; "Mme St. Clair Convicted," *NYAN*, March 19, 1930, 1.

123. Ira De A. Reid, *The Negro Immigrant: His Backgrounds, Characteristics and Social Adjustment, 1899–1937* (New York: Columbia University Press, 1939), 164; "Mme St. Clair," *NYAN*, October 30, 1929, 6.

124. Reid, *Negro Immigrant*, 162–163; Watkins-Owens, *Blood Relations*, 200, n. 31.

125. Dr. Hubert Harrison, "Hubert Harrison Answers Malliet," *Pittsburgh Courier*, October 22, 1927, 3.

126. Hubert H. Harrison, *A Hubert Harrison Reader*, ed. Jeffrey Babcock Perry (Middletown, Conn.: Wesleyan University Press, 2001), 253; A. M. Wendell Malliet, "West Indian Tells 'Why I Cannot Become Americanized,'" *Pittsburgh Courier*, July 9, 1927, 2; A. M. Wendell Malliet, "Malliet Closes, Still Crying 'I Cannot Become Americanized,'" *Pittsburgh Courier*, August 13, 1927, 5.

127. Watkins-Owens, *Blood Relations*, 4; Winston James, *Holding Aloft the Banner of Ethiopia: Caribbean Radicalism in Early Twentieth Century America* (New York: Verso, 1998), 73; Reid, *Negro Immigrant*, 204.

128. United States Bureau of the Census, Fifteenth Census of the United States, 1930. Washington, D.C.: U.S. Government Printing Office, 1933; Stephanie St. Clair (#132-16-0589), Application for Social Security (Form SS-5), Treasury Department, 1942.

129. "Mme St. Clair Gets Ten Years," *NYAN*, March 26, 1938, 1.

Chapter 3. Black Women Supernatural Consultants, Numbers Gambling, and Public Outcries against Supernaturalism

1. "FTC Charges Miss Cleo with Deceptive Advertising, Billing and Collection Practices," www.ftc.gov (accessed March 15, 2011); "Citing Fraud Federal Trade Commission Sues to Close Hotline of Phone Psychic Miss Cleo," *Jet*, March 4, 2002, 17.

2. Margena A. Christian, "Where Is Miss Cleo? *Jet*, January 7, 2008, 38.

3. John W. Blassingame, *The Slave Community: Plantation Life in the Antebellum South* (New York: Oxford University, 1972), 109–110; B. A. Botkin, *Lay My Burden Down: A Folk History of Slavery* (Chicago: University of Chicago Press, 1945); Savannah Unit Georgia Writers' Project Works Projects Administration, *Drums and Shadows: Survival Studies among the Georgia Coastal Negroes* (Athens: The University of Georgia Press, 1940); Sharla M. Fett, *Working Cures: Healing, Health, and Power on Southern Slave Plantations* (Chapel Hill: University of North Carolina Press, 2002).

4. Fett, *Working Cures*, 5–6.

5. William Wells Brown, *My Southern Home, or the South and Its People* (Boston: A. G. Brown, 1880), 70.

6. Frances Ann Kemble, *Journal of a Residence on a Georgia Plantation in 1838–1839* (1863; repr., New York: Cosimo, 2007), 72–73; William Dusinberre, *Them Dark Days: Slavery in the American Rice Swamps* (New York: Oxford University, 1995), 213.

7. Yvonne P. Chireau, *Black Magic: Religion and the African American Conjuring Tradition* (Berkeley: University of California Press, 2003), 17; Blassingame, *Slave Community*, 109.

8. McKay, *Harlem: Negro Metropolis*, 75.

9. Yvonne P. Chireau, "The Uses of the Supernatural: Towards a History of Black Women's Magical Practices," in *A Mighty Baptism: Race, Gender, and the Creation of American Protestantism*, ed. Susan Juster and Lisa MacFarlane (Ithaca: Cornell University Press, 1996), 177–178.

10. Shane White, "The Gold Diggers of 1833: African Americans Dreams, Fortune-Telling, Treasure-Seeking, and Policy in Antebellum New York City," *Journal of Social History* 47 (Spring 2014): 679.

11. Marvel Cooke, "Million Dollar Take," *NYAN*, May 25, 1940, 10.

12. McKay, *Harlem: Negro Metropolis*, 76.

13. Cooke, "Million Dollar Take," 10.

14. Harry Hyatt Middleton, *Hoodoo—Conjuration—Witchcraft—Rootwork: Beliefs Accepted by Many Negroes and White Persons* (Hannibal, Mo.: Western Publishers, 1890); Hans A. Baer, *The Black Spiritual Movement: A Religious Response to Racism* (Knoxville: University of Tennessee Press, 1984); Victoria Wolcott, "Mediums, Messages, and Lucky Numbers: African-American Female Spiritualists and Numbers Runners in Interwar Detroit," in *The Geography of Identity*, ed. Patricia Yaeger (Ann Arbor: University of Michigan Press, 1996), 273–306; Susan Starr Sered, *Priestess, Mother Sacred Sister: Religions Dominated by Women* (Oxford: Oxford University Press, 1994); Anthony B. Pinn, *Varieties of African American Religious Experience* (Minneapolis: Fortress Press, 1998); Carolyn Morrow Long, *Spiritual Merchants: Religion, Magic, and Commerce* (Knoxville: University of Tennessee Press, 2001); Jeffrey E. Anderson, *Conjure in African American Society* (Baton Rouge: Louisiana State University Press, 2005); Long, *A New Orleans Voudou Priestess: The Legend and Reality of Marie LaVeau* (Gainesville: University Press of Florida, 2006); Gayle T. Tate, *The Black Urban Community: From Dusk Till Dawn* (New York: Palgrave Macmillan, 2006); Chireau, *Black Magic*, 2006.

15. Yvonne Chireau, "Hidden Traditions: Black Religion, Magic, and Alternative Spiritual Beliefs in Womanist Perspective," in *Perspectives on Womanist Theology*, Black Church

Scholars Series: Volume VII, ed. Jacquelyn Grant (Atlanta: The ITC Press, 1995), 75–76; Chappy Gardner, "Rev. Josephine Becton Quit for Church," *Pittsburgh Courier*, September 6, 1930, 2.

16. A. M. Wendell Malliet, "We Prove What Other Churches Teach," *NYAN*, February 5, 1938, 5; Jamie J. Wilson, *Building a Healthy Black Harlem: Health Politics in Harlem, New York from the Jazz Age to the Great Depression* (Amherst: Cambria Press, 2009), 104.

17. H. Norton Browne, "You Pray for Me . . . Elder Horn, Latest Exhorter, Is Unusual Person Evangelist Professes Witchcraft," *NYAN*, October 13, 1934, 11; Demetrius K. Williams, *An End to This Strife: The Politics of Gender in African American Churches* (Minneapolis: Fortress Press, 2004), 173; "Mother Horn in Fight with Dance Hall Owner," *NYA*, December 12, 1959, 1; Edward Franklin Frazier and Charles Eric Lincoln, *The Negro Church in America* (New York: Schocken Books, 1974).

18. Chireau, *Black Magic*, 12.

19. *Soundex Index to Petitions for Naturalization Filed in Federal, State, and Local Courts Located in New York City, 1792–1989* (New York: National Archives and Records Administration, Northeast Region); Classified Ad 8, *NYAN*, September 18, 1937, 23; Ottley, *New World A-Coming*, 55.

20. LaShawn Harris, "'Madame Queen of Policy': Madame Stephanie St. Clair and African American Women's Participation in Harlem's Informal Economy," *Black Women, Families and Gender* 2 (Fall 2008): 53–76; "Mme Fu Futtam Wed to Sufi Abdul Hamid," *NYAN*, April 23, 1938, 5; Young, "Activities of Bishop Amiru"; Robert Weisbrot, *Father Divine and the Struggle for Racial Equality* (Urbana: University of Illinois Press, 1983), 43; Marvel Cooke, "Bishop Sufi A. A. M. M. S. A. H. Unveils His Universal Buddhist Holy Temple to Public," *NYAN*, April 23, 1938, 5. Marvel Cooke, "Sufi Opens Rival 'Heaven,'" *NYAN*, April 16, 1938, 1.

21. Cooke, "Bishop Sufi A. A. M. M. S. A. H."

22. Ibid.

23. Heike Raphael-Hernandez and Shannon Steen, *AfroAsian Encounters: Culture, History, Politics* (New York: New York University Press, 2006), 1; Vijay Prashad, *Everybody Was Kung Fu Fighting: Afro-Asian Connections and the Myth of Cultural Purity* (Boston: Beacon Press, 2001).

24. Phillip Brian Harper, "Passing for What? Racial Masquerade and the Demands of Upward Mobility," *Callaloo*, 21 (Spring 1998): 388; Gayle Wald, *Crossing the Line: Racial Passing in the Twentieth Century U.S. Literature and Culture* (Durham: Duke University Press, 2000); Prashad, *Everybody Was Kung Fu Fighting*.

25. Willis N. Huggins, "Second Prize Personal Experience Story," *NYAN*, June 10, 1925, 9.

26. Reid, *Negro Immigrant*, 209; Watkins-Owens, *Blood Relations*, 4.

27. Cooke, "Million Dollar Take," 10.

28. Zora Hurston, "Hoodoo in America," *Journal of American Folklore* 174 (October-December, 1931): 320.

29. "She Made 'Em Talk and Also Walk," *NYAN*, December 14, 1927, 11; "Final Rites for Rev. Broy, *NYAN*, March 15, 1961, 4.

30. Nell Dodson, "Link Forbes Girl's Death with Spirits," *NYAN*, November 25, 1939, 5.

31. Philip Jenkins, *Mystics and Messiahs: Cults and New Religions in American History* (New York: Oxford University Press, 2000), 75.

32. Display Ad 48—No Title, *NYAN*, December 7, 1932, 14.

33. See the following newspaper articles for information on fraudulent occult school founders in New York: "Promises to Help Capture Mystic," *NYAN*, March 22, 1933, 16; "Spiritualist Freed by Harlem Jurist," *NYAN*, March 17, 1934, 2; "Slick Man Lures Boy From Africa; Beats and Robs Him," *Chicago Defender*, June 13, 1914, 3.

34. Display Ad 24—No Title, *NYAN*, November 23, 1932, 7; "Spiritual School to Open," *NYAN*, September 21, 1932, 7; Prashad, *Everybody Was Kung Fu Fighting*, 90; W. F. Elkins, "William Lauron DeLaurence and Jamaican Folk Religion," *Folklore* 97, 2 (1986): 215–218; "Spiritual Church of Christ Teaching," *NYAN*, May 12, 1926, 10.

35. White, *Playing the Numbers*, 98.

36. Winthrop D. Lane, "Ambushed in the City," 693.

37. Langston Hughes, *Tambourines to Glory: A Novel* (New York: Random House Digital, Inc., 2006), 9.

38. Ira De Augustine Reid, "Let Us Prey," *Opportunity*, 1926, 277.

39. In 1923, Minott published "How to Be Beautiful and Keep Youthful." "Dr. Minott's Book," *Chicago Defender*, December 8, 1923, 10; Display Ad 17, *Chicago Defender*, February 3, 1917, 7.

40. Samuel Watson, "Prof. Adena C. E. Minott, Ph.B.; M. S.; F. A. I. P.," *Colored American Magazine*, May 1908, 525.

41. "Clio School: Institution of Mental Sciences and Character Analysis Now an Established Fact," *Chicago Defender*, January 27, 1917, 5; "Adena C. E. Minott," *Phrenological Journal and Science of Health* (May 1900): 148–149; "Clio School in Third Year," *NYA*, June 17, 1909, 3.

42. Anne Myers and Christine Hansen, *Experimental Psychology* (Belmont, Calif.: Wadsworth Cengage Learning, 2011), 28; Michael Adas, *Machines as the Measure of Men: Science, Technology, and Ideologies of Western Dominance* (Ithaca: Cornell University Press, 1990), 293.

43. Haroon Kharem, "Medical Doctor, Integrationist, and Black Nationalists: Dr. James McCune Smith and the Dilemma of an Antebellum Intellectual," in *Education as Freedom: African American Educational Thought and Activism*, ed. Noel S. Anderson and Haroon Kharem (Lanham, Md.: Lexington Books, 2009), 5.

44. Display Ad 17, *Chicago Defender*, February 3, 1917, 7.

45. Ibid.; "Doctor of Metaphysics to Adena C. E. Minott," *Chicago Defender*, April 9, 1921, 4.

46. Audrey Thomas McCluskey, "'We Specialize in the Wholly Impossible': Black Women School Founders and Their Mission," *Signs* 22 (1997): 403–426.

47. "The Thirtieth Anniversary of the White Rose Industrial Association, Inc., February 11, 1927," White Rose Mission and Industrial Association Records, Folder #1, New York Public Library Schomburg Research Center; "White Rose Home Activities Resume," *NYAN*, September 8, 1926, 5; "Centre to Give Food to Needy," *NYAN*, November 29, 1933, 4; Minott," *Phrenological Journal and Science of Health* May 1900, 148–149; "Four Hundred Delegates Attend National Association of Colored Women," *Afro American*, August 12, 1916, 1; Weisenfeld,

African American Women and Christian Activism, 87; "Marriage Announcement 2—No Title," *NYAN*, March 30, 1932, 4; "Gideon Young Highly Honored by Leadi[n]g Men," *Pittsburgh Courier*, November 8, 1912, 1; Adena C. E. Minott (the Northeastern Federation of Women's Clubs) to Oswald Villard, August 23, 1913, Administrative Files, Box 4–3, NAACP Papers, Manuscript Division, Library of Congress, Washington, D.C.; "Miss Carter Visits Mme Minott," *Chicago Defender*, August 3, 1918, 11; "Mme Minott Addresses West Side Musical," *Chicago Defender*, October 27, 1917, 11.

48. "Held in Theft of Large Sum," *NYAN*, March 1, 1941, 1; "Spiritualist Receives Chance to 'Catch Up,'" *NYAN*, April 5, 1941,1; "Court Grants Third Chance to Spiritualist," *NYAN*, July 19, 1941, 1; "Rim Flammed Out of $450," *NYAN*, March 1, 1941, 1; "Spiritualist Gets Delay in Grand Larceny Case," *NYAN*, June 14, 1941, 1.

49. Ottley, *New World A-Coming*, 87.

50. McKay, *Harlem: Negro Metropolis*, 77–80.

51. Display Ad 38—No Title, *NYAN*, March 24, 1926, 10.

52. McKay, *Harlem: Negro Metropolis*, 77–80.

53. Jessamy, "Harlem's Fakers," 11.

54. Long, *Spiritual Merchants*, xv.

55. "Policy Racket Preys on Poor," *Life*, June 19, 1950.

56. Cooke, "Million Dollar Take," 10.

57. Ibid.

58. Gilbert Osofsky, *Harlem: The Making of a Ghetto*, 1890–1930 (New York: Harper and Row, 1963), 143.

59. Long, *Spiritual Merchants*, xviii.

60. Ibid.

61. Jessamy, "Harlem's Fakers," 11.

62. Cooke, "Million Dollar Take," 10.

63. Ibid.

64. Ibid.

65. Long, *Spiritual Merchants*, 99.

66. Ibid., 99–100; Jeffrey E. Anderson, *Conjure in African American Society*, 118–119.

67. Micki McElya, *Clinging to Mammy: The Faithful Slaves in Twentieth-Century America* (Cambridge: Harvard University Press, 2007), 16; Kimberly Wallace-Sanders, *Mammy: A Century of Race, Gender, and Southern Memory* (Ann Arbor: University of Michigan, 2008), 59; Marilyn Kern-Foxworth, *Aunt Jemima, Uncle Ben, and Rastus: Blacks in Advertising, Yesterday, Today, and Tomorrow* (Westport, Conn.: Greenwood, 1994), 45.

68. Norm Cohen and David Cohen, *Long Steel Rail: The Railroad in American Folksong* (Urbana: University of Illinois Press, 2000), 104; Long, *Spiritual Merchants*, 115, 122.

69. Long, *Spiritual Merchants*, 193–194.

70. Wallace-Sanders, *Mammy*, 60–61, 68.

71. Mme Fu Futtam, *Madam Fu Futtam's Magical-Spiritual Dream Book* (New York: Empire Publishing, 1937); "Mme Fu Futtam Wed to Sufi Abdul Hamid," *NYAN*, April 23, 1938, 5; McKay, *Harlem: Negro Metropolis*, 79.

72. McKay, *Harlem: Negro Metropolis*, 106.

73. Jessamy, "Harlem's Fakers," 11.

74. Cooke, "Million Dollar Take," 11.

75. Ibid.

76. Ibid.

77. White, *Playing the Numbers*, 91.

78. William Forbes, "Billion Dollar Business," *Negro Digest*, 3 (January 1947): 64.

79. Cooke's mention of "Sufi" refers to Harlem race activist Sufi Abdul Hamid. Cooke, "Million Dollar Take," 10. For more discussion on Hamid, see Clarence Lusane, *Hitler's Black Victims: The Historical Experiences of Afro-Germans, European Black, Africans, and African American in the Nazi Era* (New York: Routledge, 2002), 121; Winston McDowell, "Race and Ethnicity," 134–146.

80. Fabian, *Card Sharps, Dream Books, and Bucket Shops*, 112, 144–145.

81. "Mme Sarah Washington, "Beauty Secrets: Dreaming the Numbers," *NYAN*, August 18, 1926, 7; "Lies Down to Sleep—Dreams Numbers," *NYAN*, November 21, 1936, 8; "Beauticians to Honor Mme Sarah Washington," *NYAN*, March 14, 1953, 10; "Mme Washington Stricken in Home," *NYAN*, January 18, 1947, 1.

82. Futtam, *Madame Fu. Futtam's Magical-Spiritual*, vi–vii, 36, 69, 73.

83. McKay, *Harlem: Negro Metropolis*, 79–80, 106; "Dream Book Author Causes Arrest Three for Copyright Infringements," *NYAN*, November 5, 1930, 1; "Oberlin Goes in for Dream Books and Policy," *Chicago Defender*, June 3, 1939, 23; United States Patent and Trademark Office, *Official Gazette of the United States Patent and Trademark Office*, 133.

84. Cooke, "Million Dollar Take," 13; Classified Ad 8, *NYAN*, September 18, 1938, 23; Futtam, *Madame Fu. Futtam's Magical-Spiritual*, vi–vii, 36, 69, 73.

85. Mme Fu Futtam Wed to Sufi Abdul Hamid," *NYAN*, April 23, 1938, 5; Futtam, *Madame Fu. Futtam's Magical-Spiritual*, iii.

86. Futtam, *Madame Fu. Futtam's Magical-Spiritual*, vi–vii, 36, 69, 73.

87. Seth M. Scheiner, "The Negro Church and the Northern City, 1890–1930," in *Seven on Black: Reflections on the Negro Experience in America*, ed. William G. Shade and Roy C. Herrenkohl (Philadelphia: J. B. Lippincott, 1969), 100–101.

88. Wolcott, "Mediums, Messages, and Lucky Numbers," 290.

89. Ibid. 294; Baer, *Black Spiritual Movement*, 17–18. Arthur Huff Fauset, *Black Gods of the Metropolis: Negro Religious Cults of the Urban North* (Philadelphia: University of Pennsylvania Press, 1944); McKay, *Harlem: Negro Metropolis*, 82–83; Ottley, *New World A-Coming*, 87.

90. Zora Neale Hurston, *The Sanctified Church* (Berkeley: Turtle Island), 1983, 103.

91. Lawrence W. Levine, *Black Culture and Black Consciousness* (Oxford: Oxford University Press, 1977), 179–180.

92. St. Clair Drake and Horace Cayton, *Black Metropolis: A Study of Negro Life in a Northern City* (New York: Harcourt Brace and Co., 1945), 476.

93. "Spiritualism Cited by 'Numbers' Player as Aid to Keeping Ahead of the Game," *NYA*, March 7, 1925, 2.

94. McKay, *Harlem: Negro Metropolis*, 106.

95. Charles Pearce, "Spiritualism—The New Racket," *Afro-American*, July 11, 1931, 20.

96. Hughes, *Tambourines to Glory*, 74.

97. Cooke, "Million Dollar Take," 10.

98. Gustov G. Carlson, "Number Gambling: A Study of a Culture Complex," PhD diss., University of Michigan, 1940, 50.

99. "Spiritual Worker Caught in Policy Net," *NYAN*, November 9, 1927, 4; Probation Department Case Files # 8599 (1927), Municipal Archives of the City of New York.

100. "Rev. Becton Shot in Head by Gang on 'Ride' in His Own Car," *NYAN*, 1; McKay, *Harlem: Negro Metropolis*, 79; "Rev. G. Wilson Becton, Noted Evangelist, Shot in Head and Beaten by Gangsters," *Chicago Defender National Edition*, May 27, 1933, 1; Lewis, *When Harlem Was in Vogue*, 299.

101. David Lan, *Guns and Rain: Guerrillas and Spirit Mediums in Zimbabwe* (Berkeley: University of California Press, 1985), 4–5.

102. Marion Kilson, "Ambivalence and Power: Mediums in Ga Traditional Religion," *Journal of Religion in Africa* 4 (1972): 171–172; Didier Betrand, "The Names and Identities of the "Boramey" Spirits Possessing Cambodian Mediums," *Asian Folklore Studies* 60 (2001): 45.

103. Reid, "Let Us Prey," 277.

104. Cooke, "Million Dollar Take," 11.

105. Weisbrot, *Father Divine and the Struggle*, 176.

106. March of Time Collection, 1934–1951, Motion Picture, Sound, and Video Records Section, Special Media Archives Services Division, National Archives at College Park; "Policy Racket Preys on Poor," *Life*, June 19, 1950, 106–108.

107. Ottley, *New World A-Coming*, 86.

108. "Time Marches Backward," *NYA*, March 27, 1937, 9.

109. Malliet, "We Prove," 5; Wilson, *Building a Healthy Black Harlem*, 104.

110. "Drive Is Planned against Spiritualist Racketeers," *NYAN*, October 26, 1935, 1; "Interdenominational Spiritualists Assembly to Open Militant Fight against Racketeers," *NYA*, October 19, 1935, 2.

111. Katrina Hazzard-Donald, *Mojo Workin: The Old African American Hoodoo System* (Urbana: University of Illinois Press, 2013), 153.

112. Owen Davies, *Grimoires: A History of Magic Books* (New York: Oxford University, 2009), 201; *Acts and Laws of the State of Connecticut* (Hartford: G. F. Warfield and Co., 1915), 1989; "Fortune-Telling Prohibited or Highly Taxed in 35 Cities," *NYT*, March 14, 1926, XX12; W. Wood, *Medical Record* (New York: The Publishers' Printing Company, 1901), 342; "Latest Legislative Bills," *NYT*, February 17, 1911, 3; *Laws of New York*, Volume 2 (Albany: J. B. Lyon Company State Printers, 1917), 1544; *The Consolidated Laws of the State of New York*, 1910–1920 (Albany: J. B. Lyon Company State Printers, 1920); Theodore Connolly et al., *New York Criminal Report* (Albany: W. C. Little and Company, 1916), 205.

113. Preacher Given Workhouse Term," *NYAN*, December 26, 1928, 2; "'Prof' Francis Kingharman and Two Others Pay Fines for Fortune Telling," *NYAN*, October 24, 1928, 2.

114. Ibid. Display Ad 55—No Title, *NYAN*, October 5, 1927, 13.

115. Wilson, *Building a Healthy Black Harlem*, 52.

116. Jessamy, "Harlem's Fakers," 11.

117. *New York State Journal of Medicine*, 39, Part 2 (Lake Success: Medical Society of New York), 1883.

118. "Inquiry on Quacks Is Set for Tuesday," *NYT*, March 27, 1926, 19; Shirley W. Wynne, "Health Advice for the People," *NYA*, May 23, 1931, 1.

119. John B. West, "Your Health," *NYAN*, June 3, 1939, 13; "Editorials," *Journal of the National Medical Association* 42 (May 1950): 182.

120. "Spiritual Faker Bleeds Victim of $1,140, Promising to Restore Health," *NYAN*, November 12, 1930, 2; *Lillian Tweed v. Audrey Dayrell* (1930), no. 184167, District Attorney's Closed Case Files (DACCF), Municipal Archives of the City of New York.

121. Ibid.

122. "Porto Rican Spiritualist Slain," *NYAN*, June 11, 1930, 2; "Voodoo Woman Killed by Victim She Did Not Cure," *NYA*, August 9, 1930, 3; "Slays Medium as Her Costly Healing Fails," *Chicago Tribune*, June 6, 1930, 21; "'Cure' Fails, Patient Kills 1, Wounds 1," *Pittsburgh Press*, June 6, 1930, 45; "Mediums Failing, Cripple Kills One, Wounds Another," *Brooklyn Daily Eagle*, June 6, 1930, 21; Palmira Savala Death Certificate #12519, Department of Health of the City of New York, Bureau of Records.

123. "Held in Theft of Large Sum," *NYAN*, March 1, 1941, 1.

124. Jessamy, "Harlem's Fakers," 11.

125. "Spiritual Healer Awaiting Sentence," *NYAN*, December 14, 1927, 18; "She Made 'Em Talk and Also Walk," *NYAN*, December 14, 1927, 11; United States Bureau of the Census, Sixteenth Census of the United States, 1930. Washington, D.C.: U.S. Government Printing Office, 1942.

126. Harriet A. Washington, *Medical Apartheid: The Dark History of Medical Experimentation on Black Americans from Colonial Times to the Present* (New York: Doubleday, 2006), 21; W. Michael Byrd and Linda Clayton, *An American Health: Race, Medicine, and Health Care in the United States 1900–2000* (Florence, Ky.: Psychology Press, 2000).

127. Fett, *Working Cures*, 6.

128. William Edward Burghardt Du Bois, *The Philadelphia Negro: A Social Study* (Boston: Ginn and Co., Selling Agents, 1899), 162.

129. Chireau, *Black Magic*, 117.

130. Cameron McWhirter, "Need a Job? Losing Your House? Who Says Hoodoo Can't Help? Tough Times Boost Sales of Spider Dust, Spells for Good Fortune, Mojo Powders," *Wall Street Journal*, December 28, 2010; http://online.wsj.com/article/SB10001424052748703989004575653102537901956.html (accessed April 22, 2009).

Chapter 4. "I Have My Own Room on 139th Street"

1. Locke, *Harlem*, 625.

2. Client MJ, Box 85, Women's Prison Association Records (WPA), 1938, Manuscript and Archives Division, the New York Public Library (NYPL). Throughout this chapter, sex workers' names were changed to fictitious names in order to comply with New York Public Library restrictions on this particular collection.

3. Marvel Cooke, "Occupation: Streetwalker," *Daily Compass*, April 16, 1950, 10.

4. Christine Stansell, *City of Women: Sex and Class in New York, 1789–1860* (New York: Random House, 1986); Ruth Rosen, *The Lost Sisterhood: Prostitution in America, 1900–1918* (Baltimore: Johns Hopkins University Press, 1982); Hill, *Their Sisters' Keepers*; Timothy J. Gilfoyle, *City of Eros: New York City, Prostitution, and the Commercialization of Sex, 1790–1920* (New York: W. W. Norton, 1992).

5. Blair, *I've Got to Make My Livin','* 8.

6. Kevin J. Mumford, *Interzones: Black/White Sex Districts in Chicago and New York in the Early Twentieth Century* (New York: Columbia University Press, 1997); Stephen Robertson, "Harlem Undercover: Vice Investigators, Race, and Prostitution, 1910–1930," *Journal of Urban History* 35 (May 2009): 486–504.

7. Reverend John P. Peters, "The Story of the Committee of Fourteen of New York," *Social Hygiene* (New York: The American Social Hygiene Association, 1918), 371.

8. Jennifer Fronc, *New York Undercover: Private Surveillance in the Progressive Era* (Chicago: University of Chicago Press, 2009), 3, 71.

9. Burton W. Peretti, *Nightclub City: Politics and Amusement in* Manhattan (Philadelphia: University of Pennsylvania Press, 2013), 30.

10. Chandler Owen, "Bobbed Hair and Bobbed Brains," *Messenger*, 1925, 112.

11. Mary Louise Roberts, *Civilization without Sexes: Reconstructing Gender in Postwar France, 1917–1927* (Chicago: University of Chicago Press, 1984), 80.

12. Patricia K. Hunt, "Clothing as an Expression of History: The Dress of African-American Women in Georgia, 1880–1915," *Georgia Historical Quarterly* 86 (Summer 1992): 459–471; Blain Roberts, *Pageants, Parlors, and Pretty Women: Race and Beauty in the Twentieth-Century South* (Chapel Hill: University of North Carolina Press, 2014).

13. Elizabeth Clement, "From Sociability to Spectacle: Interracial Sexuality and the Ideological Uses of Space in New York City, 1900–1930," *Journal of International Women's Studies* 6 (June 2005): 24–43.

14. W. E. B. Du Bois to Frederick Whitin, October 14, 1912, Box 11, Folder: "W. E. B. Du Bois Correspondence," C14. Du Bois was referring to the New York State Civil Rights Act of 1873; its amended statues of 1895, 1905, and 1909; and the 1913 Levy Law, which established that "accommodations, advantages, facilities, and privileges" could not be "refused, withheld from, or denied to any person on account of race, creed, color, or national origin." Eddie G. Burrows and Mike Wallace, *Gotham: A History of New York City to 1898* (New York: Oxford University Press, 1999), 1034–1035; *New York State Laws of 1905*, sec. 1, chap. 1042; *New York State Consolidated Laws, Civil Rights Laws of 1909*, chap. 6, article 40, secs. 40–45.

15. Gilchrist Stewart to Frederick Whitin, September 28, 1912, Box 14, Folder: St-Sz, Committee of Fourteen Papers (COF), Manuscripts and Archives Division, New York Public Library.

16. "About the Committee of Fourteen," *NYA*, November 2, 1911, 1.

17. Jennifer Fronc, "The Horns of the Dilemma: Race Mixing and the Enforcement of Jim Crow in New York City," *Journal of Urban History* 33 (2006): 13.

18. Client JJ, Box 85, WPA, 1938.

19. Hicks, *Talk with You like a Woman*, 206.

20. Report on the Blue Ribbon Chile Parlor," May 16, 1928, Box 36, Folder: 117–134th Street, COF Papers.

21. "Tenement—S. E. June 26/27, 1928," Box 36, Folder: 135–207th Street, COF Papers.

22. Client FG, Box 85, WPA, 1931.

23. Katherine Bement Davis, "Study of Prostitutes Committed from New York City to the State Reformatory for Women at Bedford Hill," in George Kneeland, *Prostitution in New York* (New York: Century, 1913), 174.

24. Greenberg, *Or Does It Explode?* 39; Clement, *Love for Sale*, 79–80.

25. Waterman, *Prostitution and Its Repression*, 51.

26. John H. Warren Jr., *Thirty Years' Battle with Crime, or the Crying Shame of New York* (Poughkeepsie: A. J. White, 1875), 110–111.

27. McAdoo, *Guarding A Great City*, 93–94, 98.

28. Hicks, *Talk with You like a Woman*, 51.

29. Hazel V. Carby, "Policing the Black Woman's Body in an Urban Context," *Critical Inquiry* 18 (Summer 1992): 747; Eleanor Tayleur, "The Negro Woman—Social and Moral Decadence," *Outlook*, January 30, 1904, 268; Hick, *Talk with You like a Woman*, 53–57.

30. "Mme Hardaway Found Guilty," *NYAN*, February 21, 1923, 1; Display Ad 1—No Title, *NYAN*, February 28, 1923, a.

31. Client RC, Box 72, WPA, 1929.

32. Greenberg, *Or Does It Explode?* 177.

33. "Frameups and Blackmail," *NYA*, June 7, 1928, 4.

34. "Beware of Dancy," *NYA*, September 6, 1924, 9; "Angry Husbands Lay Trap for Stool Pigeons," *NYA*, August 16, 1924, 1; "Threats Sent the *Age* Editor Anonymously," *NYA*, October 24, 1924, 1; "Stool Pigeon Still at Dirty Work," *NYA*, July 12, 1924, 1; "Stool Pigeon Exposure Has Stirred Folks," *NYA*, July 19, 1924, 1.

35. "Innocent Girls Arrested: Former Police Aide Says Many Were Convicted on Perjured Evidence," *NYT*, November 27, 1930, 1; Quentin Reynolds, *Courtroom: The Story of Samuel S. Leibowitz, Lawyer and Judge* (New York: H. Wolff Book Manufacturing Company, 1950), 362; Herbert Mitgang, *The Man Who Rode the Tiger: The Life and Times of Judge Samuel Seabury* (New York: Fordham University Press, 1996), 181; "Police Malfeasance," *New York Magazine*, September 21, 1970, 33; "Follow That Trial," *NYAN*, December 3, 1930, 20.

36. Gail Hershatter, *Dangerous Pleasures: Prostitution and Modernity in Twentieth-Century Shanghai* (Berkley: University of California Press, 1997), 4.

37. "National League on Urban Conditions among Negroes," *Crisis*, September 1914; Carietta V. Owens, "Investigation of Colored Women at Night Court, June 8th to August 8th, 1914," Box 63, Folder: Women's Court—Negro Cases, COF Papers.

38. "Tenement House, June 2nd and 3rd 1932," Box 35, Folder: 1932, COF Papers.

39. Steve Kramer, "'Uplifting Our 'Downtrodden Sisterhood': Victoria Earle Matthews and New York City's White Rose Mission, 1897–1907," *Journal of African American History* 3 (Summer 2006): 243.

40. Sugrue, *Sweet Land of Liberty*, 4, 12.

41. Hicks, *Talk with You like a Woman*, 41.

42. Liz Sonneborn, *The Great Black Migrations: From the Rural South to the North* (New York: Chelsea House, 2010), 8.

43. Gertrude Boyd, " Exposing a Racket," *NYAN*, March 6, 1937, 14.

44. "Seducer Jailed: Girl Accuses Him of Loving Her Sordidly," *NYAN*, September 11, 1937, 1.

45. Elsa Barkley Brown, "Woman Consciousness: Maggie Lena Walker and the Independent Order of Saint Luke," *Signs* 14 (Spring 1989): 186–187; Shaw, *What a Woman Ought to Be*, 66–67.

46. Ethel Waters and Charles Samuels, *His Eye Is on the Sparrow: An Autobiography* (New York: Doubleday, 1951), 17.

47. "Tenement—S. E. June 26/27, 1928," Box 36, Folder: 135th–207th Street, COF Papers.

48. Shaw, *What a Woman Ought to Be*, 2; Anne Valk and Leslie Brown, *Living with Jim Crow: African American Women and Memories of the Segregated South* (New York: Palgrave Macmillan, 2010), 54, 80, 85.

49. Miller-Young, *A Taste for Brown Sugar*, 10, 182.

50. "Tenement, March 30, 1928," Box 36, Folder: 107th Street–163rd Street, COF Papers.

51. Anastasia C. Curwood, *Stormy Weather: Middle-Class African American Marriages between the Two World Wars* (Chapel Hill: University of North Carolina Press, 2010), 14, 85.

52. Billie Holiday and William Duffy, *Lady Sings the Blues* (Garden City: Doubleday, 1956), 23, 24.

53. Holiday worked in a Baltimore brothel house prior to migrating to New York City. Her fellow brothel inmates referred to her as "pretty baby" on account of her age. Holiday and Duffy, *Lady Sings the Blues*, 25; Robertson, "Harlem Undercover," 499; Farah Jasmine Griffin, *If You Can't Be Free, Be a Mystery: In Search of Billie Holiday* (New York: Free Press, 2001), 52, 60.

54. Griffin, *If You Can't Be Free*, 24, 52; Julia Blackburn, *With Billie: A New Look at the Unforgettable Lady Day* (New York: Knopf Doubleday Publishing Group, 2012), 15.

55. "Weekly Topics," *NYAN*, July 30, 1938, 6.

56. Lionel Bascom, *A Renaissance in Harlem: Lost Voices of an American Community* (New York: Bard, 1999), 72–75; Kathy J. Ogren, *The Jazz Revolution: Twenties America and the Meaning of Jazz* (New York: Oxford University, 1992), 84.

57. Client IH, Box 64, WPA, 1938.

58. Owens, "Investigation of Colored Women at Night Court," 7.

59. Client TB, Box 64, WPA, 1932.

60. Cynthia Ann Briggs and Jennifer L. Pepperell, *Women, Girls, and Addiction: Celebrating the Feminine in Counseling* (New York: Routledge, 2009), 73; Peter de Marneffe, *Liberalism and Prostitution* (New York: Oxford University Press, 2010), 25.

61. Marvel Cooke, "Katie's Not Ashamed Any More—She Just Feels Hopeless Now," *Daily Compass*, April 18, 1950, 2.

62. Bascom, *Renaissance in Harlem*, 199.

63. Frank Byrd, "Prostitute," in Aaron Siskind, *Harlem Document: Photographs, 1932–1940* (Providence, R.I.: Matrix, 1981), 68.

64. Clement, *Love for Sale*, 88.

65. Thomas E. Dewey, *Twenty against the Underworld* (New York: Doubleday, 1974), 189.

66. Rosen, *Lost Sisterhood*, 166; Gilfoyle, *City of Eros*, 107; Irving Lewis Allen, *The City in Slang: New York Life and Popular Speech* (New York: Oxford University Press, 1993), 163.

67. Dan Burley, "Backdoor Stuff: The Girl in the Street Speaks—Pulse Beat of a Woman for Hire," *NYAN*, July 16, 1938, A8.

68. Ibid.

69. Ottley, *New World A-Coming*, 158.

70. *People v. Blanche Simms*, filed January 31, 1938, District Attorney's Closed Case Files (DACCF), Municipal Archives of the City of New York.

71. "Street Conditions, November 11, 1931," Box 35, Folder: 1931, COF Papers.

72. Cooke, "Katie's Not Ashamed Any More," 7.

73. Ibid.

74. "Tenement (Colored) July 18/19, 1928," Box 36, Folder: 117th–134th Street, COF Papers.

75. Shannon King, *Whose Harlem Is This, Anyway? Community Politics and Grassroots Activism during the New Negro Era* (New York: New York University, 2015), 123.

76. "Mrs. Morrison," October 1, 1927, Box 36, Folder: 107th–163rd Street, COF Papers.

77. Box 35, Folder: 1927–29, February 15, 1928, COF Papers.

78. Frank Mann and W. A. Robertson, *The Tenement House Law of the State of New York* (New York: Tenement House Department, 1921), 86–88.

79. "Report on Conditions," Box 82, Folder: Harlem Report on Conditions, COF Papers.

80. "Harlem Girl Seized in Raid on House at 66 St. Nicholas," *NYAN*, August 13, 1938, 2.

81. "Tenement—S. E. June 5, 1928 and June 21, 1928," Box 36, Folder: Rivington Street—West Tremont, COF Papers.

82. Clement, *Love for Sale*, 110.

83. "Red Light Daisy Skips Rap, but Reverend Goes to Jail," *NYAN*, December 11, 1937, 12.

84. "Tenement, October 15 1927," Box, 36, Folder: Edgecombe and Fulton, COF Papers.

85. Tenement—S. E. June 26/27, 1928," Box, 36, Folder: 135th–207th Street, COF Papers; 1920 United States Federal Census for Manhattan (New York 1920 T-625, Roll 1194, New York, Manhattan Borough, ED 441).

86. Adam Clayton Powell Sr., *Against the Tides: An Autobiography* (New York: Richard R. Smith, 1938), 55, 57–59; "Dr. Powell's Crusade against Abnormal Vice Is Approved," *NYA*, November 23, 1929, 1; "Abyssinian Pastor Fires a Broadside into Ranks of Fellow Ministers and Churches," *NYA*, November 16, 1929, 1.

87. "Dr. Powell's Crusade," 1; "Abyssinian Pastor Fires a Broadside," 1.

88. Powell, *Against the Tides*, 57–58; Powell Jr., *Adam by Adam*, 9.

89. "Title Page: Out of the Total Number of Houses of Prostitution," Box 82, Folder: Harlem Report on Conditions, COF Papers.

90. "Frances Watkins to Urban League, New York," Box 15, Folder: Urban League, COF Papers.

91. "Street Conditions (Colored)/Brooklyn January 29, 1931," Box 35, Folder: Brooklyn—INV-Z, COF Papers.

92. Gilfoyle, *City of Eros*, 243; Clement, *Love for Sale*, 89–90.

93. Peretti, *Nightclub City*, 5.

94. Erenberg, "From New York to Middletown, 762.

95. Adler, *A House Is Not a Home*, 65–66.

96. Folder: 117th–134th Box 36, COF Papers, April 22, 1927.

97. "Committee of Fourteen, Vice Reform Group, Says Many Harlem Clubs Are Respectable, as Are the Hostesses," *NYA*, October 19, 1929, 1.

98. Folder: 117–134th Street, Box 36, COF Papers, May 12, 1928.

99. Folder: 135th–207th, Box 36, COF Papers; *COF Annual Report for 1928*, Box 86, COF Papers.

100. Holiday and Duffy, *Lady Sings the Blues*, 107.

101. "Deplorable Conditions," *NYAN*, April 30, 1938, 12; "Police Deny Crime Increases in Harlem," *NYAN*, October 8, 1938, 1.

102. "Bessie Amos/Mrs. Whitfield," Box 28, Folder: 1914, COF Papers; "Real Estate Man in Custody," *NYA*, December 12, 1912, 1.

103. "Southern White Gentleman Rapes Colored Lady; Is Killed by Husband," *Chicago Defender*, November 4, 1911, 1.

104. Heap, *Slumming*, 1.

105. "Tenement, March 16, 1928," Box 36, Folder: Sa-Su, COF Papers.

106. Holiday and Duffy, *Lady Sings the Blues*, 27.

107. Folder: Sa-So, Box 36, COF Papers.

108. Brenman, "Urban Lower-Class Negro Girls," *Psychiatry: Journal of the Biology and Pathology of Interpersonal Relations* 6 (August 1943): 322.

109. Folder: Edgecombe and Fulton, Box 35, COF Papers.

110. Bertram Pollens, *The Sex Criminal* (New York: Macaulay Company, 1938), 60–61.

111. Blair, *I've Got to Make My Livin,'* 143.

112. McAdoo, *Guarding a Great City*, 99.

113. Ottley, *New World A-Coming*, 158.

114. "Loses $1,493 in 'Creep Joint,'" *NYAN*, October 9, 1937, 1.

115. Gross, *Colored Amazons*, 74, 77–78.

116. "White Pleasure-Seeker Beaten, Robbed, Stabbed," *NYAN*, May 1, 1929, 2.

117. "Loses $1,493 in 'Creep Joint,'" 1.

118. "Court Sees Harlem as Grave Vice Center," *NYT*, October 22, 1938, 34; Gross, *Colored Amazons*, 72–73, 77–78.

119. Dan Burley, "Fireman Killer Faces 20 Years," 1.

120. "Confesses to Killing Fireman," *NYAN*, July 23, 1938, 1; Burley, "Fireman Killer Faces 20 Years," 1; *People v. Blanche Simms*, filed January 31, 1938, District Attorney's Closed Case Files (DACCF), Municipal Archives of the City of New York.

121. "Chews Gum at Judge's Bench," *NYAN*, November 12, 1938, 2.

122. Bogan recorded two versions of the song. One version highlights same-sex desire and intercourse, the other heterosexual sex. Robert Staples, *Exploring Black Sexuality* (Lanham, Md.: Rowman and Littlefield, 2006), 41.

123. Hazel V. Carby, "It Just Be's Dat Way Sometime: The Sexual Politics of Women's Blues," *Radical America* 20, no. 4 (1986): 9–22.

124. Shayne Lee, *Erotic Revolutionaries: Black Women, Sexuality, and Popular Culture* (Lanham, Md.: Hamilton Books, 2010), viii.

125. Hicks, "Bright and Good Looking Colored Girl," 423–424.

126. Client MJ, Box 85, WPA.

127. Jan MacKell, *Brothels, Bordellos, and Bad Girls: Prostitution in Colorado, 1860–1930* (Albuquerque: University of New Mexico Press, 2004), 20.

128. Bascom, *Renaissance in Harlem*, 165.

129. Kelley, *Race Rebels*, 47.

130. Roberyson, "Disorderly Houses," 461.

131. Heap, *Slumming*, 233; Eric Garber, "A Spectacle in Color: The Lesbian and Gay Subculture of Jazz Age Harlem," in Martin B. Duberman, Martha Vicinus, and George Chauncey, eds., *Hidden from History: Reclaiming the Gay and Lesbian Past* (New York: NAL Books, 1989), 321; Chauncey, *Gay New York*, 250–251.

132. Blair, *I've Got to Make My Livin,'* 178.

133. "Tenement—S.E. (Colored), May 25, 1928," Box 36, Folder: 135th–207th Street, COF Papers.

134. Barry Singer, *Black and Blue: The Life and Lyrics of Andy Razaf* (New York: Schirmer Books, 1992), 160; "Repudiating Confession, Actress Denies She Shot Husband at Party," *NYAN*, July 14, 1926, 3; "'Tan Town Topics' with Rector and Cooper off to a Wonderful Start," *NYAN*, April 7, 1926, 5; Display Ad 38—No Title, *NYAN*, December 15, 1926, 12; Bernard L. Peterson, *A Century of Musicals in Black and White: An Encyclopedia of Musical Stage* (Westport, Conn.: Greenwood Press, 1993), 291.

135. Donald Clarke, *Billie Holiday: Wishing on the Moon* (New York: Viking, 1994), 79–80.

136. Dan Burley, "Dan Burley Called Harlem a State of Mind," *NYAN*, November 26, 1977, B1.

137. Ed Kirkeby, *Ain't Misbehavin': The Story of Fats Waller* (New York: Dodd, Mead and Co., 1966), 99; David A. Jasen and Gene Jones, *Black Bottom Stomp: Eight Masters of Ragtime and Early Jazz* (New York: Routledge, 2002), 116.

138. Kirkeby, *Ain't Misbehavin,'* 100.

139. "Repudiating Confession," *NYAN*, July 14, 1926, 3.

140. Mary M. Stolberg, *Fighting Organized Crime: Politics, Justice, and the Legacy of Thomas E. Dewey* (Boston, Mass.: Northeastern University Press, 1995), 88.

141. "Harlem Is Wide Open during Fair," *NYAN*, May 13, 1939, 4.

142. Gross, "Exploring Crime and Violence, 57.

Chapter 5. "'Decent and God-Fearing Men and Women' Are Restricted to These Districts"

1. "Red Light Daisy Given 6 Months," *NYAN*, November 23, 1935, 1; "Court Releases 'Red Light' Daisy," *NYAN*, December 14, 1935, 1.

2. "Red Light Daisy Given 6 Months," 1.

3. Leslie M. Alexander, *African or American? Black Identity and Political Activism in New York, 1784–1861* (Urbana: University of Illinois Press, 2011); Jane E. Dabel, *A Respectable Woman: The Public Roles of African American Women in 19th-Century New York* (New York: New York University Press, 2008).

4. "Overheard on the Avenue," *NYA*, July 30, 1908, 4.

5. "Reports of Investigation of Vice Conditions in Harlem," Box 15, Folder: Urban League, COF Papers.

6. Drusilla Dunjee Houston, "Wide Spaces Are Best for Race," *Chicago Defender*, January 2, 1932, 14.

7. Sacks, *Before Harlem*, 73.

8. Ottley, *New World-A Coming*, 180.

9. A. M. Wendell Malliet, "Survey Shows More Shacks," *NYAN*, December 4, 1937, 5.

10. "Better Apartments Shut to Race," *NYAN*, October 21, 1939, 10; "Queens Families Threaten Riot," *NYAN*, October 17, 1928, 2; A. M. Wendell, "Survey Shows More Shacks: Primitive Living," *NYAN*, December 4, 1937, 1; "Ku Kluxers Riding Again in Queens," *NYAN*, November 23, 1932, 3.

11. Ann Petry, *The Street* (New York: Houghton and Mifflin, 1943), 3.

12. Lester B. Granger, "As I Remember," *NYAN*, June 29, 1932, 13; Felix L. Armfield, *Eugene Kinckle Jones: The National Urban League and Black Social Work, 1910–1940* (Urbana: University of Illinois Press, 2011), 75.

13. Dorothy Brown, "Sugar Hill: Vice Infested," *NYAN*, February 11, 1939, 12.

14. "Little Colored Americans," *Colored American*, June 21, 1902, 7.

15. Lester Granger, "Manhattan and Beyond," *NYAN*, February 2, 1946, 10.

16. Dewey Papers, Box 4, Folder 22.

17. Dewey Papers, Box 4, Folder 13.

18. "Bootleggers Assault Minister: Series of Sermons Condemning Vice Arouses Ire of Anti-Prohibition," *Pittsburgh Courier*, August 4, 1928, A3; "Minister Beaten Who Informed on Bootlegger Gang," *NYAN*, July 11, 1928, 1; "Slashes Negro Preacher: Attacker Is Later Shot by Police while Resisting Arrest," *NYT*, July 7, 1928, 3.

19. Jervis Anderson, *A. Philip Randolph: A Biographical Portrait* (1973; repr., Berkeley: University of California Press, 1986), 178.

20. "Innocent Girls Arrested: Former Police Aide Says Many Were Convicted on Perjured Evidence," *NYT*, November 27, 1930, 1; Reynolds, *Courtroom*, 362; Mitgang, *The Man Who Rode the Tiger*, 181; "Police Malfeasance," 33; "Acuna Getting $7 a Day from Police, He Says," *Brooklyn Daily Eagle*, December 19, 1930, 1.

21. "'Human Beast,' Terror to Harlem Women for Year Past, Sentenced to 70 Years State Penitentiary, by Judge McIntyre," *NYA*, September 25, 1926, 1; "Recent Disclosures of 'Stool Pigeon' Activities in 'Framing' of Innocent Women by N. Y. Police Recalls the Dancy Exposé Made by the Age in 1924," *NYA*, December 6, 1930, 1.

22. Venkatesh, *Off the Books*, 8.

23. Ibid.

24. Benito Thomas, "Critics Criticized," *NYAN*, July 18, 1928, 16.

25. Waters and Samuels, *His Eye Is on the Sparrow*, 18–19.

26. Ovington, *Half a Man*, 156.

27. "Woman against Woman," *Chicago Defender*, December 22, 1923, 12.

28. Mary White Ovington, "The Negro Home in New York," *Charities* 15 (October 7, 1905): 30.

29. Marcia Chatelain, *Southside Girls: Growing Up in the Great Migration* (Durham: Duke University Press, 2015), 2.

30. Hicks, *Talk with You like a Woman*, 188.

31. Karen W. Tice, *Tales of Wayward Girls and Immoral Women: Case Records and the Professionalization of Social Work* (Urbana: University of Illinois Press, 1998), 111; Lee S. Polansky, "I Certainly Hope that You Will Be Able to Train Her: Reformers and the Georgia Training School for Girls," in Elna C. Green, ed., *Before the New Deal: Social Welfare in the South, 1830–1930* (Athens: University of Georgia Press, 1999), 140; Susan K. Cahn, *Sexual Reckonings: Southern Girls in a Troubling Age* (Cambridge: Harvard University Press, 2007); Hicks, *Talk with You like a Woman*, 184–185.

32. Letter from Edith Williams to William Gaynor, February 10, 1910, Box 45, Folder: Mayor William Gaynor Papers, NYMA.

33. Investigative Report of Charles Briggs, July 4, 1914, Box 29, Folder: Brooklyn/Queens—Investigative Reports, 1914, COF Papers.

34. "Conduct on the Corners," *NYA*, May 27, 1909, 4.

35. Stolberg, *Fighting Organized Crime*, 88.

36. Dewey Papers, Box 3, Folder 20.

37. Anonymous letter to William Gaynor, May 11, 1910, Box 46, Folder 402: Mayor William Gaynor Papers, Municipal Archives of the City of New York.

38. Charles "Lucky" Luciano Closed Case Files, Box 4, Folder 22: Harlem, Municipal Archives of the City of New York.

39. Folder: Urban League, Box 15, COF Papers.

40. Mother of Three, "On Deaf Ears," *NYAN*, February 12, 1938, 12.

41. "Slums, Most Deadly Foe of Harlem Masses," *NYAN*, March 7, 1942, 12.

42. Ovington, "Negro Home in New York," 2526.

43. "This Week's Guest Editor Says: Force Better Housing," *NYAN*, September 26, 1936, 12.

44. Mother of Three, "On Deaf Ears," 12; "Harlem Streets," *NYAN*, April 21, 1926, 16.

45. Dan Burley, "Below the Sidewalks in Harlem: Men Live in Misery," *NYAN*, January 21, 1939, 10.

46. "Sugar Hill Girl Tries to Kill Self," *NYAN*, October 29, 1938, 1; Ottley, *New World A-Coming*, 182.

47. "Landlords Held to Be Responsible for Permitting Bootleggers to Operate So Wantonly and Boldly in the Community, *NYA*, April, 24, 1926, 3; "Slums, Most Deadly Foe Harlem Masses; Gyps Take $4,800,000 Toll," *NYAS-N*, March 7, 1942, 12.

48. Letter from 123 West 142 Street to COF, Box 22, Folder: Citizens Complaints.

49. Charles "Lucky" Luciano Closed Case Files, Box 4, Folder 22: Harlem, Municipal Archives of the City of New York.

50. Ibid.

51. Charles "Lucky" Luciano Closed Case Files, Box 4, Folder 13: Complaints, Municipal Archives of the City of New York.

52. Hicks, "Bright and Good Looking Colored Girl," 418–456.

53. Charles "Lucky" Luciano Closed Case Files, Box 4, Folder 22: Harlem, Municipal Archives of the City of New York.

54. Clare Corbould, "Streets, Sounds, and Identity in Interwar Harlem," *Journal of Social History* 40 (Summer 2007): 859–894.

55. "Clean 'Em Out," *NYA*, April 6, 1911, 3.

56. Chatelain, *Southside Girls*, 75.

57. In 1890, there were an estimated 909 black physicians in the United States and approximately 3,885 by 1920. Ruth J. Abram, *Send Us a Lady Physician: Women Doctors in America, 1835–1920* (New York: W. W. Norton and Company, 1985), 109; Eric Homberger, *The Historical Atlas of New York City: A Visual Celebration of 400 Years of New York City's History* (New York: Macmillan, 2005), 138; Louis Wright, "The Negro Physician," *Crisis* 36 (September 1929): 305.

58. Wright, "Negro Physician," 305; *Negro Population in the United States, 1790–1915* (Washington, D.C.: United States Government Printing Office, 1925), 510; *Negroes in the United States, 1920–32* (Washington, D.C.: United States Government Printing Office, 1935), xvi.

59. "Fight for Negro Doctors at Harlem Hospital," *NYA*, June 6, 1925; "Harlem Hospital's New Policy," *NYAN*, July 1, 1925, 16; Vanessa Gamble, *Making a Place for Ourselves: The Black Hospital Movement, 1920–1945* (New York: Oxford University Press, 1995), 57; Thelma E. Berlack, "May E. Chinn Given Degree in Medicine," *NYAN*, June 16, 1926, 11; "Dr. E. R. Alexander Gets Hospital Promotion, *NYAN*, May 19, 1926, 9.

60. "Carroll Advises the Race," *Gazette*, January 15, 1898, 4.

61. Williams, *Politics of Public Housing*, 30.

62. "Citizens' Welfare Council to Give Forum Program at Abyssinian," *NYA*, April 30, 1927, 2; "Dr. Butler Tells of Welfare Work over Radio," *NYAN*, January 30, 1929, 4; Citizens' Welfare Council Adopts Constitution at Morning Meeting," *NYAN*, July 22, 1925, 9; "Medal Awards Made to Harlem Citizens for Public Service," *NYA*, February 5, 1927, 1; "Welfare Council to Meet," *NYAN*, September 12, 1928, 8; "West 137th St. Block Ass'n," *NYA*, July 28, 1923, 4.

63. "Campaign on to Clean Up Harlem Streets: Citizens' Welfare Committee Working," *NYAN*, August 5, 1925, 9; " Mrs. Sarah Gardner Dead," *NYA*, February 20, 1937, 3; "Dr. Charles Butler to Broadcast Address from Radio Station WLWL," *NYA*, May 15, 1926, 2; "136th Street Block Assn., Gets Medal for Best Kept Block Last Year," *NYA*, February 19, 1927, 1; "Citizens' Council Sponsors Clean-Up Campaign," *NYAN*, May 12, 1926, 9.

64. William F. Russell, "From 'Trouble Area' to Neighborhood," *NYT*, April 14, 1947; Federal Writers' Project, *WPA Guide to New York City: The Federal Writers' Project Guide to 1930s New York* (1939; repr., New York: Pantheon, 1982), 588.

65. "Negroes in Queens Doubled in Decades," *NYAN*, September 30, 1931, 15; Deborah Dash Moore, "Class and Ethnicity in the Creation of New York City Neighborhoods, 1900–1930," in Thomas Bender, *Budapest and New York: Studies in Metropolitan Transformation, 1870–1930*, ed. Thomas Bender and Carle E. Schorske (New York: Russell Sage Founda-

tion, 1994), 143; *Queens Borough, New York City, 1910–1920* (New York: L. I. Star Publishing, 1920), 12, 66.

66. Federal Writers' Project, *WPA Guide to New York City: The Federal Writers' Project Guide to 1930s New York* (1939; repr., New York: Oantheon, 1982), 588; "L. I. Lumber Merchant to Build Homes for Colored People in Jamaica, *NYAN*, November 25, 1925, 1; "Fifty-Two Plots Secured by Mila-Cohn Company to Erect Homes for Negroes," *NYAN*, November 25, 1925, 1.

67. Harold Cruse, "My Jewish Problem and Theirs, in Nat Hentoff, ed., *Black Anti-Semitism and Jewish Racism* (New York: Shocken Books, 1969), 149.

68. Peter Eisenstadt, *Rochdale Village: Robert Moses, 6,000 Families, and New York City's Great Experiment in Integrated Housing* (New York: Cornell University Press, 2010), 47–48; "Negroes and Jews Combine to Serve Interests of Home Buyers This Spring," *NYAN*, February 3. 1926, 8; "Residents of Long Island Should Beware of Many Things," *NYAN*, October 21, 1925, 8.

69. Artie Simpson, "Jamaica, L. I., in Spotlight because of Rapid Growth," *NYAN*, July 21, 1926, 11; "Negroes and Jews Combine to Serve Interests of Home Buyers This Spring," *NYAN*, February 3, 1926, 8.

70. United States Bureau of the Census, Fifteenth Census of the United States, 1930. Washington, D.C.: U.S. Government Printing Office, 1933; "United Front Is Formed to Elect Mrs. Chaney," *NYAN*, August 24, 1935, 15.

71. "Jamaica Civic Group Opens New Program," *NYAN*, August 9, 1933, 11; "Slum Survey Group Named: Rabbi, White Minister, and Mrs. Chaney to Outline Areas," *NYAN*, June 1, 1935, 15; Charles E. Shaw Jr. "Jamaica, L. I.," *NYAN*, November 29, 1933, 11; "Purpose to Work for Peace and Economic Equality for Women," *Pittsburgh Courier*, December 25, 1935, 1; "Branch News," *Crisis*, December 1934, 370.

72. Julie Gallagher, *Black Women and Politics in New York City* (Urbana: University of Illinois Press, 2012), 57–58.

73. Lisa Materson, *For the Freedom of Her Race: Black Women and Electoral Politics in Illinois, 1877–1932* (Chapel Hill: University of North Carolina Press, 2009), 3.

74. "Eunice Carter, Office Seeker," *NYAN*, July 28, 1934, 1; "Able Daughter of Norfolkian Defeated in N.Y.," *New Journal and Guide* (Norfolk, Va.), November 10, 1934, 12; T. E. B., "The Feminist View," *NYAN*, October 13, 1934, 9; "Eunice Carter Has Busy Time: Assembly Candidate Is Qualified for Job," *NYAN*, November 3, 1934, 7; "Six Run for Office in New York's Election Nov. 6," *The Afro-American*, November 3, 1934, 10; "Nominees in New York City Primaries," *NYT*, September 14, 1934.

75. "Alma E. Crosswaith Would Rather Lose as Socialist than Win Seat on Other Slates," *NYAN*, November 1, 1933; "Williana Burroughs to Head New School," *NYAN*, September 6, 1933, 9; "Left Wing Tickets Topped by Negroes," *NYAN*, November 15, 1933, 16; "Funeral Service Held for Well Known Negro Teacher," *NYAN*, January 5, 1046, 14.

76. "United Front Is Formed to Elect Mrs. Chaney," *NYAN*, August 24, 1935, 15.

77. "'Mayor' to Help Chaney Crusade: Aldermanic Candidate Widely Endorsed," *NYAN*, September 28, 1935, 20; Mark Naison, *The Communists in Harlem during the Depression* (Urbana: University of Illinois Press, 2004), 71, 85; "United Front Is Formed to Elect Mrs. Chaney," *NYAN*, August 24, 1935, 15; "Complete List of the Candidates in the

City," *NYT*, November 3, 1935, 42; "Supporters Urge Chaney Election," *NYAN*, October 5, 1935, 15.

78. "Candidates Lose Place on Ballot," *NYAN*, November 2, 1935, 10; "Co-Leader Out, Says Sheridan," *Brooklyn Daily Eagle*, September 26, 1935, 4; "Election Results in Borough, City, Queens and Nassau Counties," *Brooklyn Daily Eagle*, November 6, 1935, 12.

79. "The Cost of Equality," *NYAN*, June 8, 1935, 9.

80. Eisenstadt, *Rochdale Village*, 48.

81. "Jamaica Vice Drive Opened," *NYAN*, August 11, 1934, 12; "South Jamaica Project," *NYAN*, June 24, 1939, 6.

82. "Jamaica Vice Drive Opened," *NYAN*, August 11, 1934, 12; "South Jamaica Project," *NYAN*, June 24, 1939, 6.

83. "South Jamaica Project," *NYAN*, June 24, 1939, 6.

84. Robert M. Fogelson, *Downtown: Its Rise and Fall, 1880–1950* (New Haven: Yale University Press, 2008), 341; Langdon Post, "Slum Clearance Plans," *NYT*, March 28, 1935, 20.

85. "City Will Be Asked to Clean Up Slums," *NYAN*, July 17, 1934, 15.

86. "Ibid.; "Jamaicans Continue Fight for Slum Clearance," *NYAN*, August 3, 1935, 15; "Post, on Queens Tour, Opens Fight to End Slum Areas in Borough," *NYT*, January 14, 1936, 23.

87. "Slum Survey Group Named," *NYAN*, June 1, 1935, 15.

88. King, *Whose Harlem Is This, Anyway?* 154.

89. "Playground Opened in South Jamaica," *NYT*, July 1, 1939, 19; "Selects Site for Slum Clearance Project in Jamaica," *NYAN*, April 29, 1939, 13; "Jamaica Chosen for New Housing Site: Secret Slum Survey Is Made in Jamaica," *NYAN*, August 6, 1938, 1; Jamaica NAACP, *Fifty Years of Service* (Queens: Jamaica NAACP, 1977); "Branch News," *Crisis*, April 1939, 117.

Conclusion

1. Cheikh Anta Babou, "Migration and Cultural Change: Money, 'Caste,' Gender, and Social Status among Senegalese Female Hair Braiders in the United States," *Africa Today* 55 (Winter 2008): 3.

2. Sherri Day, "New Yorkers and Co.; Braiders out of Africa with a World of Woes," *NYT*, March 18, 2001; http://www.nytimes.com/2001/03/18/nyregion/new-yorkers-co-braiders-out-of-africa-with-a-world-of-woes.html (accessed November 15, 2014).

3. Babou, "Migration and Cultural Change," 9.

4. Ousmane Kane, *The Homeland Is the Arena: Religion, Transnationalism, and the Integration of Senegalese Immigrants in America* (New York: Oxford University, 2011), 81.

5. Jane E. Losby, Marcia E. Kingslow, and John F. Else, *The Informal Economy: Experiences of African Americans* (Washington, D.C.: Institute for Social and Economic Development Solutions, 2003), 34.

6. Corey Kigannon, "At 52, Still Working the Streets in Hunts Point," *NYT*, December 30, 2011; http://www.nytimes.com/2012/01/01/nyregion/at-52-a-prostitute-still-working-the-streets.html?_r=2 (accessed January 15, 2015).

7. Ylan Q. Mui and Chris L. Jenkins, "For Some Black Women, Economy and Willingness to Aid Family Strains Finances," *Washington Post*, February 5, 2012; http://www.washingtonpost.com/business/economy/for-some-black-women-economy-and-willingness-to-aid-family-strains-finances/2012/01/24/gIQAGIWksQ_story.html (accessed March 8, 2014); Courtland Milloy, "Despite 'Recovery,' Black Women Struggle to Cope with Job Losses," *Washington Post*, December 11, 2011; http://www.washingtonpost.com/local/2011/12/11/gIQAE05G0O_story.html (accessed June 1, 2014); Raine Dozier, "Young, Jobless, and Black: Young Black Women and Economic Downturns," *Journal of Sociology and Social Welfare* 39 (2012): 45–67.

8. "The African-American Labor Force in the Recovery," United States Department of Labor; http://www.dol.gov/_sec/media/reports/blacklaborforce/ (accessed October 16, 2011).

9. Matthew Philips, "Black Women Continue Making Job Gains," *Bloomberg Businessweek.com*, May 4, 2012; http://www.businessweek.com/articles/2012–05–04/black-women-continue-making-jobs-gains (accessed November 8, 2011).

10. "The State of Working New York 2012: Disappointing Weak Recovery," Fiscal Policy Institute, September 2, 2012, 15; "Black New Yorkers Not Keeping Pace," *NYT*, June 20, 2012; http://www.nytimes.com/interactive/2012/06/21/nyregion/black-new-yorkers-not-keeping-pace.html (accessed November 8, 2011); Patrick McGeehan, "Unemployment Hits 10.3% in New York City," *NYT*, September 17, 2009; http://www.nytimes.com/2009/09/18/nyregion/18unemploy.html?_r=0 (accessed October 1, 2011); Patrick McGeehan, "Study Shows Jobless Rate Varies Widely across City," *NYT*, December 30, 2009, A23.

11. F. Michael Higginbotham, *Ghosts of Jim Crow: Ending Racism in Post-Racial America* (New York: New York University Press, 2013), 153.

12. Brown-Glaude, *Higglers in Kingston*, 174.

Index

Page references in italics refer to illustrations.

McKenzie, Theodore, 49–50

Meriwether, Louise: *Daddy Was a Number Runner*, 61

Merrick Gardens (Queens), 192

middle class, black, 10, 60; community engagement among, 191; distancing from working class, 179; engagement in prostitution, 144–45, 147; on gambling, 62; monitoring of respectability, 169; supernatural consultants, 104; on supernaturalism, 104, 115–16; support for reform, 199; versions of respectability, 84

migrants, intercommunity, 171

migrants, southern, 20, 52; naïveté of, 123, 124; in New York sexual economy, 123; racial discrimination against, 135–36; supernatural consultants, 101; view of public space, 136. *See also* immigrants, black

Miller, Karen E. Quinones, 82

Miller, Kelly, 34

Minott, Adena C. E.: arrest and trial of, 106; community activism of, 105–6; education of, 104–5; metaphysical practice of, 104, 106; phrenology practice of, 105; popularity with elites, 105–6

minstrel shows, blackface, 152

Mitchell, Loften, 57

Moon, Henry Lee, 68

Moore, Fred, 77; defense of COF, 128, 129; on false arrests, 133–34

Moore, Mary Lee: prostitution of, 49–50

Morris, Vivian: study of prostitutes, 47–48, 140

Mumford, Kevin, 124

Munoz, Rita, 44; numbers banking by, 65; resistance to white racketeers, 77

National Association for the Advancement of Colored People (NAACP), 7, 31; on false arrests, 133; New York Vigilance Committee, 89, 128; on police corruption, 87; Queens chapter of, 195

National Association of Colored Women (NACW), 105

National Brotherhood of Policy Kings, 76

National Free School of Spiritualism (New York), 102–3

nationalism, black, 78; spiritualist churches and, 112

National Urban League (NUL), 7

neighborhood reform, black: community activism for, 167–71; empowerment in, 199; grassroots activism for, 17, 168, 169, 190, 198, 200, 206; Harlem Citizens Council's, 189–91; in Queens, 191–98; in South Jamaica, 196–97. *See also* vice, neighborhood

neighborhoods, black: benefits of informal labor for, 176; class distinctions in, 206; COF surveillance of, 128, 129; collective visions of, 169; communal spaces of, 178–79; community discipline in, 186; deportment in, 4; diversity in, 170; effect of brothels on, 167–68; leisure in, 30, 179; living conditions in, 172–73; moral health of, 128, 167; noise in, 172, 185–86; politicians' neglect of, 168–69; safety of, 199; socioeconomic progress of, 17; spokespersons for, 169–70; sustainability of, 200; transformative figures of, 200; white pleasure-seekers in, 151; white visibility in, 76–77

Nelson, Robert, 62

New Negro Movement, 9, 85; challenge to white supremacy, 187

newspapers, black: on false arrests, 133; on informal labor, 13; on rent, 26; St. Clair's use of, 85–86, 87, 88, 89–90; on women's gambling, 63

New York Age (NYA), 8; on brothels, 167; editorials on vice, 52; on neighborhood vice, 170, 186; on prostitution, 145–46, 186; on pseudomedical victimization, 119; on rent, 26; on state-sanctioned violence, 134; St. Clair's editorials in, 85, 86, 87, 88, 89–90

New York Amsterdam News (NYAN), 13; Harlem in, 58, 77; magico-religious advertisements in, 101; on St. Clair, 68; on UHTT, 99

New York City: black migrants' view of, 136; cost of living in, 3; cultural life of, 12, 18; dominance of, 17; extremes in, 17–18; interborough activism in, 197; jobless rate (twenty-first century), 204; Ku Klux Klan in, 171; multiethnic population of, 12, 18, 21–22; occult schools of, 102–3; sexual geography of, 125; sociocultural history of, 9; thievery rings of, 23; urban poverty in, 18

New York Department of Health, childcare inspections by, 40

New York Department of Public Welfare, 42

New York Emergency Work and Relief Bureau, 42

New York Housing Authority, 197; federal funding for, 195

New York Interstate Tattler (black newspaper), on numbers racket, 63

New York Police Department. *See* NYPD

New York state: anti-discrimination laws, 135; Civil Rights Act (1873), 232n14; prisons of, 159; supernaturalism legislation of, 117, 118

New York State Assembly, black women in, 193

New York Times (*NYT*), 13; Harlem in, 58

New York Urban League, black complaints to, 183

Nichols, Edward, 174

nightclubs: anti-vice investigations of, 149; COF surveillance of, 130; sex work in, 141, 148–49

Nineteenth Amendment, passage of, 193

noise: in black neighborhoods, 172, 185–86; creation of counterpublic sphere, 186

Norris, Mattie, 102; spiritualism practice of, 106–7

North, black migration to, 20, 52, 57, 135. *See also* migrants, southern

Northeastern Federation of Women's Clubs, Suppression of Lynching Division, 105

numbers bankers, 5; African American, 76; celebrity, 63; role of, 57; West Indian, 76

numbers players: black women, 63; use of dream books, 111–12

numbers racket, 217n1; black women in, 15, 34, 44, 65, 93; as community pastime, 61; in Detroit, 114; diverse attitudes toward, 176; income from, 61; police raids on, 114; policy slips in, 58; sale of numbers, 110, 114; supernatural consultants and, 16, 97, 104, 110–14, 122; supernaturalism and, 16, 97, 104, 110–14, 122. *See also* lotteries, illegal

numbers racket (Harlem), 54–58, 60–68, 70–93; activists' toleration of, 64; benefits of, 65; black elites in, 60; black failures in, 76; community opposition to, 68; critics of, 114; cultural significance of, 63; Dutch Schultz and, 65, 75–76; growth of, 92; harassment of employees in, 72; on

Lenox Ave., 59; male domination of, 65; male protection of women in, 66; masculine representations of, 55; middle-class blacks in, 60; NYPD ties to, 73–74; police corruption in, 60–61, 72, 73; police raids on, 86; political affiliations in, 60; popularity of, 55, 110; uniqueness of, 57; white racketeers in, 74–78, 85

numbers runners: black women, 55, 66; conduct of, 58; diversity among, 58; role of, 57; victimization of, 51

NYPD: brutality by, 87–89; Chaney's alliances with, 197; false arrests by, 131–34; harassment of black women, 131–34; informers for, 126, 130–31, 134, 175; racial violence by, 84; raids by, 68, 86, 88, 164–65; raids on brothels, 132; relations with African American women, 88; St. Clair's crusade against, 73–74, 84, 86–87, 89–90, 93; theft by, 134; ties to numbers racket, 73–74; underworld patrons among, 87; use of brothels, 87. *See also* police corruption

occult products, 97, 101; commercially manufactured, 109–10; customers of, 107–10; employment of stereotypes, 109; empowerment of users, 122; rationalization concerning, 108; sale of, 107–10. *See also* magic; supernatural consultants

occult schools, 102–3; degrees offered by, 103; fraudulent founders of, 227n33

Ottley, Roi, 2; on hustling, 31; on street children, 51

Ovington, Mary White, 26, 183

Owen, Chandler: "Bobbed Hair and Bobbed Brains," 127

Owens, Carietta V., 135

Panama Francis (numbers racketeer), 76

patriarchy: black prostitutes' resentment of, 157; debasement of black female body, 152; in informal labor, 44

Patterson, J. Franklin, 192

Payton, Philip A., 105

Payton, Phillip, Jr., 57

Pennsylvania, supernaturalism legislation of, 117

Pentecostal religious denomination, 112

Peoples, Elsie, 183

Woods, Emma, 47
working class (New York): activists on, 8;
economic pressures on, 25–26; relationship to criminal occupations, 17
working-class blacks, urban: belief in supernatural, 108; bourgeois respectability
of, 179; community engagement among,
191, 198; exploitative labor conditions of,
38–39, 178; financial stresses on, 26; and
gambling, 62; on informal labor, 175–81;
judgmental attitudes of, 178; living conditions of, 26–27, 172, 183–84; moral values
of, 178; newspapers on, 13; opposition to
neighborhood criminality, 180; outward
propriety among, 180; public/private behavior of, 169; racial uplift among, 179,
182; respectability politics among, 178–
79; use of spiritual advisors, 116
working-class women, black: bourgeois politics of, 32; children of, 39–40; documenta-

tion of, 10–15; economic disenfranchisement of, 53; employment opportunities
for, 27; historical sources for, 12–13; labor
conditions of, 25–30; labor decisions of,
34; labor identities of, 12; multiple occupations of, 34; numbers of, 34; omission from
historical record, 10–12; personal worlds of,
10; public images of, 22; resistance strategies of, 39; on sexuality, 159; socioeconomic
conditions of, 14, 207; of twenty-first century, 203–5; urban amusements of, 43, 47;
urbanized girls, 179–80; and urban poverty,
10; wages of, 28; white constructions of, 39;
white employers of, 38–39. *See also* African
American women; informal laborers, black
women
Wright, Louis T., 188
Wundus, Madge: pushcart business of, 41

Zimbabwe, supernatural consultants in, 115

LASHAWN HARRIS is an assistant professor of history at Michigan State University.

THE NEW BLACK STUDIES SERIES

The University of Illinois Press
is a founding member of the
Association of American University Presses.

University of Illinois Press
1325 South Oak Street
Champaign, IL 61820-6903
www.press.uillinois.edu